Ecological Architecture

A Critical History

A Critical History

Ecological Architecture

James Steele

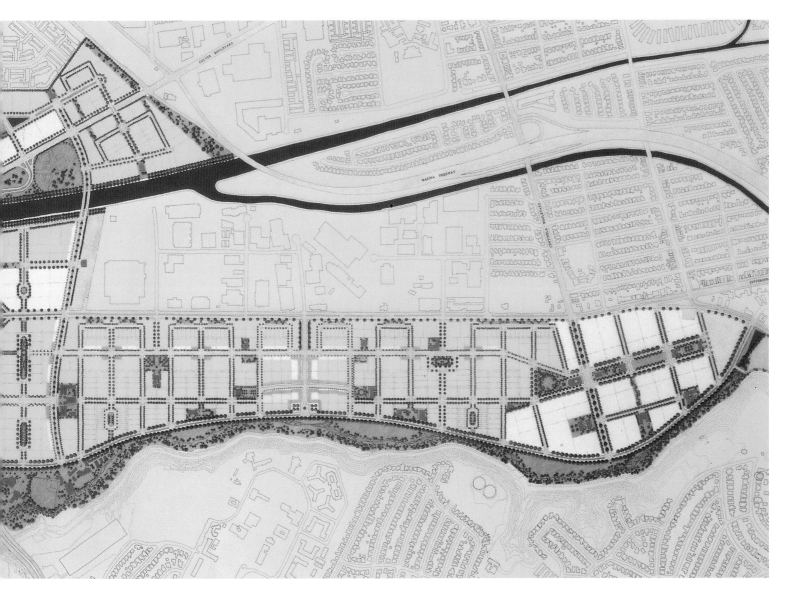

with 250 illustrations, 120 in color

Thames & Hudson

previous spread **Masterplan of Playa Vista development**, Los Angeles, Moore, Ruble, Yudell

First published in 2005 in hardcover in the United
States of America by Thames & Hudson Inc.,
500 Fifth Avenue, New York, New York 10110

thamesandhudsonusa.com

Library of Congress Catalog Card Number
2005900168

ISBN-13: 978-0-500-34210-7
ISBN-10: 0-500-34210-5

Printed and bound in Singapore by Star Standard

Contents

Preface

Nature by another Name: Coming to Terms with Terms   6

Part I: Constant Determinants of an Ecological Aesthetic

Introduction: Three Constant Themes   10

1   A Growing Respect for Traditional Knowledge   15
2   The Technological Imperative   19
3   Facing up to an Urban Future   23

Conclusion: A State of Flux   30

Part II: Leading the Green Revolution

Introduction: Reconfiguring the Modern Project   32

1   Charles Rennie Mackintosh: Reinterpreting the Scottish Vernacular   39
2   Ebenezer Howard: The Return to Paradise   49
3   Finland: The Search for a Humane Standard   57
4   The Amsterdam School: An Enduring Legacy   63
5   Frank Lloyd Wright: Close to the Land   71
6   Rudolf Schindler: Interacting with the Environment   77
7   Hassan Fathy: Reviving Ancient Techniques   85
8   Le Corbusier: The Retreat from Purism   95
9   Balkrishna Doshi: Reconsidering Modernism   107
10   Louis Kahn: Wrapping Ruins around Buildings   115
11   Rogers, Foster, Hopkins, Grimshaw: Engineering the Eco-Tech Aesthetic   123
12   Paolo Soleri: The Omega Seed Hypothesis   135
13   Buckminster Fuller: The Dymaxion World   143
14   Malcolm Wells and James Turrell: The March Underground   149
15   Edward Mazria: The Solar Cult of the 1970s   155
16   A Breath of Fresh Air   161
17   The Source of Sustainability   165
18   Ian McHarg: Passionate Steward of the Environment   175
19   A Revolution in Tent Technology   185
20   Kenneth Yeang: The Bioclimatic Skyscraper   193
21   The Aga Khan Award for Architecture: A Paradigm Shift   201
22   The New Urbanists: Building the Model Community   209
23   Jimmy Lim: The Tropical House   215
24   Rasem Badran and Abdel Wahed El Wakil: The New Traditionalists   221
25   Enric Miralles: A Critical Response to Place   227

Conclusion: Different Approaches to the Same Problem   232

Part III: Shifting Attitudes toward Tradition, Technology and Urbanism

Introduction: The Changing Landscape of a Natural Future   235

1   Digitizing the Environment   239
2   Tadao Ando: Perfecting Nature   245
3   The Greening of Los Angeles   251

Conclusion: Architecture in the Global Commons   260

Notes   263
Selected Bibliography   266
Acknowledgments for Illustrations   267
Index   268
Acknowledgments   272

Preface

Nature by another Name: Coming to Terms with Terms

The terms sustainable, ecological and green are often used interchangeably to describe environmentally responsive architecture, as they have been in this book. But at a deeper level each term is also heavily freighted with social and political implications and so we have to begin with an attempt at clarification.

Sustainability seems to be the most ubiquitous of the three terms today, and there is an entire section dedicated to the history of this phenomenon here (see pp. 165–73). It has resulted from a long series of institutional initiatives, primarily guided by the United Nations, that may be characterized as a compromise between the 'growth' and 'no-growth' factions of the environmental movement of the late 1960s and early 70s. It represents a middle ground that has allowed development, as well as the global funding of international development projects by large-scale financial institutions, to continue while pacifying the critics of such development.

Because of its institutional roots, sustainability is easier to trace and define than are the terms 'ecological' and 'green', and there has been a concerted attempt in each of the conferences that have been held since the term was first introduced in the 1970s to eliminate vague connotations. In *Our Common Future*, the proceedings of the Brundtland Commission (which was convened by the United Nations in 1987 to examine global environmental degradation), sustainability is defined as 'meeting the needs of today without sacrificing the ability of future generations to meet their own needs'. Debate soon centred around the relative value of the word 'needs' and the fact that 'needs' vary widely in different parts of the world depending on the status of development.

The Brundtland definition did, however, establish the essential intention of compromise, especially in relation to the conservation of non-renewable resources, and a more realistic understanding of the economic network that determines the use of these resources throughout the world. Because of this theoretical basis and the institutional origins of the term, sustainability embraces the following eight issues:

1 Resource Equity
Both the Brundtland Commission and the Rio Conference of 1992 stressed the need for a new approach toward resources, especially non-renewable ones, proposing a 'Green National Product' (to replace the Gross National Product) that would exclude non-renewable resources, and would put a more realistic value on others. This could also allow non-developed or developing nations to receive a more equitable return for their valuable resources, rather than forcing them to use these resources to pay off their debts.

2 Embodied Energy

Embodied energy covers all the energy needed to extract and process, transport and assemble a material or resource. There is still no single source available to those wishing to calculate such energy, showing how slowly these ideas have been implemented. Several attempts in the United States are still incomplete.

3 Global Community

The issue of resource equity extends into a larger socio-economic awareness of global responsibility for the architect, who must now 'think global but act local' in specifying materials, and understand the ramifications of choices.

4 Economics

The new ecological awareness requires the architect to be more open to other fields and to read more widely in socio-economic issues, so that more informed decisions can be made. This is not easy in a profession that can be very insular and focused.

5 Renewability

These considerations lead to a new way of looking at materials and form, replacing scarce resources with renewable materials. This often requires looking beyond fashion to a more durable approach to design.

6 Traditional Wisdom

Sustainability has led to a revision of the way we view traditional or vernacular architecture. Rather than viewing it as 'quaint' or picturesque, retrograde or primitive, we now understand that it has something to teach us, that 'local' architecture grew out of many trial-and-error attempts to deal with natural phenomena, and should be respected as a repository of wisdom.

7 Institutional Change

The architect's responsibility now extends beyond the design of buildings to the formation of policy change. An example of this is the Grameen Bank project by Muhamed Yunus in Bangladesh (see p. 205), which provided sites and services to borrowers in a micro-credit scheme that has now been replicated over the world.

8 Technology

One of the most important elements of the sustainability movement has been the new attitude toward technology that it has encouraged. There is a growing debate today as to how best to tackle environmental degradation. The 'appropriate technology' camp, building on E. F. Schumacher's book *Small is Beautiful*, proposes modest solutions to environmental problems, claiming that 'high-tech' answers just cause more problems and resource depletion. The 'high-tech' advocates, on the other hand, continue to believe that all problems can be solved by science.

Ecological Indeterminism

This precise provenance of the term 'sustainability', in relation to the built environment, makes it far less ambiguous than other terms such as 'ecological' or 'green', that are used to describe environmentally responsive architecture. Ecology itself is easy enough to understand, as it is the science of the relationship between all living organisms and their surroundings, but things get murky when the term is applied to building. Nevertheless it implies a connection to the global environmental movement that began to coalesce in the late 1960s as part of the social upheavals associated with that period. In the United States the focus began to shift away from social injustice toward pollution, toxic waste and population growth. This growing awareness diverted the attention of many young people from political issues and they were then joined by high-profile, affluent members of the upper middle class, who have remained the key supporters. This has led some sociologists to suggest that hostility to the 'limits to growth' proposals made in the 1960s by hardcore ecologists was the fuel that fed the environmental movement in the beginning; that it was a strategy for seizing control of the debate about where growth would take place, governed by economic motives, to protect personal assets.

President Nixon sensed a significant shift in the sensibilities of an influential segment of the electorate and made environmentalism one of the key issues of his administration. He went as far as to declare ecological distress a natural crisis in his State of the Union address in 1970. The National Environmental Policy Act which had been enacted the year before was followed by the Clean Air and Federal Water Pollution Control Act in 1970. The first Earth Day in America was held in June of that year, and vocal ecologists such as Barry Commoner were the heroes of the hour. By the early 1980s the Environmental Protection Agency estimated that there were thousands of environmental groups in the United States, with a combined membership of nearly ten million people.

The oil shocks of the 1970s, which saw prices escalate as supplies were cut off, confirmed political instincts about environmental issues. President Carter spearheaded an effort to make the United States as self-sufficient as possible in energy resources, and tax breaks were used to reward energy conservation. Although not affected as badly as America by the oil embargo, Europe also enacted similar measures. The result, in architecture, was that many practitioners began to jump onto the ecological bandwagon, becoming energy experts overnight in order to take advantage of a surge of new clients wishing to reap tax benefits. There were also many sincere attempts to find a new formal response to energy concerns, though these in almost every case were self-contained, self-sufficient solutions, completely lacking the global sensibility of sustainability, or even the reality of the networks evident in ecology itself.

The Green Movement

The Green Movement which began to emerge in the mid-1980s may be characterized as a radicalized variant of the ecological sensibility of the 1960s, being more assertive on political issues such as industrial pollution. In the United Kingdom the Ecology Party had only six hundred members in 1985, but grew considerably after its name was changed to the less middle-class Green Party in 1986. It was described soon afterward as 'the strongest organized hesitation before socialism'.

The association of the term 'green' with the ecological movement began much earlier, however. It can be traced back to the Grüne Aktion Zukunft (Green Action Campaign for the Future), and the Grüne Listen (Green List), which was used to identify political candidates with environmental sensibilities in West Germany in the 1970s, primarily in their opposition to nuclear power stations. In France, meanwhile, a Green Party was established in 1984, described by the press at the time as being 'in the front line of the ecological movement'. Greenpeace, the international organization that aggressively pursues issues related to environmental conservation and protection, was founded in Vancouver in 1971. It graphically personifies both the active and passive aspects of the 'no-growth' ideology. The self-described intention of the organization is to bring peace and environmental movements together, highlighting the ideological link between the two.

Contrasting the Green Sensibility with Sustainability

Three years after sustainability was put forward as a compromise in the growth/no-growth debate by the Brundtland Committee, the Commission of the European Communities released a far more holistic explanation of the reasons behind accelerated environmental degradation. Its *Green Paper on the Urban Environment* (1990), marks the beginning of environmental policy-making in urban areas within the European Union. It is an important connection to the ecological and later the green direction in architecture because it contains specific prescriptions for planning and building strategies intended to improve environmental sensibility.

Following the Single European Act in 1986, the Maastricht Treaty was ratified by all fifteen member states on 7 February, 1992. The focus of the Treaty was economic cooperation and monetary union, but it also covered common laws, as well as articles of agreement on citizenship, employment, cultures, public health, consumer protection and the environment. The treaty includes an extensive section on environmental assessment affecting planning policy, building procedures and public health. This section, which includes 'precautionary principles' that introduce the idea of preventative action into EC law, and the duties of member states, is far more specific and far reaching than its counterpart in *Agenda 21*, which stemmed from the 1992 Rio Earth Summit, in which the definition of sustainability was refined to include reparations by the G7 nations to the developing world as compensation for the use of under-valued, non-renewable resources which have been sold to manage the debt burden of the developing world.

Part I: Constant Determinants of an Ecological Aesthetic

Introduction: Three Constant Themes

Ecological considerations have generally been excluded from histories of architecture, perhaps because most studies of the built environment during the past century have focused on production. This book, an attempt to restore the balance, is only a beginning, and as such is necessarily selective. Subjects throughout the three parts have been chosen for their importance as catalysts of innovation or change, their polemical content or value as instructive contradictions to prevailing attitudes, or simply because they reveal a different aspect of a topic that many believe they already know well.

Relationships that Parallel Ecological Networks

Topics have also been chosen for their connection to each other, to provide a better understanding of the extent of environmental consciousness during a period of architectural history which is often (mistakenly) viewed as having very little. Together they begin to indicate a substantial network of connections that expanded over time, with patterns of growth that are reminiscent of the definition of ecology itself: the inter-relationship of living things to one another and their surrounding environment.

A glance at a few of the topics covered in this book immediately reveals such connections. Charles Rennie Mackintosh, for example, was considered by many to be the most effective advocate of Arts and Crafts principles, and the best able to reconcile handicraft with industrial production. He was sought out by both Hermann Muthesius and Josef Hoffmann for this reason, and his ideas eventually emerged as institutional doctrine, clearly legible in the curriculum of both the Weimar and the Dessau phases of the Bauhaus, where Walter Gropius, the founder of the Bauhaus, stressed the importance of integrating craft with new materials and assembly-line procedures. Although architectural design was not taught at the Bauhaus, the school's methods were adopted internationally and many of its faculty and alumni became teachers in architectural schools all over the world. Gropius became chairman of Harvard after leaving Germany, just before the Second World War.

Just as Mackintosh had done years previously, in the 1970s Ian McHarg again revolutionized the way in which architects perceived ecosystems and microclimates; like Mackintosh, too, he was born in Glasgow, where he was inspired by the stark contrast between nature and industry found there. After a distinguished military career he entered the Program in Landscape Architecture at Harvard soon after the war, during Gropius's tenure at that university.

Sir Ebenezer Howard, who was aware of the idealistic calls by leaders of the Arts and Crafts movement for a return to pre-industrial values, organized a competition for the design of a

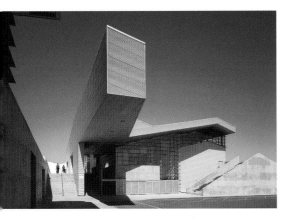

top **Katsura Villa**, Kyoto, 1624 onwards
middle **Diamond Ranch High School**, California, Morphosis, 2000
bottom **The Umbrella**, Culver City, Los Angeles, Eric Owen Moss, 2003

The notion of recycling materials or using the commonplace elements at hand is not new; rather, it was the basis of the Japanese *sukiya* style

new community outside London in 1903, intended to 'return people to their lost paradise'. Barry Parker and Raymond Unwin, who submitted the winning scheme, competed against many of the best-known Arts and Crafts architects of the time, including W. R. Lethaby and Richard Norman Shaw, and their new town, called Letchworth, was based on a cooperative model. Howard's 'Garden City' concept was the inspiration for countless attempts to reconfigure the city and integrate the built and natural environments elsewhere, becoming, for example, 'Forest Cities' in Finland. It was also the theoretical basis for the revolutionary 'Plan for the Valleys' proposed as a solution for suburban sprawl for a community near Washington, D.C. by Wallace, McHarg, Roberts and Todd in the early 1960s.

Hassan Fathy, who deliberately set out to derive a culturally based alternative to the 'International Style' for Egypt, began by conducting extensive research into vernacular prototypes to discover the reasons for their climatic effectiveness in the absence of mechanical systems. He is best known outside Egypt for his widely read *Architecture for the Poor*, a compelling account of an attempt at community building, but he actually completed more than fifty projects that constitute a repository of hard-won traditional knowledge about how to ameliorate harsh climatic conditions with what he referred to as 'appropriate technology'.

Fathy had several disciples in Egypt during his lifetime who adopted his principles and philosophy, the most notable among them being Abdel Wahed El Wakil. El Wakil extended Fathy's reach beyond Egypt, to Saudi Arabia, believing that a wealthier clientele would give these ideas greater currency. Rasem Badran, who is based in Jordan and never worked for Fathy personally, has also promoted Fathy's ideals at a larger scale, overlapping with many of the tactics (such as mixed use) being promoted by the 'New Urbanists' – Andrés Duany, Elizabeth Plater-Zyberk, Stefanos Polyzoides – in the process. Unlike El Wakil, Badran uses detailed typological studies specifically related to the region in which he is working. The work of El Wakil and Badran is discussed in Part II (see pp. 221–5).

Hassan Fathy was honoured by the Aga Khan Award for Architecture for his achievements, as were El Wakil and Badran, on separate occasions. Such prestigious winners have helped to establish the Award as an arbiter of a new, socially and environmentally based consciousness in the regions that it focuses upon, part of the global shift in this direction that parallels its beginning in the late 1970s.

As has been said, Fathy rebelled against the ahistorical and acontextual agenda of the Modern Movement or International Style (so called because it could be applied anywhere). And yet Le Corbusier, who is normally considered to be the prime exponent of the Modern Movement, and who was undoubtedly its most influential theorist, intentionally nurtured a culturally laden, place-specific alter ego, which, with its social memory and historical associations, was ecologically grounded. While he assiduously gave this alternative equal consideration to his more familiar Purist position, it has not been extensively explored because it does not conform to the heroic image that many apologists for modernism have wanted to portray. Constructing a brave new world, such historians seemed to imply, left no room for subjective sensitivity to the particular exigencies of time and place.

Louis Kahn, whose environmental sensibilities have also been largely overlooked, was greatly influenced by Le Corbusier's contextualizing, non-Purist, alternative and was as conscious of context and climate as he was of the formal spatial transformations for which he is best known. His little-known design for an American Embassy in Luanda, Angola, which unfortunately was never built, is a *tour de force* of environmental design and planning, especially in terms of the use of the roof as a parasol to mitigate heat gain (in much the same way as Le Corbusier in several of his contemporary Indian projects). The environmental strategies behind the highly complex, essentially rationalistic tectonic that Kahn created have not been investigated previously for many of the same reasons that his Swiss mentor has also not been considered to be ecologically astute: Kahn's monumentalism, which was promoted by Le Corbusier's realization that mass had to be reintroduced into architecture to retrieve a populist constituency, has tended to obscure his social and climatic conceptualism.

The free radical in the Le Corbusier–Louis Kahn equation is, of course, Balkrishna Doshi, who was one of the first Indian architects to work in Le Corbusier's Paris atelier – and who subsequently attempted through a trial and error process, to adopt Modernist principles to rapidly changing conditions in his own country. He was involved in the building of Chandigarh, and translated Le Corbusier's antithetical, earth-based alternative (perfected in the Sarabhai house in Ahmedabad – see p. 101) into a convincingly regional language at his own office, called Sangath. Kahn, who referred to Doshi as the 'wonderful architect of India', saw Sangath as an inspired synthesis of Modernist, Western, and regional, non-Western deliberations, and it is tempting to think (though difficult to prove) that Kahn adopted the barrel vault that he used at the Kimball Museum because of it.

And so the web of inter-relationships between architects continues, demonstrating that the initiatives described did not occur in isolation, but were part of a complex, ideological ebb and flow not dissimilar to that seen in all biological systems. This book is built around three recurring themes or *leitmotifs* of the recent past, which were generated by, and subsequently supportive of, much of the social theory of our time and form the focus of Part I. They are: tradition, technology, and urbanism, each a vital consideration in shaping our new conception of ecological architecture.

Tradition as the First Theme

In the spirit of its Latin origin, *tradere*, 'to carry forward', in this context tradition essentially represents the accumulated knowledge of past generations in relation to effective ways of dealing with the environment and place-specific techniques that historically have been used to control microclimates by the people that live in them.

The traditions embodied in ritual, which is used to impose a predictable pattern on the unpredictability of nature in order to give a sense of control over the unknown, have always involved technology. The cave paintings at Lascaux, for example, were rendered in pigments that the painters extracted directly from the earth and then compounded by fire. They convey, in a powerful and direct way, the complex mixture of awe and sympathy with which these early hunters regarded nature, the source of their prey. The ritual tradition also inspired the first monumental enclosures that superseded basic shelter. Warka, Stonehenge, the Pyramids at Giza, the Temple of Karnak, Yazilkaya, Chichen-Itza and all other early attempts to join with the cosmos were based on ritual related to nature.

Technology as a Second Theme

The first traditions provided the evolutionary distinction between our species and those that did not use tools as effectively. Technology, then, is inextricably intertwined with tradition, rather than being its antithesis. The agricultural revolution, as the first major technological expansion, was based on the cultivation of cereal grains and reorganized societies in different

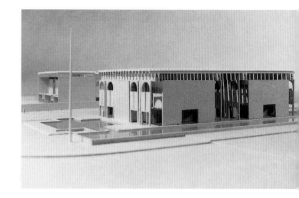

US Consulate in Luanda, Angola, Louis Kahn, 1959–62
Even architects considered to be the most staunch modernists often attempted to accommodate the environment.

Institute of Indology, Ahmedabad, Balkrishna Doshi, 1957–62
Regional adaptations on modernism, usually by architects in the developing world, often display ecological awareness of less costly, passive principles.

Roof Roof House, Kenneth Yeang, 1984
In the tropics, just providing shade alone provides considerable thermal comfort – this experimental house by Yeang uses a second baffle roof to offer extra protection from the climate.

ways at different times worldwide. It demonstrates the historical connection between tradition and technology since the growing and harvesting of grain on annual cycles required regular patterns and skills which eventually became traditions. The history of rice growing in Asia is a good example of this symbiosis. Rice grain, which began as a wild grass that grew in the Himalayan foothills, migrated to the Yangtze Valley in China over eight thousand years ago. It was well established throughout Asia by 2,000 BC, with terraced *padi* fields replacing wooded slopes, and hand cultivation methods being established that have remained basically unchanged since that time.

These methods depend on water, and in Bali villagers devised a way of conserving the rain from tropical storms in cisterns, to ensure that there would be enough to plant and grow the rice that they needed. Villages designated associations, called *subaks*, to oversee the fair distribution of the water, one of the first traditional social institutions founded on an appropriated technology.

Another example of the symbiotic relationship between tradition and technology as related to the environment comes from the Middle East, particularly the area known as the Fertile Crescent. When people began to build there during the agricultural revolution, they used the only materials available to them, mud and bitumen or oil, to best advantage, to cope with the hot, humid climate in which they lived. Thick, glazed mudbrick walls kept the heat at bay during the day and at night people slept on the roof to take advantage of cooler desert breezes. More predictable urban life also allowed manipulation of the environment to begin in earnest. The periodic burning of the savannah in Africa was relatively benign in comparison to the incremental salinization of the Tigris and Euphrates plain that took place because of aggressive irrigation (as well as because of the overgrazing of the fields that the irrigation made possible), however mitigated by transhumance. Recent discoveries of sophisticated terracing systems in eastern and south-eastern Asia, as well as extensive canal systems that supported planted raised beds in Mesoamerica, help to balance this image of systemic destruction, but the shocking message that is slowly emerging is that ancient societies were often little different from our own in their disregard of nature and desecration of the environment. It is simply a matter of scale and awareness.

Urbanism as a Third Theme

No serious assessment of the progress of an ecological sensibility can ignore the urban arena, and many of the topics discussed here relate to civic issues. By 2000, nearly half of the population of the world was living in cities, outnumbering those in rural areas for the first time in human history. Cities continue to hold out great promise as well as the potential for being the source of enormous problems; an extension of their dual, historical role as both beacon and guardian of civilization and an *entrepôt* of human misery. Rural–urban transitions, called 'the greatest migration in human history' and which accelerated during the Industrial Revolution of the late 18th and early 19th centuries, have caused serious strains. By 2000 nearly 600 million people in cities throughout the world were homeless, mostly due to decaying infrastructure or inadequate, outdated housing. The urban population is now growing three times faster than its rural equivalent, and almost all of it is happening in the developing world.

Despite these grim statistics, cities do have the obvious environmental advantage of concentrating more people on less land. They can also help their inhabitants achieve a more holistic world view and offer them the promise of a more fulfilling life by providing them with the framework they need to live it, alleviating poverty by maximizing opportunity.

As described in a United Nations study on the benefits of cities: 'Urbanization contributes to a nation's wealth (and thereby the planet's wealth) by enriching its domestic markets and international trade; (it) can create a nurturing environment for scientific experimentation and technological achievement. Cities are engines of job creation and can provide better services because they benefit from economies of scale. In reaching large numbers of people, metropolitan centres are also able to reduce energy costs, offer more efficient transportation systems, provide better educational facilities at lower cost and construct more habitable space'.[1]

The stark contrast between the promises of such advantages and the reality of city life today are impossible to overlook however, especially in the rapidly urbanizing parts of the developing world. Since a majority of the earth's non-renewable resources are also located in the developing world, comparisons between solutions to environmental problems in these regions and those attempted in the developed world, past and present, have inevitably provided much of the subject matter used in writing this book.

New strategies to cope with phenomenal city growth in both the developed and developing sphere obviously have important environmental repercussions and are increasingly predicated upon ecological considerations. The New Urbanist movement, which is considered in Part II, has been particularly effective and long lived, but is a recasting of many of the ideas put forward by Ebenezer Howard in his Garden City movement. As has already been stated, establishing such parallels is one of the key goals of this book.

1

A Growing Respect for Traditional Knowledge

Katsura Villa, Kyoto, 1624 onwards
Long admired as a perfect model of Japanese *sukiya* style, the Katsura Villa is now being studied for the environmental lessons it offers.

Tradition and technology are loaded words especially in relation to ecological architecture. There are traditions of technology in dealing with the environment and tradition itself is based in making, which is the essence of technology. To set tradition and technology against each other is to establish a false dialectic; a more accurate approach may be to try to discover where they concur or overlap and how this may be applied to environmental problems. The tendency from the beginning of the 20th century until the early 1980s was to regard traditional or vernacular architecture as primitive, quaint and unsophisticated: picturesque, perhaps, but certainly not worthy of serious research, or of informing contemporary form. Bernard Rudolfsky's *Architecture without Architects* in the early 1960s, which validates intuitive wisdom, was a courageous attempt to counter this dismissive attitude toward the vernacular, but while it did succeed in generating interest in traditional solutions to environmental conditions, the general feeling was that these solutions were unscientific (science being one of the central tenets of modernism).

When Walter Gropius and Bruno Taut wrote about the Katsura Villa, in Kyoto, they praised its aesthetic qualities and the potential of its modular system for conversion into a contemporary prefabricated system, without mention of the integral relationship between the Villa and its lake and garden, which is the main reason for its flexible system. Many non-Western critics saw this as a kind of ideological imperialism, the preferencing of one set of cultural values over others that were unfamiliar or different. This preference still prevails even through the post-modern period from the late 1960s to the late 1980s, which was supposed to have made us more sensitive to socio-historical variants. This may be because, as Robert Venturi himself finally admitted in the famous article 'Plus ça Change', post-modernism was just as exclusive as the movement it revolted against, treating history as pastiche, devoid of both context and content. Another critical point that Venturi made in that article, later substantiated by Fredric Jameson, is that the post-modern revolution was not a clean break at all, but a continuation of a pre-existing value system, deriving from an increase in commodification. History, then, was treated as a 'treasure chest' of styles to be raided at will. The superficial approach taken to style in post-modernism was similar to the modernist view of the vernacular as being picturesque.

What has changed since 'Plus ça Change'?
It is tempting to think that all this was changed by sustainability. Certainly, although sustainability can be seen as capitalism with a green face (since it, too, has been based on capital development), the fact that a majority of the non-renewable resources needed for

development happened to be located in the developing world meant that grudging respect had to be shown to poorer areas. So, while the United Nations organized one global conference after another on social issues that they determined to be related to sustainability, international lending institutions held their own meetings on the 'traditional wisdom' of indigenous peoples, announcing that only they knew how to coexist with and protect the environment. What may have arguably begun as a patronizing gesture intended to deflect criticism from 'development colonialism' (the lending of money to corrupt regimes for unnecessary, large and ecologically destructive projects, with the increased debt serviced by the wholesale sell-off of precious non-renewable resources) eventually and surprisingly led to serious research into traditional wisdom in the built environment (even if the architects doing such research often took the credit for their discoveries).

An example: when a large American firm was commissioned, as part of an international consortium, to design a new city in the desert near Yanbu, Saudi Arabia, it proposed building part of the housing underground, around planted courtyards, using evaporative cooling techniques involving misting devices and windtowers without reference to regional precedents. That same company also went through an expensive process of trial and error, exploring the use of what were eventually proven to be environmentally inappropriate conventional industrial systems for a large terminal for pilgrims in Jeddah, Saudi Arabia. They eventually arrived at a contemporary version of a Bedouin tent, a traditional solution to unforgiving climatic conditions that they could have referenced at the beginning of the design process.

Notable Exceptions

There are many people and initiatives outside the Western value system, and a few notable exceptions within it, who have respected traditional wisdom long before it became expeditious or fashionable to do so. Some have been unknown until now, some are revelatory, but all are important to a more balanced and thorough understanding of the halting but inexorable progress toward environmental consciousness, inevitably brought on by continually increasing human dysfunction and disrespect for ecological complexity.

It should come as no surprise that many of those who have explored or are exploring traditional solutions to environmental problems are in the developing and Muslim worlds (which frequently overlap). Tradition takes on special meaning in societies that have experienced colonialism or have a strong religious base. Egyptian architect Hassan Fathy, for example, looked to traditional prototypes to help him formulate a culturally relevant alternative formal language to the International Style, which he felt was exploiting his country. While his most famous followers now practice throughout the world, their philosophy and technique is solidly grounded in his language and principles, which were, in turn, directly appropriated from traditional currents at the core of Egyptian culture. Sedad Hakki Eldem, as another obvious example, was one of the first architects in Turkey to do extensive research on vernacular solutions and to extensively publish his results. His own work, concentrated in Istanbul, clearly reflects that research. Balkrishna Doshi and several other members of his generation, such as Charles Correa, trained in the West but adapted that training to local conditions in India, searching for points of concurrence between their technical education and inherited experience.

The Imperial Teahouse, Katsura Villa, Kyoto
Architecture and nature are seamlessly integrated in the teahouse, built from locally available materials and carefully oriented to maximize ventilation and views onto its lakeside site (see the site plan, below left).

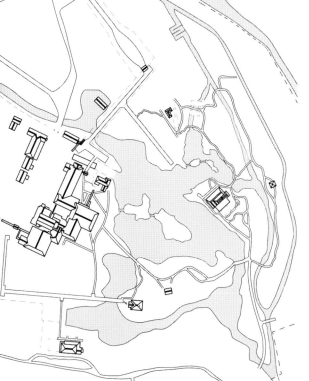

Rediscovering the Past to Move into the Future

The Award for Architecture which His Highness the Aga Khan established in 1977 (see pp. 201–207) quickly became an effective catalyst for raising public consciousness about the value of tradition. While it has continuously promoted what the Aga Khan has referred to as 'an architecture of quality', it has also typically recognized effective social programmes that improve the quality of life of common people, as well as conservation projects that preserve Islamic heritage. For those in countries which were previously colonized in this region of influence, regaining respect for tradition is no small matter since rediscovery is the only path to determining true identity. Colonial powers quickly realized that the most effective way to control their subjects was to strip them of their cultural heritage, or at least to denigrate it, to make it seem inferior.

Two Revolutions at Once

The nation state may be a threatened institution in the post-industrial societies of the information age, but the term 'nation-building' still resonates clearly in post-colonial countries in search of themselves. People in these countries need to retrace their steps, back to the point of the industrialization that made their resources so necessary and made the destruction of their culture such an effective tactic in helping to take them. This cathartic process is complicated by the fact that most of these newly minted nations are now in the process of industrialization themselves, as well as experiencing the information revolution. This adds to the difficulty of determining which traditions are real and which are preconceived, or tainted. An entire field of inquiry about the nature of authenticity in the social sciences has opened up, raising the belief among some that, because of the complex currents of globalization, there is no such thing as pure heritage today.

More Knowledge, Less Memory

In the post-industrial, developed, Western or G8 nations, tradition has a very different meaning. The exponential explosion of knowledge that they have experienced by being on the right side of the digital divide has meant that, like Alice and the Red Queen, people in these nations must now run faster and faster just to stay in the same place. They must focus on a future about to become the present and cannot ever concentrate on the past. Paradoxically, the more knowledge that electronic technology has allowed people in these societies to codify, the less historical memory those who have access to it seem to have. How else can one explain the astonishing number of museums that were built soon after the millennium, except as a collective, panicked response to an anticipated onset of cultural amnesia, akin to someone facing dementia putting nametags on framed photographs of loved ones they fear they will soon forget?

The tendency for people who are experiencing this unprecedented compression of space and time to search for relief in the past and in historical memory, was first identified by John Naisbett as the 'high-tech-high-touch syndrome'. The more technology that people have, the more human connection they seem to need. The individuals and case studies selected for review here generally demonstrate that balance, or the consequences that can result from not achieving it.

2

The Technological Imperative

Technology is not new: *homo habilis*, the toolmaker, was a critical stage in the evolution of *homo sapiens*. From the beginning technology in the best sense of the Greek root word *techné*, has been a functional adaptation, the making and using of tools to both survive in and transform our surroundings. What is new about the modern, essentially utilitarian, contract between human beings and their inventions is the magnitude of the socioeconomic transformation that technology now causes. What has led to this change, and what does it imply for architecture in relationship to the environment?

Sociologists have long been aware that technology can be used to build as well as to destroy: the chariot that the wheel made possible was used for trade as well as war, metal has been beaten into ploughshares as well as swords, and nuclear power can fuel cities as well as level them. This duality has led to the conclusion that technology isn't neutral; that tools, once invented, alter both makers and users.

What's in a Name?

There have been many attempts intellectually to accommodate the drastic changes brought on by the electronic revolution, but these have become lost in the plethora of data that they have sought to explain. This confusion largely stems from the growing influence of the media since the advent of television in the late 1940s, which has generated a public hunger for novelty. In architecture, this lust for the new has manifested itself in the search for names, the stylistic equivalent of product differentiation and brand recognition, to the extent that it soon became difficult to determine whether these names identified or precipitated the socially engendered phenomena they were intended to reflect. Did the International Style really exist before it was declared to be a cohesive idea by a self-appointed arbiter of public taste? Was post-modernism really a cultural shift just waiting to be named, as its proponents claim, or was it their branding that made it real? Was Deconstruction a valid recognition of the eclipse of institutional power and the temporal point at which technology superseded human intelligence, or merely the clever invention of a lone philosopher and his architectural acolyte, as some suspect?

A More Accurate Prediction

The term 'Post-Industrial Society,' first introduced by social scientist Daniel Bell in 1973, however, has stood the test of time as a perceptive reading of the way in which technology is regarded and has been used. Placing this change in the context of the last two centuries, Bell argues that we are in the third and final stage in the transition from an agrarian society. This transition began with the invention of steam power by James Watt in 1765 at the beginning of

Diamond Ranch High School, California, Morphosis, 2000
Technology provides architects with many tools that can be used to preserve the environment, if employed wisely. Earth-moving and material recycling were two of those used in this project.

the Industrial Revolution, a fundamental shift from the dependence on human strength and to the power of the machine. The second stage occurred during the industrial age, when steam power was replaced by electricity. And in the third stage, 'information, derived from knowledge has been encoded in comprehensive technological systems.'[1]

Bell maintains that the implications of this transformation are far reaching, since the emphasis on technological and social progress that is integral to linear, machine production is antithetical to the cyclical character of tradition and the circular, repetitive, concept of time and the established rituals that it embodies. While the technologies of the industrial age are 'transformative', the critical mass of data made possible by the computer has finally initiated an exponential reorganization in the way knowledge is used. This has created what has been referred to as the 'technological sublime': the intractable replacement of the Kantian concept of the ineffable essence of nature by its mechanistic counterpart.[2] Bell partially attributes this displacement to the 'materials revolution'; the post-industrial innovation of the technological substitution of natural resources with new, synthetic, products that have the same properties as the materials that have been replaced. This substitution accelerated our separation from nature and the social analogies of personal habit that have developed through our interaction with it. This along with the mass amnesia about the past that has paradoxically resulted from the deluge of information made available in the information age, poses a serious threat to indigenous cultures, social traditions, respect for history, and the sense of appropriate approaches to environmental degradation that these imply.

The Technological Imperative

The hope that technology really is capable of satisfying all physical and emotional needs (in spite of overwhelming evidence to the contrary) may explain the complete absence of debate about the negative impact it has had. The prevailing attitude about the increasing reliance on computers during the architectural design process, for example, is that this particular technology seems to be positive beyond question. The future it promises to shape is implicitly formulated as infinitely desirable, inevitable, and improved.

Technological determinism, predicated on the belief that social benefit is entirely dependent on scientific discovery, focuses on innovation rather than the consequences of such dependency. Tools not only change individual patterns of behaviour but also cause transformations in the institutions that are their social analogy. Technology profoundly affects the cultural, political and psychological conditions of a society and is in turn shaped by the socioeconomic forces unleashed by it. The ancient, internalized, kinaesthetic connection between tools and their makers, in which they become both physical and psychological extensions of their users, may also partially explain the lack of reflection and discussion about the possible consequences of the use of the computer in design. Just as have other tools in the past, the computer is conditioning our understanding of the world and our perception of our place in it. It is more than a pragmatic means to an end, or an inert piece of plastic and metal, it is a virtual constituent in a very real symbiotic reconstruction of the world.

The Computer is Changing the Architect's Relationship to Nature

The computer is the most powerful manifestation yet of the human ability to use technology to subdue nature. In addition to shaping behaviour, it generates powerful social consequences. Social scientists maintain that it also impacts on social structure because it

Diamond Ranch High School

In his design for Diamond Ranch, Thom Mayne, the principal architect of Morphosis, tried to work with a difficult topographical condition, which is recalled in the forms.

affects politics and culture, regulates personal behaviour through subtle coercion, reconfigures prior cultural patterns, and hinders or transforms other technologies. It also affects societies peripheral to it, by exerting a strong symbolic influence on them, reconfigures opportunities, transforms individual and collective psychological development and redirects authoritarian processes which become binding on individuals and groups.

While it does not subdue nature in the overt way that industrial technologies did, this incremental electronic shift has tended to make nature an even more abstract concept than it was already, reducing the world to the size of a monitor in a dimly lit room. There are some encouraging exceptions to these technologically induced detachments, however, which are introduced here and which can be generally categorized as the digital imitation of ecological processes. Those who are investigating this direction see the computers as the key to the final realization of humankind's long-held wish to be reunited with the natural world, and the architect's desire to accommodate this.

Kisho Kurokawa has made the point, relative to Japanese architecture, which is one of the most technologically advanced in the world, that his nation has wholeheartedly embraced the information revolution and deserves suitably up-to-date buildings. In his view, the High-Tech approach is passé, and inappropriate for Japan, because the country has moved beyond the industrialized phase of development that the High-Tech language celebrates.

But, aside from several stunning attempts in Japan metaphorically to replicate the social transformation that the electronic revolution has brought about, such as the Sendai Mediathèque by Toyo Ito early in 2001, there has not been in that country even a suggestion of the potential of the computer to replicate the natural processes in the architecture there, as there has been in Britain and the United States. This is surprising, considering the longstanding Japanese ability to transmute the technological breakthroughs of other cultures.

Norddeutsche Landesbank Headquarters, Hanover, Germany, Behnisch, Behnisch and Partner, 2002
European architects tend to side with highly technological solutions to environmental challenges, while their American counterparts seem to seek more passive proposals.

Perhaps this is precisely because technology is a socially specific structure, which can be copied in form but not in deep content, raising the possibility that the homogenous electronic revolution is just a myth and that its effects are being assimilated at different rates, in different ways, depending on cultural parameters.

These, as well as many other questions about the role that technology has played and continues to play in the evolution of ecological architecture, are discussed here in comparison to, and in contrast with, tradition and urbanism.

3

Facing up to an Urban Future

Plan Voisin for Paris, Le Corbusier, 1925
Grandiose modernist schemes such as Le Corbusier's
highly insensitive proposal for levelling much of the
historical fabric of Paris, have left the impression that
environmental concerns were absent from that
movement.

The city was established as a collective institution soon after the agricultural revolution more than four thousand years ago. In the transitional period, moving from a nomadic, hunting and gathering existence to the settlements made necessary by annual growing cycles, cities grew as a way of accommodating newly stationary populations, and the crops they had to tend, trade and store, and many of the social institutions within them, revolved around this economic base. The city remained basically the same until it was transformed by a change from an agrarian to an industrial entity at the beginning of the 19th century, when people left the farms to work in factories that were built in cities to concentrate goods, production, markets and services there.

Many of those discussed in this book have been involved in trying to understand, explain or improve the modern industrial city (and the progressive displacement of its pre-industrial counterpart), in particular the nature of the interaction between people, the city and the natural environment. Often this involvement may be characterized as ambivalent: admiration for the complexity of the city and the opportunities it offered as the incubator of civilization on one hand, disdain for its capacity for destruction on the other. Louis Kahn, who came to Philadelphia as an immigrant when he was very young, praised the city as 'the place where a child can discover what it will be for the rest of its life', and dedicated his entire life to bolstering the institutions that he first encountered within it. Le Corbusier and Ebenezer Howard can be characterized as having been diametrically opposed to each other on the issue of what the city should be, particularly in relation to the question of urban density. Le Corbusier wanted to dramatically increase density: his Plan Voisin for Paris, which he proposed in 1925, radically replaced Baron Haussmann's much-admired, uniformly scaled *maisonettes* flanking wide, tree-lined boulevards, with soaring cruciform tower blocks that Le Corbusier believed would open up large areas of green space beneath and between them, creating more parkland in the city. Ebenezer Howard thought that density could not be achieved without overcrowding and proposed his Garden Cities.

Deyan Sudjic has described these two positions as 'the two fundamental and sharply opposed recurring themes' that result in all strategies for shaping the city in the industrial era, in which 'the purpose of building has as much to do with a vision of a certain kind of state as it did with the pragmatic concerns of civic life.'[1]

Aldo Rossi advised (in his typically rational way) in *Architecture of the City*, that it is more productive for researchers to focus on the city as a subject of study when investigating the sources of architectural form, because a majority of the most enduring typologies can be found there. For Egyptian architect Hassan Fathy, who differs from others discussed here in his preoccupation with the pre-industrial city, the medieval quarter of Cairo served that purpose, becoming the research field in which he discovered the repeatedly used building blocks of what he believed could be a new more culturally representative and environmentally responsive architecture for his country. In the process, he also discovered, to his amazement, that all of medieval Cairo once functioned as an ecological entity, incrementally and collectively designed by subsequent generations of builders to capitalize on basic physical principles of convective cooling that can also be found in many other pre-industrial cities.

A Third Revolution

The city itself, however, is now undergoing a third revolutionary transformation, which affects the natural world and those building in it in unprecedented ways. To begin to understand the full extent of that transformation, it is necessary to outline how industry, which was the cause of the second urban upheaval, is changing.[2]

Global economics have undergone a fundamental shift toward an integrated and coordinated division of labour in production and trade, which has incrementally displaced conventional, assembly-line manufacturing organized within national boundaries. Fed by the electronic revolution, 'flexism', in which corporations seek out the lowest-priced production location for each component of a product in various parts of the world, has replaced 'Fordism,' the complete assembly of a product in a single factory as Henry Ford did with the first mass-produced automobiles. In the developing world, which is favoured by producers based in the developed world for manufacturing because of lower wages and costs, products for export increased from an average of 27 to 46 per cent of GNP between 1963 and 1981 during the initial phase of this new phenomenon. In mainland China, which only opened up to trade in the late 1970s, foreign import and export trade increased drastically after 1978 before acceptance into the World Trade Organization. This has also had a revolutionary impact in the developed world. In the United States, for example, total manufactured products increased by 250 per cent between 1975 and 1990, but the labour force involved decreased to 17 per cent in that same period. This has exacerbated economic differences there, between those with the digital skills to adapt to the demands of the new information economy, and those without them, who are relegated to lower paying service jobs. It has also initially resulted in the abandonment of manufacturing facilities in large industrial cities, an ironic reversal of the rural–urban migration that accompanied the Industrial Revolution one hundred years ago.[3]

Generally, globalization and the electronic revolution that has fostered it have exponentially accelerated the interaction between nations, regions and localities, setting up a dialectic of cultural interchange on one hand and reflexiveness on the other. Exchange and trade, as quantitative factors of part of the complex information age transformation, and the qualitative factors of cultural and social values, shared and protected, are far more difficult to assess.

The Death of the Nation State

Analysing the threat that new global alliances now pose to national hegemony has become something of a cottage industry among social scientists. In spite of their general sense of certainty, however, these analyses fail to take into account the real reasons behind the durability of the nation state. They fail to account for delayed development due to colonialism, in which nation-building must complete its natural cycle to allow the complex

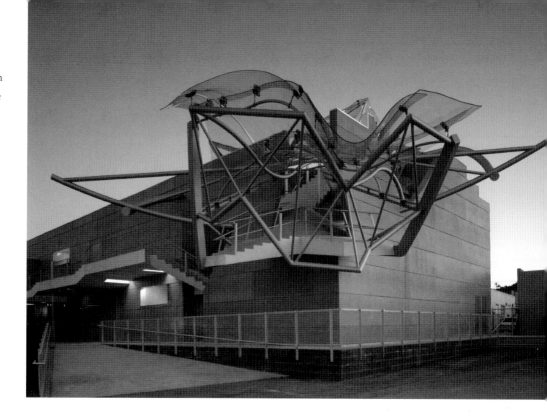

The Umbrella, Culver City, Eric Owen Moss, 2003
While avant-garde architect Eric Moss has a reputation
for high-profile object buildings, he also deserves to be
credited for recycling old structures, as here.

legacy of external domination to be assimilated. An alternative hypothesis is that the tendency
toward cultural identification that these social historians identify is more than just a
collective, frightened response to the possibility of the death of the nation state, as Kenichi
Ohmae claims.[4] It is a powerful force now operating inside the framework of the nation state,
capable of rising above the riptide of homogeneous, and mostly American, global icons that
Ohmae thinks will destroy it, and it invariably includes tradition and environmentalism as
rallying cries. This force, however, must be carefully qualified, since one faction in the post-
colonial debate about the positive or negative effects of foreign occupation believes that the
colonial experience has delayed social development in varying degrees in all of the countries
that experienced it. This has caused a layered reaction, an ideological reverberation in defence
of nationalism that is being blatantly supported by architecture in the states most affected.

Rational Argument Meets the Irrational Phenomenon of Global Cities

Kenichi Ohmae represents the extreme position of a view held by a number of economists,
a view which is very compelling on a strictly rational basis. But 'new' countries that have
experienced colonization defy rational categorization. Economic regions such as the 'Greater
Growth Triangle' of Phuket, Medan and Penang, for example, which Ohmae uses as a prime
proof of his theory, are more readily able to take advantage of instantaneous shifts of capital
and consumer awareness, fostered by the media. But nations and nationalism, for which so
many have fought and died, will not quickly disappear.

Since the phenomenon of globalization began to be recognized, the assumption has been
that not only nation states, but the cities that sustain them, would be made obsolete by
'flexism'. The wholesale abandonment of industrial areas was seen as a critical symptom of
redundant systems, and this is still a common perception. Several researchers, however, have
begun to observe a new and surprising stage in the rapid evolution of globalization. One of

the most insightful of these, sociologist Saskia Sassen, has described this significant shift thus: 'the geography and composition of the global economy has changed so as to produce a complex duality: a spatially dispersed, yet globally integrated organization of economic activity.'[5] If true, the ramifications of this argument are critically important for the future of the city, regardless of its international context.

The Duality of Dispersal and Concentration

Sassen's argument is based on well-documented evidence that in spite of an early economic decline in many cities with a strong industrial base, that trend has now reversed in many cases. The off-shoring of manufacturing, as well as migration of headquarters to the suburbs (once the need to be near factory production ended), has continued, but those who predict the demise of the city because of the absence of factories and corporate headquarters have ignored the crucial transformation of the financial industries that began in the early 1980s and has continued to accelerate. This change has involved the growing strength of investment banks and security houses, as well as a complete reorganization of the financial dispersal of factories, offices and service industries. The subsequent reorganization of the financial industry over the last twenty years has paradoxically led to the centralization of management and regulation of an increasingly dispersed global network of production sites. This has resulted in the concentration of management in large cities (where new forms of financial service are located) and a shift in institutional composition, from large corporations and commercial banks to specialized corporate service. It has also involved a shift in institutional composition, from large corporations and commercial banks to specialized corporate service firms and non-bank financial institutions.

The new forms of 'producer' services that Sassen has identified, which have found it essential to congregate in cities because they are interdependent, are: financial, legal, general management, management consulting, advertising, engineering, insurance, real estate, accounting, storage and retrieval, as well as production technology, maintenance, transport, communications, wholesale distribution, cleaning services, security and design. The result of this synergistic concentration of service facilities has been that the city has returned to, or has retained, its traditional role as production site. The difference is that this production is relatively isolated, in spite of the proximity of these facilities, because of the electronic rather than physical interaction that sustains them. This difference has had a significant impact on the way in which city dwellers now view nature. Another major difference is that, unlike the industrial manufacturing complex that existed in or near cities in the recent past, this new 'producer services complex' feeds a transnational network rather than the city in which it is located, so that each city is disconnected from its regional or national context, using the region's resources, but not making a reciprocal contribution.[6]

Global Cities and the Changing Workplace

The last critical piece of the thesis just described is that certain cities in the world were predisposed (because of singular attractors in each of them) to benefit most from this unpredicted growth in the producer services complex that has kept the urban typology intact, but each has radically changed from a participatory to an insular form. A disproportionate share of activity has been seen in New York City, London and Tokyo in the developed sector, and in São Paulo, Buenos Aires, Bangkok, Taipei and Mexico City, among others, in the developing sector, but there are other factors that are also common in conurbations that have not been designated as global cities.

A common denominator in each of these cities and others that are now joining them as global producer service zones is a radical change in the office landscape. In the early 1980s, information technology was heralded as liberating. Sociologists and technical experts alike predicted that digital technology would allow employees to work from home, checking into the office only when necessary by modem, fax or cell phone, and would provide more leisure time because time-consuming tasks could be completed much faster. What has happened instead is that digital access has increased the amount of information available as well as the ease of access to it and the time needed to assimilate it: electronic efficiency has added to employee workload rather than lightening it. In spite of the heady prospect of the freedom of a home office for everyone and the end of commuting, the harsh reality of corporate control and the panoptical view has remained unchanged, or even intensified. As Sassen has indicated, the synergistic aspect of the services industries supporting the transnational information economy, as well as the reluctance of management to allow employees to work at home and the basic human need for social contact, mean people still work from a central office. They typically spend more time there now than a decade ago, in front of a computer screen, with the expectation of higher productivity forcing them to forego overtime, since everyone is now 'outsourced.'[7]

A Further Distancing from Nature

Longer hours at the office, in relative isolation, separated from the outside world, have led to a demand for communal spaces, as places of respite, and visual distractions, when off-screen. Since more time is often spent with co-workers than with family, the office has become a surrogate home, with residential comforts now more clearly in evidence. Gathering around the coffee machine or water cooler has now been replaced by sitting around a large dining table in a home-like environment, of a scale that can accommodate a new, unlikely, digital family. This forced separation from the outside world, encouraged by architects who are now mastering new skills required to create these worlds within, adds yet another layer to the human experience of the natural world caused by both the materials revolution and the information age. Although Saskia Sassen identifies more established concentrations as the world cities of the post-industrial society, both edges of the Pacific Rim present models of a similar type, that do not exactly fit into this category.

An Exception in America

Los Angeles, for example, is redefining the global city. It does not strictly comply with the criteria cited by Saskia Sassen, and its difference from the categories she mentions is instructive. Following the immediate post-industrial period, when large areas of established cities declined and became derelict, a third reality, as opposed to the New Urbanism and the phenomenon of creeping exurbia, emerged as intrepid entrepreneurs began to reclaim these abandoned districts, prompted by the low cost of land and buildings in a depressed market. In Culver City, Los Angeles, for example, an internal, electronic city designed by Eric Owen Moss is gaining critical mass, composed of individual, hermetically sealed buildings, connected only by computers and asphalt. This burgeoning conurbation, alternatively called the 'Palindrome' or 'Conjunctive Points' by its developer, Frederick Smith, is completely unlike any previous models of urban form, and holds important clues to what the city of the future may look like. The 'Palindrome' is based entirely on a commercial premise. Its employee inhabitants rarely leave their respective digital workspaces due to the pressures of deadlines, and no public amenities exist outside their offices even if they did have time to leave. A key assumption of this harsh vision, unlike that of the New Urbanists, is that the automobile will continue to be the primary means of transport far into the future and should be dealt with realistically. While electric power may replace the internal combustion engine, the planners of the 'Palindrome' feel that nothing can replace the freedom that the automobile offers.[8]

On a more reassuring note, the Culver City initiative defines a positive future for Los Angeles, and other cities that will follow this model, even though it is less neatly proscribed than the nine to five, suburbs to office and back again, nuclear family image of the past. The Moss model, which ironically accepts the reality of the computer-bound, information-based society of the present and near future, of working indoors all day and much of the evening and then driving away for a short stay in a dormitory community, is unfortunately much more believable than the romantic vision of the future painted by the New Urbanists in their plans for the rejuvenation of the Los Angeles downtown, or other cities throughout the world, and therein lies the main danger to environmental security.

Buildings in the Palindrome are each used as a pedagogical tool by Moss, to show what can be done with the detritus of the industrial city, the abandoned factories, asphalt parking lots, highways, toxic waste zones, and steel towers that still remain. He has transformed each of these, as they used to exist in Culver City, into viable commercial buildings used primarily by companies related to the entertainment industry in Los Angeles. The Umbrella, for example, is constructed of bow-string trusses used to support an original warehouse roof, with new metal trusses, turned upside down to mirror the old structure, announcing the entry. The former Pittard Sullivan building, which is across the street, responds to, rather than ignores, a parking lot. The Stealth Building bridges a fully restored and cleaned toxic waste zone. The Samitaur Building, now a Kodak Headquarters, shows what can be done to span a highway, which has high relevance in a city connected only by freeways. The Palindrome or 'Conjunctive Points' is an assembly of real urban typologies, approached as prototypes for the future and the new automobile-based digital workplace of today, rather than a romantic fantasy centred around the patterns of the past.

An Asian Alter Ego

Perhaps the clearest example of an Asian alternative to Sassen's concept of the office tower as electronic beacon of the information age, and the adaptation of office spaces to digital concentration, is the work of Kenneth Yeang and T. R. Hamzah in Kuala Lumpur, Malaysia. To adapt the office-tower typology to the new demands made on the workforce discussed earlier, Yeang has conceived what he terms the possibility of a new 'life in the sky', shifting the focus from the technological advances that have made it possible to build taller buildings to the psychological and physiological well-being of the users. Yeang argues that 'conventional urban design carried out at the ground plane is concerned with such aspects as place making, vistas, creating public realms, civic zones, linkages, figure ground and the massing of built form. This type of thinking must now be extended upwards.'[9]

To humanize floor slabs disconnected from the ground, Yeang's sense of sustainable compromise prompts him to recommend plan layouts that address 'human habits' and

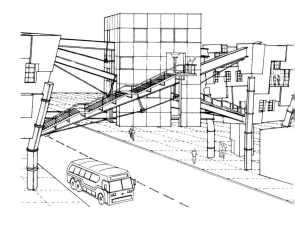

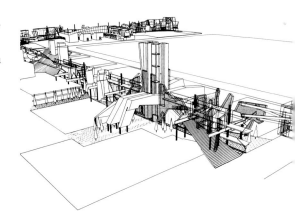

Drawings for the Culver City Development,
Los Angeles
The concentration of recycled and new buildings by Eric Owen Moss in Culver City, on the fringe of Los Angeles, which has been going on since 1988, has now reached a critical mass, to the extent that it has been designated 'The New City' by its developer.

'logical cultural patterns' as well as meeting in 'sky-courts,' or open transitional spaces between the inside skin and outside perimeter of the skyscraper. This idea was tested in Kuala Lumpur in 1992, in a headquarters for the IBM representative in Malaysia, called the Menara Mesiniaga (see p. 192). The 'sky-courts' there are three-storey-high recessed terraces cut deep into the facade, begin at the top of a high, heavily planted earth berm base and spiral around the face of the circular tower. These were originally intended to be planted, to carry the vegetation on the base upward in a verdant coil, through the structure of the metal tower. That idea has not yet been realized because of cost, but these atria do direct the convective currents of cool air rising from the heavily planted berm up, around and into the building.[10]

Conventional, curtain-wall glazing is only used on the cooler north and south façades of the Menara, and all the east- and west-facing windows are shaded by wide aluminium bands projected out from the building, which are positioned by solar chart. This animates the surface of the tower, making it a three-dimensional lesson in diurnal patterns, a high-tech sundial that shows how mute skyscraper façades have been in the past.

In other towers that have followed Menara Mesiniaga, Yeang has been able to open up the interior, and to carve his 'sky-courts' deeper into it, by placing vertical circulation on the perimeter, freeing up the inside core for atria and also using the core to act as a shield against heat gain during the hottest part of the day. Typically placed in the centre of either a rectangular or square tower in the past, the middle core was considered an immutable given in skyscraper design until recently, when architects in the Kingdom of Saudi Arabia began experimenting with different strategies to combat escalating energy costs. Two designs, by Zuhair al Fayez and Skidmore, Owings and Merrill, appeared almost simultaneously, using this idea. In their tower for the National Commercial Bank, in Jeddah, Skidmore, Owings and Merrill used an equilateral triangle as a plan form rather than the orthogonal perimeter that was typical in the mid-1980s, when it was built. They extracted the elevator and stair core from the centre and placed it on one of the sides of the equilateral triangle, to open up the inside. A similar strategy, of using an extracorporeal core connected to a U-shaped tower, lidded to provide shade for a protected central court, was used by Saudi architect Zuhair al Fayez at the same time, and both designs changed prevailing attitudes about core location, predicting Yeang's approach.

By coming to terms with the new realities that workers now face, of longer hours in closed environments, frequently in reclaimed, previously industrial urban areas or in office towers, Moss and Yeang have each created unconventional, as well as controversial alternatives to the world cities of tomorrow, that have redefined the way that nature is viewed and dealt with, in the city.

Conclusion: A State of Flux

Categories that seemed so comprehensible in the 1970s with the publication of *The Coming of Post-Industrial Society* by Daniel Bell have begun to blur and are not as neat and tidy as they were once thought to be. The 'Information Age' that Bell identified certainly became more manifest in the decades that followed but his theory was not nuanced enough to account for the digital divide: the differences between the developed and the developing worlds and each of the nations in those two spheres. It also did not predict the post-colonial sensibility that dominated theory as one symptom of the multi-faceted populism of the 1980s, to the extent that entire departments of Post-Colonial Studies were formed in many major universities.

Complex Layering

This does not diminish Bell's achievement in producing the equivalent of the Theory of Relativity in the social sciences, but his hypothesis does now beg to be updated to account for the layering that has taken place in the interim and the changing status of nations that have in the past experienced colonial intervention. Layering relates not only to the varying speeds of electronic conversion (due in turn to economic development) but also to the much bigger issue of the different rates of such development and the complicated interface between industrialism and technological transformation that all nations in the developing world now face.

Put bluntly, the developing world is by definition still in the process of industrialization, going through the same social upheavals as its developed counterpart did more than two hundred years ago, and is also in the throes of the electronic revolution: which means it is experiencing its industrial and post-industrial age at the same time. These social dislocations sound all too familiar: rapid urbanization due to rural–urban migration as people move to the city to find work, and the disruption of cultural institutions as new technologies begin to take precedence over well-established traditions. The post-colonial sensibility must also be layered over this bifurcation, in those nations which have experienced this condition, making it much harder for the developing world to cope.

Post-Colonial Patterns

As Frantz Fanon so vehemently pointed out in his polemical tracts of the 1960s, culture is the first thing that a colonizer attacks, in order to render its host country neutral – paralysed by self-doubt and an overwhelming feeling of inferiority. This includes the undermining or overt destruction of traditions that sustain that culture, and extends to indigenous architecture, one of the most enduring traditions of all, which the colonizer typically characterizes as primitive, backward, or uncivilized. This architecture, which is invariably in harmony with the specific climatic conditions in which it evolved, then also becomes anathema to the elite within the colonized country, who have been fostered and supported by the colonial power and who remain as a ruling class once it is gone. This upper class adopts the social and institutional forms of the absent authority, perpetuating the cultural destruction that kept it in power. These forms and attitudes as well as continuing economic dependence amount to colonization in absentia, after independence has been attained, for developing countries in this category.

The Implications for an Ecological Architecture

Fanon also proposed that the nation-building phase, which only began after independence in the developing world, but which is now morphing into cross-jurisdictional entities of economic or strategic convenience in the developed world, must begin with cultural rehabilitation, to recover lost identity, since physical fabrication alone is not enough.

Even though this critically important concept has not been adopted as part of a post-colonial policy, there are many indications that it is instinctively understood. A rediscovery of traditional social, cultural, religious and political forms is underway throughout the post-colonial world. Since this, of necessity, has also included architecture, and since vernacular approaches are environmentally astute, such architecture is ecologically orientated by default.

Several more insightful individuals or institutions such as those discussed in Part II have gone beyond superficial forms into substance, once they have understood the essential function of cultural regeneration in helping to re-establish national, regional, ethnic or religious identity. They have also understood that such renewal involves change, that tradition is not static but typically shows initial reliance upon a meaningful type that is improved upon, using the latest technical knowledge. Cities are the incubators of these types because this knowledge is concentrated there: it is no accident that many of those who have undertaken this search for cultural identity in architecture have used cities as study areas from which they have extrapolated ideas, rather than forms.

This process has been infectious, so that even nations in the developing world who have not experienced colonization, or have been occupied only temporarily or partially, now have architects who are engaged in this search for collective identity. This has necessitated a renewed appreciation of environmentally adept prototypes and their adaptation. In some rare cases, such as Thailand, which was spared the intentional disruption of cultural development imposed on its neighbours through its diplomatic skills at remaining neutral, cultural identity is much stronger and architecture – as opposed to building – has not moved beyond traditional types. There is great pride in the past there as well as a sense of national memory, to the extent that the legacy of the International Style is not as evident.

But whether developed or not, nations today share a deep sense of loss: their citizens are searching for ways to give meaning to the present by looking back to the past. This includes coming to terms with the increasingly imperilled and rapidly diminishing natural world through an architecture which responds to and respects it, and understanding the intentions of others who have done so, even though some of these intentions have previously been misunderstood. This book is an attempt to begin to re-examine these intentions and to clear up these misunderstandings.

Part II: Leading the Green Revolution

Introduction: Reconfiguring the Modern Project

The first phase of global industrialization, which began in the 19th century, was far more straightforward than the second phase is proving to be. Indeed, with the benefit of hindsight it now seems obvious that our blind faith in progress was unwise, but at the time invention was unquestionably considered to be the key to a better life. The light bulb replaced the gas lamp, the refrigerator replaced the ice chest, the automobile replaced the horse and carriage and daily existence became slowly but incrementally easier. This translated into enormous economic growth, of course, and competition between newly industrializing nations in this first cycle was intense as each struggled for their share of a global market, with architecture used as one of the measuring sticks of progress.

Modern architecture can be seen as the result of such economic competition, which by the beginning of the 20th century was especially keen between Britain and Germany. The Barcelona Pavilion by Ludwig Mies van der Rohe, for example, was an attempt to show the world, through the medium of an international exposition held there in 1929, that German industrial production had survived the 1914–18 war and that Germany was back in the economic race. While other countries built displays in theme pavilions to showcase specific areas of manufacturing prowess, Germany relied upon the quality, precision and level of technological advancement of its architecture alone to do that, and its tactic was very effective in conveying the message of its return from the economic abyss.

Because it is so freighted with nationalistic symbolism and cultural responsibility, the Barcelona Pavilion uniquely captures the prevalent theories of its time. It aggrandizes mechanization, but another, less overt, purpose is to advance the German architect Adolf Loos's distinction between inside and outside space (see pp. 81–3) and his view that the interior of a building should be luxurious, since it is the final refuge from an increasingly alien external world being inexorably transformed by technology. Nature was devalued in this scenario, though it was viewed with nostalgia rather than disrespect, since its destruction was seen as the inevitable result of industrialization.

The Barcelona Pavilion differs from the typical Loosian *Raumplan*, however, in its minimal use of space dividers, resulting in an open perimeter. Mies van der Rohe's breakdown of the *Raumplan*, while still retaining the Loosian premise of a luxurious internal sanctuary, seems contradictory, but in reality he simply transfers Loos's carefully controlled internal spaces to the outside. External areas, contiguous to the 'free flow of space' that Mies van der Rohe created inside the Pavilion are merely intended to define various pre-ordained processional routes, so that nature is clad in marble and reduced to being the mere servant of sensation.

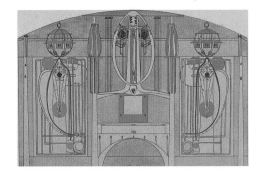

Decoration from the Music Room in the House for an Art Lover, Charles Rennie Mackintosh, 1901
This decorative scheme intended for a wall of a music room exemplifies Mackintosh's interest in organic forms, while pointing the way to modernism.

Concern for the environment was not a priority for architects caught up in a new, epic adventure of discovery. Building traditions and historical conventions, which inherently reflect natural laws, became polemical targets for many, who believed they stood in the way of a brighter, scientifically determined, future. The deliberate eradication of these traditions and conventions occurred in a remarkably brief period of time, but varied in each newly industrializing country according to its rate of growth, internal political chemistry, foreign affairs and involvement in wars.

Traditions, which typically convey respect for the environment, were not completely destroyed, however, and the hypothesis of the following section is that the history of architecture from the beginning of the 19th century until the present can also be characterized as a struggle to preserve traditions, within the process of economic competition that has just been mentioned. This subversive ideological struggle has been carried out on an individual basis with varying degrees of success and although it has recently been overshadowed by digital technology in the design profession, it has not yet been eclipsed by it.

Nationalism as a Motive for Environmentalism

While this book hopefully shows that an environmental sensibility was remarkably robust throughout a period in which it is generally considered to have been extinct, the motives of those who have demonstrated such a sensibility have often been far from altruistic, and have usually been tied to a nationalistic agenda. Those motives were further qualified by several overarching themes which are now discussed.

Many countries, such as Finland and Egypt, have produced architects that have used the reconstruction of historical identity as a weapon to protect their national integrity. It was used in Finland as a way of surviving the acquisitive intentions of more powerful neighbours, with qualified success, and in Egypt as a means of recovering the cultural authority that was lost during protracted colonial occupation. This recovery will be discussed a bit later here, as part of the post-colonial filter of nationalism.

In the United States, the search for a national architectural image suitably to reflect the democratic ideals upon which the country was founded resulted in Federal Classicism; Frank Lloyd Wright sought to revise this choice, proposing his Prairie style, and then later his Usonian house, as substitutes. The failure of each to capture the public imagination may be attributed to declining idealism, increasing consumerism, or both.

The Influence of Socialism

The role that socialism has played in both the formation and the development of the value system of the Modern Movement has yet to be comprehensively explored, and adds yet another complicated filter to the conditioning of individual environmental efforts by nationalism, within it. Any attempt at such an exploration would logically begin with the contentious questions of the extent of the transfer of the egalitarian ideals of the Arts and Crafts movement to the politics of the International Style, and of the devaluation of history and tradition in the Bauhaus curriculum and its reincarnation in other nations, after the Second World War.

In her definitive biography of William Morris, Fiona MacCarthy concisely describes his motives as being in tandem with the Young England movement of the 1840s, defined more than a decade before he took his matriculation examination at Exeter College in 1852, at

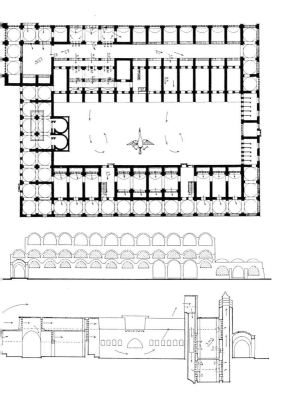

New Baris Market, Hassan Fathy, 1967
In the plan and section we can see how the wind is redirected through rows of wind catchers and circulated around the complex, then funnelled down to the basement, where perishables were to be stored. Hassan began as a modernist, but switched to a more environmentally responsive, vernacular approach.

Villa Hvittrask, Lindgren, Gesellius and Saarinen, 1903
There are striking parallels between the detailing of this
house-studio complex and the residential projects of
Mackintosh.

eighteen years of age. 'Young England', she says 'sought to emulate ideals of medieval England,
not in a regressive way but a creative one. They wanted to extract from medieval England
those elements from which the Victorian age could learn. New societies based on equality of
classes; a small-scale quasi-nomadic system of community; the return to the country; the
revival of physical activity; principles of shared work and work as holiday, like the road
building and haymaking in Morris's *News from Nowhere*; architecture as the measure of
civilization and the means by which the people reconnected themselves with the past: all these
were ideas Morris worked on and developed and in the end, during his Socialist period,
elaborated and sharpened almost beyond recognition.'[1]

William Morris joined the Democratic Federation in 1883, finally making his gradual
conversion to the Socialist cause official, a mere thirty-six years before the establishment of
the Weimar Bauhaus by Walter Gropius, who was born in the same year as Morris's
'conversion'. As MacCarthy also observes: 'Morris's ideas do permeate the Bauhaus in its early
years: the emphasis on education through doing; the principles of [the] mastering of one's
materials; the structure of the workshops; the purposeful sense of community, united in its
critique of society; the pursuit of fellowship'.[2] MacCarthy also alerts us that her observation of
this obvious connection is not the first, since Nicholas Pevsner also did so in his *Pioneers of the
Modern Movement* in 1936, where he also extends it to the proliferation of the Modern
Movement in Europe afterwards.[3]

Socialism, then, adds an additional nuance to the various nationalistic agendas behind
modernism and the ways in which these directed environmental responses, as well as the slant
of the histories that traced, or did not trace, these attempts.

Colonial and Post-Colonial Reflexiveness

The rediscovery of national architectural traditions, including their integral environmental
component, has been a common denominator in the recovery of culture in countries which

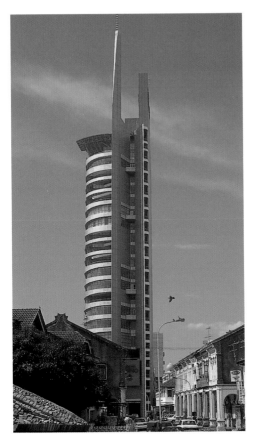

Menara UMNO, Kenneth Yeang, 2000–2001

have experienced colonial occupation. Colonialism, in the historical sense, is the conquest and political control of one nation by another for economic benefit. In theoretical terms, the study of colonialism involves the empirical investigation of the nexus between the economic and political motives that prompt and sustain such occupation and its cultural and sociological effects on both the colonizer and the colonized.

After the Second World War, resistance to colonialism, ranging from political opposition to armed insurrection, was channelled through nationalist movements and led to the dismantling of empires and independence from colonized nations. After the initial euphoria of freedom had worn off, however, these previously colonized peoples began to realize that the colonial legacy does not end with the severing of political ties with the colonizer. Economic, social, political, institutional, educational and cultural ties remain, referred to as 'neo-colonialism' in Marxist theory. These ties serve local and regional interests as well as those of the previous occupier.

In that same euphoria, as an extension of nationalism, all levels of society were united in the fight for independence, including the elite among the colonized who were most influenced by the value system of the colonizer, the so-called 'third culture' of colonialism. Once the nationalistic fervour and optimism had died down, however, this elite group began to be suspected of manipulating anti-imperialist sentiment for their own interests and this manipulation included the influencing of architectural styles by those in a position to do so. They also helped to perpetuate what have been described as 'the social formations and habits of thought' of the colonizer.[4]

In *The Wretched of the Earth*, Frantz Fanon, who unabashedly advocated violent revolution as a response to colonial occupation, graphically describes the compartmentalized zones it caused. He calls colonialism a 'manichean world' divided by 'lines of force' into areas of 'reciprocal exclusivity', of belonging and not belonging.[5] The end of colonialism meant the destruction of these zones, but the stigma of being constantly cast as inferior by the colonizer remained. Fanon eloquently compares the interaction between colonizers and colonized as a pathological maternal relationship, saying that: 'On the unconscious plane, colonialism therefore did not seek to be considered by the native as a gentle, loving mother who unceasingly retrains her fundamentally perverse offspring from managing to commit suicide and from giving free reign to its evil instincts'.[6]

The colonizer also systematically destroyed, or distorted, the culture of the country it occupied, to weaken resistance and make control easier. In a reflexive response to this, after independence was achieved, many architects chose referents from their own history and civilization, in clear recognition of the fact that colonialism intentionally negated these, and replaced them with Western models. The danger in this, as Fanon also observed, was that these architects 'who have nevertheless thoroughly studied modern techniques…turn their back on foreign culture, deny it, and set out to look for a true national culture, setting great store in what they believe to be the constant principles of a national art. But these people forget that the forms of a thought and what it leads to, together with modern techniques of information, language and dress, have dialectically reorganized the people's intelligence…'.[7]

The pitfalls inherent in assessing such translations of national culture, then, as well as the environmental components contained in them, revolve around this tendency to eliminate influences that have already been assimilated into it, or absorbed by it, in the name of authenticity and renewal.

Ministry of Foreign Affairs, Riyadh, Henning Larsen, 1987–8
Wood lattice pavilions set inside the private gardens of the Ministry are now overgrown with greenery to shade the walkways and provide secluded places to talk.

Symbols of Sovereignty

Nationalism has conditioned environmental responses within modernism, and in some cases such responses have also been slowly adapted to become symbols of national pre-eminence, or as a reminder of a more glorious past. In Britain, for example, the conservatory developed as a climatically controlled museum to showcase botanical specimens collected from all over the Empire and was subsequently expanded by Joseph Paxton to be the spectacular backdrop for an exhibition of the nation's rapidly growing manufacturing might. The conservatory, and its institutionalization in the Crystal Palace of 1851, has since served as the model for the High-Tech image that is so prevalent in much of the contemporary architecture of Britain.

At the extreme, opposite end of the symbolic spectrum, many young Egyptian architects have perpetuated the stylistic language developed by the ultra-nationalistic vernacularist Hassan Fathy, as a message to all that Western influence, along with the technologies and materials that such influence entails, has been pre-empted by local equivalents and references. In these and several other instances described here, environmental strategies are either eclipsed by or inherently integral to patriotic motives that front them and part of the challenge involved in understanding those strategies lies in deciphering such nationalistic responses.

National Self-Sufficiency

The oil shocks of the 1970s, brought about by OPEC embargos, resulted in xenophobic responses by industrialized nations, especially America and Japan, who were the most severely hurt by the cuts. Tax breaks, which were enacted in the United States to promote the development of new technologies that could promote energy self-sufficiency, fostered a brief spurt of market-driven environmental expertise among architects, but few stayed the course after the embargos were forgotten. Several of the more visionary members of the group that responded to this opportunity, however, persisted in planning for the time when all unrenewable resources will be depleted and have continued to improve upon their skills. Some of these are represented here.

Asian Values

Assuming, for the sake of discussion, that such an entity as Asia exists, it is undeniably one of the fastest-growing regions in the world, with enormous potential for negative environmental impact. The nations within it are each at a different place on the development curve, from Japan, with the highest GNP, to Indonesia and the Philippines, with the lowest. Each also has a unique history, which sometimes includes colonial experience, as well as access to a variety of natural resources.

In spite of these differences, Asian nations share a unified desire to express their national identity as well as their place in the world at the beginning of a new century which is generally assumed to belong to them. Whether or not the 'Asian Century' is a myth, the search for a means of architectural expression that matches the raised expectations and aspirations of its constituents is in full swing with varying degrees of success.

The skyscraper seems to be the typology of choice for many of the nations caught up in this scramble for power within the region, since the level of technology required to construct it unmistakably announces developed status, or at least the ability to achieve it soon. Concern for the environment usually takes back seat in the endeavour, as it does in all other areas

Earth-covered Theatre, Cape Cod, Malcolm Wells, mid-1990s

Malcolm Wells envisages that all public institutions and facilities could be built underground, resulting in huge energy savings and minimal environmental impact. This theatre, never realized, was to have been the stage for a portrayal of the first encounter between Native Americans and Europeans.

related to national advancement and progress throughout the region, and so it is remarkable that a major advancement in skyscraper design that is environmentally sensitive should come out of Asia, or specifically Malaysia, at this time. The story behind that important advance is recounted in detail on pp. 193–9.

A Religious Constituency

Religious affiliation is an additional, though certainly not the final, determinant of nationalism as a generator of architectural form derived from a traditional heritage that incorporates environmental principles, conveys meaning and strengthens identity. In the Islamic world, for example, there are many nations with completely different cultural backgrounds that are predominantly Muslim, but there is also *Dar al Islam*, the world of Islam, as an overarching reality, which binds them all.

By rewarding those individuals and organizations who have found innovative and effective ways of dealing with issues of cultural hegemony in the face of global homogenization, which so often involve environmental integrity as well, the Aga Khan Award has become the conscience of a slowly emerging, yet nonetheless profound, social sensibility that is not only confined to the Islamic world which the Award represents, but has general relevance.

That sensibility encompasses such diverse elements as the rising international tide of population, a growing awareness of the cultural value of our collective built heritage and the importance of preserving it, the function of tradition in the formation of technology and the role of each as social determinants, prioritizing people's needs above the quantitative exigencies of an architectural programme, and especially above its qualitative translation into an aesthetic statement. Each aspect of this sensibility by necessity involves environmental awareness, which becomes an unspoken agenda within such priorities.

Layering

This list is not conclusive and is further complicated by the overlapping of the issues that it raises. But, it does begin to provide several devices by which the work of the individuals and institutes that will now be presented may be better understood, placing their various environmental initiatives within diverse nationalistic contexts.

This connection between modernism and national identity has yet to be examined in great detail, but in hindsight there are multiple iterations of the movement that can be identified as being tied to regional variations. These begin to be explored here, to hint at the extent of this nexus.

above **The Hill House**, 1902–4
left **A sketch for the Hill House, north front**

While Mackintosh is today best remembered for his
sleek, stylized interiors, and as a forerunner of the
Modern Movement, much of his architecture drew on
the vernacular. In the case of the Hill House, the exposed
location meant the use of low roofs, humble pebble-dash
(harling), and smaller windows that retained more heat.

1

Charles Rennie Mackintosh: Reinterpreting the Scottish Vernacular

Mackintosh reconciled the ethos of the Arts and Crafts pioneers with the machine age, while incorporating the lessons of Scottish vernacular architecture in dealing with harsh weather

Biography

Raised in a working-class tenement in Glasgow, Mackintosh's parents insisted that he regularly visit the surrounding Highlands, and he grew up with a love of nature that remained with him throughout his life. His precocious talent won him a place at the Glasgow School of Art (which he would later famously redesign), and later a travelling fellowship. His early work is weakly Gothic in style, partially influenced by the work of A. W. N. Pugin, though also reflecting the theoretical influences of John Ruskin and William Morris, the leading lights of the Arts and Crafts movement. However, he also took great interest in vernacular Scottish architecture, which he sketched and analysed, and Japanese architecture (like later admirers such as Frank Lloyd Wright).

His rising reputation around 1900 secured some important private commissions for houses (which in typical Arts and Crafts mode were furnished according to his designs), but ultimately his uncompromising personality prevented him from enjoying greater popularity and success – his most creative period lasted only about a dozen years. He eventually retired to Port Vendres, in the south of France, to paint watercolours. He died in 1928, aged fifty-nine.

Key Projects

Glasgow School of Art, Glasgow, 1896–9

Windyhill, Renfrewshire, 1900–1901

The Hill House, Dunbartonshire, 1902–1904

Signposts

Arts and Crafts influences Part II: 2, 3, 4, 5, 16

Energy efficiency Part II: 11, 13, 16, 19

Japanese influence Part II: 5, 6, 12; Part III: 2

Local materials and techniques Part II: 3, 4, 7, 9, 12, 24

Charles Rennie Mackintosh was a true product of his time (the expansive Victorian age) as well as of his place (Glasgow, one of the primary industrial cities of empire). The reign of Queen Victoria, from 1837 to 1901, spanned a turbulent period, beginning with the enormous social upheaval caused by the invention of the steam engine and the ensuing exodus from the countryside to the city. The cottage economies that supported small communities throughout rural England could not compete with the new factories and inventions such as the power loom. The railways, which steam power also made possible, transported goods as well as people, marking the beginning of the end of local crafts based on speciality materials. Meanwhile, between 1801 and 1881 the population of London increased tenfold, forcibly mixing together a random group of separate communities. Infrastructure lagged far behind population growth, as did any organized official response to the severe social pathology that this disjunction caused (only hinted at in studies such as *Bleak House* by Charles Dickens).

Overcrowding, extreme poverty, homelessness, disease, prostitution and alcohol plagued new arrivals from the countryside as they tried to adapt to a harsh new urban way of life. Architects and engineers were also struggling to reconcile the unprecedented functional requirements and materials that they faced with prior traditions and training. While architects sought solace in scholarship, inventing eclectic stylistic responses to the design problems posed by new building types, engineers like Isambard Kingdom Brunel simply got on with building the railroad stations and bridges as well as the factories and workers' flats demanded by this new socio-economic reality. This, then, was one context for the innovations and invention of Mackintosh. However, there was also an intellectual and theoretical context.

A. W. N. Pugin

Expressions of outrage about deplorable conditions and the inequalities being caused by this changing social landscape were slow in coming, but a series of articulate critics eventually began to speak out against them. Particularly related to architecture, and to Mackintosh specifically, A. W. N. Pugin laid down an important foundation for what would later become known as the Arts and Crafts movement in an intellectual riposte to the cultural depredation of industrialization. Pugin's father Augustus came to England during the French Revolution, working for urban planner John Nash. Pugin was born in London in 1812, and worked as a stage designer at Covent Garden as a young man, while becoming increasingly convinced that a restoration of Christian spirituality would heal the growing social problems of England.

He was sure that the Gothic style could be the means for this revival and in his *True Principles of Pointed or Christian Architecture*, 1841, set several rules that would later become the cornerstones of the Arts and Crafts philosophy. These, which he saw as being exemplified in Gothic architecture, were that there should be nothing in a building that was not necessary to its function or its construction, and that ornament should serve a functional or structural purpose and not be used for decoration alone, being appropriate and significant to its use and based on natural forms. His passion for discovering the true basis of Gothic design prompted him to make many excursions across the Channel to France to sketch and record intricate details of cathedrals and other medieval structures. His expertise led Sir Charles Barry to hire him as a consultant on the design of the new Houses of Parliament in Westminster, London, on which he worked on until his death in 1852.

The connection that Pugin made, between social ills and spiritual crises and the principles behind the Gothic palliative that he proposed to cure these ills, profoundly influenced social critics such as Thomas Carlyle and John Ruskin as well as Ruskin's disciple, William Morris.

Craft as a Redemptive Force: John Ruskin

Pugin's impassioned espousal of a return to the piety and public spirit of the Middle Ages and his attempts to judge a work of art by the moral worth of its creator, in spite of difference in their religious affiliations, greatly influenced writer and critic John Ruskin. Ruskin, who was tutored at home, had a strong Protestant background and channelled an almost fundamentalist zeal into the formulation of a social and moral theory that he proposed as an antidote to the increasingly commercial values of industry. In his first book, *Modern Painters*, published in 1843, Ruskin argued that art should not only be judged aesthetically, but in a social context as well. And in his second, *The Seven Lamps of Architecture*, in 1849, he extended that premise to building, saying that it contributes to 'mental health, power and pleasure'.

Defining architecture as 'those characteristics of an edifice which are above and beyond its common use', he echoes Pugin in identifying it as the symbol of a 'spiritually unified' society. While a chapter in *The Seven Lamps* called 'The Lamp of Truth' is based on the issue of honesty of expression, material and workmanship and an admonition against 'architectural deceit', it is in 'The Lamp of Life' that Ruskin issues a clarion call that he would later expand upon in 'The Nature of the Gothic' in his third book *The Stones of Venice*, 1851, which would become the manifesto of Arts and Crafts belief. In it he says:

> We are not sent into this world to do anything into which we cannot put our hearts. We have certain work to do for our bread, and that is to be done strenuously; other work to do for our delight, and that is to be done heartily [but] he who would form the creations of his own mind by any other instrument than his own hand, would also, if he might, give grinding organs to Heaven's angels, to make their music easier. There is dreaming enough, and earthiness enough, and sensuality enough in human existence, without overturning the few glowing moments of it into mechanisation; and since our life must be at best a vapour that appears for a little time and then vanishes away, let it at least appear as a cloud in the height of heaven, not as the thick darkness that broods over the blast of the furnace and the rolling of the wheel.[1]

William Morris

When he first read *The Stones of Venice* as an undergraduate at Oxford, William Morris was inspired by its idealism, and especially by 'The Nature of Gothic', which he would later describe as one of 'the few necessary and inevitable utterances of the century'. In this chapter, Ruskin restates Pugin's belief that Christian, specifically Gothic, architecture is superior to its Classical, pagan, equivalent, but expands on it by saying that architecture should express its human origins and reflect the individuality as well as the flaws of its makers, without the expectation of perfect finish that can only be achieved by a machine. Morris was drawn to Ruskin's (and by extension Pugin's) thesis of a social basis in architecture and after leaving university joined the firm of Gothic Revivalist George Edmund Street in Oxford in 1852. In the summer of 1856, Street moved from Oxford to London and Morris, encouraged by Pre-Raphaelite founder Dante Gabriel Rossetti, took up the production of crafts.

In 1859, Morris and his wife Jane Burden, moved into Red House, at Bexleyheath, Kent, a medieval-type residence designed for them by Philip Webb, whom Morris had met while the two were working for Street. In 1861, Webb was also a founding partner in Morris, Marshall, Faulkner & Co., along with Edward Burne-Jones, Rossetti, Ford Madox Brown and Arthur Hughes. The firm won several gold medals for furniture appearing in the London International Exhibition of 1862. It was very reminiscent of designs by Pugin, but few could have predicted the financial success it would soon enjoy. It was reorganized as Morris and Co. in 1875 and moved to Merton Abbey in 1881. Morris first concentrated on embroideries, then expanded to stained glass, wallpapers, printed and woven textiles, carpets, tapestries and furniture.

He established a workshop at Hammersmith for hand-knotted carpets in 1880, and set up looms for tapestries at Merton Abbey in 1881. In 1890, he established the Kelmscott Press to publish hand-produced books, at a medieval farmhouse he had purchased of the same name near Oxford. His dilemma was that while he promoted art for all, not only the rich, he worked mainly for wealthy clients and became rich himself (or richer, since he inherited family money as well). The dichotomy he never reconciled was that the hand-made products his firm produced cost too much for ordinary people, encouraging a retreat into dreams of a utopian future such as that described in his book *News from Nowhere*, where machines were abolished and medieval guilds restored. In 1892, C. R. Ashbee discussed the formation of a guild of hand-workers with Morris, but was discouraged, and Morris also expressed hesitation about the movement that began to grow out of the Arts and Crafts Exhibition Society, founded in 1888. His political activity increased in the 1880s, he joined the Democratic Federation in 1883, and then left to form the Socialist League in 1884, and concentrated increasingly on a post-revolutionary future, until his death in 1896.[2]

A Complex Legacy

Far more than simply establishing crafts as a means of opposing mechanized mass production, Morris synthesized the ideals of social theorists attempting to find a correlation between architecture and its related arts and morality, to counter the increasingly commercial values of the industrial age. The paradox of his use of technology for commercial gain rather than social, polemical purposes was overshadowed by the impression that craft could become a weapon of liberation, but now a more balanced view, related to his call for a symbiotic, joyful relationship between craft and the machine, has began to emerge.

This positive viewpoint offers a more useful introduction to the contribution of Charles Rennie Mackintosh than the contradictions so often referred to in Morris's life, aptly described by one critic as: 'the fusion of revolutionary Marxism looking forward to a new and more just society, and rural romanticism wistfully looking back to a pre-industrial age, which exemplifies the dichotomy inherent in Arts and Crafts thinking, where avant-gardism and nostalgia seem to be found in almost equal parts'.[3]

A Love of Nature

This abridged description of the theoretical heritage of Pugin, Ruskin and Morris is a necessary prelude to an appreciation of the contribution of Charles Rennie Mackintosh, who, unlike the founders of the Arts and Crafts movement, was not upper class. His father, a police superintendent, tried to make up for the lack of play space for his large family by making arrangements to use a vacant lot nearby. A garden that the family planted in this plot as well as long walks outside the city prescribed for the young man to build up the muscles in a deformed foot, gave Mackintosh an early and enduring appreciation of nature, so dramatically presented in the stark contrast between Highland and city in Scotland. After attending Glasgow School of Art, he won a travelling fellowship as well as a position in the respected firm of Honeyman and Keppie. His first project for them, the Glasgow Herald Building, is vaguely Gothic in style, reflecting the firm's sympathy with the arguments put forward by Pugin, Ruskin and Morris in favour of a non-Classical language, but the swelling tower is reminiscent of Italian campanile that he sketched on his grand tour.

Other projects completed while he was with Honeyman and Keppie, such as Queen's Cross Church, also coincide with rules put forward in Pugin's *True Principles*, with the additional influence of vernacular Scottish typologies layered over them. Queen's Cross, for example, is broadly based on sketches that Mackintosh made on the many trips he took to the Highlands, showing the influence that traditional forms had on him.

Baronial Precedents

Mackintosh is perhaps best known for the Glasgow School of Art, hailed by critics Nikolaus Pevsner and Thomas Howarth as a nascent indication of the Modern Movement, but two

right (above and below) **Designs for the House of an Art Lover**, 1901
far right and below **Windyhill**, Renfrewshire, 1900–1901

These two projects date from exactly the same time, but show two very different approaches by Mackintosh. While the House for an Art Lover is more typically Mackintosh, with its large windows and lavish interior, Windyhill responds to its harsh exposed site with low roofs, small, efficient windows, and practical harling.

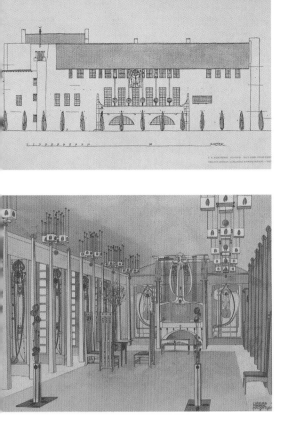

private residences that he designed show this traditional influence even more clearly because of their rural references. The Hill House, which was the first, was built for a wealthy publisher named Walter Blackie, who had given his architect free rein in budget and style. Mackintosh surprised him with a simple country farmhouse, using typical local details. Instead of cut stone, which Blackie expected and certainly could have afforded, Mackintosh used harling (a cement and plaster mixture with pebble aggregate), saving golden Glaswegian sandstone for important details such as entry lintels and cornerstones. This humble pebble-dash is more practical in wet Scottish weather and also allowed Mackintosh to spend more on built-in furniture and custom-made details. Everything in the house shows Mackintosh's sensitivity to context, awareness of the Arts and Crafts aesthetic, practicality and thrift. For example, the window that overlooks Loch Lomond (and lights a settee where Blackie would sit to review manuscripts), is smaller than might be expected, to reduce the infiltration of cold air.

Efficiently designed minimalist coal-burning fireplaces, which became a patented Mackintosh trademark, are balanced by delicately detailed tilework and stencilled murals contributed by both Mackintosh and his wife Margaret Macdonald, and built in, as well as occasional furniture throughout the house, confirms the overall impression of exquisite austerity found in other Arts and Crafts projects further south. Windyhill (see p. 43), which is

Sketch for the Hill House, 1902–4

Mackintosh's private commissions show a great sensitivity to place, while the spare, minimal lines of his drawings betray the influence of Japanese design.

near Hill House, is based on the same ideas as its better-known neighbour: coated in humble pebble-dash wrapper, with small windows. But the roof on the north side, facing the wind, snow and rain, sweeps right down, close to the ground, to deflect the worst of the weather. A broad chimney on this side which indicates more than a passing familiarity with Arts and Crafts protagonist C. A. Voysey, also serves as an effective shield against the elements as much as it makes a statement about the rural roots of the house.

Japanese Inspiration

Like many of their contemporaries, Mackintosh and Macdonald were determined to simplify the clutter of Victorian life and to clean up the interiors of their houses. In this they were inspired by the traditional Japanese aesthetic, just then being introduced to an international audience after Japan had been forced into a trade treaty in 1854. However, they married this minimalist approach to the vertical room divisions typically found in Scottish Baronial and English country houses: the dado rail running around each room at chair height to save the plaster from damage, and the picture rail about two thirds of the way up the wall, from which the family portraits were hung. Dividing each room in three horizontal bands in this way, gave them a modular, proportional guide to go by, and made each item of furniture and lighting and each fixture seem visually to interlock, either coming down from the ceiling, up from the floor, or out from the wall, to match one of these horizontal lines of reference.

A Seamless Mixture of Technology and Tradition

Because he was seen as provincial and working class, Mackintosh was never really accepted by the Arts and Crafts establishment and his irascible personality also eventually marginalized him even in Glasgow. Elsewhere, however, he was recognized as one of the most talented of the British Arts and Crafts architects, especially in Germany and Austria where his work was well-known through exhibitions. Hermann Muthesius, who was sent to Britain as a glorified industrial spy, to learn all he could about production techniques that allowed the British to monopolize global market share, determined that the secret to British industrial success could best be uncovered by studying the Arts and Crafts house, as the *summa* of all manufacturing skill, an attitude that would prevail in modern architecture for decades afterward. In *Das Englische Haus*, Muthesius argues that the reason for British domination of world trade was the synthesis of handicraft and machine work that the Arts and Crafts movement had made possible, most evident in the houses designed by Mackintosh. Muthesius identified him as one of the best of these because his circumstances had made it natural for him to mix craft and machine production in his work and Muthesius as well as Josef Hoffmann made a pilgrimage to Glasgow to seek him out.

Unlike Ruskin or Morris, who sent mixed messages about what they called the 'machine', vilifying it one minute and yet using it the next, Mackintosh was clear in his acceptance of industrial method from the beginning. This is perhaps because Clydebank, where many of the ships in the White Star and Cunard lines were built, is near Glasgow and was a key source of the craftsman who worked for him. The big ships that were built there exemplify the mixture of the handicraft and machine aesthetic that is essential to Mackintosh's sadly limited body of work. These ships, which were engineering marvels, were built of the latest industrial materials available, using the newest technologies, but still retained their connection to previous shipbuilding methods in the way that those materials were put together and those technologies were implemented. While the hulls of these ships, for example, were made of riveted steel plate, their camber was still set by eye following guidelines established when ships were made of wood.

Even the parts of Mackintosh's masterwork, the Glasgow School of Art, which are singled out as being proto-modernist by Pevsner and Howarth – such as the large studio windows on the north side of the building – were also made in this way. While the oversized steel frames of these windows are a continuation of the same conservatory tradition that led to Joseph Paxton's Crystal Place of 1851, each of the brackets that brace them was handmade by blacksmiths who set up their forges on site while the windows were being built. The elegantly curved brackets, which double as supports for the window-washers' scaffolds, each have a different finial but they all symbolize the Scottish rose and serve as a poetic reminder that Mackintosh was also part of the Celtic Revival movement led by city planner Patrick Geddes. The theme of the rose can be found throughout the work of Mackintosh and Macdonald, but is never put to such functional use as it is here, in close adherence to Pugin's caveat about the application of ornament.

Tradition is not Antithetical to Technology

The most important legacy of Mackintosh, then, in relationship to the general themes introduced here, is the way in which he demonstrates that accumulated vernacular knowledge need not be antithetical to technological innovation.

He embraced, rather than denied, the new materials and processes then becoming available to him, and rather than wishing them away as the philosophical stalwarts of the Arts and Crafts movement seemed to do, looked for pragmatic ways in which they might enhance the vernacular traditions he sought to perpetuate, through innovation. The lesson offered by his relatively small but extremely influential body of work is not only that he was precocious, predicting the incremental stripping away of referential elements that would accelerate soon after his death, but, more importantly, that he realized that technology, used appropriately, could perfect rather than replace the traditional knowledge imbued in vernacular architecture.

opposite, top **Entrance, the Hill House**

opposite, below **Service wing, the Hill House**, from north east

right **Glasgow School of Art**, 1896–9

The comparison between the well-known School of Art and the Hill House is revealing. Where the School uses huge windows and a highly stylized vocabulary of forms, the house opts for small, economical windows and a solid, rugged construction fitting to its location.

above **Typical worker's housing, Rushby Mead, Letchworth Garden City**, Hertfordshire, *c.* 1911–12
left **Housing near Ludwick Centre, Welwyn Garden City**, Hertfordshire, from 1919

Emerging from the smog and overcrowding of 19th-century London, garden cities such as Letchworth and Welwyn offered good-quality housing for all classes in a semi-rural environment. Meandering roads, widespread planting of trees and the careful preservation of existing natural features all contribute to a feeling of bucolic tranquillity.

2

Ebenezer Howard:
The Return to Paradise

Appalled by the overcrowding and squalor in cities caused by the Industrial Revolution, the planner Ebenezer Howard advocated the development of 'garden cities', between city and countryside

Biography

Born in 1850, Ebenezer Howard moved to the United States when he was eighteen to pursue a life as a farmer. However, realizing that this was not his calling, he moved to Chicago, and then back to London, working producing parliamentary reports (a profession he continued for the rest of his life). He developed a private interest in social conditions, and in 1898 published the groundbreaking book *Tomorrow: A Peaceful Path to Real Reform*, which was reprinted in 1902 as *Garden Cities of Tomorrow*. In this he called for the creation of new, properly planned, suburban towns of limited size,

surrounded by an inviolable 'belt' of agricultural land ('greenbelt', as it would later be known). In this he was aiming at a synthesis of the benefits of the country and those of the city. His ideas attracted enough attention and financial backing to begin Letchworth, a garden city in suburban London in 1903. Other schemes followed, including Hampstead Garden Suburb in 1907 and Welwyn Garden City in 1919, just after the First World War. The influence of the 'garden city' continued to be felt in planning throughout the 20th century, especially in projects such as Milton Keynes.

Ebenezer Howard was born in London and was well aware of the appalling social cost of progress: in his early career as a Parliamentary reporter in the late 19th century, he must have heard many debates about how to improve the urban blight of homelessness, vagrancy, overcrowding, prostitution, crime and disease. He was also conscious of the utopian attempts by enlightened industrialists to provide amenable and decent community housing and facilities for their workers – in milltowns such as New Lanark by Robert Owen, Saltaire by Titus Salt, Cadbury's Bournville and Lever's Port Sunlight – and became determined to create a prototype of his own.

Bedford Park as a Model

The most immediate model for Howard's 'garden cities', since it was speculative as well as altruistic, is Bedford Park, begun in 1875. Considered to be one of the first garden suburbs built for rental rather than company employees, this community, named after the local Georgian residence Bedford House, was launched by builder Jonathan Carr on a forty-five acre parcel at Turnham Green. Intended for families with incomes in the range of £300 to £1,500 a year, Bedford Park was initially hailed by *The Building News* as 'a very laudable scheme that will supply for the middle classes that which the Shaftesbury Park Estate has

Key Projects

Letchworth Garden City, Hertfordshire, from 1903
Hampstead Garden Suburb, North London, 1907
Welwyn Garden City, Hertfordshire, 1919

Signposts

Arts and Crafts influences Part II: 1, 3, 4, 5, 16
Garden cities Part II: 3, 18, 22
Town planning Part II: 3, 4, 8, 9, 11, 12, 18; Part III: 3
Community building Part II: 4, 12, 21, 22

Welwyn Garden City, 1919
Critical to the success of the Garden Cities was effective transportation – which in the early 20th century meant easy access to rail.

partially done for the labouring classes – namely, houses well-planned, conveniently arranged and constructed with regard to both stability and comfort and architectural character each house will have a plot of ground about 50ft frontage and 75ft deep, with gardens filled with shrubs surrounded by oak fencing and rents will vary from £45 to £65'.[1]

The new town was seen as very experimental because it was self-contained, with communal public facilities such as St Michael's Church, the Tabard Inn, an art school, club and tennis courts. Its individually designed detached and semi-detached homes also had the latest sanitary facilities, with sewer traps, no basements (to eliminate dampness), central heating and cooling, and external drainpipes. The nearly nine-hundred houses, on a plot which eventually increased to 113 acres, were built with varying floor plans in the Queen Anne Style. The choice of style is significant, deliberately failing to identify either with the Gothic Revivalists or with the Classicists.

In addition, by choosing the Queen Anne Style, with its vaguely Dutch curved gables, red-brick walls, elegant chimneys and tall windows specifically sized to provide maximum daylight to each room, Jonathan Carr and his primary architects, E. W. Godwin and Norman Shaw, were appealing to an upwardly mobile segment of the market. They were not interested in taking a polemical position in the growing struggle between management and labour exacerbated by the Industrial Revolution, but in capitalizing on the change in lifestyle. Although Norman Shaw is often identified with creating the style as well as the entire plan of Bedford Park, the first eighteen houses were provided by Godwin, with additional contributions by E. J. May and Maurice B. Adams. The association of Shaw and Godwin with the Aesthetic Movement that thrived between about 1875 and 1885 and included the artist Whistler and writer Oscar Wilde, as well as the commercial basis of their new community, further separated Bedford Park from the high idealism and political agenda of the Arts and Crafts advocates.[2]

The social and commercial foundation of Turnham Green Terrace as an integral community conceived and realized within a short train ride from central London is due to the financial acumen and good timing of Jonathan Carr, and his decision to choose architects and a style associated with an avant-garde aesthetic to specifically appeal to middle-class clients

Letchworth Garden City, 1903
Arts and Crafts ideals are evident in each of the garden cities, especially in the use of vernacular styles.

anxious to escape back-to-back housing estates closer to the city. But his formation of the Bedford Park Company Ltd., in 1881, as well as his ceaseless personal involvement in this pioneering project, was also critical to its success. Ebenezer Howard used similar techniques – of brand recognition, public relations, incorporation and individual commitment – in launching his own experimental utopias, first at Letchworth in 1903, then Hampstead Garden Suburb in 1907 and Welwyn Garden City in 1919, but he expanded on the principles that had been so effective at Bedford Park in several key ways.

Carr understood marketing, but Howard grasped even more fully the power of the media and advertising, choosing concentric circles as the image, or logo, of his grand plan. Following an idea in the book *Looking Backward* by Edward Bellamy, Howard saw the need to include industry in his plan, allocating it to the outer ring in a series that began with civic buildings in the centre, followed by residential areas, playing fields, shops and an agricultural belt (to feed the village), connected by wide boulevards. Unlike Carr, who took advantage of a singular opportunity, Ebenezer Howard wanted to enact Bellamy's vision of 'a movement – a corporate migration of overcrowded cities into green pastures, to return people to their lost paradise'.[3]

Letchworth Garden City

Like Bedford Park, Letchworth was speculative and self-contained, designed to project an image of exclusivity and individuality, but larger in scale than anything attempted before. A competition for the new town was announced by Howard in 1900; the plan by Barry Parker and Raymond Unwin was selected in 1904. The competition was illustrious, since in addition to Parker and Unwin, Richard Norman Shaw of Bedford Park fame, as well as W. R. Lethaby, Halsey Riccardo, Geoffrey Lucas and Sidney Cranfield, were asked to prepare plans by the directors. The Parker and Unwin plan was selected mainly because it most specifically conformed to the topography. Raymond Unwin described the site as '3800 acres of undulating land with comparatively few level acres situated on the Cambridge Branch of the Great Northern Railway which almost bisects the site. Other existing features which greatly influenced the planning were the Hitchin and Baldock Road and the Norton and Wilbury Road and the Icknield Way between them, running approximately parallel to the railway.'[4]

Parker and Unwin proposed individually designed houses in a 'cottage' style, based on the pre-existing estate village of Old Letchworth, which, in addition to Letchworth Hall and St Mary's Church, still had several blocks of 17th-century cottages, a town centre and a main north–south axis through the centre. Parker and Unwin used this axis to full advantage, having residential areas of detached and semi-detached houses fanning out from it. They had intended to use a uniform palette of materials throughout their new village, but the onset of war and the pressure for housing afterward introduced unintended features into the planned community. The planners did manage to save almost all existing trees, boasting in promotional brochures that only one was cut down during construction. They also identified a level plateau at the highest part of the site near the town centre as the ideal location of the Common, with roads spreading out from the circular strand around it offering impressive vistas into the surrounding countryside as they slope down in all directions.

Paradise, plc

Letchworth was the first of what Ebenezer Howard envisioned as a series of Garden Cities, each with a population limit of 32,000, which would surround industrial cities throughout Britain. To ensure the success of his enterprise, Howard determined that Letchworth should be incorporated and that any increase in property value should be shared by the entire community, and formed a Garden Cities Association in 1899 to implement his plan. The association purchased Letchworth estate in April, 1903 from fifteen different owners totalling 3,818 acres, for £155,587, buying the parcels in ways that would prevent the individual owners from realizing they were contributing to a unified development. On 1 September 1908, First Garden City Ltd. was registered and Howard's idea of public ownership in a public company in which the owners and tenants held shares and received dividends on their property was finally realized.

The Cheap Cottage Exhibition

Since Howard, Unwin and Parker were among those owners with shares in Letchworth, their vision was not completely altruistic; this was no Erehwon, even through Raymond Unwin was a fervent supporter of the Socialist League and a vocal advocate of affordable, working-class housing. Both Parker and Unwin built houses for themselves on Letchworth Lane in 1904 in what they referred to as a 'Yeoman' Tudor style and in 1907 Parker designed a thatched studio on Norton Way South in East Anglia vernacular, which now houses the First Garden City Heritage Museum. The unlikely pairing of egalitarian ideals and speculative motives is further personified by Howard's efforts to have Edward Cadbury, planner of Bournville, and W. H. Lever, who built Port Sunlight for company employees, on the Board of Directors of a public company from which he hoped to profit. It is also epitomized by the Cheap Cottage Exhibition, which was ostensibly intended to demonstrate that affordable workers' housing was a key component of the Letchworth community. The insistence on including these houses also demonstrates Howard's realization that, in spite of his dream of a return to a pre-industrial paradise, manufacturing was necessary for financial success. It was vital to his goal of self-sufficiency, since employment in the community would be needed to sustain it.

A sales brochure for the Garden City Concept included a circular diagram entitled 'The Three Magnets' separated into pie shaped divisions labelled 'Town,' 'Country' and 'Town-Country.' Garden Cities represent the final combination, having all of the advantages and

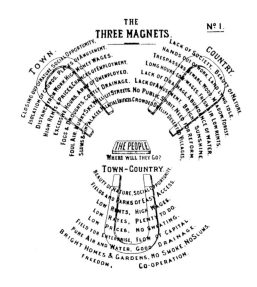

'The Three Magnets' diagram, 1902
Taken from Howard's book, *Garden Cities of Tomorrow*, this ingenious sales material shows how garden cities reconcile the advantages of the country with those of the city. These were, of course, commercial as well as idealistic ventures.

Proposal plan for Hampstead Garden Suburb, 1907
Hampstead Garden Suburb was the result of a grass-roots movement established by Henrietta Barnett to save London from vulgar overdevelopment. While it was led by Raymond Unwin, the planning was more cooperative than in other developments. The suburb was deliberately open to all classes, and aimed at total silence – even church bells were banned. Buildings grew out of the contours of the ground, and hedgerows were preserved wherever possible.

HAMPSTEAD GARDEN SUBURB

none of the disadvantages of the first. Unlike the 'Town', Garden Cities would have 'Low Rents' and 'High Wages', 'Field for Enterprise' and 'Flow of Capital.' Unlike the 'Country', they would also have social and cultural activities as an attraction for prospective residents.[5]

The press was invited to the unveiling of 114 houses built especially for the exhibition, advertised at £150, using every new construction method possible to lower costs without compromising the standards of quality or style originally established by Parker and Unwin for the rest of Letchworth. The exhibition attracted nearly 60,000 visitors, but it is unlikely that many of these had agrarian aspirations, given the location of the houses. The contrived attempt to make the cottages seem bucolic was a strategy intended to make them appeal to middle-class urbanites looking for an inexpensive retreat in the countryside.

Letchworth was administered by the Hitchin Council as a rural district until after the 1914–18 war, when it was elevated to urban status, due to rapid growth. After the Second World War, development pressures drove property values up even higher and to protect this first example of Howard's Garden City concept from takeover, the Letchworth Urban District Council backed a private bill enacted into law in 1962, which established the Letchworth Garden City Corporation.[6] It continued to administer profits for community benefit as before, but enforced stricter controls on development. Administration transferred to the Letchworth Garden City Heritage Foundation in 1992, again through a Private Bill in Parliament, creating an Industrial and Provident Society with charitable status.

An Important Precedent
The missionary zeal of Ebenezer Howard's 'back to the countryside' movement was diverted into nationalistic favour prior to the First World War, and lost its impetus because of the social and economic consequences of that conflict. Its importance as a precedent for various

Inside the map border:

ROAD · & · RAIL · COMMUNICATIONS ·

SHOPS · PUBLIC · BUILDINGS · OPEN · SPACES · ETC ·

DIAGRAM · OF · TOWN · PLAN · SHEWING · ZONES

WELWYN · GARDEN · CITY

Residential Areas   Factory Areas   Open Spaces   Shopping Areas.

LOUIS · DE · SOISSONS · FRIBA
SADG · ARCHITECT ·

Promotional plan of Welwyn Garden City, 1920
'Agricultural belts' are marked, reinforcing the rural location, but also setting limits on further growth. The map shows the division between Residential Area, Factory Area, Open Space, and Shopping Area. Again, the rail connection is important to the success of the venture.

aspects of the environmental sensibility that has begun to become so pervasive, however, cannot be overemphasized, especially in view of the three themes of tradition, technology and urbanism that have been put forward here as the framework for understanding that pervasive growth. The reasons for the importance of the Garden City movement as a precedent may be outlined as follows.

First of all, it was unarguably the prototype for suburban growth, and the urban flight that went with it, beginning in the late 1940s and early 50s, but different from those developments in having a more traditional approach to nature. Rather than the ubiquitous, finely

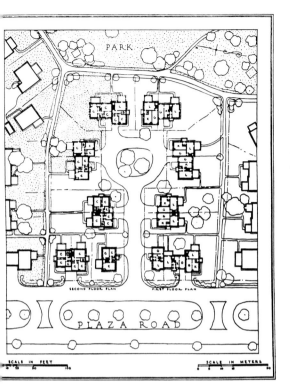

top **Plan of Burnham Place, Radburn New Town**, Clarence Stein and Henry Wright, planned 1928–9

above **Radburn New Town in the 1950s**

Called the 'First Town for the Motor Age', the Radburn layout segregates traffic from pedestrians, one side of every house opening onto communal gardens, while the cul-de-sacs used by vehicles were also planted with trees.

manicured and watered lawns with which suburb developments have now become synonymous, and which separate each detached house from its neighbours as well as the sidewalk, the Garden Cities that Howard completed were designed to fit into their environment, and were respectful of existing contours, trees and vegetation. They were compactly organized, with semi-detached as well as detached houses provided.[7]

The construction of the Garden Cities movement in America, led by Clarence Stein and Henry Wright, perpetuated Howard's ideals and planning tactics, but they could not withstand the economic forces unleashed by the baby boom that followed the Second World War and the speculative opportunists that took advantage of them. Howard's dream, carried forward by Stein and Wright, of profits from property serving the common good and providing affordable housing for all, fell victim to market forces, and architects who held to Howard's ideals withdrew from popular housing completely.

There was a short-lived rebellion in southern California, just after the Second World War, referred to by Reyner Banham in his classic *Four Ecologies* about Los Angeles as 'the style that nearly', because it almost prevented the defection of architects from the mass-housing market. Concentrated in an effort called the Case Study House Program, organized by John Entenza, this campaign was intended to convert people to modernism by using prefabrication to lower costs and make houses available to all. What Entenza and his chosen Case Study architects failed to appreciate, which Ebenezer Howard and Jonathan Carr before him did, was the power of image on the public consciousness: the need for people to feel that they were escaping the city to a bucolic cottage in the countryside, rather than a machine in a well-mowed garden.

This leads to the second reason why the Garden City movement is an important precedent to include here: while it ostensibly appears to be anti-urban, many of its principles have now been adopted by the New Urbanists as part of their strategy to repopulate inner cities in a more humanistic way. Howard did not visualize his communities as refuges from the city but as alternatives to the urban conditions of the times, which is why he planned to have an outer belt of light industry surrounding each one. Mixed use, which is now one of the New Urbanists' most frequently repeated mantras, was a central idea of Garden City planning, to reduce traffic and promote a closer sense of community.

The third reason why the Garden City movement is an important precedent is the idealistic legacy it has left. Howard's dream of having an egalitarian framework that would allow everyone to return to the land has endured in spite of the suburbs and the sprawl that are its more prevalent common denominators. That dream is evident in the early modernist emphasis on workers' housing and the numerous *Siedlungen* that resulted from it. It was also the basis for Frank Lloyd Wright's ambitious Broadacre City plan, which he envisioned as a prototype for American cities of the future, as well as for the groundbreaking Plan for the Valleys, put forward by McHarg, Wallace and Todd in 1962 (discussed in detail on pp. 175–83).

In spite of several impressively effective local ordinances in the United States, such as those enacted in parts of Oregon, to contain sprawl, the general tendency, abetted by population rise and economic opportunism, is toward exurban growth as well as movement back into the cities. Howard's model is relevant to each of these trends and offers valuable lessons on how to accommodate all of them.

above **Saynatsalo Town Hall**, Alvar Aalto, 1949–52

left **Villa Hvittrask**, Lindgren, Gesellius and Saarinen, 1903

Because of the low population to land ratio, as well as the drama of the landscape, it is perhaps unsurprising that architecture in Finland should be particularly responsive to context. These two projects, built fifty years apart, share a commitment to a humane architecture that embraces rather than shuts out nature.

3

Finland: The Search for a Humane Standard

The quest for national identity and a love of nature have combined in Finland to create an ecologically sympathetic and humane architecture

Background

Key Projects

Villa Hvittrask, Lindgren, Gesellius and Saarinen, 1903
Paimio Sanatorium, Alvar Aalto, 1929
Villa Mairea, Alvar Aalto, 1937–39
Saynatsalo Town Hall, Alvar Aalto, 1949–52
Diploma Student Union, Otaniemi University of Technology, Raili and Reima Pietila, 1966

Signposts

Arts and Crafts influences Part II: 1, 2, 4, 5, 16
Local materials and techniques Part II: 1, 4, 7, 9, 12, 24

Ecological sensitivity and contextual awareness in architecture are arguably more legible in Finland than in any other Nordic country. Because of its singular physical conditions and tumultuous history, the 'land of a thousand lakes' has distinct seasonal changes and a low population/land area ratio with vast areas of forest and tundra untouched - indeed around two-thirds of Finland is covered in forest and about a tenth by water. This has engendered both a love of nature and a high degree of individuality and independence, clearly legible in the stylistic evolution of its architecture.

This evolution is also closely tied to its history, noticeably accelerating after the country gained independence in 1917. Prior domination by both Sweden and Russia spurred a search for collective identity that coalesced in National Romanticism at the turn of the 20th century, well exemplified in the music of Jean Sibelius. Industry grew rapidly in Finland after independence in 1917, and after a depression in the 1930s it rebounded more quickly than most of Europe, with a significant shift from wood to metal and reinforced concrete construction. This surge was halted by the devastating winter war with Russia in 1939-40, as well as the World War that followed in 1941. In the Treaty of Paris of 1945, Finland not only lost its beloved Karelian heartland, but was also forced to pay reparations to Russia that drained its resources and spirit until the early 1950s and caused a critical housing shortage as refugees fled from Karelia.

The Finnish struggle for self-determination in the face of threats from both Russia and Sweden was quick to take visual form – as early as 1900 the country's overtly *Jugendstil* entry in the World's Fair in Paris was a clear symbol of the search for a national identity. This search extended to architecture, with the documentation, most notably by Gustaf Nystrom, of the indigenous architecture of Karelia, the spiritual heart of the aspiring nation. These explorations were then expanded upon by Armas Lindgren (1874–1924), who concentrated on a vernacular construct paralleling Medievalism in countries such as Britain. As a partner with Herman Gesellius (1874–1916) and Eliel Saarinen (1873–1950), Lindgren's knowledge of the indigenous 'carpenter' style soon emerged in projects such as the Villa Karsten in Helsinki (1900) the Suur Merijoki Mansion in Viipuri (1903) and the Villa Hvittrask (1903).

This latter project in particular (which the partners used as a communal house and studio) is a compelling symbol of a determination to create a national architectural style as

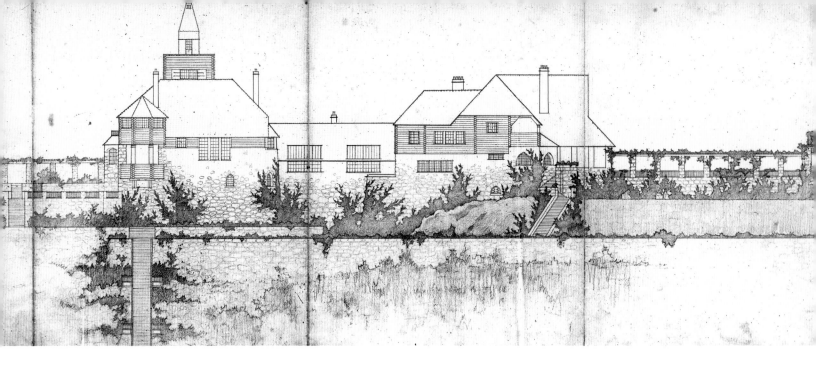

well as a convincing exercise in contextual sensitivity. Named after the 'white lake' far below the mountaintop it commands, Hvittrask was originally crowned by a distinctive, steepled tower, accentuating the designers' intention both to sanctify and to protect their new architecture studio overlooking the lake. The massive, random, rustication of its exterior walls seems to fuse it to the rocky mountaintop. These stones establish the connection to H. H. Richardson, who is known to have been a favourite of Saarinen at that time, confirmed by extensive references in his library.[1] Arts and Crafts references are equally pronounced, especially after the rebuilding of the house following a fire in 1922, when the tower was replaced by a gable roof and the rough-hewn, horizontal logs were covered with shingles in an echo of the style seen in 1880s America. These changes reinforce the original courtyard plan, which makes the villa seem like a castle, in the medievalist manner of Ruskin and Morris. The open, minimal studio, acting as a link between the north and south wings, has pride of place near the courtyard on one side, and the best views of mountains and the lake on the other. The potential plastic flow of space that begins to emerge in the Saarinen south wing is overwhelmed by materials, detail and furnishings. While the exterior was mostly shingled over, the logs of the Finnish Handicraft Style still predominate on the walls and ceiling of the living room, contributing to the heavy rustic atmosphere of this wing.

National Romanticism in Finland flickered out after Saarinen's epic design for Kalevala House failed to be realized and he left for America after his second prize in the Chicago Tribune Competition in December 1922. Yet their purist approach in several apartment buildings such as the Doctor's House at 17 Fabianin Kata (1900) and Olopborg in the Katajanokka area of Helsinki (1902), are reminiscent of other precursors of modernism, such as the Michaelerplatz project by Adolf Loos at the same time in Vienna.

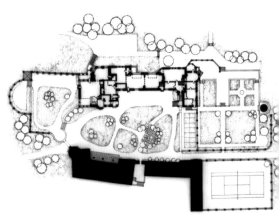

Elevation and plan of the Villa Hvittrask, 1903
Named after the 'white lake' that it overlooks, Hvittrask was designed as an architecture studio, a place to inspire the designers with dramatic scenery. Lindgren, one of the architects, sparked the equivalent of the Arts and Crafts movement in Finland, and was especially interested in the vernacular tradition. The design was later altered after a fire.

Aalto Leads the Nation

In parallel with the rapid industrialization of the new nation, the 1930s saw the emergence of a confident Functionalist direction, initiated by Alvar Aalto, Erik Bryggman and Sigurd Frosterus. Aalto's Paimio Sanatorium (1929) combined the latest research in medicine and

Villa Mairea, Alvar Aalto, 1937–9

Like the Kings Road House by Rudolf Schindler (see p. 76), this early project by Aalto blurs the line between inside and out, while part of the roof was turfed over.

psychology with new structural technology supported by an innovative load-bearing concrete pillar frame. The sanatorium is divided into four wings to maximize sunlight, with one of these being a seven-storey open-air ward with a partially covered roof terrace that provides stunning views out over the forest below. The architect's humanistic concern for the patients' wellbeing goes beyond this direct physical and visual contact with nature to the materials and colour used throughout and the accessibility of the communal spaces which easily orient each of the wings at the building's base.

The Paimio Sanatorium set a new standard for a social view of public architecture that transcended purely functional requirements and uplifted the spirit through direct contact with the environment. Aalto's Villa Mairea in Noormarkku (1937–9), for Harry and Maire Gullichsen, was equally innovative at a residential scale. Raised up on a plinth to lift it slightly above the surrounding forest, the garden court bracketed by the L-shaped plan blurs the demarcation between inside and outside, effectively integrating house and site. This juncture, particularly related to social space, is visually reinforced by the predominance of natural details, such as the clusters of slim columns that replicate the thin trunks of the pine trees outside, the sod on a portion of the roof, and the lake-like pool.

The latitude for experimentation offered by the owners of the Villa Mairea allowed Aalto to consolidate his ideas about the importance of a synthesis between functionalism and humanism stated so emphatically at Paimio, and both the Villa Mairea and Paimio had a profound impact on the next generation of architects then being trained in Europe and America. This sensibility was further refined in the general plan for Otaniemi in Espoo which occupied Aino and Alvar Aalto for twenty years after they won a competition for its design in 1949. They presented a scheme that was notable for its integration with nature, by using changes in topography to separate pedestrian and vehicular traffic.

An Integration of Nature and Architecture

The Saynatsalo Town Hall (1949–52) won in competition at the same time as Otaniemi and also rendered in red brick, to underscore its institutional role, is the civic equivalent of the

Villa Mairea in international influence. Like the villa, it also has a courtyard (really a raised *parterre*) to negotiate between the elemental extremes of shelter and wild nature, though here the centre is more enclosed. Aalto describes the concept as a building 'on a steep ridge alternating with one and two storeys around a central courtyard patio. The courtyard forms an elevated level, which was achieved by utilizing the excavated foundation soil for the raised courtyard – the lower level of the building was reserved for business premises – by using two levels, street level and the patio, the administrative building itself was set free, with its accommodation around the patio, of the vulgar influence of the business premises.'[2] As at the Villa Mairea, a fountain replicates nature at Saynatsalo, as do interior details such as the wooden butterfly roof beams in the council chamber, which mimic a treetop canopy.

A Year of Miracles

The year that Saynatsalo was completed, 1952, has been described as an *annus mirabilis* for Finland.[3] War reparations to Russia were finally paid off, rationing ended, and a pervasive sense of prosperity replaced years of privation. New construction materials, made possible by rapidly expanding industrial production became more accessible. The Olympic Games, meant to be held in Helsinki in 1940, but cancelled because of the war, finally became a reality, and the games village (1948–52) also opened up many other opportunities for architects, increasing their influence. Unfortunately the growth in wealth and status prompted a rural–urban migration, leading to the construction of new communities to house a growing population. The demands of this sudden growth led to standardized parts and construction systems being favoured over traditional methods and crafts, with prefabricated components replacing site-specific materials. However, environmental sensibilities remained strong, and the interrelationship between the new garden suburbs and their natural surroundings was taken very seriously.

Sunila and Tapiola

Finland's first modern housing development, at Sunila, was planned by Alvar Aalto before the Second World War, in 1936. Both a formal and social model, it was generally considered to be a breakthrough, with interaction between buildings, landscape and people of all economic levels being the operative principle. This is legible in what began to be called 'forest cities' in Finland, where the vision was to provide urban amenities in the countryside close to nature.[4] A booklet published by Heikki von Hertzen called 'A Home or a Barracks for Our Children?' places such cities in the tradition of Finnish wood-built towns, as well as the Garden City movement. The Population and Family Welfare Bureau along with the Housing Foundation commissioned Aulis Blomstedt, Aarne Ervi, Viljo Revell and Markus Tavio to work with urban planner and garden-city proponent Otto I. Meurman on the first housing phase in 1952 at Tapiola, also in the forest cities category.[5] As initiated by Aalto at Sunila, their guiding principle was social diversity and the integration of architecture and landscape, and open spaces were as carefully designed, as outdoor 'rooms,' as the buildings. Housing was sited around the parkland near the meadows, increasing in scale from terraced flats and single family units to higher apartment blocks beyond to increase access to public areas, while higher slopes were left unbuilt. Landscape was also used to blur the distinction between public and private zones and edges, with nature invited in rather than being tamed and kept at bay. These ideas, today proclaimed as revolutionary by the New Urbanists, attracted much

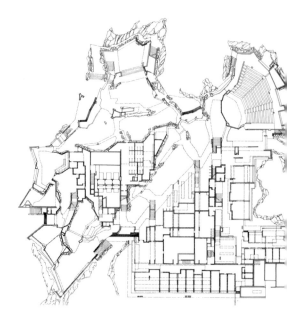

Dipoli Student Union, Otaniemi University of Technology, Raili and Reima Pietila, 1966
While made from concrete, this project largely confines itself to the existing contours of the site, meaning minimal visual interruption.

international attention in the 1930s. But the hidden revolution at Tapiola was the designer's decision to use it as a testing ground for new construction materials and prefabrication methods. Aarne Ervi and Viljo Revell, who had both worked in Aalto's office in the 1930s, were particularly interested in technical innovation.

Revisionism Sets In

By the mid-1960s, a new generation of architects had begun to revise the forest-city notion, claiming that instead of giving residents the best of the city and the country, it separated them from both, causing isolation and depression. Finland was as susceptible as ever to outside influence and the megastructures movement, led by Buckminster Fuller, is legible. A glass-enclosed extension to the Tapiola Centre by Erkki Juutilainen, Erkki Kairamo, Kirmo Mikkola and Juhani Pallasmaa proposed in 1967, shows the extent of this insurgency.

Examples of the Finnish 'carpenter' style in old towns which had survived intact because of economic hardship prior to the 1950s were also destroyed in the 1960s. A notable exception to the trend toward rational efficiency (and the psychological distancing from the environment that this encouraged) can be found in the Dipoli Student Union at the Otaniemi University of Technology designed in 1966 by Raili and Reima Pietila. It is mostly *in situ* concrete, but the formwork was pre-soaked and shaped by hand to conform to the contours and character of the site, with boulders used as a base, as at Hvittrask, to complete the impression of organic growth from the ground.

An idealistic search for egalitarian shelter supported the growth of prefabrication or 'element building' from the early 1950s until the late 1970s. By the early 1980s however, slower growth, overproduction and criticism of technical performance caused by rapid industrialization, led to proposals for a return to the crafts that had atrophied in the interim, to be used in conjunction with industrial production. This sensibility then expanded to include energy-saving strategies such as active and passive solar heating, once again emerging as a counterpoint to the glass and steel language promoted throughout Finland in the later part of the 20th century.

Enduring Traditions in Architecture and Urbanism

Mention of Finland to those in the design professions outside Scandinavia inevitably elicits reflections on Alvar Aalto or the Saarinen family, or on the High-Tech business parks funded by Nokia. But, as this overview hopefully shows, Aalto and the Saarinens were part of a much broader, environmentally based tradition, in which the High-Tech office complexes of the late 1990s are an anomaly. That grand tradition extends to 'forest cities' such as Sunila and Tapiola, which are among the few successful implementations of Ebenezer Howard's Garden City concept in the world, but are generally overlooked today when precedents for new urban typologies are sought out.

Alvar Aalto, who was viewed circumspectly by mainstream modernists, is also a clear example of the main thesis of this book: that there are many designers who tried to promote ecologically sound principles during the ascendancy of the International Style, including several leaders of the movement, but these efforts have received far less attention than progress-, or product-based work.

Saynatsalo Town Hall, Alvar Aalto, 1949–52
The unusual layout of the town hall is designed to allow unbroken access to the natural surroundings, while a central courtyard was artificially raised using the material excavated for the buildings' foundations. The relationship with the surrounding woods is reinforced by gaps between buildings that allow vistas, while the dark red brick, and angular roofs allow the complex to become lost in the surrounding rugged landscape.

above **Hilversum City Hall**, W. M. Dudok, 1924–30

left **De Dageraad (The Dawn)**, Michael de Klerk, 1919–22

The architecture of Amsterdam in the 20th century balanced cutting-edge design with traditional materials (notably brick) and a traditional approach to the division of land.

4

The Amsterdam School:
An Enduring Legacy

Topography, late industrialization and progressive housing policy combined to create a city eagerly receptive to ecological and community-based architecture

Background

Key Projects

Amsterdam Stock Exchange (Beurs), Hendrik Petrus Berlage, 1898–1903

Amsterdam South Plan, Hendrik Petrus Berlage, 1907–

Shipping House, Van der Mey with Kramer, De Klerk, 1913–16 and 1926–8

Spaarndammer series, Michael de Klerk, 1913–20

De Dageraad (The Dawn), Michael de Klerk, 1919–22

Hilversum City Hall, W. M. Dudok, 1924–30

Open Air School for the Healthy Child, Johannes Duiker and Bernard Bijvoet, 1929

Signposts

Arts and Crafts influences Part II: 1, 2, 3, 5, 16

Local materials and techniques Part II: 1, 3, 7, 9, 12, 24

Town planning Part II: 2, 3, 8, 9, 11, 12, 18, Part III:3

Community building Part II: 2, 12, 21, 22

The public architecture of Amsterdam, in the present-day Netherlands, makes a revealing case study. The city's specific topography is unusual: like much of the country, it has been reclaimed from the North Sea, making it a man-made landscape to the extent that for a long time it was believed that the name Holland came from 'hollow land'. Meanwhile, the division of the Lowlands into the Netherlands and Belgium in 1831 delayed the onset of industrialization, which proved both a curse and a blessing.

The lack of any material for building except clay meant that the early architecture of the Netherlands literally sprang from the earth: the Dutch word for brick, *baksteen*, means 'baked stone', and it remained the material of choice for much of the 20th century. Other specific qualities of architecture in Amsterdam, such as large windows, also reflect the particular characteristics of the geography, and lend historical continuity to the city's fabric. Finally, there is in Dutch culture a longstanding commitment to peaceful, communal cohabitation. This meant that while countries such as Britain struggled to house rural-urban migrants, Amsterdam launched a series of innovative public housing projects.

The history of society-based housing in the Netherlands goes back many centuries. With no historical tradition of Roman law or feudal fiefs to guide planning, egalitarian organizations were established to assess the productive capacity of land, and systematically to allocate and manage it. These organizations also determined the location and spacing of settlements as well as the distribution of fields, and these patterns in turn responded to the scarcity of land. One of these patterns is the *hofje*: four or five rows of small, party-wall houses which each have little courtyards, clustered around a garden court.[1]

Construction of these houses was typically in brick, the quintessential Dutch building material. The shortage of timber and necessity of using party walls (access to natural light restricted to the shorter ends of rectilinear units) resulted in small windows, and generally caused a rhythmic grid and the repetition of rectilinear forms. Proximity to the North Sea as well as the uniform flatness of the land both contribute to the phenomenon known as 'Holland light', an evenly distributed glow that led early builders to conclude that the size of windows was more important than their orientation.

In the division of the Lowlands in 1831, Belgium obtained the majority of the region's coal and iron deposits, while Amsterdam lost its predominance as a port because the shallow channel to the Zuiderzee could not accommodate the bigger ships then coming into service. The delay of industrialization in the Netherlands has had important consequences in making the country a paragon of environmental consciousness, since rural–urban migration has been far less severe than elsewhere in Europe. This, in turn, has meant that there has been less pressure put on the historical fabric of Dutch cities, where those migrating from the countryside usually settle because of lower rents. Unlike Britain, which concentrated on textile manufacturing during the Industrial Revolution, the Netherlands' holdings were predominantly agricultural, which fostered greenhouse horticulture at home. Late industrialization also allowed brick construction to become well established and for the Netherlands to learn from Britain's mistakes in so readily embracing new technology. The Arts and Crafts movement, which arose in direct response to Britain's industrialization, had a profound influence on pre-modern architecture in the Netherlands especially under P. J. H. Cuypers, who was the local equivalent of William Morris. He promoted the integration of architecture, art and craft and the virtues of brick as an indigenous material.

Light and Truth
Modern architecture in the Netherlands was unquestionably established by Hendrik Petrus Berlage (1856–1934) in conjunction with three younger Cuypers disciples: J. L. M. Lauwerks (1864–1932), K. P. de Bazel (1869–1923), and William Kromhaut (1864–1940). While not joined in practice, these four were similarly committed to Theosophical Anthroposophy, a belief that began in the United States in the 1870s, based on the concept that geometry and proportion are sacred and represent a fundamental truth. The movement had its own journal in the Netherlands called *Licht en Waarheid* (Light and Truth) to which the four contributed regularly.[2]

The Amsterdam Stock Exchange or Beurs (1898–1903) by Berlage, which is generally considered to be one of the most important precursors of modernism (along with Henri Labrouste's Bibliothèque Nationale, the Glasgow School of Art by Mackintosh and the Carson Pirie Scott Store in Chicago by Louis Sullivan), most clearly exemplifies the quality of *Vormharmonie* (Form Harmony) central to theosophical theory. After a series of competition entries submitted in a first round in 1883 and a second in 1885, during which the design changed considerably, Berlage was finally able clearly to express his wish to use homogeneous wall planes (*muurslak*) to enclose and protect an internalized plaza. Described best as creating the 'paradox of going outside by going inside' through a carefully choreographed sequence of incrementally expanding passages, which reverberated when the trading floor was still in operation, these walls are intentionally reminiscent of ancient Roman masonry, which Berlage greatly admired. The mass of the brick planes and piers is accentuated by the relative delicacy of the arched steel trusses supporting the protective glass roofs, a sympathetic marriage of traditional and industrial materials on a par with Labrouste's Bibliothèque in Paris.[3]

The Housing Act of 1901: the Woningwet
In 1854, King William III commissioned the Koninklijk Istitut van lngeniers (KIVI) to study housing in the Netherlands and to report their findings to the government. The Institute was determined to avoid the pitfalls that other European countries had encountered in their earlier industrialization cycle, and surveyed as many of its neighbours as possible. Among

Amsterdam Stock Exchange (Beurs), Hendrik Petrus
Berlage, 1898–1903
Berlage's Beurs is generally seen as a forerunner of
modernism in its marriage of massive, homogeneous
wall planes (built of brick) and vast glazed roof.

many other findings, the most significant standards that the KIVI finally recommended were
that all dwellings should be aligned on a north–south axis, have no closed courtyards, not be
stacked too high and have individual gardens. Their findings never became law, but did
establish conventions against which all new housing was measured, until the National
Housing Act expanded on the KIVI findings in 1901.

With the exception of housing built and managed by philanthropic organizations that
evolved from the charitable groups that ran the traditional *hofjes* and several other
enlightened projects, the inevitable pressure of overcrowding which was then endemic in the
cities of other industrialized countries, began to cause slums in urban centres throughout the
Netherlands. Calls for reform led to the National Housing Act (*Woningwet*) in 1901, with
three main provisions intended to provide everyone with affordable housing. These
provisions were that all municipalities with ten thousand or more residents be required to
submit an expansion plan before development; that detailed national housing standards be
established; and that municipalities and cooperative associations receive housing subsidies.
These provisions, intended to allow the cooperative associations to remain a viable
institution, were soon tested in the comprehensive plan for Amsterdam South.[4]

The Amsterdam South Plan

Initially conceived and coordinated by Berlage, the Amsterdam South Plan represented a fifty
per cent expansion of the city, an intricate interlocking network of inward-looking
neighbourhoods that is as important to the nation and its place in the early history of
modernism as the architectural contribution of the Beurs. Following the guidelines of the
newly enacted Housing Act, Berlage submitted a plan in 1907 that established the basic
framework for the district until his death in 1934.

Berlage was impressed by *City Planning According to Artistic Principles*, written by Camillo
Sitte in 1889, and he used Sitte's idea of implementing demonstrably effective typologies in a
balanced, egalitarian way. His plan, adopted in 1917, is based on mixed use, with provision for
commercial and office functions, but is predominantly made up of housing units that serve

occupants of different economic means. The application of Sitte's typologies includes his recommendations for town squares, but Berlage still achieved densities of up to 150 dwellings per hectare.

The Amsterdam School

The Netherlands remained neutral during the First World War, which allowed it to retain a relatively stable economy and labour force and ensured the continuation of the principles Berlage had implemented in Amsterdam South as well as their expansion throughout the country. This came at a time when a steadily increasing population needed more housing. Three architects who had apprenticed with E. Cuypers and are now considered to be the nucleus of the Amsterdam School, put an expressionistic spin on Berlage's principles in public buildings and housing projects produced just prior to, during and soon after the 1914–18 war. Johan Melchior van der Mey (1878–1949), Pieter Lodewijk Kramer (1881–1961) and Michael de Klerk (1884–1923) presented their first declaration of allegiance to *Vormharmonie* in the Shipping House, a five-storey office building near the Amsterdam Central Station, in 1913. Although Van der Mey is the architect of record, the other two members of the group participated in the design of this abstractly ornamented, neo-Gothic monument to *Jugendstil* nostalgia, in which an intricately detailed brick wrapper conceals an ascetic core.

The combination of the organic use of brick and the abstract ornamentation of the Shipping House, in expressive contrast to Berlage's personal evolution toward the stripped-down frame of Holland House in London that same year, was given even freer reign in several subsequent 'garden villages' (*tuindorp*) which have come to define the Amsterdam School style. The Spaarndammer series, which occupies three entire blocks in northwest Amsterdam, is the most spirited of these. Phase I (1913–15) which encloses a rectilinear park, has a flat facade periodically interrupted by parabolic renditions of traditional Dutch *klokgeval* (clock gables) like the cramped attics typically found in medieval canal houses. De Klerk extended the upper story of this block into a relatively window-free horizontal brick band that unites all of the units under one uniform roofline.

De Klerk used this same staccato rhythm of vertical volumes and planar facades terminated by a horizontal band in Phase II (1915–16) but a projecting, cylindrical oriel window and swirling volumes above the door mark a transition to Phase III (1917–20) which Reyner Banham has described as 'one of the most violent architectural experiences of the 20th century.'[5] The internal courtyards of Phase III, built under the auspices of the Eigen Haard (A Hearth of One's Own) housing foundation, combine the comprehensive protectiveness of the *hofjes* with cubist disjunction, layering traditional and modernist interpretations on the interpenetration.

De Dageraad (the Dawn) housing foundation sponsored an eponymous residential complex that marks the next stage of stylistic development of the Amsterdam School (see p. 62). It was completed by De Klerk and Kramer along Tellegenstraat in Amsterdam between 1919 and 1922, just prior to De Klerk's death from pneumonia in 1923. The curvilinear forms of the Dawn recall the close connection between the Netherlands and the sea. De Klerk's death caused a re-evaluation of the principles of the Amsterdam School by its growing number of adherents, who continued on in a more conservative way in filling up the empty spaces still left at Berlage's overall plan for Amsterdam South and its extension to the west. With the exception of the Ons Huis (Our House) housing foundation by J. F. Staal (1879–1940) in

above **Shipping House**, Van der Mey with Kramer, De Klerk, 1913–16 and 1926–8
An essay in *Vormharmonie*, like the Beurs, the Shipping House uses brick in an organic way.

above, right **Phase III ('The Ship'), Spaarndammer development**, Michael de Klerk, 1917–20
right **Phase I, Spaarndammer development**, Michael de Klerk, 1913–16

The Spaarndammer development was one of the most important social housing programmes in the 20th century. The forms and materials reflect the traditions of the city: the phase known as 'The Ship', for example, uses undulating forms to allude to Holland's past naval glories. Such character or attention to detail has rarely been seen since in housing projects.

1919–20, in the Watergraafsmeer district, the source of creative energy of the school, based in a naturalistic marine idiom rendered in brick, seemed to die with De Klerk.

A Prairie Style for the Polders

The planar expressionism that had been initiated by Berlage and then organically interpreted by De Klerk, Kramer and Van der Mey has a Wrightian variant that appeared in parallel to the Amsterdam School. This variant, which eventually led to De Stijl, was also generated by Berlage, who associated Wright's *In the Cause of Architecture* (1908) and the *Wasmuth Portfolio* (1911, with its introduction by C. R. Ashbee), with the long use of masonry construction in the Netherlands. *Wendingen* magazine, edited until 1927 by its founder Theodorus Hendricus Wijdeveld (1885–1986), was an important conduit for the Prairie Style. Wright corresponded with Wijdeveld in the early to mid-1920s and Wijdeveld designed a poster for the first exhibition of Wright's work in the Stedelijk Museum in Amsterdam in 1931. Robert van 't Hoff visited Wright in America in 1914 and paid overt homage to him in the Verloop residence (1915) and the Villa Nora for A. B. Henry (1916) before being asked to join De Stijl as a founding member, along with Theo van Doesburg and J. J. P. Oud. Although Van 't Hoff only remained a part of the triumvirate for two years, he contributed to the basic theory of this singularly Dutch movement during a critical period in its growth.

Dudok Monumentalizes the Wrightian Aesthetic

William Marinus Dudok (1884–1974) was the most enthusiastic Wrightian in the Netherlands in the early 1920s. He became Director of Public Works in Hilversum in 1915, just before the city became an important broadcasting centre, attracting the production companies, foundations and technical facilities associated with the industry. This put Dudok in a strategic position to contribute to the rising status of the city. Hilversum City Hall (1924–30), for which he was both client and architect, has both Wrightian and Amsterdam School themes. Its flat, light ochre, Roman bricks and carefully choreographed entry sequence leading through a tightly compressed entrance into an expansive reception hall establish these precedents clearly.

The connection between Wright and De Stijl is critical to an understanding of subsequent architectural developments in the Netherlands. In addition to Van 't Hoff, Oud also published an article on Wright, praising the 'dematerialization of the corners' in his houses in De Stijl magazine in 1910; the 'breaking of the box' for the De Stijl group, as for Wright, was intended to unify inside and outside space and was not an exercise in abstraction for its own sake. Van Doesburg, Oud and Van 't Hoff transformed Wright's concept of 'organic' architecture, or assimilation of natural processes, into a theory more congruent with contemporary scientific method, as a continuation of the traditional regard for nature in the Netherlands, rather than a negation of it. Although not part of De Stijl, Johannes Duiker (1890–1935) explored similar ideas of combining interior and exterior space, in industrial materials, most notably in his Open Air School for the Healthy Child in Amsterdam South, designed with partner Bernard Bijvoet (1889–1980) in 1929. The southern corner of the innovative concrete and glass cube is left open on the upper three levels to provide outdoor classrooms. Not all the work of Duiker and Bijvoet was as severe as the Open Air School: the same sensibility for humane contextualism in more natural materials appeared five years before in a wood frame villa in Stammerskade, Aalsmeer, built to extol the integrity of rural topologies.

The Delft School Confronts Nieuwe Bouwen

The westward spread of the *Neue Sachlichkeit* or New Objectivity was hastened by the participation of Berlage, Rietveld, Stam and Cornelis van Eesteren in the founding of the Congrès Internationaux d'Architecture Moderne (CIAM) at La Sarraz in 1928. Under the joint sponsorship of Le Corbusier and Van Eesteren, CIAM adopted resolutions denouncing the Amsterdam School and De Stijl as 'too emotional', and restricting the scope of city planning to the 'four functions' of work, housing, recreation and transport without regard for the historical role of cities as repositories of culture. This view was swiftly implemented when Van Eesteren became chief architect of the newly formed Amsterdam Municipal Planning Department in 1929 and Chairman of CIAM in 1930. Van Eesteren promoted long, linear units of the *Siedlung* variety called *stroken bouw* or 'strip buildings' in the Netherlands and advocated that traditional, small-scale garden plots and internal courts be replaced by communal 'public space'. The lower density implicit in the mid-rise units, however, caused more land use and the public spaces made private gardens difficult to cultivate.[6]

Marinus Jan Granpré Molière (1883–1972), a professor at the Technical University of Delft, led a counterattack against the growing influence of the New Objectivity as well as what he considered to be the excess of the Amsterdam School. He used his considerable influence as a high-ranking academic to lead what has since become known as the 'Delft Dictatorship' in favour of traditionalism. Vreewijk, built in 1913 in Rotterdam, is clearly based on Arts and Crafts principles, overlaid with Molière's prescription to preserve the masonry tradition of the Netherlands. It defines the Delft School agenda of perfecting the garden village model, domestic scale brick craftsmanship and geometric proportion. Molière's former students, in powerful administrative posts after the German occupation, were strategically positioned to address the critical housing shortage as well as the massive destruction of industry and polders throughout the Netherlands after the Second World War ended. These conditions were especially severe in Emmeloord, Middlebury, Rhenen and Zandvoort.

Team Ten

By the time the ninth CIAM Congress convened in 1953, opposition to the original Le Corbusier and Van Eesteren concept of the 'four functions' of a city led to a counter manifesto in favour of fostering a sense of community instead. Supporters from the Netherlands included Aldo van Eyck (1918–99) and Jacob Berend Bakema (1914–81). Bakema had replaced Molière as the resident conscience of the Delft School at that university when Molière retired in 1953. At the tenth CIAM Congress in Dubrovnik in 1956, this group, which also included Peter and Alison Smithson, Jill and William Howell and John Voelcker, Gorges Candilis and Shadrach Woods and Rolf Gutmann consolidated its position, published as the *Team Ten Primer* in 1968.

Van Eyck, who designed over seven hundred children's playgrounds for the Amsterdam Public Works Department between 1947 and 1978 carried the childlike capacity for wonder and discovery characteristic of this primary clientele over into his architecture. His 1957 design for a municipal orphanage in southwest Amsterdam reveals the Team Ten vision. The love of small-scale courtyards and cellular tendencies that the brick construction tradition fostered in the Netherlands is clearly evident. The repetition of two basic typological units has allowed the building to adapt to various uses over time, a perfect example of the perpetuating permanence that Aldo Rossi describes in *The Architecture of the City*, at small scale. Van Eyck

Open Air School for the Healthy Child, Johannes Duiker and Bernard Bijvoet, 1929
Designed to allow in the maximum amount of fresh air and natural light, this project bridges the (not inconsiderable) gulf between cubistic modernism and nature. It remains a school to this day.

also participated in the campaign to construct 70,000 new housing units in Amsterdam between 1968 and 1986, distributed on either new or reclaimed sites throughout the city. Van Eyck's contributions, along with those of others, such as Stytze Visser Kees de Kat, Dick Peet and Ruud Snikkenburg, were categorized as launching a second Amsterdam School.

Accurate or not, the comparison underscores the durability of a core set of values in Netherlands architecture: love of the land and light translated into telluric materials, respect for human scale, historic continuity and reference, social equity and interaction translated into housing, compact neighbourhood structures and mixed-use (that the New Urbanists are trying, with difficulty, to legislate into existence in other countries).

Herman Hertzberger (1932–) who has achieved international recognition on a par with Team Ten members such as Van der Broek, Bakema and Van Eyck, has continued to emphasize archetypal, cellular units, masonry construction, social intention and responsiveness to communal patterns. His concrete and brick office building in Central Beheer, Apeldorn (1967–72) is based on stacking up square units nine metres long on each side, with a three-metre gap between them, in an irregular cluster that rises to six levels at its highest point. There was an option to use either open or closed corners, reminiscent of Duiker's Open School, to allow visual and verbal interaction from one unit to another as well as the ability to experience the vertical spaces between them. Although repetitious and much smaller in scale, the interior of Central Beheer recalls the weighty massiveness and spatial excitement of Berlage's Beurs: both share the quality of being a covered internal plaza.

The Amsterdam School and Anthroposophist Resurgent

In spite of the same flirtations with High Tech steel and glass modernism also described in other countries, such as Finland, with a strong environmentalist heritage, many Netherlands architects continue to pay homage to the free form masonry tradition by the Amsterdam School. The headquarters of the NMB Bank in Amsterdam built between 1979–86 by A. Alberts (1927–99) and M. van Huut (1947–) was hailed as the most energy-efficient building in Europe when it was dedicated, because of its superinsulated perimeter and innovative use of high interior spaces as solar chimneys. More than a single office building, the complex is divided into ten wings that are each subdivided into smaller work spaces, to ensure privacy and quiet. The wings surround an open, protected internal commercial plaza which has become a gathering place for both the people working in the complex and the surrounding community. The NMB Bank is a testimony to the ongoing influence of the Amsterdam School in the Netherlands, which continues its leadership in environmental issues in Europe.

Taliesin West, 1938–59

The shapes echo the surrounding mountains, while the
materials were largely gathered locally, the walls built by
filling the formwork with local volcanic rock, and then
pouring in concrete.

5

Frank Lloyd Wright: Close to the Land

Frank Lloyd Wright created an 'organic' architecture that drew on indigenous Japanese traditions which he tailored to specific climatic conditions

Key Projects

Barnsdall House (Hollyhock House), 1917–20
Jacobs House (Hemicycle House), 1943
Taliesin West, 1938–59

Signposts

Arts and Crafts influences Part II: 1, 2, 3, 4, 16
Japanese influence Part II: 1, 6, 12; Part III: 2
Solar energy Part II: 11, 14, 15

Biography Frank Lloyd Wright has long been included in the canon of proto- or early modernists, but his long career covered many different approaches to architecture. He moved to Chicago aged twenty to pursue a career in architecture, serving as a draughtsman for Adler & Sullivan where he gained an understanding of abstract masses. This combined with an interest in Japanese architecture to forge a low, horizontal type of building which Wright likened to the flatness of the Midwestern prairie – in most cases it was also characterized by a play between solid and glazed walls, inside and outside.

From the outset most of his commissions were for houses, often for wealthy patrons. However, over the course of his career, he designed churches and temples, hotels and skyscrapers, as well, of course, as Taliesin, the utopian community where he lived. The original Taliesin was founded in Wisconsin, but at the age of seventy, in 1936, Wright contracted pneumonia, and decided to found a new colony, Taliesin West, near Phoenix, Arizona. He was still working on this project at the time of his death in 1959. His workshop launched the careers of many other architects, including that of Rudolf Schindler.

The Prairie House that Frank Lloyd Wright is so closely associated with in the early part of his career and that he and his Prairie School followers promoted as being genuinely American, was actually inspired by the traditional Japanese house. The raised base, wide, open main floor and overhanging roof used in his best-known residences in Oak Park and River Forest, near Chicago, owe an obvious debt to the tripartite *Sukiya*-style villas he was familiar with from his frequent visits to Japan, even though he never acknowledged this, or any other link to historical or indigenous precedents.

The Prairie House was exemplary in a contemporary environmental sense, because of its traditional Japanese roots: its wide eaves provided shade for outdoor 'rooms' associated with interior spaces and prevented heat gain inside; the predominant use of wood meant that they had low embodied energy in a renewable material; and the lack of a basement gave them a lighter, less oppressive footprint, causing minimal disturbance of the site. Wright also excelled at orientation, a rudimentary but very effective form of diurnal zoning which made optimum use of climatic factors to heat or cool each space at the time of day in which it was being used.

In spite of the fact that Wright's Prairie houses are inspired translations of an effective traditional adaptation to specific environmental conditions, he designed two other projects later in his long career that exceed this considerable achievement, without relying on any specific vernacular precedents. The Jacob Hemicycle, in Middleton, Wisconsin, finished just before the Second World War, is the first of these: a passive solar residence with a semi-circular plan that predicts the mania for thermal augmentation that would follow, more than thirty later, because of a series of disastrous oil embargos in the mid-1970s. Taliesin West, built at the same time, is the desert equivalent of his Hillside, Wisconsin, home, and is a second ecological paradigm: it fits seamlessly into its difficult surroundings, and demonstrates an exceptional understanding of material processes in its design. Before reaching this point of ecological awareness, however, Wright went through a transitional phase, in which he was searching for a new direction.

Coming to terms with the Machine

After scandal prompted him to leave Chicago, the opportunity to build a house, theatre and actor's colony for Aline Barnsdall in Los Angeles allowed him to explore what he considered to be a more authentic national heritage: Barnsdall's 'Hollyhocks' has Mesoamerican, rather than Asian, roots. The *talud-tablero* profile of the main elevation is distinctly Mayan, and this also launched a 'school' of its own in that city, continued by Stacey Judd. Wright, who referred to the Barnsdall House as his *romanza*, a one-off attempt at something different, made it the first in a limited series that also included the Ennis Brown bastion, which shares the same profile, and the Milliard house, also made of concrete block. He referred to these houses as attempts to come to terms with 'the machine', marrying industrial materials with handcraft.

The Usonian House

After he completed his Mesoamerican explorations, he was still searching for a genuine American Style. His Usonian (meaning democratic) series is yet another attempt to find an appropriate national language. Like the Prairie style, it was also organized horizontally, although not raised on a plinth. The difference was in its relationship to the outdoors: the Usonian type was intended to be varied to suit different sites, and to have an even more open plan than the Prairie house, which was his first attempt to 'break the box'. The Usonian model was the result of Wright's ongoing attempt to derive what he called an 'organic' architecture, which he viewed as achieving more than just designing a home that responded to climatic conditions to create internal comfort by natural means, instead becoming an organic whole as part of a dynamic ecological process. Wright stressed that the Usonian, organic house was not to remain in a static state, and would never be finished, just as nature was always changing.

A First Attempt

The first Usonian house was built for Herbert and Catherine Jacobs in Madison Wisconsin in 1936. At 150 square metres (1,500 square feet), it was relatively small, and cost approximately $5,500. Shortly afterward, the Jacobses moved to a 52-acre farm in Middleton Wisconsin, and asked Wright to design another home for them there. While his first house was rectilinear, the topography of this more wide open site suggested a curvilinear or semi-circular plan, the first of a series of houses that Wright built with curved plans. By early 1944 he had produced a house that was unlike anything he, or anyone else up until that time, had done, and which is now seen as a pioneering attempt at passive solar design. The house is a half circle with its rear, north, wall, protected from the cold winter wind by a berm that rises to the top of it.

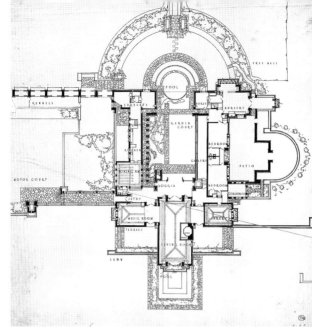

top, left and right **Barnsdall House (Hollyhock House)**, 1917–20
This project seems to be an early attempt by Wright to find an authentic American architectural language, one that responds to the environment and climate. To achieve this, he uses a Mesoamerican vocabulary of forms. The left-hand photograph shows the east façade.

above **Olive Hill Residence**, 1921–3

The entire south façade has large windows and glass doors covered by the deep eave of a flat overhanging roof, to let the low winter sun in, but to block higher summer solar angle. This is in response to a Midwest, north-east temperate zone where temperatures can range from sub-zero to more than 30°C (86°F) and where summers can be very humid.

In this humid zone, which has higher temperatures than are typical in the Midwest, Wright realized it was especially important to open up to cooling breezes, and so these large doors on the south side open wide to connect the long, narrow interior space to a sunken, outdoor garden protected by the hill and the curved form of the house. The interior is basically one large room, 5 metres (17 feet) wide and 24 metres (80 feet) long, with a kitchen and bathroom kept apart in a masonry core. There are bedrooms on an upper level, reached by a narrow stair in a circular stone core; but to keep the lower level open, this floor is suspended from the roof beams by steel rods. These beams, which are relatively small 1 by 12s (about 30 centimetres by 3.5 metres), radiate out from the buried berm wall on the north and are doubled up to embrace the mullion posts of the glazed south wall, to which they are bolted on either side.

A Lesson, Ahead of its Time

The second Jacobs house is in perfect harmony with its surroundings and is a model of passive solar design, which was not to become popular for another thirty years. It integrates a relationship to its particular context with strategies for natural energy and spatial organization in many important ways. Burying the back of the house in the earth protects it from the prevailing wind and keeps it warmer, because of thermal mass, and the limestone walls and floor serve the same purpose. Rather than being coincidental, the curved shape derives from the structural requirements of this earth berm, which is very heavy. The orientation toward the south/south-east is ideal for passive solar gain, captured by clever use of glazing.

The curved shape of this façade is also the most efficient in increasing solar gain. The large roof eave protects the interior from direct solar radiation in the summer and allows it in during the winter when the sun is lower on the horizon. The irregularly laid limestone bricks, rather than being a stylistic gesture, also increase the surface area of material used for thermal storage, soaking up heat during the day and re-radiating it into the interior at night. The suspended second floor, recessed 1.2 metres (4 feet) back from the south window wall, allows heat to rise from the lower level to heat the upper floor during the winter. During the summer, the wall on the north as well as the windows on the south have openings that allow the house to be cross ventilated, and this natural ventilation, combined with the thermal inertia created by the stone walls and floor contribute to a cool interior environment. The Jacobs Hemicycle was followed, in rapid succession, by the Martin house in Akron, Ohio (1947), Meyer house in Galesburg, Michigan (1948), Laurent house in Rockford, Illinois (1949) and Pearce house in Bradbury, California (1950), as well as similarly shaped houses for his sons David, in Phoenix, Arizona (1950), and Robert Llewellyn, in Bethesda, Maryland (1953). None of these, however, has the direct simplicity of their pioneering predecessor.

A Second Environmental Model

Just before the second Jacobs house was built, Wright was also consulting on the Arizona Biltmore Hotel, designed by a former employee at the Oak Park Studio, Alfred Chase McArthur. Wright stayed in Phoenix for four months and while he was there, also received a commission for another hotel, San Marcos in the Desert. Escaping the cold Wisconsin winters in 1929 he established a site, which he called Ocatilla, at Salt River Mountains, as a studio and living quarters for fifteen people who came from Taliesin. It was built of readily available, inexpensive materials appropriate to its temporary status: wood and canvas units laid out in an angular geometrical plan that echoed the mountain peaks nearby, grouped around an internal courtyard, which offered some protection from the harsh desert landscape.

The San Marcos project was sidetracked by the stock market crash, but the brief experience at Ocatilla, and a bout of pneumonia, planted the idea of establishing a permanent studio there.[1] In January 1938 Wright bought 800 acres, twenty-six miles northwest of Phoenix in Paradise Valley, and the entire Wisconsin studio travelled west to help construct Taliesin West. It is angular, like Ocatilla, in reference to the McDowell Mountains, which form a 1,300-metre (4,000-foot) high backdrop on the north side of the site.

The materials used in the construction of Taliesin West were also mostly taken from the site, as they were for the Ocatilla Camp, but are more permanent: volcanic stones at hand were placed in rough wooden forms and concrete was poured in around them, to hold them together without using steel reinforcing bars. Heavy redwood truss frames were placed at intervals along these walls holding up a sliding canvas panel roof between them, giving the impression of what has been called 'a savage and yet luxurious tent that is sympathetically responsive to the desert landscape'.[2] Several biographers, such as Brendan Gill, have broken the unofficial and unspoken code of silence that surrounded Wright for years after his death in 1959, imposed by his inner circle, especially his wife Olgivanna Labovich, who was very protective of his image and reputation. Gill has written about Wright's paradoxical character – his ability to endure great hardships for the sake of his work and his equivalent love of luxury – and Taliesin West is a symbol of that ambivalence.

After the first phase was completed, in 1941, the 'campsite made permanent' included a residence for the Wrights, drafting room and workshop but also a 'teaching theatre' for performances and films, where Wright and his wife were the centre of attention. There was also a communal kitchen, consistent with Mrs Wright's idea of a fellowship in which people

top and above **Imperial Hotel**, Tokyo, 1919–21
Wright first visited Japan in 1905, and was a keen collector of Japanese *ukiyoe* prints. Having been so influenced by Japanese architecture, it was fitting that he had an opportunity to build in that country.

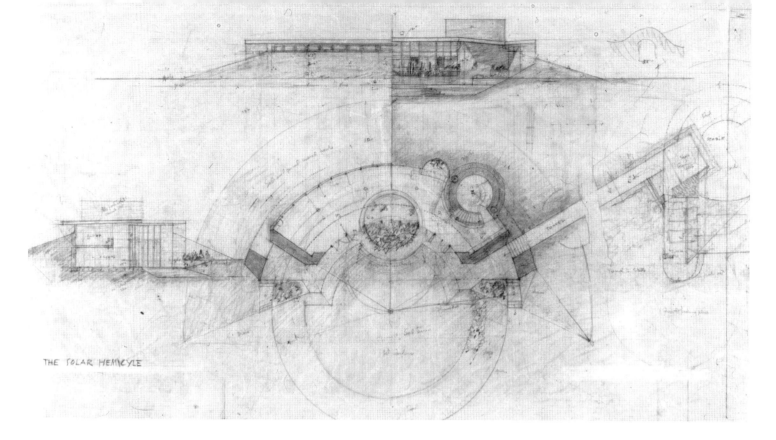

THE SOLAR HEMICYLE

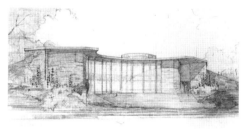

Jacobs House, 1943

Known as the 'solar hemicycle' house, this was the second house built for the Jacobs family. In perfect harmony with its surroundings, it is also a model of passive solar design, well ahead of its time.

lived and worked together. She had been a Gurdjieff disciple at his Institute for the Harmonious Development of Man. Her involvement in the formation of Taliesin West introduced a spiritual component into Wright's idea of an organic architecture, taking his notion of unity with nature to an almost mystical level, by enhancing human perception.[3]

After Phase I was completed, there was an annual western migration from Wisconsin to Arizona until Wright died. Photographs and films taken during the early days at Taliesin West show the contrasts best: one indelible image is of Wright and his wife in a Cherokee Red Lincoln Continental Cabriolet, in front of their elemental rock, wood and canvas commune.

An Anti-Urban Sensibility

No discussion of Frank Lloyd Wright would be complete without mention of Fallingwater, generally considered his masterpiece. In spite of its close integration with the site, Fallingwater was an anomaly for Wright, a deliberate attempt to show that he was as capable of producing modernist syntax as the European architects who were getting media attention at that time. His decision to have it cantilever over Bear Run made it necessary to use reinforced concrete, which he restricted to horizontal planes. This was offset with local stone, steel and glass, reflecting his concern that nature, craft and 'the machine' be balanced.

The focus on Fallingwater is further proof of the historical emphasis on progressive forms, often to the exclusion of those with a less industrial basis. Wright's claim that Fallingwater was his final victory over 'the machine', however, is also a reminder that his spiritual affinity to the Arts and Crafts movement remained long after he first opened his studio in 1898.[4] That affinity extended to a distrust of the city, and in spite of the fact that he designed and built several skyscrapers and is considered part of the Chicago School, he was essentially as anti-urban as the founders of the Arts and Crafts movement themselves.

Kings Road House, Los Angeles, 1922

Built by the architect for himself and another couple, the
Kings Road House exemplifies his inside-outside
approach that blurred the boundaries between internal
and external.

6

Rudolf Schindler:
Interacting with the Environment

The architecture of Rudolf Schindler shows an early interest in the relationship between inside and outside, as well as the value of natural ventilation

Biography

Key Projects

Kings Road House, Los Angeles, 1922–
James Eads How House, Silverlake, completed 1925
Buck House, Los Angeles, 1934
Rodakiewicz House, Los Angeles, 1937

Signposts

Japanese influence Part II: 1, 5, 12; Part III: 2
Self-build Part II: 7, 9, 12, 21
Natural ventilation Part II: 7, 11, 16, 20, 23, 24
Sensitivity to site Part II: 10, 25; Part III: 2

Born in Vienna in 1887, Schindler studied painting and engineering under the seminal modern architect Adolf Loos, before moving to Chicago in 1914, drawn in large part by Frank Lloyd Wright. In fact he arrived in the United States at a critical time. As historian Kathryn Smith has explained, 'with only a few months until the outbreak of war, in 1914, Schindler sailed for America. Although he was not fleeing Europe, like later refugee architects, but simply seeking his American prospects, his choice at that pivotal moment in history would set him apart from Le Corbusier, Gropius, Mies and even his friend Richard Neutra, for the rest of his life.'[1] While, like Neutra, Schindler had been exposed to Otto Wagner's ideas about the necessity of using contemporary materials, he retained a more humane, less mechanistic, outlook, perhaps because he escaped the impact of the war and its aftermath.

Three years after arriving in the United States, he began to work in Wright's studio, until he was sent to Los Angeles to supervise an important project. Upon completion he decided to remain in that city, and after marrying built the Kings Road House, essentially a manifesto for the rest of his career. Most of his commissions were for private houses or villas, almost all in California, and particularly around Los Angeles. However, in spite of his importance - and the fact that his work was widely emulated by the Californian 'Case Study' house architects of the 1940s to 1960s - he attracted little attention or acclaim at home or abroad, and was not included in the seminal 1932 'International Style' exhibition curated by Philip Johnson at MOMA. He died in 1953, and at his memorial exhibition was described as 'the least understood of the American pioneers of modern architecture.'

Rudolf Schindler, whose work only began to be more widely recognized in the late 1990s, had a profound influence on what came to be known as the 'California house' in the post-Second World War period, especially in the recognition that during warmer times of the year a direct connection between inside and outside should be encouraged. His first exposure to architecture in America, working for Frank Lloyd Wright at his Taliesin Studio in Spring Green, Wisconsin, was in this context serendipitous, since Wright's rural Arts and Crafts aesthetic must have reinforced Schindler's own more inclusive view of nature. Schindler's next stroke of luck came when Wright sent him to be project manager at Olive Hill, where the patron Aline Barnsdall was feeling rather neglected, since Wright was spending so much time in Japan. The older architect correctly guessed that Schindler's charm would soothe the frayed nerves of the disillusioned oil heiress, who understandably felt abandoned by her architect.

When the Barnsdall house was finished Schindler and his new bride, Sophie Pauline Gibling, vacationed in Yosemite National Park and upon returning to the city they decided to try to recapture the freedom they had felt camping out in the wilderness and sleeping under the stars in a house they planned to build in Los Angeles. They bought a 33 by 66 metre (100 by 200 foot) lot on King's Road for $2,750 in November, 1921, and together with close friends Clyde and Marian Chace, they began construction in the spring of 1922 with $2,350 borrowed from his wife's parents. Chace was an engineer and was working for Irving Gill at the time the Kings Road House was started. He had experience with tilt-slab concrete construction and he and Schindler devised a similar system for the exterior walls of their house, since it was such a quick and inexpensive way to build. The panels used to make the wall were themselves made by digging a shallow depression in the ground which could be used as a mould. When the concrete had set the panel could be stood upright. The panel size was dictated by the weight that Schindler and Chace could lift with a rudimentary wooden tripod and rope winch. Schindler turned the necessity of having a joint between the panels into an asset by making them wider in the middle, for over half their length and inserting glass in the gap to let in the light. The house plan is based on the idea that each couple would have their own private section, and that each person would have a separate space within that section.

Interior–Exterior Relationship

The King's Road House is organized into L-shaped segments which each wrap around their own outdoor courtyard and pinwheel out from a kitchen and laundry room core at the centre with a tented open sleeping 'basket' above it, on the roof. As Schindler described it in a letter to his wife's parents: 'the basic idea was to give each person his own room – instead of the usual distribution – and to do most of the cooking right on the table – making it more a social 'campfire' affair, than the disagreeable burden to one member of the family... The rooms are large studio rooms – with concrete walls on three sides, the front open (glass) to the outdoors – a real California scheme.'[2] While each couple could be alone, or each person could have *right* **Plan, Kings Road House**, 1922

The cleverly interlocking plan makes little distinction between inside and outside, to the extent even of putting fireplaces in external areas.

below **Kings Road House**, 1922

The need for quick and simple construction meant that the concrete slabs used to construct the wall were cast on-site – thin strips of glass were inserted in between each to disguise the joins, though Schindler clearly chose to turn this to his advantage. Such inventiveness is a hallmark of much good ecological architecture.

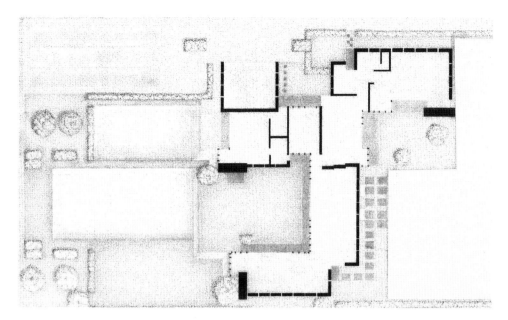

privacy if they wanted it, the social potential of the house was an important feature. The pinwheel plan also allowed each 'L' to have a hard public concrete face and fragile wood and glass sliding screen that opens up to its respective interim garden, the private outdoor room of each couple that lived there. Each garden is treated as the natural extension of its interior counterpart when the *shoji*-like walls are pushed open to join them, with a fireplace on the outside wall to contribute to the domestic feeling of the garden and make it usable most of the year.

An Efficient Module

The sliding glass walls facing each interior garden, which are obviously influenced by traditional Japanese domestic architecture and the idea of *shaki* (borrowed landscape), are also based on a modular system like their Japanese counterparts; however, instead of being the *ken* and the *tatami* they are governed by American timber sizes. Schindler's logical modular system of two-foot (60-centimetre) increments makes construction much easier, and lowers cost because it reduces waste. This is startling compared to customized timber-frame houses which are designed without regard to standard lumber sizes, with waste factors of twenty per cent or more. Schindler introduced this system at King's Road and used it throughout his career. Starting from the break required by the ceiling height, Schindler introduced a long horizontal sill above the full-height sliding panels, and projected a narrow roof from this sill out over an extension of the interior concrete floor, corresponding to the Japanese *engawa*. Like the *engawa*, this covered transitional space joins inside and outside as a thin linear neutral zone that blurs the demarcation line found in conventional houses. The actual roof at King's Road is 60 centimetres (two feet) higher than this sill, again because of timber sizes, and because it begins as the line of the sliding *shoji*-like walls, it makes each of the elongated studio-rooms seem to rise, while still accentuating the human scale. The final impression is paradoxical: an uplifting intimacy that is enhanced by the resonating duality between inside and outside space.

A Model of Environmental Awareness

The King's Road House inspired countless steel-and-glass replicas in Los Angeles during the post-Second World War era, especially in the 'Case Study' house series organized by editor John Entenza to be published in his *Arts and Architecture* magazine. It anticipated and defined the idea of casual, outdoor living that an entire generation of young Americans sought after surviving the horrors of war in Europe and Asia, in spite of its communal quasi-socialist roots. But, it also presages all of the environmental principles later labelled as 'sustainability' in the late 1980s and early 90s: low embodied energy, high thermal mass in the concrete outer walls and floor, natural ventilation induced by sliding screen internal walls, and the efficient use of a renewable resource in its timber structure. More important than that, of course, is its mixing of inside and outside, the reverse of the early modernist attitude that nature must be kept at bay.

Refracting the Integration of Interior and Exterior Space

This attitude toward the relationship between material and human made space was underscored in the James Eads How House, completed in Silverlake in 1925. Because of the steeply sloping plot, Schindler was forced to internalize the spatial relationships that a

James Eads How House, completed 1925
By working with the gradient of the site, and by orientating the roof beams diagonally, Schindler created visual relationships with the surrounding mountains.

relatively large and flat site had allowed him to explore more freely on King's Road, and he uses a stunning view of mountains in the distance to maximum effect. Closing down the entry sequence to emphasize the final surprise of this view (in the best tradition of his mentor Frank Lloyd Wright), Schindler intricately manipulates the plan to create a series of alternating chevrons that emanate from a small central light shaft, linking all of the storeys of the compact building. By doing so, he accentuates the visual experience of seeing through the entire house, on a diagonal axis, from the front door after entering it, across the central light-well to the mountains in the distance, reiterating the startling impression with an intricate, interlocking series of beams on the ceiling above.

Unable physically to connect the interim spaces to exterior counterparts, he decided to use every visual means possible to make the same connection psychologically, refracting a paradigmatically natural mountain scene through a deliberately crafted series of glass prisms to make his point. Although a fairly conventional foreground garden was later added between the road and front door by his erstwhile friend and eventual nemesis Richard Neutra, Schindler's vision of using formal interaction to make nature palpable inside the house remains the indelible impression and it is more memorable than any actual juxtaposition between building and landscape could possibly be because it intentionally connects at a deep subconscious perceptual and psychological level.

The Buck House

In 1934, more than a decade after his breakthrough at King's Road and its refracted internalized equivalent for Eads How in Silverlake, Schindler designed a house for J. J. Buck that codifies many of the principles first established in that pair. Although he concentrated on residential design throughout his career and completed many houses in the interim, the Buck House represents a point of resolution in the same way that Hill House does for Charles Rennie Mackintosh, or Fallingwater does for Frank Lloyd Wright. If the King's Road House may be said to have anticipated the California style patented by the 'Case Study' house architects between the late 1940s and the mid-1960s in Los Angeles, the Buck House is the recognizable prophetic model for them, in its elegant, minimal, cerebral lightness, openness, structural clarity and fundamental relationship to the climate and to the land.

Many of Schindler's spatial interpretations in other houses have been profitably compared to those of his Viennese mentor, Adolf Loos, whose *Raumplan* was an attempt to retain rather conventional room arrangements and designated times in plan, while 'breaking the box' in terms of section. Loos's reason for not breaking down traditional room patterns stemmed from a profound reading of the radical disjunctions caused by the rural to urban migration of the late 18th and early 19th centuries and the belief that, even though the loss of community caused by the Industrial Revolution could justify an anonymous, mask-like exterior wrapper (because few in their new urban condition knew of or cared about the status of anyone else), the inside of a house should remain a familiar sanctuary from the trauma of dealing with strangers in the city every day. Sectional dislocations, however, such as interlocking half levels and open mezzanines served to remind the rural refugee of the tectonic social changes that had taken place and the psychic dangers lurking outside the deceptive safety of the front door. As the prototypical city without a centre, Los Angeles seems an even likelier candidate for the domestic reassurance offered by the *Raumplan* than Vienna, were it not for the climate, which occasionally reduced Schindler into abandoning his mentor's subtle rationale.

The Buck House, like his own on King's Road or the better-known Lovell House, is one of those significant exceptions replacing the *Raumplan* with a reunion with Paradise itself (or at least a reasonable facsimile of it). The Buck House is more mainstream than the King's Road campsite and was more easily assimilated by architects eager to cater to a freshly minted middle class. The 'Case Study' architects served clients in search of a less traditional, more casual lifestyle acted out under a perennially shining sun.

The durable myth of Richard Neutra's comment to Philip Johnson (made while Johnson was scouting the West Coast for talent to include in his landmark MOMA exhibition on International Style) that there was no-one, other than himself, doing truly modern architecture in Los Angeles, makes a good story. But it does not completely explain why Schindler was not only excluded from the show, but also from the pantheon of modernists that this media coup helped to create. Had Johnson known about the Buck House, which was completed after the 'International Style' exhibition had closed, he may have changed his mind, but a more plausible explanation is that modernism and nature did not mix at that time – that the Brave New World was irreconcilable with the most elemental processes of our shared human past.

The 'Case Study' architects were chosen by John Entenza because of their modernist credentials, and they, ironically, responded by doing less-than-inspired versions of the Buck House. What had changed? Le Corbusier's parallel exploration of two diametrically opposed philosophies (discussed on pp. 95–105) provides a key clue, of doubts, or rather ambivalences, among the founders of the heroic phase about the extent of the exclusion of history and the natural environment from the future of architecture. The 'Case Study' architects enter at this point of ambivalence; they finally found that they could not exclude the

top and above **The Buck House**, 1934
The Buck House is a building very much of its place – California – responding to climate and surroundings, uniting the building with its gardens in a way that would have great influence on the later 'Case Study' architects.

most prevalent fact affecting their design, and turned to Schindler's ideas for guidance and direction. But he himself was gone before his instincts were vindicated and never experienced the reaffirmation he deserved.

Reconciling Modernism with the Environment

Using the lens of the parameters introduced earlier here, to best determine Schindler's contribution to green sensibilities today, there are several salient points to recall. First of all, his two famous mentors, Loos and Wright, represent diametrically opposed positions on urban theory. Loos was urbane, but shared what Anthony Vidlier has described as the early 20th-century paranoia caused by urban *anomie*, making the interiors of his city houses refuges from what he and many other social therapists at that time considered to be alien territory, however civilized.[3] This attitude had an enormous impact on early modernists such as Mies van der Rohe, whose use of luxurious materials, such as chrome, marble, mahogany and leather in his interiors, and glass planes to divide inside from outside, reflect the Loosian notion of an outer and inner self. The 'free flow of space' that Mies and then others announced as a benefit of using the frame, instead of the bearing-wall system, extended to the outside; the curtain wall that the steel frame made possible, allowed a new freedom of interaction between interior spaces as well as between inside and outside. But as this system matured, in the Farnsworth House in Plano, Illinois, for example, the internal–external relationship was reduced to visibility only, and the use of a patio, now and then. The Loosian distrust of the outside world, in other words, was translated into luscious interiors and glass walls that put nature on display, keeping it at an abstract distance behind crystal panels.

But Schindler took away a different interpretation of Loos's insight, related to that part of his theory which argued that the expulsion from pre-industrial communality has made the search for vernacular integrity a meaningless, if noble, endeavour. Schindler fastened onto the tragic implications of that paradox (which is recalled in German Romanticism), the loss of our ancestral rural home and the continuous search for it. Schindler decided to carry out that search using a complex strategy largely provided by his second mentor Frank Lloyd Wright.

Unlike Loos, Wright was distinctly anti-urban, having been indoctrinated in the rural ethics of middle America by the Lloyd Jones side of his family, in Wisconsin. Although he can be said to have participated in the evolution of the Chicago School and its urban ethos, since he also designed several skyscrapers, the majority of his designs were for single-family residences and in the beginning of his career these were located in Oak Park and River Forest, which were then suburbs of Chicago. His Prairie-style house type was based on a Japanese prototype: the *Ho-o-den* teahouse, which he had seen at the World's Columbian Exposition, and used a similar tripartite division of raised base, open middle, and large overhanging roof as organizing principles. Wright's and Schindler's adaptation of a Japanese model leads to the second reason for Schindler's current relevance to us now. Specifically by removing the intervening walls of glass that Mies van der Rohe had imposed, Schindler finally managed to sweep away Loos's fears, providing the prototype for a liberated modernism that others in Los Angeles were able to follow.

Windcatches, Souk, New Baris, 1967
The development of New Baris, an entirely new
settlement in the Egyptian desert, miles from anywhere
and lacking electricity, posed considerable challenges to
Fathy. These windcatches were used to create natural
ventilation.

7

Hassan Fathy: Reviving Ancient Techniques

The Egyptian architect Hassan Fathy did more than perhaps any other architect in the Middle East to encourage a return to traditional building techniques

Biography

Key Projects

Hamdi Seif Al-Nasr Villa, Fayum, 1945

New Gourna Village, Luxor, 1945–7 (partially constructed)

New Baris, Kharga, 1967 (partially constructed)

Dar Al Islam, town plan, 1980 (unfinished)

Signposts

Local materials and techniques Part II: 1, 3, 4, 9, 12, 24

Self-build Part II: 6, 9, 12, 21

Natural ventilation Part II: 6, 11, 16, 20, 23, 24

Climate control Part II: 8, 9, 10, 12, 15, 19

Hassan Fathy was born on March 23, 1900 near Tanta, in the delta region of Egypt, close to the Mediterranean coast. His Egyptian father was a moderately wealthy landowner; his mother was Turkish. After a private, Lycée-based education, he entered Cairo University as an Agricultural major in 1922, switching to Architecture after he found he had no aptitude for farming. The majority of his instructors were British, who followed an Ecole des Beaux-Arts curriculum based on classical principles and prototypes.

After he graduated in 1926, Fathy opened his own practice in Cairo. His first project for a private school in Talka, in 1927, was Beaux-Arts in style. Over the next ten years he designed a number of private homes and offices in Cairo, gradually moving away from his Beaux-Arts training toward a modernist language. The flat roofs, severe, angular forms, industrial

materials and lack of ornamentation common to all of these projects indicate more than a passing familiarity with changes then taking place in Europe and cohesively developed at the Bauhaus in Dessau, Germany.

In 1936, partially in response to a growing nationalist tendency in Egypt, he broke decisively with the modernist school in favour of early Islamic Egyptian styles and forms. This won him commissions for private houses, and later entire town plans, as well as many public buildings. His lasting achievement in print has been the book *Architecture for the Poor* (1963): this outlined his theory of mud-brick building, which he developed in conjunction with a group of Nubian masons using traditional techniques. Clashes with conventional builders led him to move to Athens, in 1955, though he returned to Egypt in 1962, where he worked until his death in 1989.

Hassan Fathy's moment of revelation came in 1936 as a result of his involvement with a circle of intellectuals attempting to channel an emerging Egyptian nationalism. Previously a rather conservative architect, in that year he exhibited in a gallery in what was then a suburb of Cairo called Mansouria a series of non-commissioned projects that are remarkable in their uniform proclamation of difference from the Bauhaus style. The projects exhibited what might be described as lyrical fantasies of Egyptian architectural history, concentrating on the period after Islam was introduced in AD 626. The apparent objective was to declare independence from foreign sources, and to find an authentic means of Egyptian expression instead. The exhibit was very controversial. Reactions ran the gamut from derisive disbelief through concern about Egypt's image as a developing nation should the exhibition be published abroad, to moderate support.

Undaunted by the furore, Fathy began soliciting clients willing to enact these new, nationalistic images, and found several among the wealthy landowning class of which he was a part. Owners of large agricultural holdings, similar to those of Fathy's own family, typically were absentee landlords, using tenant farmers to care for the land and oversee production. These were ideal clients because they only visited their properties occasionally, to collect revenues. They needed large houses to accommodate them while they were there and act as symbols of authority when they weren't and didn't want to spend much money building them.

Urban Typologies Adapted to Environmental Purpose

After the structural failure of a dome in the first of his projects, Fathy intensified the research that he had begun several years before the Mansouria exhibition, concentrating on spatial typologies and local construction methods. Because the areas of focus and the selective thought process behind them are critical to his development, these typologies and construction methods require some brief explanation.

In his effort to derive a more authentic, Egyptian architecture, Fathy concentrated on researching the existing Fatamid, Mamluk and Ottoman palaces in the medieval quarter of Cairo, also described in Orientalist classics such as *Description de l'Egypt* and Emil Pauty's *Les Palais et les Maisons d'Epoque Musulmane au Caire*. In 1936, he bought one of these palaces, known as Beit Labib, restored it, and lived on the fifth floor. He discovered similarities in the houses that he studied, mainly the Beit Souheimi, Beit Kathoda and Beit Gamal adin Dahabi, which are within walking distance of his residence.

These similarities were orientation toward a prevailing northwest breeze, and the use of two courtyards, one planted and the other paved, which were placed in sequence to take maximum advantage of this prevailing breeze. The planted courtyard, placed first in the sequence, trapped cooler night air in the surface area of the leaves of the plants and trees, releasing the cool air to the paved courtyard by convection current as the sun moved overhead and heated the paving stones. He also discovered a similar use of an opening between the two courtyards, called a *taktaboosh*, which allowed this convection current to transfer, and a room spanning over the *taktaboosh*, with floor vents that allowed some of the cool air to be directed into it, where the family would meet for the midday meal. He also noted a raised open loggia, facing the prevailing breeze at the end of the second paved courtyard, called a *magaad*, which was coolest in the late afternoon, where the family would sit at the end of the day. Finally, he discovered a tall windtower, called a *malkaf*, directing the prevailing breeze into the main, formal, social space of the house and a consistent shape of this social space, called a *qa'a*. Fathy traced the evolution of this social space, and wrote several articles about it.

The *qa'a* is a classic example of a traditional archetype. Beginning as an open courtyard flanked by opposing T-shaped iwans in the residential quarter of the Ukhaider Palace, which was built by an Abbasid prince in the 8th century near Kerbala, Iraq, the *qa'a* surfaced in Egypt four centuries later, inside the tightly compressed houses of Fustat, after possibly undergoing further development in the cities of the Hijaz in Arabia. In Fustat, the position of the open, central courtyard seen in the Ukhaider Palace remains intact but the T-shaped space on either side began to become more simplified in response to the need to adapt to urban conditions. In the course of this change, a fountain was also added to cool the air coming into the courtyard. In its final form, in Fatamid Cairo, the *qa'a* became completely internalized as a result of the increased density and noise of the city. The flanking iwans, which eventually

Taktaboosh, **or covered seating area**
This photograph of the Beit Souheimi, a traditional building in Cairo, shows a *taktaboosh*, a covered seating area situated between two courtyards. The heat differential between a hot paved courtyard and a cooler planted one creates a breeze by convection, which cools the seating area.

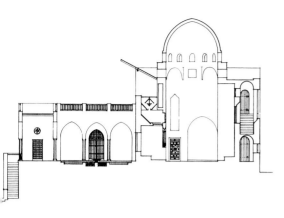

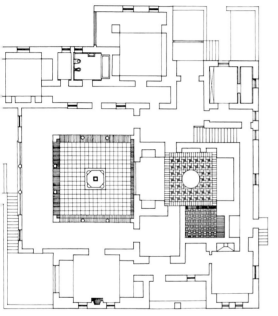

Preliminary plans for the Hamdi Seif al-Nasr House, 1942

The windcatch appears to the left of the dome, directing a current of air past a cooling plate wetted by a constant trickle of water, providing humidity. Such devices had been used for hundreds of years, but had fallen victim to the vagaries of fashion.

dropped the cross-bar of the 'T' to become a simple alcove on each side of the higher covered central court, ultimately created an integral, unified architectural component that was perfectly suited to the social needs of the emerging merchant class of Cairo.

As adapted by Fathy, the *qa'a* took on a new significance as a formal residential reception area, as he began to carefully scale down the high central tower of the Mamluk and Ottoman houses to allow it to fit contemporary domestic needs. While the first use of this composite form in such houses as the Hamdi Seif Al-Nasr villa in Fayum shows that Fathy was initially inspired by the monumental scale of such *qa'a* as that of the Beit Kathoda, later drawings indicate a more reasonable approach.

An Ancient Ecologically Integrated Construction System

At the same time that he was making these typological determinations, Fathy was also actively searching for a construction method that would convey the same degree of cultural authority as the spatial system he had pieced together in medieval Cairo. This part of his search is documented in his book *Architecture for the Poor*, where he tells how, at the prompting of his brother Aly, he went to Upper Egypt to visit the Nubian settlements around Luxor and Aswan.

His re-telling of that discovery in *Architecture for the Poor*, which was written nearly three decades after the event, still conveys that sense of discovery, as well as his initial excitement in finally finding a structural system that would allow him to build with mud brick without the need for any supports for roofing. His enthusiasm for a system which thereby reduced construction costs to zero if a cooperative building method was used, is totally understandable. The architect was also extremely impressed by the natural comprehension of engineering principles displayed by the Nubian masons in their use of this technique. As he said later, 'it is remarkable to find that the builders of these vaults were working according to the laws of statics and the science of resistance of materials with extraordinary intuitive understanding. Earth bricks cannot take tensile or bending stresses, so they make the vault in the shape of the parabola, conforming to the shape of the bending movement diagram, thus eliminating compression. In this way it became possible to construct the roof with the same earth bricks as for the walls.'[1]

Villages like Gharb Aswan, which is on an island in the Nile across from the village of Aswan, and others such as Aboul-Riche nearby, are the final remnants of the Nubian culture. Their towns once covered the area now flooded by Lake Nasser, built in a mud-brick method that can be traced back to the time of the Pharaohs. In using this system, Fathy solved his structural and economic problems, but also consciously re-established a link to the distant past that he felt was in danger of being broken. In addition to being inexpensive, mud brick also performs extremely well in the hot, dry Egyptian climate, providing the thermal mass necessary to keep building interiors cool most of the day. When combined with his Cairene 'thesis of space', this language was ideally suited to climatic response.

Attracting Attention

The series of country houses built between 1937 and 1940 using this typological Cairene spatial system and Nubian construction method rendered in mud brick that Fathy believed would make them authentically Egyptian, brought him to the attention of the Department of Antiquities, which was looking for a solution to a public relations problem that arose in early 1940. A large Pharonic basalt statue, detected by customs officials before being shipped from Alexandria, was traced to the village of Gourna, built on a mountain slope directly above the tombs of the Valley of the Kings and Queens in Luxor. The Gourni had long been suspected of tomb robbery, but the scale of this incident, which was picked up by the international press, forced the Department of Antiquities into action. They decided to relocate the village several kilometres east, toward the Nile, and Fathy's self-help mud brick system appealed to them because it was inexpensive and fast.

In the end only a portion of the new village was built because of repeated sabotage by Fathy's reluctant clients and bureaucratic lethargy that seemed to increase once the public furore over the theft of the statue had died down. Fathy's own recounting of the frustrations he experienced in his idealistic effort to complete New Gourna appeared in French in 1963, in Paris, republished by the University of Chicago Press as *Architecture for the Poor* in 1973, thirty years after work on the village had ended. It coincided with the first oil shock caused by an OPEC quarantine, which brought home the fragility of energy supplies in the West and prompted heightened awareness of the urgent need for conservation. Due to a general feeling of helplessness in losing a resource so vital to their lives, the public was perhaps more able to identify with Fathy's tale of duplicity by both the Gourni and the government and his self-characterization as a victim of forces beyond his control. William Polk, who was a close friend of Fathy, and was responsible for obtaining *Architecture for the Poor* for publication by the University of Chicago Press, has said: 'I have long considered Hassan Fathy's *Architecture for the Poor* to be the intelligent, heartfelt and contextualized architectural counterpoint to earlier twentieth-century manifestos. I still hold this belief and think of Fathy as an architectural icon.'[2]

After New Gourna ground to a halt, however, and before his near cult status had been established by *Architecture for the Poor*, Fathy found that the high profile of the project within Egypt had made him many powerful enemies. Osman Osman, owner of a large contracting firm, was one of these and was to become Fathy's nemesis. He saw the self-help mud brick approach as a threat to the well-entrenched, fee-based system used by the construction trades and tried to ensure that Fathy's intention of using New Gourna as a prototype, to alleviate the housing shortage in Egypt, was never realized. Temporarily thwarted on the housing front, Fathy turned to the development of a prototype village school at Faris, on an island near Luxor, that might be built inexpensively by local residents throughout Egypt. However, claimed misrepresentations about costs in the press by the 'contractor establishment' prompted him to leave Egypt in 1955.

Since he had close ties to the court of King Farouk and was rumoured to have had a romance with the King's daughter, Fatima, it would seem that his reason for leaving the country might have been due to the revolution and fear for his life. But according to William Polk: 'In 1957 King Farouk had been out of the country for five years and royalists were no longer a problem for Gamal Abdul Nasser, who became president in 1954. Fathy was driven out by the socialist reforms of Nasser, initiated after the nationalization of the Suez Canal in 1956 and not by a purge of royalists.'[3]

Self-Imposed Exile
Fathy accepted an invitation by Constantinos Doxiadis, Director of the Architecture and Planning firm of Doxiadis Associates in Athens, to join its research arm, the Centre of Ekistics. Soon after his arrival, Fathy became part of a project entitled 'the City of the Future' an

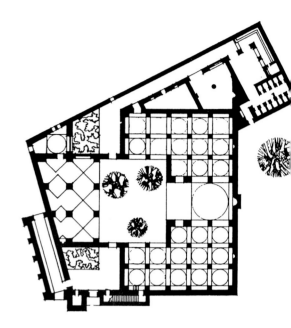

Plan of the Mosque, New Gourna, 1945–7
Though the New Gourna project was never finished, it provides an excellent example to architects of how to overcome the harshest of climates, through a combination of ingenuity and an awareness of traditional building methods – the repository of considerable wisdom.

attempt, as described by Doxiadis, 'to try to help the understanding of what is going to happen to our human settlements and what we can do to save them.'[4]

Doxiadis envisioned the 'City of the Future' project within the global parameter appropriate to the topic, with a large panel of experts from different disciplines including Margaret Mead, Buckminster Fuller and Arnold Toynbee, recruited to join the study with Fathy. Doxiadis divided the initiative into four headings, which, in addition to the 'City of the Future' were, 'A City for Human Development', 'Building Entopia' and 'Action for Human Settlements'. Fifteen years after the start of the project, each subject area was presented as a book by the key participants to the United Nations, during a meeting of the General Assembly. The 'City of the Future' book alone was a synthesis of 260 internal reports totalling nearly 10,000 pages and 1,600 charts, maps and graphs.

Sadly, Fathy's contribution to that book was not clearly defined or attributed, his own unpublished 250-page report subdivided into 21 sections or chapters did not conform to Doxiadis's view of an increasingly urban future. As part of his research, which focused on Africa, he visited Khartoum, Sudan, Kano and Lagos, Nigeria, Accra, Ghana, Abidjian and Bouake; the Ivory Coast, Ouagadougou, Upper Volta, Bamako, Mali, Guinea, Monrovia, Liberia, Lome, Togo, Cotonou, Porto Novo, Douala, Youndè, Cameroon and Tripoli, Libya, finishing in Cairo in time to present a paper at the Conference on the Arab Metropolis in December 1960, that crystallized many of the issues raised during his trip.

Return to Egypt

While direct influence cannot be substantiated, it is tempting to consider that Doxiadis had some bearing on Fathy's surprising ultra-modernist approach to a housing block he designed in Mussayib, Iraq, at this time, as well as his relatively regimented layout for New Baris, Egypt, begun on his return to Cairo in 1962.

New Baris, which is his second major town-planning project, differs completely from New Gourna in several important ways. Firstly, it was speculative, being based on the discovery of a vast artesian well beneath the Qattara Depression in the central desert, opening up the possibility of an agricultural community, far removed from Cairo, that could alleviate population pressure and reduce food imports. This meant that, unlike New Gourna, Fathy had no demographic data to work with, and could not personalize his plan. Secondly, the climate is much more extreme in the central desert without the ameliorating effect of the Nile to temper it. Third, there was little probability of major electrical service being available until long after the settlement was complete, requiring almost total reliance on natural, rather than mechanical, cooling systems. The success of the community was also completely dependent on the efficiency of these systems, since potential occupants would have to be convinced they could live in comfort in the middle of the desert and perishables would have to remain fresh in storage until shipping, without air-conditioning, as their primary means of economic support.

Social Activism as a Model for Environmental Involvement

Fathy worked almost exclusively on the New Baris project for five years, overseeing the completion of the central market and food processing and storage facility, before war with Israel brought construction to a halt. The Aswan High Dam, nearing completion at the same time, allowed him to channel his disappointment at having his second major community

thwarted into a hotly debated social issue, important to him. Nearly 250,000 Nubians living in the valley that would be inundated by the dam had to be relocated; half of that number would remain in Egypt near Aswan, and the other half would move to Sudan. The Egyptian government offered those relocating to Aswan the option of financial compensation or a new house that the government would provide, little more than a concrete box with a few windows and a door. Fathy argued that the Nubians should design and build their own houses in mud brick, with the government only facilitating the process and cited the long Nubian building tradition and the environmental advantages it had over concrete in making his case, but to no avail.

Tragic Irony

Ironically, Fathy was chosen to be part of a select team of scientists, architects, archaeologists, historians and artists who were sent to Nubia by the Ministry of Culture just before the final inundation to compile a cultural synopsis of a society about to be destroyed, the same society that had provided him with the key ingredients of the structural system he was using. In spite of his scathing criticism, which was picked up by the local press, the concrete units were built, but Fathy followed the issue, using subsequent reports of high infant mortality rates due to overheating to substantiate his position. He also predicted many of the negative ecological side-effects that the Aswan High Dam would cause, including the disruption of the annual cycle of topsoil renewal by the Nile flood. To save money, Russian and Egyptian engineers constructed a massive rock and earth dam, rather than a concrete steel barrier with sluice gates, which would allow soil, picked up by the river in its course from Uganda to pass through. As a result, this soil is now dropped on the upriver side of the dam, and the topsoil on the fields beside the river must be completely supported by fertilization.

A Stone Phase

A ban on the use of mud brick, which was imposed because of this change in topsoil supply, forced Fathy to rethink his structural system. Following a resthouse for President Sadat in

above, left and right **Market, New Baris**, 1967
Two views of the market at New Baris, perhaps the most important part of the development. Here, food was stored in underground chambers that were cooled by redirected breeze.

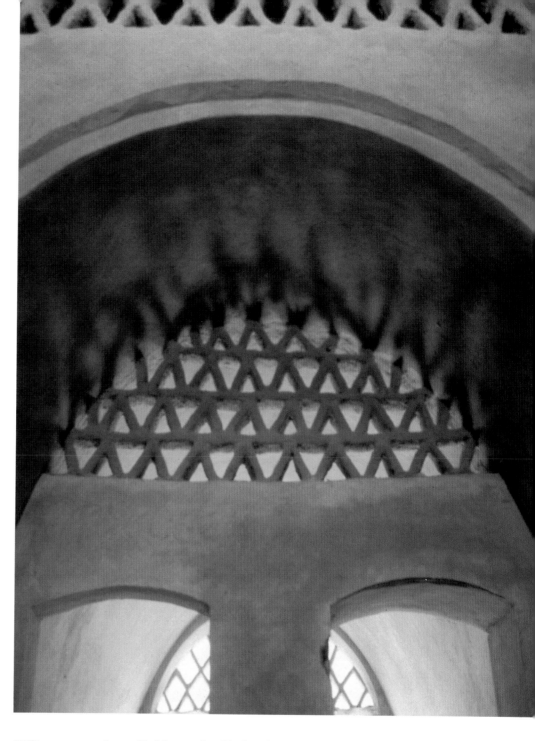

View inside a *malkaf* (wind catch), New Baris

1973, a swansong in mud brick completed before the ban took effect, Fathy built a series of houses in stone for wealthy clients in Shabramant, a suburb of Cairo near Giza. The Fuad Riad, Murad Greiss and Kazrouni houses have the same spatial combination of double courtyard, *taktaboosh*, *magaad* and *qa'a* used previously, but the Nubian system of mud vault and dome construction has been altered slightly to accommodate additional weight.

The Shabramant houses brought Fathy around full circle to the beginning of his career, when he was building resthouses for wealthy clients, and using them to test his ideas. By this time, however, *Architecture for the Poor* had established his international reputation as a

champion of the economically disadvantaged, in sharp contrast to the reality of his failure to
implement his ideals on a large scale and his final success at once again becoming the architect
of the rich, in Cairo.

Dar Al Islam

His third major town-planning project, called Dar al Islam, or 'the world of Islam', in the
United States, underscored this failure, and the unsettling discrepancy behind it. Just before
his death in 1989, Fathy was invited to design this new community, near Abiquiu, New
Mexico, for American Muslims in the region, and he accepted the commission without a fee.
He visited the barren site with three Nubian masons to give demonstrations of his self-help
system to prospective residents and also gave a series of lectures about his philosophy during
his visit. After he and his masons left, however, problems began to crop up, primarily due to
the sociological differences between the American residents and the expectations of their
Egyptian architect.

   The self-help system that Fathy proposed was only marginally successful, at best, at New
Gourna and New Baris; residents in each of these communities were not enthusiastic about
building their own houses and the system never really worked as Fathy intended. In America,
this lack of enthusiasm was compounded by unfamiliarity with the cultural lineage of the
process as well as reluctance to provide labour necessary to make it work. This unfamiliarity
extended to construction methods as well, the omission of several critical techniques used by
the Nubian masons initially resulted in failure of the mud brick vaults and the substitution of
plywood forms which were left in place until the masonry set. These as well as radiant heating
in concrete slab floors requested by the residents and local building codes which required
concrete foundation walls and a concrete coating over the mud brick caused costs to sky
rocket and the Saudi backers withdrew.

Sadat Resthouse, Gharb Husayn, 1981
This building was designed for the President of Egypt, Anwar Sadat, to be used on official trips to the region.

A Valuable Legacy

New Gourna, New Baris and Dar al Islam each remain unrealized for different reasons, not directly related to the efficiency of Fathy's hybrid system (although it could be argued that unfamiliarity with it caused the Abiquiu community to falter). Nevertheless, he is unfortunately held responsible for their failure, the common refrain being that he chose the wrong historical typologies, or misread the willingness of people to try to help themselves. What is incontestable is that he was one of the first of only a few architects during the early modern period to seek an alternative solution to the economic disparities caused by the onset of industrialization, while recognizing the cultural erosion it was causing and the insensitivity of the International Style to the aspect of technological growth. Questions remain about provenance – the fact that he chose a medieval city as his field of inquiry – and these overshadow environmental performance, which is exceptional, especially in the marketplace of New Baris, which has been overlooked for too long. In the discussion about sustainability on pp. 165–73, the realization that traditional architecture has something to teach us about environmental responsiveness and performance, rather than being seen as quaint and picturesque, is described as a recent phenomenon. When Fathy proposed using Fatamid, Mamluk and Ottoman houses as models for a new architectural language, in 1936, he was generally considered to be a misguided romantic who was completely out of touch with the realities of industrial production. In retrospect, he was a visionary, far ahead of his time.

High Court, Chandigarh, 1951–5

Le Corbusier is best-known for his Brutalist concrete structures, such as those at Chandigarh. However, looking beyond materials, he makes an array of references to the environment, to climate and to Indian culture.

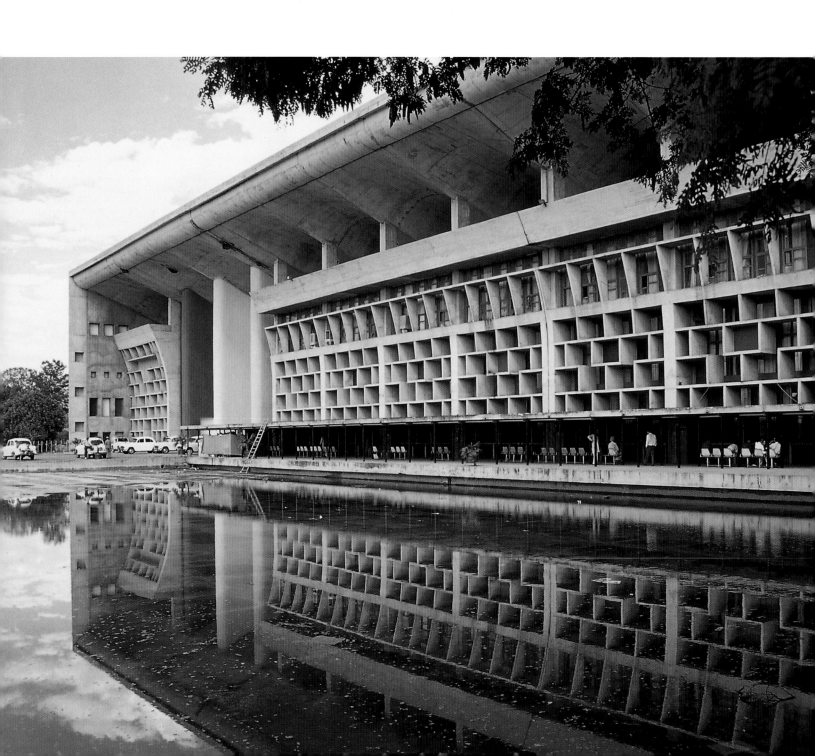

8

Le Corbusier: The Retreat from Purism

Though Le Corbusier is remembered as a modernist of the heroic school, his architecture can show great sensitivity to context and an interest in more earthy forms of building

Biography

Born in 1887 to a French-speaking Swiss family, Le Corbusier (originally Charles Edouard Jeanneret-Gris) was the most influential architect of the Modern Movement. After initially training as a watch engraver, he switched to architecture when he was nineteen, and almost immediately began to work on local commissions, which show a strong Arts and Crafts influence. He temporarily moved to Paris, where he served his apprenticeship with Auguste Perret, who pioneered the use of *beton armeé* or concrete reinforced with steel, and certainly this was to remain Le Corbusier's material of choice for the rest of his life (though not exclusively). In 1910 he studied trends in German architecture, and around the time of his *Voyage d'Orient* – a tour of European culture and industry – was deeply impressed by Ruskin's *Seven Lamps of Architecture*. He died in 1965.

Le Corbusier is generally associated with the machine aesthetic of Purism that he introduced soon after the First World War. The Villa Savoye in Poissy, near Paris, completed in 1929, is the iconic apotheosis of that philosophy, a constructed demonstration of the 'Five Points' which he used as a shorthand list to describe the opportunities made available to architects by the Industrial Revolution. High-strength steel, he argued, dictated a switch from the masonry bearing wall to the columnar frame, predicting the first and most important of his points – the grid – from which all others follow. The grid made it possible to have a free plan (the second point), since structural loads are no longer carried by partitioning walls. The third and fourth points: a free elevation, or external skin, and long horizontal strip windows (rather than small rectangular openings punched out of a bearing wall) logically follow since internal columns (rather than continuous masonry exterior bearing walls) carry the load of the roof. And this roof, which is the fifth point, can become a garden to replace the land on which this new, lightweight trabeated structure is raised. From this he developed his own reinforced concrete post-and-slab system, which he named *Dom-i-no* because of the resemblance of the pattern of the columns on plan to the numerical designations on the game pieces of that name.

The *Monol* Topples the *Dom-i-no*

Considering Le Corbusier's determined advocacy of the *Dom-i-no* idea, perfected through many built examples prior to final fruition in the Villa Savoye, it is, initially, difficult to

Key Projects

'Maison de weekend', Saint-Cloud, 1935

Roq and Rob development, Cap Martin, 1949

Chandigarh (city plan), 1950–65

Maisons Jaoul, Neuilly-sur-Seine, 1952–4

Millowners' Association Building, Ahmedabad, 1954

Signposts

Town planning Part II: 2, 3, 4, 9, 11, 12, 18; Part III: 3

Climate control Part II: 7, 9, 10, 12, 15, 19

reconcile his development of an alternative bearing-wall system called the *Monol*: he was, after all, possessed of an exceptional, visionary grasp of the potential of the new materials made available at the end of the 19th century, making him the leader of the Modern Movement. When viewed against the political and intellectual climate of post-First World War France, however, this second system begins to make sense as a complement to rather than a contradiction of his trabeated theory. This less abstract, more humane and environmentally sensitive, direction adds richness and depth to the enormous contribution of this singular figure, revealing him to be even more complicated than commonly believed.

Le Corbusier proposed a variant of the *Dom-i-no*, or 'Citrohan' system to the French government as a solution to the housing crisis following the 1914–18 war. It was initially conceived as a panel system connected by metal channels that could be easily transported and erected as formwork to be filled with concrete made with crushed stone aggregate from the area in which the houses are built. The roof was a slightly curved, or vaulted corrugated steel sheet, also covered with a thin layer of concrete; the long narrow houses were intended to be parallel and share walls for additional support.[1] The *Dom-i-no* and *Monol* systems of 1919 then, were structurally antithetical, but each was the result of a search for an easily replicable standard. Each alternative was subsequently explored, the *Dom-i-no*, or 'Citrohan' approach most notably in the early to mid-1920s, in the *Esprit Nouveau* Pavilion at the 'Arts Decoratifs' Exposition in Paris (1925), the Ozenfant House in Paris (1922), the Fruges garden city in Pessac, near Bordeaux (1925), two houses in the Weissenhofseidlung in Stuttgart (1927), the La Roche/Jeanneret house in Paris (1923), and the Villa Stein in Garches (1927), prior to its culminating statement in the Villa Savoye in Poissy (1929).

The radical futuristic images of the projects of Le Corbusier's 'White Period' have fixated public perception to the point that the *Monol* has not been given the consideration as the counterpoint it was intended to be. He described the *Dom-i-no* approach as 'a strong

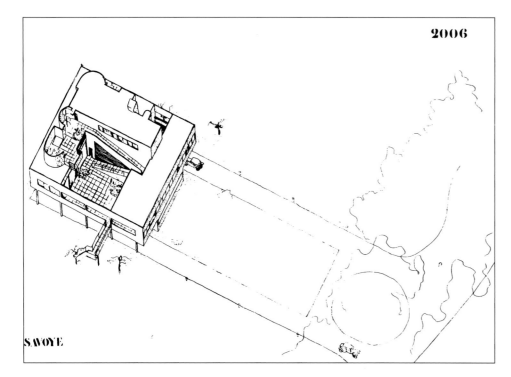

Axonometric drawing of the Villa Savoye, 1929
The archetypal 'machine in the garden', the Villa Savoye stands for the triumph over nature, even its subjugation – it was also the ultimate statement on the *Dom-i-no* system.

Isometric drawing of the Maison de weekend,
Saint-Cloud, 1935
This simple, single-storey weekend house just outside
Paris looked back to the *Monol* house, rather than the
Dom-i-no system. Hidden away behind a mound of
earth, built from brick, and covered with turf, today it
looks like a model 'green' building. It was to remain
influential for the rest of his career.

objectivity of forms, under the intense light of a Mediterranean sun: male architecture,'
and the *Monol* as 'limitless subjectivity rising against a clouded sky, a female architecture.'[2]
Following its appearance in 1919, the *Monol* system didn't surface again in a significant
way until it was used in a small, stone, sod-covered 'Maison de weekend' in Saint-Cloud
(a suburb of Paris) in 1933 – it then appeared in a Village Cooperative five years later, then
in a residential complex in Cherchell, North Africa (1942), a house in Sainte-Baume, La
Tourade (1945), the Roq and Rob Housing Project in Cap Martin (1949), the Fueter House
in Constance, Switzerland (1950) and the Maisons Jaoul in 1952, before its *denouement* in
the Sarabhai house in Ahmedabad, India, in 1955. The Sarabhai house may be considered
to be the equivalent of the Villa Savoye, the final evolution of an idea – in this case, the
Monol concept.

Not By Androgyny Alone

These two alternatives – the light, frame, modular system of reinforced columns and beams
that culminated in the Villa Savoye and its massive, vaulted bearing wall alter ego, finally
realized in Ahmedabed – represent more than the tectonic equivalent of a balance of x and y
chromosomes, however. They represent a consistent search for elemental types by a
committed rationalist. Over and above the political and social motivation of finding a
practical and inexpensive solution to the post-war housing shortage, Le Corbusier was also
motivated by the intellectual debate taking place in the early part of the 20th century, centred
in the art world, being carried out in the café society of Paris. He explored his formal and
spatial innovations in a variety of media, in addition to conventional architectural means,
much as his groundbreaking contemporary Pablo Picasso did in his art.

Primitivism

In a broader sense, the typological experimentation represented by Le Corbusier's frame and
bearing wall antipodes is best understood against the background of the aesthetic revolution
initiated by Cézanne and then expanded by Picasso, culminating in the *Demoiselles d'Avignon*
in 1907. The advent of Cubism which had a relatively short lifespan, ending with the First
World War, was symptomatic of the disaffection that Picasso, following Cézanne, and a small

group of *avant-garde* artists felt with conventional, perspectival methods of describing reality, as well as with the social system that such a singular view of the world represented. At the time of this breakthrough the Marxist critiques of capitalism, as well as its Arts and Crafts equivalent as a riposte to industrialization, were still fresh issues. The appeal of a simpler pre-industrial world had been eloquently evoked by William Morris and John Ruskin as well as by Dante Gabriel Rosetti, the leader of the Pre-Raphaelite movement, but Cézanne, Gauguin and Picasso wanted to go back further, in search of the 'noble savage' described by Rousseau, and found inspiration in tribal art such as that exhibited in the Musée d'Ethnographie du Trocadéro which opened in 1882.[3] Rousseau also provides the link with the rationalist traditions of which Le Corbusier is a part, since his writing distills the dissatisfaction of Enlightenment *philosophes* with the excesses of the *ancien régime*, much as Abbé Laugier did in his *Essai sur l'architecture*, in which the concept of the 'Primitive Hut' is introduced.

The paradigm shift prompted by tribal or primitive art has been described as being from the perceptual to the conceptual: of using simple forms and symbolism as a critical 'instrument', a lens through which to examine a preconceived worldview. Primitivism is defined as 'deriving its energies from differences and their cancellation, creating a charged division by recognizing the significance of that which is distinctly *other*'.[4] It does not view this *other* as inferior, only different, seeing purity and virtue in simplicity, in contrast to the perceived artifice and superficiality of civilized society. Primitivism is also based on the idea 'of a beginning or original condition, and the irreducible foundation of a thing or experience. (referring) to that which is most deeply innate within oneself.'[5]

Irreducible Types

Le Corbusier investigated the new potential of such rational perception in his own art, capitalizing on the wide rift opened by Picasso. He separated mimetic means of representation used in the past from an active, organized processing of visual information that was analogous with industrial production creation and invention. He was sympathetic to the Primitivists' use of elemental symbols for an attempt at an accurate depiction of nature, using painting as scientific method in doing so. Both the *Dom-i-no* and the *Monol* forms coincided with the crest of Cubism, in 1919: the redefinition of place in each as a distribution of floor plans experienced through shifting patterns of light and movement is analogous to the Cubist recognition of non-Euclidian possibilities of spatial description.

Le Corbusier also sought a 'fourth dimension' of reality as processed through relative multiple points of view rather than a stationary point. He also tried to create a new structural system, the *Monol*, to meet the new aesthetic urgency he felt, to substitute forms for the artists' impressions of reality rather than using an inherently imperfect method of depicting it. He also wanted to establish a baseline of irreducible types with these two polarities of *Dom-i-no* and *Monol*, as a way of rediscovering traditional ways of building that would force a redefinition of technology and re-establish contact between human beings and the environment. All this can be read in Le Corbusier's key projects between 1949 and 1955.

Roq and Rob

Roq and Rob, an apartment-hotel project intended for a steeply sloping site on the Côte d'Azur but never realized, is a good example of Le Corbusier's intention to use the *Monol* model as a synthesis of vernacular forms and the latest construction technology. The units,

Roq and Rob, 1949

This development of high-density, low-rise housing was intended for the southern French coast, though was never realized. It attempts to bridge the gap between the built and natural environments by responding to the slope and using a more primitive building technique.

which stretch out in horizontal ranks along the hillside, on either side of a central, open access stair, are based on a prefabricated modular 226 centimetre (89 inch) cube that the architect called *le brevet*. Each unit is composed of three cubes in a row, perpendicular to the hillside. The vaulted roofs, which are reminiscent of sketches Le Corbusier had made of houses he had seen in desert villages in North Africa, were intended to be curved corrugated aluminium sheeting supporting a thin concrete layer covered with earth sown with grass. Portions of the modular grid would have been left open to create an irregular chequerboard pattern of courtyards stepping up the hill. Hellenistic Priene is an obvious historical precedent and the organizational principles are very similar in each case. Horizontal terracing is used in both to adapt to the sheer, cliff-side site as is a central stepping spine, and public plazas carved out of a dense, honeycomb pattern of houses, allowing light and air to penetrate into the midst of the lightly structured, cellular texture of the community.

The defining feature of the Roq and Rob project is structural thinness to the point of frailty and a relentless modular regularity, compared to the relative weight of the earth on the roof. The challenge that this dichotomy presents to previously held images of barrel-vaulted, bearing-wall buildings, is deliberate. The long, narrow interior of the units, with interlocking upper level balconies, recall those of the Unité d'habitation in Marseilles, also proposed as a mass-produced solution to post-war housing shortages, but the most obvious difference between the Cap Martin and Marseilles proposals is lightness, airiness and a much more humane relationship to, and connectedness with, the environment in the Roq and Rob project. The Unité d'habitation almost singlehandedly launched the New Brutalist movement and the tower blocks that are arguably its grim inheritance. It is particularly regrettable that Roq and Rob was never realized, to provide a more human alternative.

Maisons Jaoul

In 1952, Le Corbusier did build a weightier version of the Cap d'Antibes community at Neuilly-sur-Seine using a different modular interval. The Jaoul houses on the rue de Longchamp lack the wire-frame thinness of the Roq and Rob structures, having rough concrete piers, beams and vaults, with brick infill and coloured glazed tiles pressed into the underside of the vaults which are exposed as the ceiling of the interior spaces. The beams, which are the end of an enormous vaulted concrete roof, are scaled to support the exposed brick walls on top of them, and so are lateral members taking the thrust of the tiled arches and longitudinal bond beams at the same time. An interwoven arrangement of formwork on the exposed outer edge of these beams creates a basketweave pattern that intentionally offsets their massiveness, and visually defrays their critical structural role as the containing frame that holds everything up. This is one of many small but revealing details that show Le Corbusier's innate understanding of structural forces. Like the Roq and Rob experiment, the Jaoul houses also have sod and grass roofs, but in this instance concrete seems more suitable for the heavy loads that the earth transmits.

The Sarabhai House in Ahmedabad

Le Corbusier's intellectual search for a historical, environmental and technological synthesis, as well as a balancing of the polarities in his own personality as revealed in his paintings, sketchbooks and diaries, came to fruition in Ahmedabad, India, in a house designed for Mrs Manorama Sarabhai, in 1952. Having been commissioned by Nehru to design the capital city of Chandigarh in East Punjab soon after independence in 1947, Le Corbusier began a series of biannual trips to India, which he was contractually obliged to make.[6] Sketchbooks from these trips, like those he religiously kept from all his travels, reveal a number of important impressions of sites he visited, beginning with the capital complex in New Delhi by Sir Edwin Lutyens and the Jantar Mantar astronomical observatory built by Maharajah Jai Singh in the older section of that city. These initial images were followed in quick succession by those of the *Diwan-i-Am* inside the Red Fort in Delhi, the Mughal city of Fathipur Sikri, the Palace at Sarkej, near Ahmedabad, and especially the pillared pavilion near the palace mosque, and the step well in that city, among other sites.

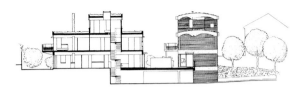
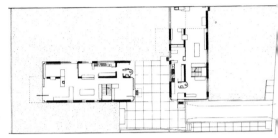

Maisons Jaoul, 1952–4

The twin Jaoul houses (seen at top in section and plan) have a very simple, almost unfinished, construction. Interestingly, the British architect James Stirling commented that he could find no reference to 'the machine' in these buildings, and that, aside from glass, they were constructed without synthetic materials.

Balkrishna Doshi, who worked in Le Corbusier's Paris office for five years in the early 1950s, was heavily involved in both the planning and construction of the capital city of Chandigarh. Born in Gujarat and based in Ahmedabad, he was a natural guide to these critical historical monuments and a source of information about them. He is discussed on pp. 107–113. Ahmedabad was destined to play an important role as a manufacturing centre in newly independent India, because of its well-established textile industry, and was a fertile source of commissions for Le Corbusier because of the wealthy Jain families – the owners of the textile mills – who lived there. Through Doshi, he soon met members of the four leading mill-owning families, Kasturbhai Lalbhai, Chinubhai Chimanbhai, Surottam Hutheesing and Gautam Sarabhai, all of whom supported the growth of cultural and educational institutions in Ahmedabad. They saw the opportunity of having buildings designed by this world-famous architect as a rare chance to enhance their city, and acted decisively to engage him. The optimism and syncretism of Le Corbusier and his prospective clients overlapped to a remarkable degree, both he and they wanted to preserve the rich traditions of the region and advance them with the most up-to-date technology.[7]

During Le Corbusier's first visit to Ahmedabad in March, 1951, Chinubhai Chimanbhai commissioned him to design both a cultural centre, which included a museum, and a house, while Surottam Hutheesing, the president of the Millowners' Association, asked for a new headquarters overlooking the Sabarmati River, as well as a house for himself. The Chimanbhai house was never realized, and only the museum portion of the cultural centre was built, in greatly altered form. The Millowners' Association was built as designed, but the Hutheesing house was abandoned by its intended owner. The plans were acquired by fellow millowner Shyamubhai Shodan, and built exactly as originally designed, for another site. Both the Millowners' Association Building and the Shodan House fall into the category of the Maison Citrohan model: frame and flat-plate structures fitted with either a deep egg-crate or *brise-soleil* façade and a separate, elevated, 'parasol' roof to adapt them to the extreme climate of India. As innovative as these adaptations are, the basic type remains substantially unchanged in them, but his approach to the Sarabhai House advances the diametrical, *Monol*-type considerably. Where the Roq and Rob project had been an attempt to render indigenous pattern in a light, modular frame, and the Maisons Jaoul use a much more muscular concrete frame and brick infill rendition of the Cap Martin idea, the Sarabhai House is organized within a series of parallel bearing walls (with pieces left out to allow cross-ventilation), with the vaults in line with the front and back of the house, implying circulation patterns between public and private areas.

Far from being constant, the climate in Ahmedabad has drastic swings from a monsoon season from June to August, when rainfall averages 125 centimetres (50 inches), temperatures vary between 32 and 49°C (90 and 120°F) and the prevailing wind is from the south-west, to a winter season which is dry and cool with temperatures as low as 21°C (70°F), and prevailing winds are from the north-east. The gaps in the parallel bearing walls allowed Le Corbusier to accommodate these extreme shifts, but also provide diagonal views, recalling the Cubist viewpoint which Le Corbusier began to explore thirty years earlier. In Primitivism, as discussed earlier, reality is perceived as cyclical and episodic rather than teleological and predictable, just as time is understood in traditional societies, and these diagonal views encourage a similar reading of diurnal cycles. Rather than framing linear views, the staccato walls layer them, as well as creating shifting patterns of light and shadow, depending on the

Millowners' Association Building, 1954
The distinctive *brise-soleil* façade and separate 'parasol' roof – of a type also used by Louis Kahn in his Luanda US Embassy proposal – ensures that the building does not overheat.

time of day and season. In stark contrast to many of Le Corbusier's object buildings, which stand in isolated grandeur apart from or above their natural surroundings, as indeed do the Shodan house and the Millowners' Building, the Sarabhai residence is so seamlessly integrated into its lush tropical setting that it seems to be part of it, an impression strengthened by a planted sod roof and a green courtyard in the midst of the house. The earthen roof is refined as an insulative cooling device here with the addition of water channels that traverse it, perhaps inspired by the Mughal gardens that Le Corbusier had seen nearby.

Both this and the *parasol* introduced at the Villa Shodan (and later made the key design concept of the High Court at Chandigarh) show a concerted effort to come to terms with the lethal power of the sun in India, which is directly overhead well before midday, making the roof the main built surface most susceptible to heat gain. Water troughs running across a planted, vaulted roof were later the basis for the Sangath studio of Balkrishna Doshi, also in Ahmedabad, a long work in progress finally finished in 1981. Although air-conditioning is used in part of the Sarabhai House, installed long before it was generally commercially available in recognition of the client's wish to be comfortable at the hottest time of year, the house is oriented to maximize natural ventilation and wide wooden doors that pivot 180 degrees are used to present as little of an obstacle as possible to air moving through the house. Cross-ventilation, then, as well as the prevalence of concrete, masonry and stone to increase thermal mass, and the water-cooled earthen roof, are the key environmental strategies used here.

Chandigarh

Named after Chandi, the Hindu goddess of power, the new capital city of the Indian side of recently partitioned Punjab region was intended by India's first Prime Minister to announce separation from the past and symbolize hope for the future.[8] Based on his earlier position on

Secretariat, Chandigarh, 1951–8

Le Corbusier stressed in his writings the ways in which he had tailored this building to Indian conditions, including *brise-soleil*, and large ramps that would serve all floors. He was particularly proud of the windows, which he claimed saved an enormous amount of money and maintenance.

urbanism, made manifest in his Plan Voisin for Paris (1925), Plan Obus for Algiers (1932), and a plan for war-ravaged Saint-Die (1945–6), Le Corbusier seemed to be the perfect choice as a *tabula rasa* city planner who would completely ignore history, culture and context. With his Plan Voisin, he had almost singlehandedly launched the modernist myth that by concentrating activities in tall towers, the land below could be returned to nature or parks and gardens for the people (resulting in less-enlightened hands in the desolate, wind-swept plazas in central business districts today). The Brave New World he envisioned with his Plan Voisin towers flanking multi-laned expressways has become a reality, a familiar sterile concrete landscape that is remarkably the same, whether it is encountered in Bulgaria, Buenos Aires or Riyadh. In his previous plans, Le Corbusier had also demonstrated his eagerness to break with the past: his political views aligned with those who considered historical structures to be nothing more than a regrettable, tangible record of social divisions and class struggle. The Plan Voisin occupied and required the destruction of the entire medieval centre of Paris and his plan for Saint-Die assured the demolition of everything not levelled by Axis bombing, rather than the restoration of an ancient core that had been thoroughly documented and could have been at least partially rebuilt.

Urbanism for the People

But Chandigarh would be different, because it was a *tabula rasa*, in which the architect had to find parameters to anchor it to its vast, open plain. The axiom that restrictions are a blessing in design is proven by exception here: Le Corbusier chose to rely upon themes prevalent in 'A Poem to the Right Angle' that he wrote at the time of this commission. In it, he describes the place of the human being in nature and the cosmos, in an attempt to make sense of the boundless parameters presented to him in the Punjab. At Chandigarh, he relied first on immutable, seasonal patterns and the sun as the most predictable of these, to establish boundaries: a 'tower of shadows' remains as a shrine dedicated solely to his study of solar patterns. His opening moves in designing this city reveal an elemental strategy traceable to Stonehenge as a means of establishing a place in a trackless universe and inform his first steps in conjuring a specific vocabulary of architecture for Chandigarh. The Sarabhai House shows that he came to realize that the sun is not always an enemy in India, that it is welcome for four months during the winter and that the sunshades which he was adapting as a critical part of his urban vocabulary, based on regional precedents, could accommodate that need.[9] As Le Corbusier later wrote of this realization: 'besides the administrative and financial regulations there was the Law of the Sun in India: a calendar of sensational temperature, extraordinary heat, dry or humid according to the season or the location. The architectural problem consists: first of all to make shade, second to make a current of air (to ventilate), third to control hydraulics (to evacuate rain water). This necessitated a real apprenticeship and an unprecedented adaptation of modern methods.'[10]

This 'law' dictated every move he made, from the choice of material with sufficient thermal mass to withstand the withering heat, to the orientation of streets in what was then still a relatively automobile-free country to avoid having to drive into the sun in the future, and burrowing into the ground for protection from it. His response to this 'law' in his design for the High Court of Justice was particularly inspired, an institutional application of the 'parasol' roof that he had introduced in the Villa Shoden on a monumental scale. At the High Court, it is supported on arches shaped to generate and accelerate the flow of air through it, so

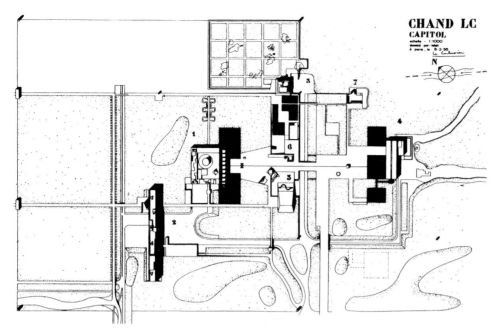

left, below **Masterplan and model of the Capitol, Chandigarh**, 1950–65
Le Corbusier's plan was for an entirely new type of city, but perhaps unlike his earlier plans (say, the Plan Voisin), this one shows far greater sensitivity to context, and to the needs of the users – for example, Chandigarh was designed for the pedestrian rather than the motor car.

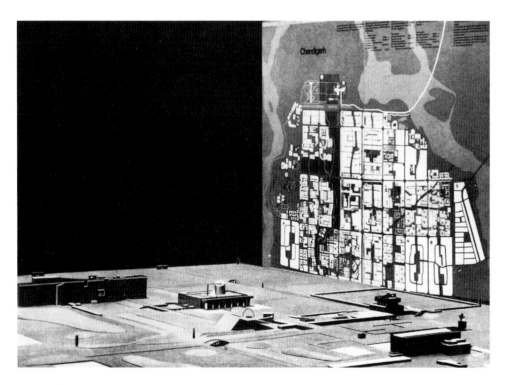

it both shades the second, closing roof below it and washes it with a steady laminar flow of air. The main entrance is also sized and oriented to catch and direct as much breeze as possible, the remainder of the interior converted into a soaring cool, dark, cave-like space in which ramps are used to reduce the amount of heat-generating, calorie-burning effort needed to reach the upper levels. Relegating the majority of the interior of the High Court of the portion not allocated as office or courtroom space, to darkness, reflects Le Corbusier's realization that cross-ventilation is useless as a cooling strategy during the hottest time of the year, and that the only effective tactic was the 'creation of cool interiors, as large as possible, and as amply protected from the southwest sun as ingenuity and funds permit.'[11] During this critical super-heated period, he found, 'the only defence is to retreat behind massive walls or their equivalent, with every aperture closed, and if possible sealed.'[12]

Le Corbusier chose concrete to provide the thermal mass necessary to create these massive walls and cool interiors, but this technological part of his tradition-through-science equation resulted in a high investment of human capital. A reporter observing construction described how more than thirty-thousand men and women, working seven days a week, poured concrete from buckets carried on their heads, climbing up bamboo scaffolding and mixing mortar with their feet. Aggregate was made from boulders that were broken with hammers, and asphalt was poured and spread on roads individually, by workers who wrapped their hands in burlap sacks to keep them from being burned.[13]

Primeval Inspiration Recalls Tradition

The financial restrictions which made this hand labour necessary, become Le Corbusier's second parameter, after 'the law of the sun' and climate. The third parameter he chose, to bracket the infinity of choices made possible by an open-ended site and ambitious nationalistic brief, was symbolism, referring back once again to his earlier, Cubist roots. At Chandigarh, Le Corbusier relied heavily on universal, primitive phenomenology, cosmological themes and iconographic references specifically drawn from regional sources, to an extent not seen in his earlier architecture or planning projects. The governmental centre contains especially overt anthropological analogies, but more than being straightforward gestures of respect to Indian heritage, they have been identified as 'being in accord with Le Corbusier's definition of "types" that is, forms that have been refined over a long period of everyday use resulting in a careful selection based on utility, function and aesthetics'.[14]

The City as a House, the House as a City

As a true rationalist Le Corbusier saw the historical city as not just a random assemblage of buildings, but rather a laboratory full of specimens waiting to be classified, with the most successful of these, as proven through evolution, fit to be selected and refined for future repetition. In his final city, he determined that traditional responses to physical as well as psychic wellbeing were far more effective than forms alone and that technology should be assigned a supporting rather than a leading role in providing those benefits.

As Chandigarh has matured, Le Corbusier's intentions have become clearer, as residents' satisfaction with their city continues to grow. Focus on the centre in the media during and just after construction, for many of the same reasons that have already been discussed here, tended to obscure the fact that most of the master plan is given over to housing, organized along green fingers that extend out from the more megalithic and photogenic palm. These wide pathways are now filled with trees and are much appreciated by those that live and work along the shaded streets that connect the public residential parts of the capital. In a sense, Chandigarh is the urbanistic realization of the *Monol* experiment, finally proven in the Sarabhai residence in Ahmedabad, with its residential part being a model for the green city of the future.

far left **Aranya Low-Cost Housing Project**, 1983–6
left **Sangath Studio**, 1979–81
below **Hussein-Doshi Gufa**, 1992–5

Doshi's approach to design has changed considerably
over fifty years, gradually moving away from a Western,
Corbusian conception of architecture towards the
idiosyncrasies seen in the Hussein-Doshi Gufa (below).
However, from the beginning there was an interest in
tailoring building to specific conditions, in appropriate
materials (as in the broken china seen here), and in the
power of architecture to change, or unify society.

9

Balkrishna Doshi:
Reconsidering Modernism

Doshi reconciles Western modernism with environmental responsiveness, and has been particularly concerned with improving the quality of low-income housing

Biography

Born in Poona, India, in 1927, Doshi first studied at the School of Art in Bombay before travelling to Paris in 1950 to meet Le Corbusier – who promptly hired him. He became a senior designer on Le Corbusier's projects in Ahmedabad and Chandigarh, then in 1956 established a private practice in Ahmedabad. In the 1960s he was instrumental in founding the School of Architecture in Ahmedabad University.

As his career progressed he became increasingly influenced by mystical thought (as seen in the Bharat Diamond Bourse project), but also by environmental concerns, and in 1962 established the Vastu Shilpa Foundation for Environmental Design, next to his studio, Sangath (which means 'coming together' in Sanskrit). He has focused on low-tech solutions to the oppressive climate of India, such as natural ventilation, building on the advances made by Le Corbusier in that country. He has also found innovative, low-tech answers to problems with non-native and modernist materials such as concrete, and has sought to bring a more humane attitude to town planning.

Key Projects

Institute of Indology, Ahmedabad, 1957–62
Sangath Studio, Ahmedabad, 1979–81
Aranya Low-Cost Housing Project, 1983–6
Hussein-Doshi Gufa, Ahmedabad, 1992–5
Bharat Diamond Bourse, Mumbai, 1998

Signposts

Local materials and techniques Part II: 1, 3, 4, 7, 12, 24
Town planning Part II: 2, 3, 4, 8, 11, 12, 18; Part III: 3
Self-build Part II: 6, 7, 12, 21
Climate control Part II: 7, 8, 10, 12, 15, 19

The cultural cross-fertilization that resulted from the commissioning of Le Corbusier to design Chandigarh was extensive, and affected an entire generation of young architects in the newly independent Indian nation. Balkrishna Doshi was more determined than most in his exploration of the implications of breaking away from imperial control on the one hand, but at the same time recognized the importance of the French-Swiss architect and planner, and was instrumental in inviting him to translate the legacy and aspirations of an entire nation into an urban form. Doshi joined Corbusier's rue de Sèvres office at the critical period of the design of Chandigarh, and he not only proposed new strategies that improved the environmental performance of several of the major institutions in the central core of that city, but also facilitated introductions to members of the mill-owning families in his hometown of Ahmedabad, which led to several private commissions for Le Corbusier, whom Doshi would later call his 'guru'.

A Marriage of Modernism and Tradition

Doshi's first projects on his own, after his return to India, understandably reflect Le Corbusier's principles. Tracing his attempt to reconcile those principles, which are the bedrock of the modernist position in its heroic phase, with the richness of his own culture, the overwhelming problems of a large, developing nation, and the climatic extremes of India's various regions, defines the essence of the struggle that architects in the developing world face in trying to assimilate the technology of the developed world. The building Doshi designed to house the School of Architecture at Ahmedabad University continues the dialectic integration of modernist materials and formal attitudes with a wide range of regional realities, an attitude first seen at Chandigarh. In Ahmedabad, however, there is more humidity due to its proximity to the Indian Ocean, and this caused the concrete to quickly sprout a slimy green mould. Doshi's unerring instinct for siting to achieve optimal orientation, however, and his strategic positioning of wide openings on each of the long walls of the rectilinear envelope to maximize cross-ventilation, ensures a steady stream of fresh air through the studios, public spaces and administrative offices of what is now regarded as a venerable institution in India.

The Institute of Indology

His Institute of Indology, also on the campus of Ahmedabad University, was built soon after the School of Architecture and suffers from the same discoloration. It is also configured and sited to capture and funnel the prevailing breeze. In this case, however, the need for natural cooling, which is so important in a country in which budgets for mechanical equipment and its maintenance are low or non-existent, was even more critical, since this is an archive of rare Buddhist manuscripts which require careful temperature and humidity control. That Doshi has achieved this without the benefit of the complex climate-control systems typically found in comparable facilities in the West is testimony both to his intuitive grasp and factual knowledge of the complex physics of the local environment and to his understanding of how to harness it for the client's benefit. Here, too, he has elevated to a fine art the rudimentary technique of positioning a paved public space on one side of a building and a rolling lawn on the other, which together generate a convective current through differential cooling. The lush garden on the windward façade is lowered to make it a memorable formal entrance to the research centre. Paved courts, on the opposite side of the long narrow building envelope, are a visual focal point for the director and his staff, whose offices are located directly above, and these courts help generate the convective current. Subsidiary projections from the main rectangle are sculpted to form a variegated, if somewhat severe, perimeter, consistent with the noble mandate of the Institute as well as the courtyard's role as a thermal sink.

The Hussein–Doshi Gufa

A museum dedicated to the work of legendary Indian artist, M. F. Hussein, which is the third major project by Doshi on the Ahmedabad campus, is a startling departure from this earlier work, organic evidence of the philosophical distance that Doshi has travelled in the three or so decades that separate his school and the Buddhist archive from the Hussein Gufa. Compared with the pared-down Corbusian frame system that he used in the 1960s, the Gufa represents a radical departure in Doshi's construction language. It is based on an amalgamation of inexpensive, locally available materials assembled using innovative adaptations of vernacular techniques, on which the architect's self-described and exponentially expanding cultural awareness is literally writ large. Rather than being cast in concrete, the expressionistic, vaguely anthropomorphic shells were first formed in fine wire mesh and then thin slurry of concrete was hosed onto them, similar to the construction of a swimming pool (though concave). Strands of local clay were then manually coiled into ropes

Institute of Indology, Ahmedabad University, 1957–62 Similar to Le Corbusier's approach, but using far less material, this design incorporates a very effective passive cooling system. The basement of the Institute is home to a collection of very important manuscripts, which require specific atmospheric conditions: Doshi achieved these conditions by creating a convective current through careful positioning of a lawn on one side, and a pavement on the other.

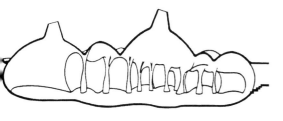

Sketch for the Hussein-Doshi Gufa, 1992–5
The highly unorthodox forms of this gallery building, which bring to mind Gaudí, are derived in part from the use of local, inexpensive materials and techniques.

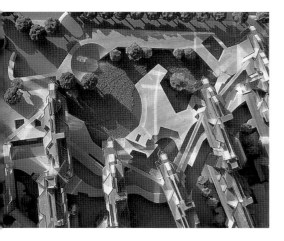

Bharat Diamond Bourse, Mumbai, 1998
Doshi was able to apply his principles on a much larger scale in this project. Each part of the complex – actually the size of a small city – is designed to present as little of the façade as possible to the sun, while open spaces were used for cooling.

by a small army of labourers whose low pay scale was an important factor in Doshi's transformation, because these techniques would not be possible with intensive handiwork. Layered over the shell, these acted as insulation, then a final ceramic carapace was added.

This final shell is an inspired adaptation of a technique commonly used on streets shrines seen throughout Ahmedabad and elsewhere in India, on which pieces of broken ceramic plates and cups are meticulously pressed into a rapidly hardening medium, such as partially cured concrete, to create a colourful mosaic surface that is impervious to mildew and mould. This skin can also be easily washed, making it an elegantly simple alternative to the high-maintenance methods needed to clean concrete. Doshi's recent movement toward mysticism and reliance upon visions to inform his design concepts resulted in the uncoiled snakelike pattern that undulates in dark curves over the white shells of the Hussein museum, recalling a dream in which Doshi wrestled with a cobra: the Naga of Buddhist mythology. Hussein was so enthralled by his womblike gallery that he decided to move into it soon after completion.

The Bharat Diamond Bourse
Similar visions informed one of the largest projects of Doshi's long career, the Bharat Diamond Bourse in Mumbai (Bombay). This prominent centre of diamond trade in India was critically overcrowded; the new headquarters that Doshi designed provides much more space and room for future expansion, as well as heightening the Bourse's status and identity, by concentrating all of its activities into one prestigious and highly visible location. Sales rooms, cutting laboratories and offices are organized into long, linear towers once again positioned to take full advantage of prevailing winds that are channelled through a planted park for as much natural cooling as possible. At the start of excavation, however, the location of a bedrock strata turned out to be very different to what was expected, and the jagged, crystalline formations that were uncovered by the earth-moving equipment caused Doshi nightmares until a solution to these new subsurface conditions was discovered. Finding inspiration in adversity in a way that is consistent with his increasingly mystical outlook, he chose to accept the craggy bedrock as a portent, which he described as emerging like a spectre during floodlit night-time construction. He redesigned the external skin of the finger-like towers to complement their hidden subterranean geological base, based on the forms he saw under the floodlights.

A Struggle
Balkrishna Doshi's personal struggle reconciles the glaring discrepancies that he found to exist between principles learned during his apprenticeship with one of the founders of the Modern Movement, and the rudimentary realities of building in the developing world. It is perhaps best resolved in his own studio in Ahmedabad, called Sangath, which, means 'coming together' in Sanskrit. This complex, which includes his office as well as the Vastu Shilpa Foundation, a research organization which also informs his work, is located on a flat 2,425 square metre (26,100 square foot) site on the fringe of Ahmedabad. It consists of a series of long, terraced entrance courts which have fountains and pools inside them. The vaults are covered in the same mosaic of broken ceramic pieces set in clay over a thin reinforced concrete shell that Doshi used on the Hussein Gufa, with the main difference being an even more aggressive application of environmental strategies.

Sangath is based on a prototype first developed by Le Corbusier in his *Monol* series, which culminated in the Sarabhai House in Ahmedabad. The Sarabhai House, described in detail on pp. 100–101, is remarkable in Le Corbusier's oeuvre because it represents the consolidation of decades of experimentation with an alternative typology intended as an indigenous complement to his more familiar mechanistic *Dom-i-no* model. At Sangath, Doshi engages in an extension of the environmental strategies introduced at the Sarabhai residence, substituting water running in the troughs between the vaults for the sod roof, and partial burial of the units for optimal orientation as a cooling device.

An Urban Model

Rather than being primarily used to channel prevailing breezes as the Sarabhai vaults are, those at Sangath are positioned to make the most of natural light within each space and to syncopate the progressive experience of vertical scale throughout the enclave. In a characteristically rationalistic way, Doshi also views Sangath as work in progress and an example of what Ahmedabad, and by extension the rest of India, could be like if the principles used there were extrapolated. He believes what is now becoming a chaotic, ugly urban wasteland might be transformed into the ecologically synergistic and indigenously adaptive, tranquil oasis similar to the one he has designed.

While the Sarabhai project had a profound impact on several other influential architects, such as Louis Kahn and Arata Isozaki, none seems to have grasped the full theoretical or environmental implications as well as Doshi. Kahn's Kimbell Art Museum, for example, consists of a series of parallel barrel vaults that pay obvious homage to Le Corbusier's formal investigations and Doshi's commentary on them, but aside from progressively sinking elongated galleries into the ground, Kahn does not move this typological evolution forward, except by consolidating the position of the barrel vault in the rationalist pantheon of preferred forms. By the time Isozaki appropriated Le Corbusier's argument in a series of built essays, such as his Fujima Clubhouse, the clarity of Le Corbusier's formal statement had been obfuscated. It was further obscured by the semantic manifestos of Robert Venturi and Michael Graves, who began to suggest that all platonic solids had subliminal linguistic meaning, with the barrel vault simply relegated to a suggestion of entry.

Aranya as Another Urban Model

The Aranya Low-Cost Housing Project in Madhya Pradesh, which Doshi has designed for the Indore Development Authority, is an urban prototype of a different sort, intended to address the acute housing shortage throughout India. Indore, which is a commercial centre for the region, is located 600 kilometres (375 miles) south of Delhi, and was an ideal place for such an experiment because of the acute housing shortage and slum conditions that exist there. Working through the Vastu Shilpa Foundation, Doshi approached the problem in a characteristically contrary way by considering the existing slums as a resource rather than a detriment, and then used the clues he found there, behind the chaotic overlay, as guiding principles for his new settlement. He found that what might superficially be considered random clusters of huts were actually small neighbourhoods, which included shops; and that each house opened onto the vestiges of public space in specific ways.

His most critical insight was that the roads through these clusters were social as well as transportation conduits, along which people met, sat and talked; and that these were places

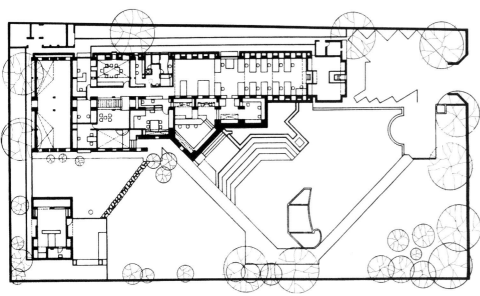

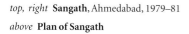
top, right **Sangath**, Ahmedabad, 1979–81
above **Plan of Sangath**

Meaning 'coming together' in Sanskrit, Sangath is the studio campus of Doshi's practice, and the Vastu-Shilpa Foundation. At the centre of the complex are troughs containing water and covered with the trademark broken china. Pots and sculpture are dotted around the campus, reminders of Indian handicraft, while the semi-circular vaults are based on the Golden Section.

Model showing density, Aranya Low-Cost Housing Project, 1983–6
Doshi's initial approach to the Aranya Project was to divide the 85 hectares into six zones, that might function like separate villages. Cheaper housing was distributed among the six zones, while the high-end, expensive houses were to be found on the arterial roads.

where casual interaction as well as commercial activities took place. Doshi divided the 85-hectare site into six sectors, with houses in each zone clustered in groups of ten. A staggered hierarchical street system branching out from a similarly irregular central spine is an attempt to replicate vernacular patterns, and to avoid a regular grid. Paved open spaces act as transitional zones between houses and these streets mimic the local habit of eliminating conventional distinctions between indoor and outdoor space, institutionalizing a regional pattern in architectural form. Doshi accommodated economic variations within this loosely interpreted system by locating the poorest residents in the middle of each sector and the less poor along the central spine, with the poor making up a majority of 40,000 people in the city. More importantly, a series of larger public spaces intermittently positioned along each of the branching connections create places where people of different economic circumstances and different religions can meet, promoting tolerance and understanding.

The design tactics used at Aranya were all part of a deliberate strategy to reverse what Doshi felt was a trend toward an imbalance in low-cost housing projects, due to a disregard for efficient land use, lack of a sense of community, ignorance of the traditional habits of people, lack of recreational space, and no allowance for flexibility or future growth. By way of contrast, Doshi characterizes his approach at Aranya as reflecting regional historical patterns by replicating overlapping land use, interlocking built areas with open space, and respecting human scale by promoting street life. He does this through the introduction of an *offa*, an outdoor platform that is a transition space between each house and its street.

Doshi has moved the search for a solution to the chronic problem of housing low-income families forward in his design of the residences at Aranya by perfecting a 'sites and services' approach in which a service core is provided first, allowing prospective residents relative freedom in choosing a series of optional plans. The variations that Doshi has provided, which are essentially based on a 'kit of parts' idea, allow the incremental addition of parts to a basic unit, all of which are predicated on optimum orientation, light, ventilation and climatic control, as well as the possibility of commercial use and subletting, to offer each family the

Aranya Low-Cost Housing Project, 1983–6

India suffers from chronic housing shortages, and much social or emergency housing is poorly designed. Doshi made intensive studies of how people live in slums – of how a community lives together – when designing Aranya. One of the key innovations was to limit the widths of streets (interestingly, this has also been a preoccupation of the New Urbanists – see pp. 209–213).

widest economic opportunities. The significant advance made here is the realization that slum clearance and the relocation of the poor into publicly built, government-subsidized, standard housing units is a failed idea, and that a shift from clearance and relocation toward environmental improvement, in which slum dwellings also constitute part of the housing stock, is a more realistic approach. Aranya represents an acceptance by the public sector, that it is more effective and financially sound for them to provide streets, water supply, sewer systems, storm water drains, electricity and other infrastructure, and to leave the construction and upgrading of houses to the people involved. It is better to view housing, as Doshi has said, as 'a process rather than a product.'[1]

A Bridge Between the Past and the Present

Balkrishna Doshi, then, stands out among other architects of his generation in the developing world as an exemplary conduit, interpreter and innovator, translating core principles from the source of the Modern Movement into a meaningful traditional regional language that is appropriate to his own context. This allows his work to serve as a valuable resource for those who are searching for an integral bridge between East and West, or tradition and technology, in response to the irrefutable and perhaps inevitable dislocations now being caused by globalization. He has demonstrated that it is not only possible but creatively preferable to allow syncretism to inform design decisions and his later work has also shown the extent to which such assimilation can open up new interpretations of indigenous standards. Sangath, which is his greatest achievement, certainly stands on the theoretical shoulders of Le Corbusier's *Monol* series, but also introduces fresh insights that no outsider could have realized.

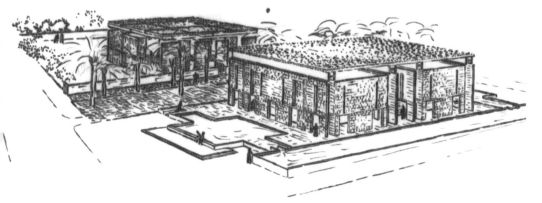

above **Salk Institute**, 1959–65

left **US Consulate and Residence**, Luanda, 1959–62 (unbuilt)

While the well-known Salk Institute took great care to orient itself towards the sea, perhaps the clearest example of Kahn's environmental awareness is the consulate in Luanda, with its double roof, layered walls, and central court oriented to catch the prevailing breeze.

10

Louis Kahn: Wrapping Ruins around Buildings

Louis Kahn reintroduced to modern architecture a sense of humanity and sensitivity to site and function

Biography

Louis Kahn was born in Estonia in 1901, but moved with his family to the US just four years later. He grew up in Philadelphia in difficult economic circumstances and graduated from the University of Pennsylvania in the mid-1920s when modernism was about to come into full flower in Europe. The Great Depression and subsequent onset of the Second World War were epic obstacles to the beginning of a promising career. However, the extreme poverty of his youth, which at one point forced his family to move seventeen times in two years in the heavily industrialized Northern Liberties neighbourhood in Philadelphia because they

couldn't pay the rent, made him resilient and inventive. His first major public building, the Yale University Art Gallery (1954), immediately placed him among America's most outstanding modernists.

At the same time Kahn worked hard to counter the alienation associated with modern architecture, showing a new sympathy for the inhabitants of the building, and for the site. He was a passionate advocate of the use of natural light, insisting that every room have natural light, while projects such as the US Consulate for Angola show an understanding of the cooling effect of a second skin. He died in 1974.

Key Projects

US Consulate and Residence, Luanda, 1959–62 (unbuilt)

Salk Institute for Biological Studies, 1959–65

Indian Institute of Management, Ahmedabad, 1962–74

Mikveh Israel Synagogue, Philadelphia, 1961–72

Signposts

Sensitivity to site Part II: 6, 25; Part III:2

Climate control Part II: 7, 8, 9, 12, 15, 19

While many of his contemporaries were caught up in the search to expand the structural possibilities inherent in lightweight industrial materials, architect Louis Kahn wrestled with more substantial issues, such as historical continuity, basic human values, social relevance and environmental appropriateness. Because he was initially unable to reconcile the basic premise of modernism, defined by one of the movement's leading lights Mies van de Rohe as the expression of the technology of the times, with its poor performance and lack of popular appeal, Kahn sought a clearer mandate in qualities he described as monumentality and timelessness. The economic hardships and instability faced by Kahn as a child had made him tough, and on graduating from Pennsylvania he laboured away in the trenches for more than two decades, doing housing projects and planning commissions with little notoriety. When major building commissions did finally materialize in the 1950s, this meant, however, that he was singularly qualified to redirect the anti-populist course of modernism, write the final chapter of its heroic phase and prepare the ground for greater diversity. In sharp contrast to Frank Lloyd Wright, who was the only other American architect of sufficient stature at that time to have effected such momentous change, Kahn felt a real connection with the European birthplace of the Modern Movement, and had a more common touch. Unlike Wright, who was the third generation of a Welsh family from the American heartland and began his career as a society architect in the exclusive Chicago suburb of Oak Park, becoming a pillar of the upper-class, white Anglo-Saxon Protestant establishment, Kahn was an outsider, the first generation of his working-class family to be educated in the United States, with a radical set of social sensibilities. His political views were quite unlike the exclusive notion of equality that Frank Lloyd Wright tried to express in what he cryptically called 'usonian' architecture. While Kahn was also exposed to American philosophers that extolled the virtues of independence at the expense of social norms and the common good, the exigencies of his background did not allow him to indulge in the same flamboyant behaviour that Wright exhibited. Wright seemed to relish scandal; Kahn fought hard to avoid it. Even while breaching similar social constraints, he kept up the appearance of a normal family life, since marriage was among the institutions that be believed should be protected.

Coming of Age

Louis Kahn graduated from architectural school at an auspicious time. Americans experienced unprecedented change in the three decades between 1920 and 1950. The Depression, followed by the Second World War, created a pent-up demand for housing, exacerbated by the baby-boom that followed. Significant legislation discouraged renovation of inner-city dwellings, encouraged the construction of new single-family houses in the suburbs, and facilitated the building of a highway system to reach them, giving a new breed of property developers the opportunity to supplant the architect as arbiters of public taste. Architects in general failed to anticipate this change and reacted with disdain when it occurred, abdicating responsibility for mass housing, the domestic future of their country, and one of the major components of the modernist agenda as a result.

At the end of his career, Frank Lloyd Wright boasted of having built houses in every state in America, but they were all custom-designed preserves for the rich. Aside from his admittedly visionary Broadacre City plan, which was a utopian proposal for organizing the suburbia that he then knew was inevitable, Wright led the retreat away from popular architecture. Kahn's enlightened activism, on the other hand, offers an inspiring alternative, leading the inexorable shift from high to popular culture now being fuelled by globalization.

Love of the City

In the 1950s, during the presidency of Dwight D. Eisenhower, the United States experienced an economic surfeit, but this prosperity was selective. Throughout his early career, Kahn attempted to make the suburbs accessible to the economically disadvantaged as well as the middle classes. In housing projects such as Pine Ford Acres, Pennypack Woods, Carver Court, Stanton Road, Lincoln Highway, Willow Run, Lily Ponds and Mill Creek, he showed that he understood the threat that the demographic shift to exurbia posed to the modernist ideal of equal access to shelter. His attempt to redefine that ideal was recognized by his peers, who accepted him as the architectural mediator of rapid sociological change. He dearly loved the institution of the city, because Philadelphia had given him so many life-changing opportunities, and he revered the subsidiary institutions it had historically fostered. He also understood that the organizations that had evolved from social interrelationships in the past would have to adapt to the changing cultural and moral framework from which they had historically claimed authority. He also believed that in spite of such changes, certain elemental

Model for the City Tower Project, Philadelphia, 1952–7
Influenced by the work of Anne Tyng, Kahn's design for
the Philadelphia City Hall was intended to describe
visually the problem of wind load.

aspects present in tacit social contracts should remain immutable. During his redefinition of
what an institution should be, he was fascinated by what he called 'beginnings', thinking back
to when the institution first started.

Tumultuous Times

From the time that Kahn's first major public building, the Yale University Art Gallery,
appeared in 1954, until his death in 1974, the United States experienced the Kennedy version
of Camelot, his space programme, the lunar landing and his tragic assassination in Dallas in
1963, Vietnam, Lyndon Johnson's Great Society, the War on Poverty, the Civil Rights Act of
1964, Project Head Start and the Model Cities Program of 1966, as well as racial riots in
Harlem and Philadelphia in 1964, Watts, Los Angles, in 1965 and Detroit in 1967 – with the
Detroit riot determined by the Kerner Commission to have been caused by the existence of
'two societies in America, one white and one black.'

Kahn's major projects during this period of unprecedented upheaval demonstrate his
visionary anticipation of the 'multivocality' that emerged from it, which has now become a
global chorus. During those same twenty years from 1954 to 1974 – the crucial span in which
Kahn moved from houses and housing to the design of monumental public buildings all over
the world – his output was unbelievably prodigious and remarkably diverse. Many of his most
visionary offerings, however, sadly remain unbuilt, since he lavished as much or more
attention on long shots and lost causes as he did on conventional commissions, saying that
once a project was visible in his mind it was as real for him as one that had been, or could
be, built. The most significant of both built and unbuilt efforts in this period tell the story,
starting with the City Tower Project of 1952–7 that would have drastically upset existing
Philadelphia tradition of not building higher than the eclectic Victorian pile it would
replace.

The City Tower Project was followed by the American Federation of Labor Medical
Services Building (1954–7), now tragically demolished, that definitively revised the prevailing
modernist language of steel, glass and concrete, continuing the departure from this reductivist
vocabulary began at the Yale Art Gallery. Then, the Jewish Community Center in Trenton, New
Jersey, of which only a few of the bathhouse units were actually completed (1954–9), provided
an effective exploration of how one unit, or building block, can be repeated to accommodate
many functions, countering the modernist dictum that the form of a building should honestly
express, or 'follow' its function. Trenton overlapped with the Alfred Newton Richard Medical
Research Building and Biology Building (1957–65), which was the second stage of Kahn's
rocket to fame, reaching the international audience that the Yale Art Gallery missed. This
project incorporated a historical metaphor, a reference to the Italian hilltop towers of San
Gimignano, offering an alternative to minimal ahistoricism. The Tribune Review Publishing
Company Building in Greensburg, Pennsylvania (1958–62), built of low-cost masonry block,
continued both the Trenton use of pragmatic materials in exalted ways as well as Kahn's
general tendency to turn every project into a lesson.

A Breakthrough in Luanda and a Built and Unbuilt Legacy

Had it been built, the United States Consulate and Residence in Luanda, Angola, designed
1959–62, would undoubtedly have been recognized as an unprecedented attempt at
environmental response for the period. In it, Kahn employed a second, detached, outer skin to

protect the windows from glare and a raised metal roof daringly used to protect a second one below it and soak up solar heat so that it could be wicked away by the wind, as it is in the radiator of an automobile. An open central court oriented to capture the prevailing breeze was also intended to distribute it into the interior. By layering the walls, and deciding to work with natural forces rather than treat them as an adversary, Kahn broke through an entrenched psychological barrier erected in modernist doctrine that a second skin was somehow dishonest and redundant.

The Salk Institute for Biological Studies (1959–65) followed Luanda. Only the laboratory portion was built, but it consistently ranks, along with the Kimbell Art Museum, as one of Kahn's best-loved buildings. Perhaps this is because it most closely approximates his goal of making architecture 'timeless,' rather than inextricably tying it to fashion or function, which can change. His association with Dr Jonas Salk, who had recently risen to fame with his discovery of a polio vaccine, proved to be a meeting of the minds: they challenged each other, and the friendly (and sometimes not so friendly) competition forced the architect to stretch his aesthetic range. Limited finances unfortunately prevented the completion of the educational and residential pieces that Kahn believed were essential to the totality of his concept, prophetic of the client restrictions that he decided to use to his advantage, again as a pedagogical exercise, in this next project for a Unitarian Church and School in Rochester New York built between 1959–69. He referred to this Church in an instructive set of diagrams as an example of what client demands could do to an ideal formal construct: the 'form follows function' stratagem was intentionally amplified in Rochester to create lyrical exterior walls that rise and fall like musical chords. His first idea for assembly, here expressed as a circle, was eventually changed by the client, but was finally realized at Dhaka, as proof of his perseverance in the search for the perfect form.

Kahn's interest in music, as a pianist who paid his way through the University of Pennsylvania by playing in theatres and movie houses, as well as art, which tempted him as a career prior to architecture, was partially responsible for his involvement in the Fine Arts Center, School and Performing Arts Theatre in Fort Wayne, Indiana. Only the theatre and offices, however, were built between 1959 and 1973. Once again recycling an idea which was part of the process of his search for an approximation of perfection, he returned to massing diagrams in an unrealized design for the Philadelphia College of Art (1960–66). Tall towers there were intended to create an internal street, and emerge again in the fly tower of the theatre at Fort Wayne, a symbol of this particular institution and its 'inspiration to express.'

The next two projects to be considered were commissioned for specific social groups: the first, showing a slightly romanticized, slightly regressive, approach, was Eleanor Donnelley Erdman Hall, a women's dormitory at Bryn Mawr College (1960–65); the second, the Levy Memorial Playground for children, was designed in collaboration with the sculptor Isamu Noguchi between 1961 and 1966. Erdman Hall, like the City Tower Project, was developed with Anne Tyng and exhibits geometric intricacy as a result, layered over historical references to Scottish castles. Although his attitude now seems dated and quaint, Kahn thought the castle metaphor was appropriate as a symbol of protectiveness for a women's dormitory, just at the time that a new feminist consciousness was beginning to emerge. The Levy Memorial Playground, however, which has an organic and spontaneously free form, even today is far ahead of its time in offering a natural alternative to the ubiquitous manufactured swings and metal playsets that children are mistakenly thought to prefer.

First Unitarian Church, 1959–69
The massive brick walls that became Kahn's trademark first appeared at this project and the Richards Medical Towers.

Indian Institute of Management, 1962–74
Kahn chose to use local brick to lower construction costs
and to associate the building with its surroundings more
closely. The brick has not fared well over time, but the
use of deep openings and the provision of shade has
proved effective.

Layering in Response to Context rather than as a Conceit

The idea of layering exterior walls, which Kahn explored at the Luanda Embassy and Salk
Institute, moved inside in his Synagogue for the Mikveh Israel Congregation in Philadelphia,
designed between 1961 and 1972, but never built. Rather than serving an environmental
purpose, as the layering was intended to do in Africa and San Diego, however, it manifests
itself as light shafts that bracket each corner of a central rectangular worship space, with
sections cut out to serve as overflow spaces for the congregation as well. These were to be the
realization of his vision of habitable structure, here expressed as columns that expand and are
hollowed out to become rooms. This concept, which is a philosophical rather than functional
construct, increasingly manifested through compartmentalized spaces, is an important key to
understanding Kahn's apathy with structure.

Those two intentions, of climatic response and structural animism, finally coincide in the
Indian Institute of Management in Ahmedabad, India (1962–74, a commission secured
through Kahn's friend Balkrishna Doshi), and Sher-e-Bangla Nagar, the capital of
Bangladesh, in Dhaka, began in 1962, but completed by David Wisdom and Associates in
1983. Arguably the apotheosis of his long search for appropriate monumentality and
grandeur suitable for the modern age, these two projects also represent the multicultural
bridge that Kahn almost single-handedly constructed during the course of his career. Each
project was completed at a critical point in the history of these nations: the Management
Institute supporting a rising middle class in India by providing badly needed administrative
support for the rapid industrial growth the country was experiencing; the capital of
Bangladesh provided a much-needed sense of identity for a newly formed Muslim nation,
struggling to find its way in the world.

Because of his multi-faceted background and exposure to a variety of theories which he saw as having a surprising degree of coincidence, he was just as qualified and comfortable in conceptualizing a Convent – the Dominican Mother house of St Catherine de Ricci, in Media, Pennsylvania (1965–9, unbuilt) – as he had been in designing a Unitarian Church, several Synagogues and a Mosque. His skill as a mediator between cultures is particularly evident in his renditions of the religious institutions which are one of the most manifest of all traditional determinants. Those related to his own background, however, understandably had more profound resonance for him. In addition to the unrealized Mikveh Israel Synagogue, the Temple Beth-El in Chappaqua, New York (built between 1966 and 1972), and the Hurva Synagogue in Jerusalem (1967–74, but not built), make this clear. Perhaps one of the most moving images of Kahn's entire career is a sectional drawing of Hurva rendered in charcoal on yellow tracing paper, cut through the hilly site, showing his massive Synagogue on the left edge of the long, horizontal sheet, and the Church of Holy Sepulchre (c. AD 326) and the Dome of the Rock (AD 688–91) in sequence to the right. The primitive forms of the Synagogue ably represent Judaism with sufficient power in the presence of such psychologically charged monuments of Christianity and Islam. Comparisons between Hurva and the Temple of Solomon, which was undoubtedly its inspiration, are myriad and Kahn said that this study forced him finally to come to terms with his past. The Memorial to the Six Million Jewish Martyrs intended for Battery Park in Manhattan, but also sadly never realized, was in progress at the same time (1966–72), representing the most tragic chapter of Kahn's own ethnic history. It commemorated the victims of the Holocaust and included nine square pylons, equally spaced, inside a raised, square precinct to allow passage between them. These

Hurva Synagogue, Jerusalem, 1974–6

Kahn's synagogue was destined for one of the most sensitive sites in the world, one which accommodates the remains of the Temple of Solomon, the Dome of the Rock, and the Church of the Holy Sepulchre. His proposal responded to the history of the area but also to its climate.

were to be rendered in glass, representing ethereal purity, reaching out, as he said 'to something primordial, something that existed before.'

The Importance of Natural Light

Natural light was sacred to Kahn: he insisted that no space in his buildings be without it. From the sublime purpose it was intended to serve in the Holocaust memorial to its more pragmatic, but nonetheless exalted, appearance in all his work, light is introduced in countless, inventive ways. In the library and dining hall of Phillips Exeter Academy in Exeter, New Hampshire, completed between 1965 and 1972, the great central hall is awash in light through an aedicula, or freestanding tower inside the main volume, perforated with a huge circle on each side to defuse the glare, predicting the use of a similar device at a much larger scale at Sher-e-Bangla Nagar.

His last three major projects – an office building in Kansas City (1966–73, unbuilt), a Palazzo del Congressi, or Congress Hall, for the Biennale in Venice (1968–74, unbuilt), and the Yale Center for British Art (1969–74, with design and construction completed after Kahn's death by Pellecchia and Meyers and Architects) – convincingly and conclusively demonstrate the extraordinary range of his imagination and talent as a great architect capable of assimilating the most complex brief. For Kahn, however, timeless architecture demanded much more than this purely functional synthesis, which he called 'the immeasurable' realm of unlimited design possibilities, through the necessarily inescapable process of contending with a client's 'measurable' requirements. And then, with hard work, empathy, intuition, and full knowledge of the past as it relates to the present, he believed architecture can transcend necessity and return to the realm of the immeasurable once again.

Nobility of Purpose

A more focused understanding of Kahn's work is important now because he succeeded in adding that immeasurable dimension back into architecture, beyond his expectations, making contemporary pluralism possible and prefiguring the gamut of issues that are germane today. Particularly in its last mature phase, Kahn's contribution marks an important reconciliation between modernism, in which contextual, climatic, historical or stylistic reference, colour, ornament and symbolic content were noticeably absent; and the more liberal period of post-modernism, which enthusiastically embraced these concepts, directly after him. His hard-won credentials as a modernist, gained through decades of social activism, gave him added authority when he questioned the validity of modernist asceticism, and that authority now extends to imbuing environmentalism with the nobility of purpose that it frequently lacks.

UK Pavilion, Expo '92, Nicholas Grimshaw, 1989–92
Based in Seville, and visited by thousands of people
every day, the main problem in the design of this energy-
efficient pavilion was temperature control. In typical
High-Tech fashion, the answer lay in solar-powered
pumps, which sprayed water onto the glass walls.
Together with other technological innovations, this
resulted in energy savings of around one third.

11 Rogers, Foster, Hopkins, Grimshaw: Engineering the Eco-Tech Aesthetic

The 1960s and 70s saw the emergence of a new High-Tech approach that looked to science for answers to environmental management and integration

Biographies

Norman Foster

Nicholas Grimshaw

Michael Hopkins

Richard Rogers

Richard Rogers

Born in Florence in 1933, Rogers studied at the Architectural Association, London, then Yale University, before establishing Team 4 with Norman Foster. He came to prominence with the Pompidou Centre, Paris, co-designed with Renzo Piano. His work since shows an abiding interest in large, uninterrupted spaces, in the modernist tradition. Other key projects include the Lloyd's of London headquarters, the National Assembly of Wales, and the Millennium Dome, London

Michael Hopkins

Michael Hopkins and Partners was founded in 1976. His buildings are typified by an intelligent use of materials and a generally unfussy approach, and like the other architects here defy easy categorization, although there is a recurrent interest in 19th-century engineering and prefabrication. Recent important works include 'Portcullis House' in London, a beacon of sustainable architecture.

Norman Foster

Like Rogers, Foster completed postgraduate studies at Yale, before establishing Foster Associates in 1967 (now Foster and Partners). Like Rogers he has worked globally and has been awarded prizes internationally. Recent projects include the Reichstag in Berlin, and, in London, the Great Court of the British Museum, the Swiss Re building, and the Millennium Bridge. His work tends to rely on technological solutions, something that all of these architects have in common.

Nicholas Grimshaw

Founded in 1967, Grimshaw and Partners' science-led aesthetic has proved to be internationally popular. The practice early on specialized in airport design, but a recent development of particular relevance to this book was the Eden Project in Cornwall, UK, a collection of 'biomes' made from unorthodox materials, which house samples of the entire world's ecologies.

Key Projects

Richard Rogers

Mallorca Development Project, Mallorca, 1994

Pudong Development Plan, 1992–4

Law Courts, Bordeaux, 1992–8

Michael Hopkins

Inland Revenue Centre, Nottingham, 1992

Portcullis House, 1998–2000

Norman Foster

Sainsbury Centre for Visual Arts, Norwich, 1974–8

Hong Kong Shanghai Bank Tower, 1979

Commerzbank Tower, Frankfurt, completed 1997

Nicholas Grimshaw

UK Pavilion, Expo '92, Seville, 1989–92

Eden Project, Cornwall, 2001

Signposts

Energy efficiency Part II: 1, 13, 16, 19

Town planning Part II: 2, 3, 4, 8, 9, 12, 18; Part III: 3

Solar energy Part II: 5, 14, 15

Natural ventilation Part II: 6, 7, 16, 20, 23, 24

'Eco-Tech' Part II: 17, 19

Sustainability Part II: 15, 17, 20, 21, 23

Biospheres Part II: 13

The growth/no-growth conflict of the 1960s, which centred around the amount of development that was appropriate in view of increasing ecological problems, was supposedly neutralized by the compromise of sustainability. However, there remained disagreement over the proper architectural response to environmental degradation. Some believed that technology can be effective only if it is applied in doses that are appropriate to present needs; others, sharing the modernist trust in scientific progress, believed that technology could solve any environmental problem, no matter how severe. Several High-Tech architects in Britain personify this latter approach. They can be identified as a cohesive group because of a common stylistic direction, and a unified belief in the effectiveness of science. They have each now also assumed the mantle of sustainability, trying to align natural forces with industrial production. They seek to make the compelling myth of the machine in the garden a reality, finally exceeding the standard set in 1851 by Joseph Paxton's Crystal Palace.

Richard Rogers

Richard Rogers first achieved international fame – or notoriety – with the Pompidou Centre in Paris, on which he collaborated with Renzo Piano in 1977. The Centre perpetuates and expands upon the main tenets of the Crystal Palace code – mass production; standardization; industrial materials; rapid construction; long spans and the clustering of services to ensure flexibility; panoptical space; the denial of context in favour of a man-made climate-controlled, utopian interior; and an intentionally mechanistic image – all combined in an unfettered celebration of technology. In the Lloyd's of London Headquarters, which Rogers completed on his own soon afterward, prefabricated metal trusses have been replaced with a heavier precast concrete frame, increasing the contextual insult to this historically fragile section of the City, just adjacent to Leadenhall Market. But the same message that was sent earlier in Paris – that any external sacrifice is justified in order to create a more perfect and controlled internal world – is repeated even more emphatically here, to the extent that Lloyds employees later complained that they had no privacy.

A More Contextual Approach

Later projects by Richard Rogers Partnership, such as a development scheme for the island of Mallorca and for Pudong, Shanghai, are more humane, indicating a softer approach in keeping with claims of newly adopted ecological principles. The Mallorca project, in particular, demonstrates the most promising aspects of a total reliance on science to solve environmental problems, in the hope that knowledge can cure the ills that human intervention in natural processes has caused. The hot, dry Mediterranean climate that prevails on the island for most of the year, along with constant north and northwest winds that are slightly buffered by a mountain range running the entire length of the island from Palma to the sea, have restricted agriculture and economic growth, keeping Mallorca in poverty. Because of this lack of rainfall in summer, one of the key strategies proposed by the Richard Rogers Partnership was to provide a systematic network of cisterns that would be capable of storing 10 per cent of the rain that falls during the winter, and would normally run straight into the sea. Choosing a 30 square kilometre (11 square mile) zone around a 1.5 square kilometre site area connected to a 50-hectare natural habitat zone as a territory of study, Rogers determined that this was the amount necessary for both irrigation and residential use during the summer, with any extra diverted back into the ground to recharge the aquifer.

Several other methods of collecting the precious water that the island needs to survive its dry summers were investigated. Open lakes were found to be least expensive but also require aeration systems to prevent mosquito infestation. Hence weirs, sized according to the daily variation in river levels, below which no water is taken off, were chosen as another effective method of collection. Water storage facilities have been located at optimal points to facilitate a gravity irrigation system, eliminating the need to pump water, with distribution constantly monitored by a computer-controlled system. Agricultural terraces, on the steeper slopes of the study area, help contain the gravity-fed water, while flatter land to the south is irrigated by a network of pipes. This improved water storage and irrigation system has made possible a diverse range of new crops, as well as improving the yields of traditional varieties, which are expected to increase tenfold in some cases. Trees to be planted along the edges of the terraces protect the crops from the excess wind and storms that are typical on Mallorca. Quick-growing crops, such as willow and sorghum, will provide renewable sources of energy to generate local power.

Mallorca as a Prototype

In a way that is typical of the high-technology approach, the Mallorca Development Project is intended to be a pilot project that can be applied to the entire island. But it is unusual in that the architectural component of the plan is considered only one part of a complex system that includes water and agricultural management, energy strategies and social issues. The built component is based on a compact neighbourhood concept, with narrow streets used to create a sense of community, provide shade and reduce travel distance.

Housing has been inserted into the hillside, with heavily structured roofs allowing terraces to be extended above. Vents placed between rows of deciduous trees allow light and natural ventilation into the houses and are positioned for maximum cooling in the summer and solar gain in the winter. Growth toward the town centre intensifies in relationship to bands of use, from these agricultural terraces on the perimeter through residential areas, then a working zone, to a mixed-use public area including small plazas encircling a lake. During the summer, when water levels drop, cascading terraces around the lake area are exposed one by one, becoming stepped public promenades that allow people to walk near the water's edge.

Pudong as an Environmental City of the Future

Pudong is the commercial heart of a new Shanghai, and a source of a great civic pride because it is entirely a Chinese construct. Rogers was invited at a relatively early stage in the growth of this area to propose ideas that would overturn accepted concepts of city planning, to arrive at a prototype for a futuristic city based on environmental principles. His response was that Pudong should be integral to Shanghai, rather than isolated from it, and be based on streets rather than singular object buildings, which seem to have become the norm in city-planning models proposed by Shanghai officials. This focus on the street is based on the premise that the circulation of people and goods is a key factor in the success or failure of any city and the first place to start to conserve energy.

Rogers saw this as an opportunity to design an urban centre with a coordinated transportation strategy, an efficient building layout, management of vehicular circulation and the provision of an efficient and reliable public transportation system. To that end, a strategy was developed that included subways, rapid light rail, trams, taxis, buses, bicycles and cars,

while still giving precedence to pedestrians, creating an overlapping system of separate but interrelated networks. A mix of activities was seen as having significant environmental advantages, since a good balance of commercial and residential use tends to even out demands on infrastructure, especially power generation and transport. To achieve this mix, commercial development was placed along a light rail loop, cultural and social facilities were concentrated around open spaces, housing was clustered at the sub-centre and shopping was located along the primary routes leading to river crossings. The height and profile of the buildings in the environmentally engineered new town was defined by two complementary objectives: the need to maximize daylight, and the views from all buildings. A model was made to optimize sun angles with the understanding that natural daylight can dramatically reduce dependence on artificial lighting, thus reducing energy use.

Law Courts, Bordeaux

The Rogers Partnership has also applied sound sustainable principles at a much smaller scale in their dramatic extension to the Palais de Justice in Bordeaux, France. The 14,000 square metre (150,000 square foot) addition clearly demonstrates an ongoing commitment to elegantly crafted mechanistic object buildings in the Pompidou–Lloyds tradition, with a new overlay of environmental sensitivity. A linear, glazed, five-storey office block, for judges and administrative staff, is shaded by a thin independent copper umbrella that creates an open, Corbusian roof garden along the top . Seven independent courtrooms, contained in bulbous 15-metre (50 foot) high wooden pods, are evenly spaced along this bar with the top of each of the red cedar-clad bulbs having an oculus that lights the interior of the court, and assists in the natural convective cooling system that naturally ventilates most of the building. The courtrooms are clearly visible from a central landscaped courtyard that has a large fountain used to moderate external temperatures.

Norman Foster

Norman Foster travelled across America with Rogers when they were both students, and recalled that they were both most impressed with the Eames House, in Los Angeles. Like the Crystal Palace, it embodies the technologist's ideal of rational, pre-planned effortless

top **Model of mixed-use area, ParcBit, Mallorca,** Richard Rogers Partnership, 1994
above **Diagram of Mallorca development**

Rogers' concern in the development plan for Mallorca was integration of systems and networks: transport, utilities, resources – all typical High-Tech themes.

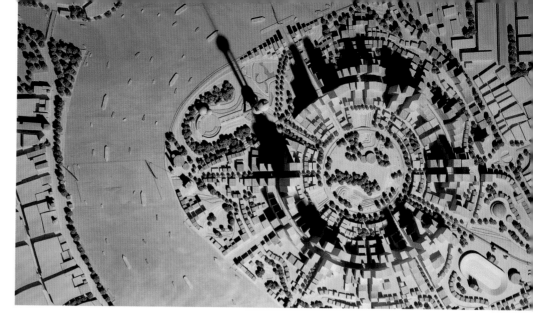

Model of the Shanghai Masterplan (Pudong), Richard Rogers Partnership, 1992–4
Rogers was invited to propose a new approach to city-planning, based on environmental principles. His key recommendations were to focus on the street rather than isolated buildings; to develop an efficient transport system; to promote mixed-used; and careful planning to maximize daylight.

construction: Charles and Ray Eames had all the steel for the house pre-cut and erected by crane in a few days. Like Rogers, Foster has also produced many landmark ultra-modernist buildings: the Willis Faber Headquarters in Ipswich, the Sainsbury Gallery at Norwich University, and the Hong Kong Shanghai Bank are the most prominent. The major discernable difference between the two is that Foster has always made a point of responding to context, while still conforming in every way to the unwritten High-Tech code of internal autonomy, Miesian universal space, and the external celebration of cutting-edge hardware. In Ipswich, the contextual premise is brilliantly implemented by making the sizable Willis Faber Headquarters virtually invisible during the day by wrapping it in an elegant glass veil that reflects rather than competes with its venerable surroundings. After sunset, however, strategically placed backlighting makes the veil seem to disappear, and a muscular concrete core emerges behind it, essentially providing the insurance company with two buildings for the price of one and allowing the architect to claim clandestine victory over local constraints.

The Sainsbury Centre
The Sainsbury Centre at Norwich University, nearby, is equally sensitive to its surroundings with the glazed ends of its aircraft hanger-like form intentionally oriented toward the best light and views. To maximize each of these, the ends of the long, rectilinear museum have no obstructions, with silicone joints used to increase glass area. This allows visual reference to the centre of the campus, at one end of the axis that bisects the rectangle, and a river that flows past it, on the other, linking the man-made and natural contexts in which the building has been placed. The U-shaped aluminium shell that encases the top and long sides of the rectangle, however, constitutes the High-Tech component of the project, since it is made up of individual panels that can be removed and reconfigured by the client to provide different levels of natural light inside the gallery. Once the panels, which are either solid, louvered or glazed, are changed, computer-driven blinds on the inside of the structural truss that supports the aluminium skin are reset to react to new light levels and to prevent glare. This combination of glazed, unobstructed ends which mirror context and sleek, computer 'smart' skin which regulates climate with sophisticated technology, is typical of Foster and Partners' approach to each project.

The Hong Kong Shanghai Bank Tower as Urban Gateway

The Hong Kong Shanghai Bank Tower, one of the first of a series of skyscrapers that Foster has designed, continues this theme of technology softened by sensitivity to place. Inspired by the Golden Gate Bridge in San Francisco, the tower has floors which are suspended from two masts, to allow physical and visual access at ground level from the Star Ferry pier in front of the tower to a large urban park behind it. By using this suspension structure to create a gateway at this critical point in the city, Foster has also ensured that the main technological strategy that they have used is fully visible (another recurring theme in the High-Tech lexicon). The masts also facilitate the clustering of services on the ends of each suspended floor to allow complete flexibility in the middle, which fulfils another article of faith. Through these various considerations – positioning on the critical axis, exposing the suspension structure, calling attention to service clusters – Foster and Partners have made the tower seem much more imposing than it actually is.

New Environmentally Friendly Towers

After this *tour de force* in Hong Kong, Foster and Partners have designed increasingly taller towers that have come to define the state of the art in high-rise construction in their respective cities, with the added agenda of increased ecological awareness. The Commerzbank building in Frankfurt, Germany, which was billed as the world's tallest environmentally conscious high-rise tower when it was completed in 1997, is triangular in plan and is 300 metres (985 feet) high. It mimics Ken Yeang's innovative notion of 'sky-courts' (discussed on pp. 193–9) in its use of nine four-storey-high sections that spiral up the sides of its sixty-storey elevation. Foster and Partners have also utilized Yeang's strategy of moving structure from the centre of the tower to the perimeter, to create an atrium, while utilizing their extensive access to research facilities to study more thoroughly the convective forces that result from such a tall vertical court. This led them to place a horizontal glass screen on every twelfth floor to prevent stack effect from disturbing airflow. They have augmented these fundamental typological shifts with triple-layered (single and double sheet) glazing that makes it easier to control the day lighting and ventilation of the interior. The Commerzbank and the Swiss Re Tower in London signal the determination of Foster and Partners to use the latest scientific findings in the design of the building envelope for 'smart' climatic control.

Michael Hopkins

Michael Hopkins (who, like Foster, often works in conjunction with Ove Arup and Partners) has taken a decidedly different approach in his search for an ecological paradigm. He has developed several key ideas through a series of major commissions which began with Bracken House, were improved at the Mound Stand in Lord's Cricket Ground, the David Mellor Cutlery Factory, Glyndebourne Opera House, and the Inland Revenue complex, and coalesced in the New Parliamentary Building at Westminster (known as Portcullis House) in 2001. Precast concrete beams and panels were used at Bracken House in the City of London and at Glyndebourne, before circumstances prompted a quantum leap in Hopkins' use of this technology. Pressure to complete the new Inland Revenue centre in Nottingham was high because it was re-commissioned in 1992, due to a decision by the government to abandon an earlier project by another architect. This was due to public outcry over what was believed to be its unsuitability and the need to accommodate 1,800 employees who had uprooted

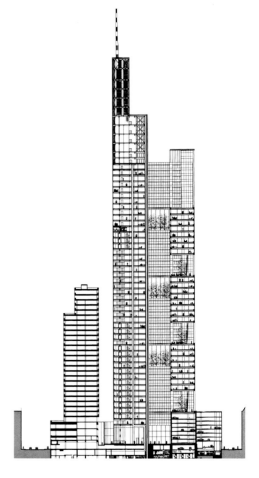

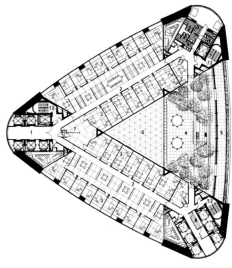

Section and floorplan of Commerzbank Tower,
Foster and Partners, completed 1997
The floorplan shows the space given to terrace (5) and 'sky garden' (4), while the entire interior is lit by the atrium (6). It has been called the world's tallest environmentally conscious high-rise tower.

themselves in the process. This pressure provided the crucible that Hopkins needed to push these adaptations of precast technology to the next level.

For speed, Hopkins Architects divided the huge complex, located in Castle Meadow near the Nottingham Canal, into six discrete blocks, four of which are L-shaped and bracket the ends of the lozenge-shaped site, with another two shaped as contorted squares surrounding a courtyard in the middle of the site adjacent to Wilford Road. A fabric 'amenity' building for receiving visitors, staff and community facilities is at the centre of the northern part of the complex, deliberately crafted to stand out in the midst of the other massive brick monoliths on the site. The decision to break the project down into disparate elements, was made on the basis of increasing the feasibility of prefabrication as much as it was for aesthetic reasons – as well as the desire to find an appropriate humanely scaled contemporary expression of the local brick vernacular that dated back to the Victorian period.

Paradigm Shift

In Nottingham, Hopkins Architects broke away from the usual High-Tech reliance on industrial materials, while substantially advancing the science of prefabrication. This makes the collective High-Tech claim of sustainability far more convincing, since energy conservation is only one of the many complex interrelationships that the principle entails. It also encourages other technologists to consider the use of telluric rather than non-renewable resources that require a great deal of embodied energy to manufacture. This breakthrough was largely due to Arup's proposal that in order to meet strict deadlines the brick piers had to be prefabricated off-site, along with the wave-form folded-plate floor panels which span from wall to wall without intermediate support. The piers were built around a single steel bar anchored into a stainless steel baseplate, all meant to serve as a cradle for lifting the 1,032 piers into place by crane. Warm, dry, well-lit factory conditions, as well as a template, allowed the bricklayers to achieve high-quality work to a tight schedule. As each pier was completed, precast base and cap pads were added, before it was placed in storage, awaiting transport to the site and final installation, onto pre-levelled pads. Once the piers were in place the 13.6 by 3.2 metre (45 by 10 foot) vaulted precast floor units, each weighing 26 tons, were lifted into place, locking each building together laterally.

Four Strategies

The use of brick was one of the four basic strategies behind the environmental approach to the Inland Revenue project, and together with the precast concrete floorslats provide the thermal mass necessary to counter erratic temperature fluctuations. The other three goals – a high-performance façade, solar-assisted ventilation and good daylighting levels – were also based on the central premise that low energy use would logically result from the close integration of these ideas. The deep brick piers shade the triple-glazed, fully operable windows, while a light shelf bounces daylight far into the interior. Cool outside air is drawn through each building by a combination of convective suction and solar-assisted towers or chimneys. The exposed concrete soffit also helps to reduce peaks and valleys in temperature scorings. As Arup point out: 'natural ventilation has become a generalization with no meaning, simply opening windows is not in itself a solution, other factors such as solar shading to minimize heat build-up, thermal mass to dampen temperature fluctuations, exposed surface area for heat transfer, adequate volume for ventilation flow, tall rooms for stratification and a means of controlling airflow during the day and at night for capacitive pre-cooling also need consideration'.[1]

Exceeding All Expectations

Completed in late 1993, in the Inland Revenue Centre Hopkins Architects not only met, but clearly exceeded, their original objectives. By breaking the brief down into seven separate buildings, rather than one 37,000 square metre (400,000 square foot) monolith, they have extended the urban grain across the canal, revitalizing a previously desolate area to the south. Tree-lined 'streets' and partial or full courtyards branching out from a mini 'boulevard' running through the site that links with the canal tow paths, create and extend a garden landscape onto the site. (The potential disposal of separate buildings in the event of privatizing elements of the Government Departmental user was also a consideration.) A structural module, used on all seven buildings, provides a legible, flexible organizing device. The extra effort expended in reviving Victorian brick-building techniques (the clay beds in Nottingham were worked out and the architect had to go to Cumbria to find a material of similar consistency) not only energized a vernacular tradition, but also demonstrated that such materials can meet the structural challenges of major civil engineering projects as well as providing a more thoroughly sustainable environmental solution.

Public Clients Now Promote a Green Agenda

Hopkins Architects have credited the political climate that made the Inland Revenue Centre possible to the rapidly evolving environmental awareness of the European Union and its implementation of green policies. Public clients now take a long-range view of occupancy and energy investment. Hopkins believe that this commitment also led to their commission to design the New Parliamentary Building in Westminster, giving them the opportunity to further investigate the complications presented by building in a heavily urbanized context. Following advances already made at the David Mellor Cutlery Factory, the Mound Stand at Lords, and the Inland Revenue Centre, Hopkins Architects increased their resolve to take an approach to environmental amelioration that is different from the modernist obsession with the artificial filtering out of adverse climatic effects.

They found that even though they had pragmatically began to use structural elements to moderate climatic performance in the Inland Revenue project, they still had some way to go to fully integrate as many functions as possible into each single construction element to maximize its overall environmental effectiveness. Again concentrating on the twin goals of optimum thermal mass and daylight, the designers of the New Parliamentary Building provided large radiant surfaces in high rooms to create a thermal fly-wheel effect. Surfaces and height stratify ventilation, exploiting low-grade ambient energy sources such as fresh air and groundwater for cooling and passive solar gain for heating. Voids between the top of the exposed reinforced concrete slab and the floor turn it into a hypocaust radiator. Hopkins Architects also decided to bring fresh air into the building at roof level to avoid pollution, circulating it with fans and expelling it through rotating chimney turrets. This has given the New Parliamentary Building a very different profile to conventional office buildings, as novel as the more humane comforts it offers to those working inside. It marks a formal as well as a theoretical shift from the fragmented modernist approach of separating a steel frame structure from a glass enclosure and from the equipment used to heat and cool a building.

opposite, top **Central courtyard, Portcullis House (New Parliamentary Building), London,** Hopkins Architects, 1998–2000
opposite, below left **Section, Portcullis House**
opposite, below right **Inside central courtyard, Portcullis House**

The designers of this highly visible building, which provides offices for Members of Parliament, were preoccupied with optimum thermal mass and daylight, as well as security. Fresh air is dragged in by fans at roof-level (to avoid pollution), while stale air is exhausted through the distinctive chimneys.

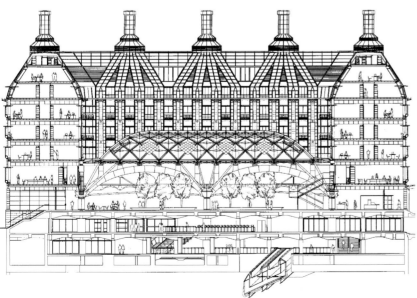

Grimshaw & Partners

If any doubts remained by the end of the 20th century that High-Tech was the architectural language of choice in Britain, the UK Pavilion at Expo '92 in Seville, by Nicholas Grimshaw & Partners, certainly dispelled them. Like the Crystal Palace of 1851, the goal of the Seville Pavilion, as articulated by the British Department of Trade and Industry, was to 'promote the UK as a strong, resourceful and open economy by displaying British enterprise and to demonstrate the excellence of British design'. And also like the Paxton model, this pavilion was intended to do that through an overt display of technological might. The initial brief given to Grimshaw and Ove Arup and Partners in March 1989, stressed the need for unobstructed floor space to handle up to 20,000 visitors a day, seven days a week for six months, as well as an exterior that the public would immediately identify as bring British. The design team responded by looking to the distinctive climatic restraints presented by the location, where summer temperatures regularly reach 30°C (86°F) and sometimes exceed 45°C (113°F), with minimal rainfall; and where hot dry winds are directed across the city from April to October by mountains nearby. Site constraints dictated a rectangular plan dimension of 64.8 x 32 m (213 x 105 ft) and a height of 24.8 m (81 ft) from lower ground floor to the roof, with the long walls of the rectangle facing the major heat gain on the east and west.

Because of orientation and the requirement for specialized exhibition areas, Grimshaw and Arup took a hierarchical approach to environmental control, rather than heating the interior as a uniform space. The temperatures that visitors might experience from the queue outside to an air-conditioned interior were moderated, to allow people gradually to adjust. The designers dealt with heat gain on the long east wall, which was also the major public face of the pavilion, by shielding the glass with a continuously flowing sheet of water, which kept the glass temperature at a constant 24°C (75°F). Submersible pumps, powered by photovoltaic arrays on the roof, operating in tandem with conventionally powered motors raised the water 17.5 m (57 ft) from a lake running along the entire east elevation, to pipes fitted with nozzles that sprayed it on the glass. Solar energy provided about 50 per cent of the power needed by the pumps. Stacked steel tanks filled with water were used to provide the thermal mass necessary to stabilize the opposing west wall. Heat absorption was further controlled by painting these tanks and insulating them, making it possible to maintain a constant 30°C (86°F) temperature throughout the day. Air was exhausted naturally through louvers located near the roofline, in a negative pressure zone, operated by wind-monitoring sensors, and the upward movement of air within the envelope contributed to the desired stratification necessary to maintain the optimum temperature conditions at concourse level.

In a final assessment of the performance of the UK Pavilion at the Seville Expo '92, Arup noted that 'the high internal heat gains from exhibits, and the organization of internal spaces required by the client meant that the Pavilion was not the ultimate low-energy building. However, within the constraints it demonstrated how these techniques, some long established, are appropriate in the context of modern materials, industrial methods, pre-fabricated buildings and modern user needs. Energy savings of about 33 per cent, relative to a more conventional building of similar size and purpose, were achieved'.[2]

Eden Recreated

Perhaps the project that Paxton would most easily recognize as the rightful heir of the Crystal Palace, however, now exists in two biomes in Cornwall. Billed as 'the largest glass house in the

Eden Project, Nicholas Grimshaw, completed 2001
The giant biomes of the Eden Project house three
different ecosystems under a super-lightweight
membrane structure that owes something to
Buckminster Fuller.

world', the Eden Project, by Nicholas Grimshaw and Partners, in St Austell, covers 123 acres of a former clay quarry and is intended to be a showcase for global bio-diversity and human dependence on photosynthesis. Plants from three of the world's major ecosystems have been relocated into two conservatories and one external ground on this site. The first is a light biome, or 'climate controlled transparent capsule' that covers 3.9 acres and soars to 55 metres (180 feet) high, replicating rainforest ecosystems with trees and plants from Malaysia and the Amazon. The second biome, covering 1.5 acres, has plants from the subtropical zones of the Mediterranean, South Africa and California. A third, roofless biome mimics temperate woodlands, housing plants from such zones. More than 800,000 tons of soil were placed in all three zones to grow the 250,000 plants in them.

Prefabrication Once Again a Prime Consideration

The biomes have the appearance of an alien biomorphic organism but Grimshaw, in the best High-Tech tradition of a concern for speed, precision and breaking existing barriers, says the design was driven by fabrication, transportation and construction considerations, rather than metaphorical references. In this case that meant creating a lightweight structure that covers the most volume with the least surface area. To achieve this Grimshaw used straight tubular compressive membrane joined by standard cast connections, forming hexagonal cell geometry with a 9-metre (30-foot) span. This cladding is covered by transparent air-inflated foil pillows that result in an envelope of unparalleled lightness.

An Ongoing Scientific Campaign

The range of approaches that these projects represent, from comprehensive microclimatic manipulation in Mallorca though the attempt to improve on Ken Yeang and make skyscrapers in major European cities more sustainable, to imprisoning messy, elemental, unpredictable nature under the largest bubble-wrapped glass house in the world, demonstrate a continuing firm belief that science still has the power to keep environmental degradation at bay. Against all odds – unchecked population growth, unprecedented loss of non-renewable resources, and undeniable evidence of global warming, as well as the growing realization that science is a double-edged sword, and not the shibboleth it was once considered to be – proponents of High-Tech continue to seek heroic, mechanistic solutions to the problems of the earth.

Integrating Traditional Technology in the Urban Context

As the examples just cited, and many more since, clearly show, however, it is those now engineering the 'Eco-Tech' aesthetics who are most aggressively confronting the central issues put forward in this book: trying to come to terms with the integration of appropriate traditional and sophisticated new technologies for ecological benefit, mainly in an urban context. Some attempts may be faulted for being overzealous, while others demonstrate a more creative fusion of vernacular principles and materials with the High-Tech dedication to prefabrication, rapid construction, clear-span spaces and the celebration of structure, but each represents a dedicated search for solutions to mounting environmental difficulties, using time-tested principles.

Model of Cosanti, 1951

Soleri's visions have always seemed to exceed his ability to achieve them, but the pieces of the original Cosanti that have been built provide an indication of his holistic view.

12

Paolo Soleri: The Omega Seed Hypothesis

The architecture and planning of Paolo Soleri shows an early interest in self-sufficiency, taking Wright's utopian Taliesin a step further towards genuine sustainability.

Biography

Key Projects

Ceramics Factory, Vieti sul Mare, Italy, 1950

Cosanti Foundation, Arizona, 1951

Mesa City (plan), 1959

Arcosanti, Arizona, 1962

Valetta Spring, Arizona, 1980–85

Signposts

Local materials and techniques Part II: 1, 3, 4, 7, 9, 24

Japanese influence Part II: 1, 5, 6; Part III:2

Town planning Part II: 2, 3, 4, 8, 9, 11, 18; Part III: 3

Community building Part II: 2, 4, 21, 22

Self-build Part II: 6, 7, 9, 21

Climate control Part II: 7, 8, 9, 10, 15, 19

After receiving his degree in Architecture from Turin Polytechnic in 1946, Paolo Soleri used a travel grant to go to the United States and join the Frank Lloyd Wright Taliesin Fellowship in Arizona. He was dismissed after an eighteen-month apprenticeship for daring to suggest that, instead of Wright, he should establish a branch of the Taliesin Fellowship in Italy. Soleri set off on his own in 1948; his first independent commission was a house in the desert for Eleonora Woods, at Cave Creek north of Phoenix. She selected Soleri because estimates she had received from Wright for the house were too high. His later projects, including the groundbreaking Cosanti, built on the utopian ideals of Wright's Taliesin colony. Like Wright he was interested in making the desert habitable, and saw these new communities as essential if the world was to deal with the population explosion. Unlike the biospheres that followed him, his emphasis was almost always on the low-tech.

After his early years in the United States, working for Wright, Soleri returned to Italy for a couple of years, in which time he designed and built a ceramics factory for the Sulimene family in Vieti sul Mare, and became proficient in ceramics techniques as a result. This modest commission was in a sense to influence the rest of his career, since most of his building projects have been funded by selling handmade ceramics. In 1951, returning to the United States, he established the Cosanti Foundation in Paradise Valley, Arizona. He began experimenting with what he calls 'earth-casting' techniques, which involve using mounded desert sand and soil as the framework for a layer of reinforced concrete, with the mound removed once the concrete has cured. He has used this technique successfully to build a large, sculpted vault at the centre of the five-acre complex. The organizational and physical similarities between the Cosanti Foundation and Wright's Taliesin West are striking. Both were founded on a utopian social structure, under one leader, with the expectation of free labour by resident apprentices, built from material found on site. The difference is Soleri's desire to use his community as a prototype for a sustainable city of the future, able to adapt to regional variations.

Mesa City Milestone

In 1959, Soleri consolidated several hypotheses about the increasingly urgent need to concentrate rapid population growth into ecologically harmonious earth-cast

Aerial view of Cosanti, 1951
The Scottsdale headquarters of the Cosanti Foundation has continued to grow from modest beginnings, a monument to the success of self-build.

megastructures to conserve precious arable land in an urban regional plan he called Mesa City. Intended as a prototypical city for two million people that could be located on any flat arid or semi-arid region, Mesa City predicts many of the components of the megacities or 'Arcologies' that Soleri designed later. These components, summarized by Soleri as density, self-sufficiency and three-dimensionality, appear in Mesa City as mixed-use, with natural energy generated by sun and wind, an agricultural region designated to supply the city with food, and the strategic positioning of industries to avoid polluting water supplies.

Cosanti II

In 1962, shortly after completing the Mesa City plan, Soleri implemented many of these ideas on a site north of the original Cosanti Foundation near Scottsdale, which he called Cosanti II. Rather than being dispersed, as Mesa City was, Cosanti II, later named Arcosanti, more closely approximates Soleri's principles of three-dimensionality, compactness or density, and self-sufficiency, with functions divided between a 'macrostructure' containing public assembly spaces and a 'microstructure' intended for living, studio and workshop spaces. The earth-cast shell, first attempted at Cosanti, is modified at Arcosanti into two enormous half domes or 'apses' which Soleri determined to be more suited to the hot-arid climate of this desert region.

The Omega Seed

By the time the second Cosanti had been built, Soleri had developed a complicated philosophical framework for his utopian planning projects, which he calls the 'Omega Seed Hypothesis.' His theory is divided into a 'metaphysical' component and a physical

Mesa City design, 1959
Soleri envisioned entire cities being built on the most inhospitable parts of the earth's surface, saving valuable farmland for food production.

counterpart. The metaphysical part is based on an evolutionary view of the progressive dematerialization of the universe that he describes as having begun with the Big Bang and is now moving through the phase of a delicately balanced biosphere toward the spiritual state of the ionosphere. The physical component of this metaphysical evolution is characterized by Soleri as progressing from the 'mineral reality to the living reality to the compassionate reality of the Omega Seed.'[1] Soleri believes the final stage in this conjectural process is a mental, rather than physical, reality in which 'mass energy and space time' will be replaced by 'the mind.'[2] He calls this final stage the Omega Seed since he sees it as the beginning rather than the end, a view shared by many advocates of artificial intelligence who believe that electronic technology will make it possible to achieve a supernatural state.

The MCD Paradigm

Soleri believes that the physical component of the metaphysical evolution he envisions operates on the principle of incremental sophistication and richness through a process of increasing miniaturization, complexity and duration. This is what he refers to as the MCD Paradigm and the 'urbanization of matter.' Arcology, the combination of architecture and ecology, is the tangible representation of this paradigm, his attempt to participate in the evolutionary process he has diagrammed. Arcology presents the city as a human ecosystem, which saves valuable land by having a compressed footprint, reinforces the human need for a sense of place and community, and reduces pollution by discouraging traffic and the infrastructure needed to support it.

'In nature,' Soleri observes, 'an organism increases in complexity as it evolves and it also becomes a more compact or miniaturized system. The city, too, is an organism, one that should be as alive and functional as any living creature. It must follow the same process of miniaturization and complexification to become a lively container for the social, cultural and spiritual evolution of human kind'[3]

Five Phases

After the founding of Cosanti in 1951 and the construction of Cosanti II ('Arcosanti'), in 1965, there have been three more experiments intended to test the fundamental principle of Soleri's theory. A third design, called Critical Mass, began in 1971, was built to refine the apse form as well as to test horticultural techniques, the use of internal greenhouses, solar chimneys and heat sink effects. In fine-tuning the apse form, Soleri found that the sectioned dome proved to be an ideal way to capture the shallow angle of solar radiation during the winter while protecting the interior from sun during the summer, if oriented due south. Horticultural techniques involve an overall strategy for a self-sufficient food supply, using planted terraces inside the apses in combinations with agricultural fields around the periphery of the city. The terraces are planted with fruit trees, irrigated by a misting system that provides residents with a cooling shield of atomized water that reduces desert temperatures by as much as 17°C (30°F). The greenhouses are separate structures which support solar collectors that generate electricity and augment the fruit grown on the terraces with vegetable production. Solar chimneys capture the warm air rising up through these stacked glass enclosures, using it to provide heat during the winter. The thermal mass of the apses absorbs the heat during the summer, releasing it slowly at night, which can be very cold in the desert, and provides warmth during the winter.

Valetta Spring

The fourth stage of Soleri's Arcology prototype, built between 1980 and 1985, was an attempt to improve the economic base of the desert community. A two-part complex called Valetta Spring, connected by greenhouses, contains housing for two hundred people, above an open-air market and performing arts centre, as well as an educational complex that includes a School of Architecture, Urbanism and Ecological Design, a School of Theology and Religious Studies and a School of Agriculture and Forestry.

In the Valetta Spring complex, Soleri continued to fine-tune the apse form by truncating it and juxtaposing it with another apse to create what he refers to as a 'double exedra'. This form has now been combined with 'garment architecture' of transparent shading screens that control air circulation and provide moisture retention inside the exedra.

In 1991 the fifth and final generation of Arcology evolution began with the addition of three ten-storey double exedras on a flat plateau behind the original complex, intended to bring the total population of Arcosanti to six thousand. Progress has been slow because finances are restricted to revenue from the sale of ceramics as well as from construction services, silt-casting workshops, lodging facilities, student fees and donations from visitors. In its final form, Arcosanti will occupy about 20 acres of the 4,000-acre site on which the project is located. The surrounding land is used for food production and as a nature preserve. Arcosanti, which was originally conceived as a compact self-sustaining city or 'urban implosion' that is a polemic against urban sprawl, is automobile free and residents have easy access to work, parks, educational and cultural events as well as public and private greenhouses. It is an ongoing social experiment, just as Taliesin West was. Like Wright, Soleri

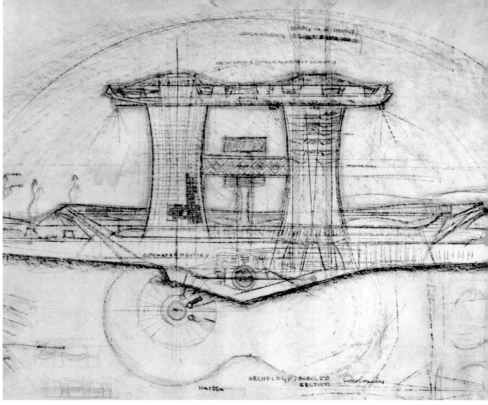

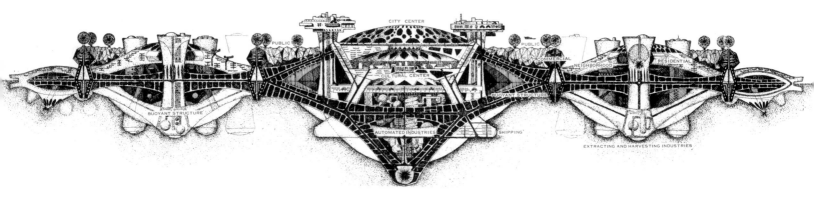

The labels within the image read: CITY CENTER · PUBLIC · PUBLIC · COMMERCIAL · NEIGHBORHOOD · RESIDENTIAL · CULTURAL CENTER · BUOYANT STRUCTURE · BUOYANT STRUCTURE · AUTOMATED INDUSTRIES · SHIPPING · EXTRACTING AND HARVESTING INDUSTRIES

also relies heavily on human resources: disciples help plan, construct and maintain Arcosanti, as well as providing teaching, cooking, farming, gardening and communications assistance.

Cities in Marginal Zones

To save as much arable land as possible for future use, in anticipation of a rapidly growing worldwide population, Soleri has deliberately modelled his Arcologies to work in marginal environments. Arcosanti tests the possibility of living in the desert, but other designs adapt to mountain, tundra, and arctic regions, as well as to oceans and space, ranging from twenty to 150 storeys high, accommodating between 160 and 600 residents per acre. These alternative Arcologies are aptly named: a floating city series called Novanoah, in which energy is generated by the hydraulic action of the ocean; a tower, called Babel, which can be located on uneven terrain anywhere on earth; and a crystalline city called Hexahedron.

Each of these has structures which adapt to their unique contexts. Soleri remains in the forefront of those preparing doomsday scenarios for the hypothetical time in which the population of the earth has taken over all of the conventionally habitable places. He also stands in stark contrast to other megastructuralists in wanting to coexist with those contexts, rather than being isolated in huge, hermetically sealed containers. In the late 1950s and early 1960s,when his ideas first came to public attention, alternative megastructures proposed by architects such as Buckminster Fuller were generally speculative, but during the course of his long career, the alternative, hermetic proposals have become much more sophisticated, to cope with the projected growth of the earth's population to nine billion in 2050.

Biosphere

In 1990, for example, Texas oil tycoon Edward P. Bass built a self-sustaining, artificial ecosystem in the Arizona desert, called Biosphere II. Bass wanted this experiment, simplistically modelled on the life systems of 'Biosphere I,' the earth, to be a 'cyclotron for the life sciences' a hermetically sealed closed-loop mesocosm, producing all of the elements necessary for human survival inside a glass shell. The main structure of Biosphere II is a universal node system (UNS) space frame, chosen because of its low cost, ease of construction, low toxicity and trouble-free maintenance. Basically a 12,000 square metre(130,000 square foot) greenhouse, with a 7.5-metre (twenty-five-foot) deep stainless steel tray foundation to prevent the intrusion of outside air, Biosphere II was designed to include seven 'Biomes' that replicate the most prevalent ecosystems on earth. The plants and water in these biomes were intended to produce oxygen levels high enough to support human life inside the five-story high structure indefinitely.

Novanoah proposal, 1960s
Among the habitats Soleri designed for is the ocean, which he envisioned as providing the energy for this floating city through hydraulic power.

After three years, however, the eight 'bionauts' chosen to live inside the sealed glass ark discovered that oxygen levels dropped precipitously, forcing the experiment to be abandoned. At first, unseasonably cloudy weather and a lack of photosynthesis seemed to be the reason for the sudden oxygen decrease. But subsequent studies have determined that concrete flooring caused the drop. Cores taken inside the Biosphere, at various points across the ten thousand square yards of concrete floor, revealed ten times more calcium carbonate than cores taken outside the structure, up to two centimetres deep in the interior cores after the first two years of habitation. Carbon dioxide, needed to sustain plant life, was being drawn into the concrete due to the chemical reaction between the calcium hydroxide and calcium carbonate.[4]

Eden

Since Biosphere, advocates for the insular alternatives to Soleri's contextual Arcologies have become much more daring, as demonstrated by the biomes of the Eden Project, designed by Nicholas Grimshaw to occupy an abandoned tin mine in Cornwall. Described in detail on pp. 132–3, these biomes break down the various ecosystems that were internally segmented in Biosphere II in Arizona into separate components, appropriately scaled to accommodate the vegetation in each; in addition, Grimshaw is less concerned with total separation from the outside environment than was Bass. This difference is significant, since during the decade that divides the two projects a certain amount of resignation has set in over the question of atmospheric degradation, as seen in the difference between the Kyoto and New Delhi declarations on global warming. While the Kyoto Accords recommended strict limits on greenhouse gases and carbon dioxide emissions, the proposals put forward in New Delhi in 2002 were more lax, reflecting naive confidence that technological solutions can be found to offset inevitable climatic change in the future.

Since the Eden Project, Biospheres have proliferated, with an increasingly pedagogical agenda replacing the earlier emphasis on sheer survival. The Cornwall biomes have proved enormously popular with the public that they were intended to instruct, but the Biosphere and Flower Pavilion in Postdam, by Berlin-based architects Barkow Leibinger, built for the German Horticultural Show in 2001 drew two and half million visitors during the exhibition, before it was turned into a permanent research facility for the study of rare plants.

Low-Tech Cities for the Future

After sixty years of literally struggling in the wilderness to find an ecologically sound solution to the problem of rapidly shrinking human habitat, Soleri seems to be less successful at gaining public support for his ideas that those who are building Biospheres, perhaps because the technological imperative is more persuasive than the low-tech direction he has consistently taken. His clear-headed insistence on exploring the possibility of building cities in those parts of the earth that have typically been considered to be uninhabitable, out of local materials if possible, has placed him in a category by himself. He may most usefully be compared to Buckminster Fuller, since Soleri has persistently insisted that appropriate technology, rather than the complex kind that Fuller used, offers the best hope for our collective survival.

Expo '67 Dome, Montreal, 1967

The geodesic dome is, without doubt, Buckminster
Fuller's trademark. Born out of his attempts to create
lightweight, transportable, cheap and efficient
structures, it also came to inspire a generation of
'biospheres'.

13

Buckminster Fuller:
The Dymaxion World

Fuller dedicated his life to efficient, low-cost, low-energy housing, looking to science and geometry for answers

Biography

The paragon of the can-do, Yankee inventor, Richard Buckminster Fuller was born in Milton, Massachusetts on 1 July, 1895 to a wealthy, well-respected New England family, which had produced a number of ministers, military officers and lawyers. Following family tradition he entered Harvard University in 1913, but did not do well: considered a non-conformist, he was dismissed in his first term after failing to turn up for exams. Enlisting in the Navy, however, he was able to develop his innate and considerable engineering skills, and soon set up the first of many, largely failed, ventures to develop low-cost, mass-produced, housing.

Among his best-known projects are the Dymaxion House, and, of course, the later geodesic domes. Throughout his career his works characteristically emphasize efficiency, and use unusual materials, often aluminium.

His career highlight, as Fuller saw it, was the dome raised at Expo '67 in Canada, the largest of his geodesic domes, and a clear statement of his faith in geometrical units. However, he planned even larger projects, including a dome that would cover Manhattan, a forerunner of the later biospheres. While, as with so many of his projects, the plans came to nothing, his legacy is still felt today.

Many of the architects discussed in this book shaped their philosophies at a young age, and this was certainly true of Buckminster Fuller. After a failed first attempt at university, his family sent him to apprentice as a mechanic, repairing the looms in a cotton mill in Sherbrooke, Quebec, which he later described as one of the happiest times of his life, 'a self-tutored course of engineering exploration'.[1] He revelled in manual labour, the task of assembling imported looms and the chance to invent ways to replicate or repair broken parts, and learning new skills from experienced machinists.

He re-entered Harvard, but was dismissed again and decided to enlist in the army. He was rejected at first because of his poor eyesight, but applied again in 1916, and because of apprehension about German invasion, he was accepted by the United States Navy and began his active service on a ship patrolling the coast of Maine. A year later, he married Anne Hewlett, daughter of the well-known local architect James Monroe Hewlett. While serving in the Navy, Fuller invented a mast, boom and grappling system that used pulleys to lift planes that had crashed in the ocean, keeping them out of the water long enough for pilots to be rescued before they drowned. He was granted admission into the United States Naval Academy at Annapolis for this service, and did much better there than he had at Harvard,

Key Projects

Expo '67 Dome, Montreal, 1967
Dymaxion House, 1928 (first built 1945)

Signposts

Energy efficiency Part II: 1, 11, 16, 19
Biospheres Part II: 11

because he saw practical applications for his efforts. He was promoted to lieutenant, and helped conduct experiments on radiotelephones for use on ships at sea.

After the armistice, Fuller left the Navy, and after several short-term jobs, started a company called Stockade Building Systems with his father-in-law Hewlett, inventing a number of lightweight construction components. In spite of having over two hundred houses built using their construction materials and methods, the partners were forced to sell the company in 1927, due to financial problems. Such problems followed Fuller throughout his career: he was much more interested in invention than wealth.

Mass Housing in a Can

His experience with the Stockade Building company, however brief, convinced Fuller that the stick-and-nail, custom-made, platform or balloon-frame houses that were then (and still remain) the norm in North America, and are based on archaic, wasteful and expensive practices unchanged since Colonial times, deprived the economically disadvantaged of shelter. It was while he was involved with this company, he said, that 'I really learned the building business. And the experience made me realize that craft model building, in which each house is a pilot model for design which never has re-runs, is an art which belongs in the Middle Ages'. Moreover, he determined that he would approach this anachronism from a global, rather than just a national, perspective consistent with the wider viewpoint he had taken as early as grade school. With missionary zeal, he set out to discover latent technologies that would revolutionize the building industry at a critical time when there was a shortage of housing to meet the demands of those returning from the war. He declared that he would find a way to 'make the world work', through 'spontaneous cooperation, without ecological offence or causing disadvantage to anyone.' During his time in the Navy, he had been impressed by the efficiency of lightweight aluminium aircraft, and the mass movement of troops and cargo over great distances in relatively short periods of time that they facilitated. He decided to apply the advantages of this new material to the global housing crisis, to invent a housing system that could be mass produced and delivered anywhere in the world by air. Since aluminium was so expensive to manufacture, it was also necessary to use a minimum amount of material to contain a maximum amount of space.

The Dymaxion House

Fuller had sketched out a circular metal house in 1928, but refined the concept with the intention of mass-producing what he called the Dymaxion House at an aircraft factory in Wichita, Kansas, in 1945. It was based on the idea of a bicycle wheel, held up by a prefabricated central mast from which wire cables were suspended that support the exterior walls and floor of the structure, and were anchored to the ground. The interior space was completely flexible, with movable screens that could be adjusted to change room sizes.

The Dymaxion was far ahead of its time in ecological terms as well, and had many features that would only enter the environmentalist lexicon more than two decades later. In spite of the fact that it can now be criticized as having an aluminium shell made from a non-renewable resource that requires an enormous amount of embodied energy to manufacture, the main advantage of this model from an environmental point of view is that the Dymaxion was intended to be mass produced and erected by ten labourers in only two days using a crane, allowing an impressive saving of human resources.

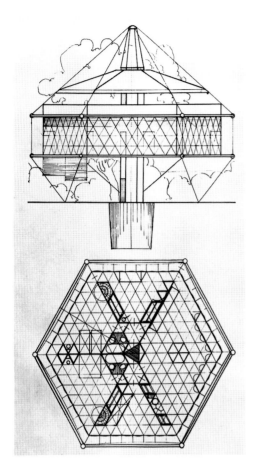

top **Initial Dymaxion House drawing**, 1928

above **The Dymaxion House as produced**, 1945

Buckminster Fuller was long fascinated by new materials and the possibilities they offered for producing low-cost housing. While the aluminium shell would be frowned upon today by environmentalists, the Dymaxion House required very little energy to assemble, recycled its water, and had good heat conservation and natural ventilation.

Even though the 11-metre (36-foot) diameter house contained 92 square metres (1,000 square feet) of floor space, its light aluminium shell kept its weight under three tons. Fuller planned to ship its three thousand main components to buyers in a steel cylinder. It was also relatively self-contained, requiring only a small amount of piped-in water and gas to operate. It used an atomizing filter that was able to sterilize and re-circulate up to a quart of grey water every ten minutes. The aerodynamic shape of the house and its circular, deep plan was specifically intended to prevent heat loss in winter. Cool air, produced by a rooftop ventilator that was one half the diameter of the house, circulated throughout the flexible, open interior spaces in summer, and the curved aluminium panels were designed to slide open to allow cross ventilation. It also stood a greater chance of surviving the tornadoes that regularly roar through the Midwest, where the houses were to be produced, since it had no corners for the wind to catch.

Ahead of Its Time

Like the pioneering Case Study House architects behind what Reyner Banham referred to as the 'style that nearly' in the post-war Los Angeles, Fuller was promoting mass-produced, metal housing at the wrong time in the wrong place. He formed a company, Fuller Houses Inc., operating out of the Beach Aircraft factory in Wichita, and built two prototypes. One was erected outside the factory for field-testing and another, built inside, was furnished for marketing. Although public interest was strong and the media gave the Dymaxion favourable coverage, substantial changes would have been necessary to meet Fuller's goal of producing the house for 25 cents a pound, about the same price as a luxury automobile at the time. When engineers at Fuller Houses Inc. suggested that the aluminium panels be replaced with Fiberglas and most of the movable parts be scrapped to cut costs, Fuller gave up, defeated by finances once again. Beach Aircraft still believed in the prototype and tried to continue, but could not raise the $10 million they estimated was necessary for full production.

The Dymaxion Deployment Unit

Undaunted, Fuller teamed up with Phelps-Dodge Corporation, working with ship architect W. Starling Burgess and several engineers at Rolls-Royce to turn the technology developed in the assembly of the Dymaxion House toward the production of an automobile. He considered the conventional combustion engine and axle, transmission and four wheels system to be as anachronistic as custom house building in wood and proposed a car with three wheels which could turn independently, allowing it to travel sideways and to complete a 360-degree turn. The rear wheel also acted as a rudder, and its streamlined watertight body enabled it to float, like a ship. A prototype was built that was nearly 6 metres (20 feet) long, held a driver and ten passengers, had a 90 horsepower engine and travelled at up to 120 miles an hour. Cost overruns as well as the bad publicity Fuller received after being involved in an accident in New York City sealed the fate of the Dymaxion car, but his design for emergency housing, called the Dymaxion Deployment Unit was more successful because it was adopted by the United States Department of Defense. The circular unit was inspired by metal grain silos Fuller had seen throughout the American Midwest, its form made the shell self-supporting without any additional structure. As with the Dymaxion House, the Deployment Unit was designed to be transported easily in a kit, and erected quickly. These qualities made it an ideal for military use and it has remained in service since the Second World War.

Energetic Synergetic Geometry

Throughout his life, Fuller had been fascinated by natural geometries, especially those of crystals. He was convinced that the engineering breakthroughs of the future would not be achieved through adaptations of new materials, as was the case after the Industrial Revolution, but through the translation and magnification of the geometric building blocks of nature. He believed that engineers should not make structures out of materials, but should make larger structures out of smaller structures, that is, that they should adapt the foundation geometries of life. He believed these geometries had the potential to allow him to realize his life-long dream of being able to create a new order of structures that would be much more efficient, enclosing the maximum amount of space, using a minimum amount of material. Rather than using conventional bearing-wall or column, beam and girder frame systems as supports, he developed what he called an 'Energetic Synergetic Geometry'. It was based on crystal formations, in which the surface of the structure itself provided support, leaving the interior open and free. By using tetrahedrons, octagons and hexagons broken down into triangular segments, Fuller was able to realize the structural efficiencies he wanted. In 1953, he tested his idea for a 'geodesic' system made up of one hundred and seventy struts weighing a total of sixty-five pounds (30 kilos), and found it could support a compressive load of six tons. He tried the same geometry in different materials and found the stability to be equally impressive. In 1954 he built a Fiberglas dome that was 16.7 metres (55 feet) in diameter and 12.1 metres (40 feet) tall, and which could withstand extremely high wind loads.

First Kabul and then the World

Seeing the public relations potential in his invention as the perfect symbol of progressive, national scientific advancement, the United States Department of Commerce chose the geodesic dome for its pavilion at the International Trade Fair in Kabul, Afghanistan in 1956, advertising the structure as the product of 'American ingenuity, vision and technological dynamism' on the doorstep of its arch Cold War enemy. Advertisements also touted its efficiency of production and construction: that it could be built in two days from a kit of parts that only took one month to manufacture. This firmly placed the geodesic dome within the Pantheon of high-technology engineering marvels, along with Paxton's Crystal Palace of 1851, and the Pompidou Centre by Piano and Rogers, which were also erected in record time. Proving its versatility and mobility, the same dome was rebuilt in Tokyo, by Shoji Sadao, in May 1957, initiating a number of subsequent dome designs that led to the United States Pavilion for the World's Fair in Montreal, Canada in 1967 (see p. 142). This dome, which Fuller viewed as vindication for the failures that had preceded it and his highest achievement, was 76 metres (250 feet) in diameter, built in a double-layered system of steel rods, configured in a hexagonal pattern on the inside and in triangles on the outer shell. The outer layer was inset with transparent acrylic panels equipped with computerized sunshades that adjusted to allow a specific amount of light to enter the interior space at different times of day, for precise climate control.

A Self-Contained Urban Ark, A Technological Victory

Since this image coincided with several highly publicized ecological disasters, which fuelled a radicalized no-growth movement and the proclamation of the first Earth Day in the United States three years later, Fuller became the focal point of a mania for megastructures, seen by

Harlem Redevelopment Plan, 1964

Fuller's later fantasies show the same concern for high-density housing as many of Soleri's projects, but his main concern was prosaic enough: to alleviate substandard housing. Unlike Soleri, his answer was quarantine.

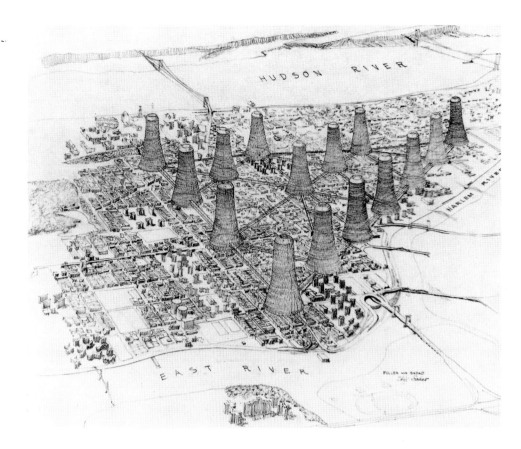

some as the Ark that would save the human race from a climatic Armageddon. The Expo '67 dome is an important milestone for those who support the position that technology alone can counteract environmental degradation, with self-contained climate-controlled megastructures being the final refuge on a dying planet. It is the progenitor of a growing family of 'Biospheres', of which Biosphere II, funded by billionaire Edward P. Bass in the American Southwest, and the Eden Project in Cornwall, are more sophisticated examples. But Fuller's agenda differed from these later permutations in a significant way. He saw the future as being inexorably urban. He outlined this idea most eloquently when he attended the City of the Future conference on Delos organized by Ekistics founder Constantinos Doxiadis, in July, 1963, four years before the Expo '67 dome appeared. It was intended to be the prototype for a new city, or city within a city.

He went on to develop this idea in actual models, such as the Tetrahedronal City, near Tokyo, which also included more conventional configurations. His unforgettable images of a Two Mile Diameter Dome for New York City and fifteen turbine-like towers he proposed for Harlem intended to alleviate substandard housing conditions there, remain as a haunting vision of a final refuge, inside a technological cocoon, from an increasingly hostile environment, poisoned by human disregard. He shared Paolo Soleri's fear of the population pressures of the future, but he believed that this pressure could be overcome by placing people in technologically refined, hermetically sealed, megacities.

Roden Crater, James Turrell, 1972–
On his frequent flights over the Arizona desert, artist
James Turrell noticed an extinct volcano that he
eventually made a test case for his ideas about light and
underground architecture.

14

Malcolm Wells and James Turrell: The March Underground

The 1970s saw a growth in interest in underground building as an energy-efficient form of construction, but many obstacles had to be overcome

Biography

Malcolm Wells

Wells is one of the original pioneers of underground – or as he calls it, 'earth-sheltered' – building. Initially he found it very hard to get commissions, but the oil shocks of 1973 and 1976 awakened public interest in self-sufficiency, and in 1975 Wells was commissioned to build a government office complex in Moorestown, N.J., which led to other projects. Like many of the architects discussed in this book, he is an active champion of environmental issues, spreading the word whenever he can, and to this end he has published widely on living underground, the books illustrated with his distinctive annotated drawings. However, by the early 1990s the tide had again turned, as oil crises became distant memories, and underground building ground to a halt. He still lives and writes in the US.

James Turrell

Turrell came to prominence as part of a group of artists in the 1960s producing Land Art. His largest, and most prolonged, work has been Roden Crater, an underground series of tunnels with special alignments. While not strictly architecture, this sort of project has captured the public's imagination, and popularized underground building.

Key Projects

Malcolm Wells

Architect's Office, Cherry Hill, 1974

City Hall, Moorestown, 1975

Locust Hill, Ohio, 1989–

James Turrell

Roden Crater, Arizona Desert, 1972–

Signposts

Solar energy Part II: 5, 11, 15

Underground construction Part II: 25; Part III: 1

Material recycling Part II: 23

One of the most obvious, but least pursued, options open to architects trying to find energy-conscious solutions to the energy crises of the mid-1970s was to investigate underground structures. The advantages that this option offered were numerous, the most important one being the stabilization that occurs at more than one metre below grade, when temperatures level off at around 18°C (mid-60s°F). The second advantage is that the land that would normally be covered by building is freed up, to be left in its natural state or planted. As global warming, caused by carbon dioxide emissions and the re-radiation of solar heat from paved surfaces, increases, and the earth's population continues to grow exponentially, this advantage becomes more and more attractive and will take on greater urgency, as time goes on. But the disadvantages of building underground were equally striking: no-one was sure how to do it well enough to prevent moisture penetration, infestation by insects or vermin, or more prosaically, complete collapse due to the excessive weight of wet earth. In America, where tax incentives were being offered by the government to encourage architects to implement energy-conscious solutions, an increasingly litigious society left little room for experimentation. Finally, there was the secret fear among architects that building underground would involve a loss of identity, that building a non-building, or at least one that could not be easily photographed would not contribute to reputation or fame.

However, in the early 1970s several brave souls, mostly in temperate countries, weighed the benefits and took the risk, believing that future demands would make it necessary to build underground and that the initial steps had to be taken soon. In America, Malcolm Wells was in the forefront, concentrating on proselytizing rather than doing a one-off demonstration project to be published in the alternative culture press. He focused on reaching as many people as possible, by writing as well as building. In his writing, he aimed for a popular market, producing books himself, usually in his own distinctive, handwritten script. From the mid-1970s through to the 1990s, he wrote fifteen tracts, including one children's book, extolling the virtues of going underground, most of them during the flurry of interest in natural systems that followed the oil shocks of 1973 and 1976.

Sounding (and looking) like a lone prophet in the wilderness, Wells found it difficult to get commissions, in spite of his public relations blitz, mostly due to public fear of the architectural unknown; and so he began experimenting on himself. In 1974 he built his own office in Cherry Hill, N.J., using all of the tactics expected of those promoting a self-sustaining lifestyle: passive solar orientation and exposure, active solar panels, vegetable garden, dry plumbing and high thermal mass. But few people beat a path to his partially buried door.

Sketch for Locust Hill project, Malcolm Wells, 1989– This large house-office complex is still under construction in Ohio, where a group of ten people bought over 1,000 acres of mature forest land to preserve it. The land supports organic farming, and the complex is powered by windmills and photovoltaic arrays.

LOCUST HILL FROM THE SOUTHWEST
MALCOLM WELLS, ARCHITECT 8/89

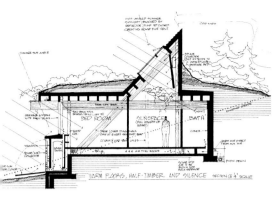

Cross-section of an earth-covered house,
Malcolm Wells
One of Wells's typically didactic drawings. These aim at explaining rather than baffling, though his lighthearted approach has not always been fashionable. He later abandoned timber construction (seen here) in favour of concrete, which is less prone to rot.

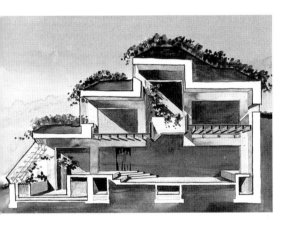

Cross-section of Locust Hill, Malcolm Wells, 1989–
This cross-section shows just how deeply earth-covered – and thus insulated – this project is.

Public Clients

In 1975, however, government officials of the Moorestown, N.J., Municipality approached him to build their administrative complex – the equivalent, in underground architecture, to the De Montfort University breakthrough in naturally ventilated design in Leicester, England, described on pp. 161–3. This was followed, one year later, by the Plant Science Building at the Cary Arboretum of the New York Botanical Garden; Locust Hill, a multi-family complex in Beausville, Ohio; a factory for Construction Fasteners, Inc., in Reading (Penn.), in 1979; and a large underground art gallery in Brewster (Mass.), in 1987. Then, in spite of requests for consultations on several private homes, his lone revolution ended. While Wells was perfecting his earthly art, many bottle and bale enthusiasts built really ugly underground homes for themselves, which got more exposure in the populist press than his public buildings did, creating a negative impression that, in addition to all of the disadvantages mentioned earlier, scared many architects and potential clients away. And, as the trend toward ever more massive single-family homes and vehicles in the run up to the millennium showed, energy consciousness dropped off considerably once fossil fuel prices levelled off and the oil embargo became a reasonably distant memory. Business as usual meant building as usual as one quarter of the world's population got back to the habit of using three quarters of its resources.

Being Perfectly Clear

In a long article in a professional publication in 1991, entitled 'Being Perfectly Clear', Wells vented his frustration at public wastefulness and apathy and admitted that after more than twenty years of trying, 'underground architecture is still virtually unknown'. But, he countered, his basic premise remained unchanged: that 'the surface of the earth is meant for plants and animals, not for naked buildings, shopping centres, roads and parking lots'. Remaining adamant, he then predicted that 'we are moving into Energy Crisis II' in an ongoing environmental disaster that will finally work its way into our consciousness. For those who criticized his projects for being too expensive, he responded: 'The cost of environmental destruction is much higher. In the buildings I've built, construction has been virtually trouble free, and my God, the benefits: living wild gardens instead of asphalt overhead, rain water considerations, silence, sunlight, low fuel bills, little maintenance, slow temperature changes, freedom from vibrations, clean air; and perhaps best of all, the feeling of having done something right for the planet. There is a sense of mission, by moving up as you go down, to the next stage of life on earth'.

Land Art as Public Policy

Wells, in his search for elusive details, such as the knife-edge lip that would blur the line between earth and architecture as a final sign of respect, was perfecting an art form, but as his published appeal made clear, he had failed to sufficiently penetrate an increasingly distracted public consciousness. The Land Art movement, which began at the same time that Wells was designing his first underground project, may eventually succeed in achieving that. In 1969 Michael Heizer gouged a pair of slashes in a canyon wall in Nevada, each about 460 metres (1,500 feet) long, called *Double Negative*, beginning a long series of such temporal and memorable statements about human interaction with the earth. This was followed by Robert Smithson's *Spiral Jetty* in Utah in 1970, Walter De Maria's *The Lightning Field* in New Mexico in 1977, and James Turrell's epic *Roden Crater* on the Colorado Plateau in Arizona.

Proposed sewage treatment plant, Malcolm Wells
This chemical-free, solar-powered and non-polluting sewage treatment plant is based on John Todd's 'Living Machines' designs. The glass domes are reminiscent of Fuller.

Roden Crater

Of these, Turrell's twenty-million dollar excavation of an extinct volcano may finally convince a reluctant and distracted public that going underground need not be depressing and can be aesthetically exhilarating. As a child, Turrell became fascinated by light, poking holes in curtains so he could see constellations of his own making during the day. In the 1960s, he joined a group of artists working in Venice, California, that included Richard Diebenkorn, Robert Irwin, Larry Bell, Bruce Newman, Peter Alexander, Billy Al Bengston and Ed Moses, the so-called 'Light and Space' group that are now a local legend. They were drawn to the exceptional light in Los Angeles, especially close to the Pacific Coast and produced work related to the effects of light on various materials. They became minimalists dedicated to form, defined by light.

Turrell became involved in making *Ganzfelds* (total fields) in which all the usual visual and aural clues to space determination are eliminated, in indeterminate light. He also began flying and in one of his runs over the Arizona desert, at the edge of the San Francisco Peaks volcanic field, he found a 180-metre (600-foot) high red cinder cone at an elevation of 1,500 metres (5,000 feet) called Roden Crater. Using funding that he received from several foundations, he bought the crater, and over twenty-five years began excavating what he called 'a cathedral to the heavens and light'. He became a cattle rancher, using the land around the crater to stay close to it while he worked on the project, which in many ways recalls prehistoric preoccupations with seasonal changes and the channelling of natural light into predetermined directions.

Comic Inspirator

Turrell's choice of precedents in planning his underground universe is revealing. One space was inspired by the Great Temple of Rameses II at Abu Simbel near Luxor, in which the sun

Roden Crater, James Turrell, 1972–
Having moved from large-scale land art projects, Turrell now builds 'light spaces' for eager clients throughout Southern California.

shines on his statue, through a tunnel carved into the cliff wall, on the summer and winter solstice. In Roden Crater, the light of the moon is directed through the oculus, and down a 260-metre (854-foot) long tunnel every 16.8 years, to be directed onto a 4.8-metre (16-foot) tall monolith. Once a year the sun passes through a hole in this same room to light the other side of the stone in the 'Sun and Moon Space'. In all, Turrell removed 920,000 cubic metres (1.2 million cubic yards) of earth to create the tunnel, which gently rises from one side of the crater toward the central circle of light at the crater oculus. The approach goes through a keyhole-shaped doorway, reminiscent of an ancient ruin. The 'Sun and Moon Space' is only one of what Turrell calls 'ambient' spaces inside the crater, which elevated the argument for building underground to a new level.

Moving Toward the Mainstream

Despite Malcolm Wells' disappointment that more underground architecture has not been built as a result of his proselytizing, there are signs that both he and James Turrell have succeeded in making it more acceptable. Gunnar Birkert's University of Michigan Library indicates institutional acceptance of this approach, which accounts for a substantial savings on energy costs during the cold winters there, and Hans Hollein has shown increasing enthusiasm for underground solutions, in his unbuilt Guggenheim Museum in Salzburg, and the Museum of Vulcanology in the Auvergne region of France. Such growing acceptance bodes well for an ancient building technique found as far afield as Northern China and Mali in the past, where traditional societies found it to be a highly effective way of levelling out extreme environment, and Malcolm Wells's prophecies may eventually become an accepted part of the lexicon of environmental architecture after all.

Rio Grande Botanic Garden Conservatory,

Albuquerque, 1995

The conservatory contains two temperate zones, desert
and Mediterranean, both of which need to be carefully
controlled: computer modelling was used to obtain the
correct balance of heat and light, and has ensured that
little or no outside energy is required to keep the
temperature a consistent 10–15°C (20–30°F) above
outdoor lows.

15

Edward Mazria:
The Solar Cult of the 1970s

Environmentally friendly legislation in the 1960s and 1970s favoured the use of solar power, but Mazria also understood the dramatic benefits of passive solar gain

Biography

The oil embargos enforced by the OPEC countries in 1973 and 1976 sent shockwaves through the industrialized nations that were heavily dependent on this scarce natural resource, particularly Japan and the United States. America responded by searching for ways to become more self-sufficient, with government tax incentives made available for energy conservation. The favoured form of alternative energy was solar power, primarily because it could be collected scientifically and used conventionally. However, architects such as Edward Mazria understood the true potential of solar energy lay in passive solar gain. His observations were fully laid out in *The Passive Solar Energy Book*, published in 1980, and were then tested in buildings such as the Stockebrand house, and a public library in Mt. Airy, N.C., which was sponsored by he US Department of Energy – the results showed that effective use of daylight and solar gain could drastically reduce the amount of energy needed to light and heat a building. In more recent years Mazria has concentrated on 'open' systems to achieve further improvements in energy efficiency.

Key Projects

Stockebrand Residence, Sandia Heights, 1980
Mt. Airy Public Library, North Carolina, 1984
Rio Grande Botanic Garden Conservatory, Albuquerque, 1995

Signposts

Solar energy Part II: 5, 11, 14
Climate control Part II: 7, 8, 9, 10, 12, 19
Sustainability Part II: 11, 17, 20, 21, 23

While environmental activism may seem to have appeared out of nowhere in 1970s America, the country in fact has a tradition of vocal opposition to the destruction of nature. John Bartram, who is considered the first American-born naturalist, campaigned for the protection of the Florida Everglades in 1767, writing eloquently about the need to save a vast wetland that eventually cost far more to fix then to destroy. About the same time, founding father and President Thomas Jefferson wrote in praise of 'agrarianism', that 'contract with the land is good for the spirit.'[1] President James Madison led a movement to establish the first Federal Forest Reserve in 1817, setting a precedent for what would become an extensive national park system that spread throughout all the states of the nation. The Transcendentalists, led by Ralph Waldo Emerson and Henry David Thoreau, provided the theoretical structure for the preservation of the wilderness in the mid-19th century, popularizing the idea of public land and the particularly American notion that areas of environmental significance or great scenic beauty should be set aside for the common good.[2] President Ulysses Grant signed the legislation that established Yellowstone National Park in 1872, followed by the formation of a Forest Service in 1891, and the National Parks Service in 1916. The Conservation Movement, which was at its height between 1890 and 1920, found its champion in President Theodore Roosevelt who fought hard to establish National Parks.

A Deluge of Environmental Legislation

The radical 1960s, however, definitely unleashed a flood-tide of environmentally related legislation in America, beginning with the Wilderness Act of 1964, the Land and Water Conservation Act of 1965 and the Wild and Scenic Rivers Act of 1968. The Clean Air, Clean Water, Resource Conservation and Recovery and Toxic Substances and Control Acts were all passed in the early 1970s, followed by the Forest Management and Federal Land Policy Management Acts of 1976.

This partial list of the most formidable environmental legislation of this halcyon period indicates the growing awareness of what have come to be called the 'four p's' of pollution, poisons, pesticides and population at that time, redirecting the attention of an entire generation of young people angered by social injustice, indeterminate wars and political corruption toward the much more comprehensible task of saving the earth.[3]

Sensing this substantial shift in public opinion, politicians who had been the main cause of such disillusionment, such as President Richard Nixon, fed this cycle by making environmentalism a central part of his agenda, identifying ecological destruction as a national crisis in his State of the Union message in 1970.[4] He also promoted the acceptance of a natural recognition of the importance of global environmental health by designating the first Earth Day to be held in June 1970. While it has since failed to achieve the exalted status enjoyed by Christmas, Thanksgiving, Mother's Day or Valentine's Day in America because it is not as easy to market, Earth Day began with great promise. Environmental superstars of the time, such as Ian McHarg and Barry Commoner gave public addresses and a whole generation of young people felt, for the first time, that there was some hope, as well as an alternative direction possible in architecture. By the early 1980s, the Environmental Protection Agency estimated that there were close to twelve thousand environmental groups of various sizes in the United States, with a combined membership of almost ten million people.[5]

The demographic of this rapidly growing segment of American society, however, was almost exclusively upper middle class: the growth/no-growth divide of the 1960s had been transformed into the haves and have-nots and the have-nots were beginning to feel excluded. The haves, it seems, were more interested in preserving the suburban enclaves they had struggled so hard to achieve and to prevent others from moving next door than they were in protecting the environment.

Caught by Surprise

This groundswell of interest in the environment, and the political support that both fed it and was fed by it, caught architects by surprise, but they were not long in realizing its potential. Only solar energy, however, was quantifiable enough for architects responding to the 1970s energy crisis to be comfortable using it. Natural ventilation has a distinguished historical lineage but had not been accommodated to the new, glass-enclosed building types introduced as a result of industrialization at the beginning of the 19th century. Geothermal power was costly and complicated to harness. Construction with or below the earth, which has the same endurance in vernacular architecture as natural ventilation, was also difficult to adapt to modern conditions and tastes. But solar energy had empirical potential: it could be measured, collected, converted, stored and transformed in technologically acceptable ways that were predictable enough for it to be classified as an active energy source. Despite its techno-friendly capacity, active solar power was not without its faults, including plumbing problems, cloudy

top and above **Stockebrand Residence,** 1980
Incentives offered in the late 1970s for energy efficiency led to a boom in interest. The Stockebrand Residence is exemplary not only in harnessing active and passive solar energy, but also in responding formally to the peaks of the surrounding mountains.

above, left and right **Mt. Airy Public Library**, 1984
Through thoughtful positioning of windows and lightshelves, this library uses around four-fifths less artificial lighting than an equivalent conventionally built commercial building. Moreover, its light and inviting interior has been tremendously popular with local users.

days, initial installation cost, maintenance and repairs, as well as the wide array required to produce minimal energy requirements. Despite all of these disadvantages, however, the tangible and fairly predictable characteristics of active solar power attracted many enthusiasts throughout the industrialized world. Partial use, for hot-water heating, became popular in the developing world as well.

A Passive Alternative

The lure that the plumbing and hardware of active systems had for some, as well as the science and pseudo-science supporting them, tended to obscure the fact that solar energy is a casual force like wind and water and that technology can be a barrier to the true integration between architecture and nature. *The Passive Solar Energy Book* by Edward Mazria which appeared in 1980, demystified the alternative to active systems, cataloguing techniques to be used in conjunction with, or exclusive to, them in such a way that even technophobes could understand them. The real possibility of using these techniques was verified by built examples from the architects' own work, especially the Stockebrand Residence in Albuquerque, New Mexico, which had subliminal as well as visceral appeal for a generation of architects who were eager to explore other possibilities. The subliminal pull of the house was its setting in the foothills of Sandia Mountains, which provided a rugged backdrop to the adobe-walled compound in all published photographs. It exemplified the American dream of a solitary, self-efficient outpost at the edge of the western frontier, the essential image of rugged, individualism which bubbles just below the surface of the national psyche. Unlike the sustainable initiative which was to begin soon afterward, the active solar movement and its passive supplement or alternative, which Mazria championed, targeted personal rather than the communal aspirations and needs: the possibility of off-the-grid independence rather than the 'think globally, act locally' mantra of intra-personal awareness that would emerge in the late 1980s. Architects fed these solo fantasies, and it took a concerted institutional campaign, led by the United Nations to shift the focus to a global, communal prospective.

Thomas Stockebrand, who commissioned this epitome of passive principles, was a director of engineering for Digital Computers in Albuquerque at the time the house was built and he designed and constructed active collectors to be used on it. This part of New Mexico has near-perfect conditions for both kinds of solar energy collection and was a thriving centre of research and experimentation. Local zoning codes in Sandia Heights prohibited the alteration of the natural contours or the appearance of the land, so Mazria shifted the plan footprint to conform to the topography, while taking advantage of the best views and solar angles, both toward the southwest. A 210 square metre (2,250 square foot) pool was used as the social centre of the house, which is quite unusual for this part of the United States. Rather than simply being a luxury, however, the pool is also a heat-storage medium and an uninsulated wall which separates it from the rest of the house serves as an internal radiator, with rigid waterproof insulation extending half a metre (two feet) below grade around the foundation wall to prevent any heat stored in it from being conducted to the outside. Sawtooth skylights are the major strategy for passive solar gain and were generally recommended and used by Mazria in this and subsequent projects, along with some south-facing windows to balance the daylighting, and light-coloured surfaces were used to offset heat gain and prevent overheating. Trombe walls, which he also included as a key component of an overall passive strategy, were not feasible at Sandia Heights because they would have blocked the view.

Architect and client both planned that the combination of active panels, passive collection through sawtooth monitors and additional windows, aquatic heat sink and masonry radiating wall and wood-burning stove, would reduce the remaining percentage of electricity needed for heating to a fraction of the conventional amount usually required in this region and they were right. The main problem, they were to find, was not underheating but overheating, especially in the summer months.

Soon after this residence was finished, Mazria was able further to test the ideas put forward in *The Passive Solar Energy Book* in a large public library in Mt. Airy, North Carolina, in completely different environmental conditions, on the opposite side of the country. Mazria/Schiff and Associates advised the library to take advantage of funds that the Department of Energy had made available in 1979, in response to the energy crisis, for public or private commercial projects in which solar principles were integrated into the design, with the stipulation that results be monitored and evaluated. As in the Stockebrand Residence, the plan was restricted to one level, not only because of topography but because that was the easiest way to collect and distribute sunlight to all the spaces. The basic challenge in a library is how to eliminate the ultra-violet rays and glaze that destroy books, so the sawtooth clearstories were angled, as always, so that higher summer sun was blocked and lower winter sun was captured. Lightshelves, on the south face of the library, located above recessed view windows which they shade, reflect sunlight deep into the interior, assisted by light coloured materials in these spaces.[6]

Surprising Results and Valuable Lessons

Subsequent evaluation, required by federal grant, proved that these tactics worked here as well: compared to a commercial building of equivalent size, which would typically use 105,000 Btu per square foot each year, the library only used 23,149 Btu per square foot – or about one fifth as much energy annually. The daylighting strategies used in the library were also dramatically effective, since it was found that it used 86 per cent less artificial light than a building of comparable size each year, which reduced energy costs substantially. The information provided by these experimental public and private projects as well as the wide distribution and popular acceptance of the publications that accompanied them, helped to bring passive solar strategies into the mainstream. Follow-up evaluation in each case showed that rather than providing enough heat, a major concern was overheating, opening up secondary studies on the materials and colour used in interiors to avoid heat build up. By using lighter masonry surfaces, the heat that each vertical and horizontal space receives can be more accurately calibrated, allowing balanced re-radiation into each space. Another surprising realization was the psychological role that light plays in an overall perception of warmth, making darker surfaces less functional for this reason as well.

Architecture as an Open System

By the late 1990s Mazria had formulated a theory for a new kind of environmentally responsive architecture, based on this empirical experience, which would operate as an open rather than an isolated system. In his view, most contemporary buildings, like machines, are provided with the energy they need to run, and do so according to the Second Law of Thermodynamics: they import energy, convert it to run equipment and lighting fixtures, and then dissipate that imported energy as waste heat. Without an uninterrupted supply of imported energy such isolated systems become uninhabitable, and are intentionally isolated against the environment for as long as possible to preserve artificial internal conditions. In contrast to this he has proposed an architectural approach which mimics nature more closely.

Living organisms, he contends, are open systems, maintaining a continuous flow and exchange of energy with their surrounding to survive, adapting to any environmental changes that take place. Unlike an isolated system, which will shut down if its source of imported energy is interrupted, or if one part of the system fails, a living organism will fluctuate, repair and renew itself to adapt to changes in its environment. Each element in an open system compensates for a change of capacity in one of its parts. Each open system is also distinct, with a boundary that filters the elements. It has a recognizable order of internal relationships. This order gives each system a unique form or pattern of relationship that makes it unique.

Technology is Necessary to Replicate Nature

This sensibility was not new, having also been the driving force behind the explorations of Buckminster Fuller, as well as the interest, among late modernists like Louis Kahn, in studies such as *On Growth and Form* by D'Arcy Thompson, who likened vernacular configurations to natural systems. What was new at this point in the late 1990s, was its persistence. But realizing the need to make architecture organically compatible and converting inert materials into environmentally responsive networks are entirely different things. Ironically, it would take a computer programmed with genetic algorithms as described in Part III here, finally to bring that elusive goal within reach.

left and above **School of Engineering, De Montfort University**, Leicester, Short and Associates, built 1991–3

The School of Engineering marks an important breakthrough in ecological design, proving that a large building could be ventilated without expensive air-conditioning. Its design combines elements of Neo-Gothic, High-Tech and local traditions, while the distinctive chimneys act as exhausts for stale air. Widely studied, it won the 1995 Green Building of the Year Award.

16

A Breath of Fresh Air

Natural ventilation is one of the key tenets of ecologically minded architecture, at once energy saving and healthy

Background

While techniques of natural ventilation have been used by many of the architects and designers in this book (for example, Le Corbusier or Jimmy Lim), the first large-scale application was at the School of Engineering at De Montfort University, Leicester, UK. This groundbreaking building dispenses entirely with air conditioning – which uses large amounts of energy and is in any case less healthy – in favour of an ingenious system of intakes and exhausts, ensuring circulation of fresh air. It was also discovered that the ability to control the environment, to open windows, or switch on heating, which has been lost in so much modern architecture, greatly influences the user's perception of the building's comfort.

It occasionally happens that a single architectural statement is so well timed that it comes to represent an entire era or movement: the Villa Savoye, Fallingwater, or the Barcelona Pavilion are all good examples. To this list can be added the Leicester Engineering Building by James Stirling, since it seemed to show, when it was built in the early 1960s, that modernism could have a new lease on life – and as such was one of the most important sources of the British High-Tech aesthetic. It is ironic then, that a milestone of ecological architecture should be built in the same city nearly thirty years later.

The Unlikely Symbol of a Quiet Revolution

In 1992 Leicester was designated as the United Kingdom's Environment City, and so when the leaders of De Montfort University came to build a new School of Engineering they wanted to depart from the conventional institutional approach to energy. In particular they were keen to use natural sources of heat, light and ventilation. The Vice Chancellor of the University had actually commissioned the design in 1988, and it was finalized following Government review in 1989, but official consensus could not be reached at that time. In addition to architects Alan Short, Brian Ford, Anne Goldrick and Peter Sharratt, an impressive list of advisors had been recruited to assist in the design process, including the Department of Architectural Research at Cambridge, the Environmental Computer Aided Design and Performance Group at De Montfort, Thomas Lawson from Bristol University, and Max Fordham Associates, who provided direction on everything from general ventilation and air-flow physics to advice on building services. What they were all proposing was nothing less than the construction of the

Key Project

School of Engineering, De Montfort University, Short and Associates, built 1991–3

Signposts

Arts and Crafts influences Part II: 1, 2, 3, 4, 5

Energy efficiency Part II: 1, 11, 13, 19

Natural ventilation Part II: 6, 7, 11, 20, 23, 24

largest naturally ventilated building in Europe at the time, using only minimal mechanical equipment for dampers and fans to induce stack effect as well as minimal heating by a two-pipe weather-compensated system – what the experts would refer to as 'top up and trimming'. This achievement is especially remarkable considering that the new building was sited in an area with a strong tradition of high technology and a very conservative approach to energy.

An Integral Approach

In spite of all the expert input, the initial concept proposed by the architects remained relatively unchanged throughout. They advocated an integrated approach to tempering the internal environment of the University that was new at the time. It linked site layout, built form, materials, services and controls, and the daily and seasonal patterns of occupants. In form, the building is a series of narrow, daylit, naturally ventilated volumes, carefully arranged to maximize orientation according to function, so that, whenever possible, rooms are lit from the side by shaded windows. When side-lighting is not possible, north lighting or top lighting is used. A north-east/south-west orientation of the entire complex was dictated by prevailing winds and a thin profile to encourage cross-ventilation.

Functional requirements – for example, that two separate auditoria be located centrally, amid the various laboratories strung out along them – caused complications which Short and Ford solved with a central linear 'concourse' that allows air to escape through the deepest mid-line of the plan. This is where the majority of the distinctive ventilation chimneys are located, since stack effect rather than normal air currents had to be the main cooling strategy in this part of the complex. The comfort levels required in the auditoria, where large groups remain for extended periods of time, made this section even trickier. Computer simulations indicated that the most important factor was the size and position of the chimney openings or 'extracts'. This analysis indicated, as the architects have described, that 'the opening had to be sized so that the boundary of the one-metre-thick layer of hot polluted air was below the top lip of the extract opening, but above head height on the top row of seats. The system comprises a fresh-air plenum serving grilles under the raked seats, the ventilated air being exhausted through a 13-metre (43-foot) high stack. In winter, finned tubes located behind the inlet grilles heat the fresh air. A carbon dioxide detector controlling automatic dampers in the stack is intended to prevent excess ventilation in winter. Temperature sensors will control the heating and override the carbon dioxide detector to open the dampers as space temperature rises'.

Other concerns, such as unexpected opposing eddy currents and backflow caused by external cooling of the chimney surface, also had to be accounted for. The general design goal throughout the complex was to maintain an internal mean temperature of 19°C (66°F), a minimum of 13°C (55°F), and a maximum of 25°C (77°F) and this has been maintained, with only rare extreme cases of 28°C (82°F) temperatures in summer, when school use is low.

An Internal Street

The school is organized along a 50-metre (165-foot) long, full-height internal street (inspired by the medieval scale of Trinity Lane in Cambridge), which gives access to all the teaching rooms of the University at the ground level. The engineering school is located on the upper level of this spine, with a glass-enclosed walkway at the first floor and bridges on the third floor linking each side of the concourse. A double-height general laboratory with a gallery providing access to offices is on the south side of the spine and two auditoria, with design

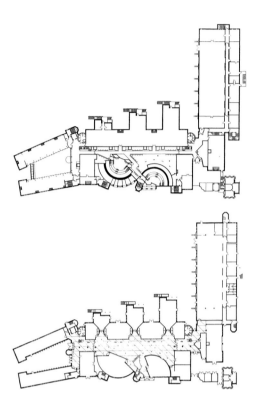

above, top and below **Ground and first floor plans of the School of Engineering**
opposite **Axonometric diagram of the School of Engineering**

We can clearly see the two semicircular lecture theatres, the chimneys (which reach to the 'internal road' at the heart of the complex), and the laboratories at the top with their roof vents.

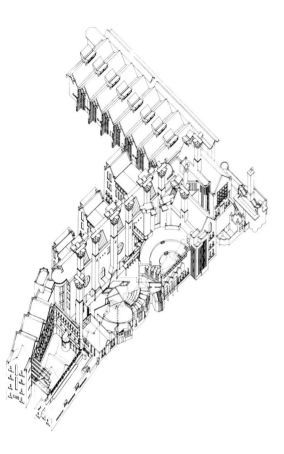

studios above them, are on the south. Electrical laboratories are at the east and of the concourse and mechanical labs on the west, both ventilated by vertical intakes on the walls and outlet vents in the roof.

The Perception of Control is an Important Factor

The architects and their consultants realized that the occupants of their building would have to deal with a much wider temperature variation than is found in air-conditioned buildings which are kept at a fairly constant 21°C (70°F). Naturally ventilated buildings are designed around the maximum allowable temperature; De Montfort uses natural ventilation to keep the inside temperature at least 1°C (1.5°F) below that outside. Perception of control seems to play a key role in temperature: surveys show that in air conditioned buildings occupants considered a change of 4°C (7°F) uncomfortable, but in buildings in which occupants would open windows if it got too warm, or turn on radiators if it got cold, changes of 10°C (18°F) were tolerable.

Apart from huge energy savings, naturally ventilated buildings are far healthier than air-conditioned offices. According to a 1992 report for the Health and Safety Executive in the UK, ozone can cause 'sick building syndrome', irritating eyes and throat, and causing headaches and lethargy. Statistical data gathered since the building was first occupied will provide a valuable resource for future designs, since it has over nine-hundred control points to allow fine tuning as time goes on. It also provides students with a built-in research source, proselytizing for natural heating and cooling by its performance.

A Difference in Intent

While some may see obvious parallels between Leicester's two iconic buildings, the difference is one of intent. Stirling's listed modernist monument has proven to be an environmental disaster, its stress on formalized function having little to do with climate. The choice of materials, especially glass for the laboratories and offices, forced dependence on a mechanical air-handling system. Short and Ford, however, have allowed air dynamics to shape their building, with brick chosen as cladding to assist in providing thermal mass rather than to act as a visual foil. This difference in intent speaks volumes about the philosophical transformation that has taken place in basic architectural principles in the intervening period.

The essence of that transformation, as it is spelled out at Leicester, is that after the post-modern debacle, the expression of traditional forms became acceptable once again on the condition that those forms are contextually connected and functionally viable. De Montfort University is especially apropos as a case study here because Short and Ford have deliberately selected both a palette of local materials and an indigenous style for a polemical as well as a practical reason. It was the first major civic project in Britain in a century built in the Gothic Revival style – with straightforward functional planning, emphasis on traditional materials, and steeply pitched roofs – but also the brick they have used has a specific historical connection to the city, as well as working extremely well environmentally. The tall ventilation towers, which are the main breathing apparatus of the building, recall those on the ovens that used to make those bricks, reinforcing local memory. These towers have an equally essential purpose, not only replacing dependence on costly and energy-intensive mechanical systems, but also demonstrating to a sceptical global public that this dependence can be broken through a return to traditional methods augmented by appropriate new technologies.

Norddeutsche Landesbank Headquarters, Hanover,
Behnisch, Behnisch & Partner, 2002
A publicly accessible ground floor is landscaped with
water elements while the offices are not air-conditioned,
but rather cooled using a soil–heat exchanger located
beneath the foundations that draws up cool air, and
a double façade. Other energy-saving measures reduce
carbon dioxide, control exhaust air, and optimize
day-lighting.

17

The Source of Sustainability

From the 1970s onwards there has been a flood of commissions, legislation and international agreements dealing with the issue of sustainability

Background

Since the 1970s the hope of politicians and ecologists alike has been placed in the concept of sustainability. This suggests that there need not be any inherent conflict between economic growth and ecological awareness, and offers, in principle, a compromise between the 'growth' and 'no-growth' factions. From 1977 onwards a number of international commissions have been convened, each to look at a key issue: the Brandt Commission investigated the economic divide between developed and developing countries; the Brundtland Report saw a direct link between environmental protection and economic development; the Earth Summit, perhaps the most important convention yet, outlined a programme for change that encouraged efficient use of the earth's resources and traditional forms of building.

What has emerged is a picture of complex interrelations, which bind together human rights, environmental destruction, living conditions and economic growth. Architecture, which deals with questions of materials, appropriate technology, landscaping and housing has a crucial role to play in shaping this discourse, but must also learn from it.

Earth Day in June 1970 was an important event, the first consensus to arise out of the growing ecological concerns that began to be voiced in the 1960s. That consensus seemed especially prescient three years later when supplies of fossil fuel from the Middle East were curtailed and prices drastically increased, with public anger at shortages finally prompting minimal conservation efforts. A report entitled *Limits to Growth*, published by the Club of Rome think tank in 1972, focused on the idea of progress and, in particular, on the fact that global industrial activity was increasing exponentially, predicting drastic consequences if such growth were not altered, such as the irrevocable loss of non-renewable resources. This report, although later considered naive in several of its assumptions, firmly put the spotlight on resources, and succeeded in popularizing the axiom of 'zero growth' which has been the subject of debate among environmentalists ever since.

The basic environmental issues raised on the first Earth Day – of resource degradation, population growth and agricultural limits leading to global famine and pollution of air and water, as well as the disastrous potential climatic effect of the concentration of greenhouse and ozone-depleting gases in the atmosphere – have all been examined in exhaustive detail, and incontrovertible evidence of the irreparable damage being inflicted on the planet mounts daily. The subtle but significant philosophical shift that has taken place since that first Earth

Key Events

The Brandt Commission, 1977–83

The Brundtland Report (*Our Common Future*), 1987

Rio Earth Summit (*Agenda 21*), 1992

Beijing Declaration, 1995

Habitat II, Istanbul, 1996

Signposts

'Eco-Tech' Part II: 11, 19

Sustainability Part II: 11, 15, 20, 21, 23

Day has been an emphasis on the concept of sustainability rather than ecology, making it important to understand where this term has come from and its implications for the future, particularly for those in the design professions.

The first use of the word 'sustainability' in connection with the environment was in 1980 in a publication produced by the International Union for the Conservation of Nature (UCN) entitled *World Conservation Strategy*, in which sustainability was inextricably linked to development. This was intended to diffuse the growth/no-growth debate that had raged throughout the 1970s between those who argued that economic progress was necessary to finance environmental protection on the one hand and those who were against such growth because its inevitable result was resource degradation and waste on the other. However, *World Conservation Strategy* had a limited impact on governmental policy. A more effective initiative was the Brandt Commission, named after Willy Brandt, then also chair of the Social Democratic Party of the Federal Republic of Germany. In a speech delivered in Boston in January 1977, then president of the World Bank Robert S. McNamara proposed the formation of a Commission on International Development, also to be chaired by Willy Brandt, and repeated the call during his address at the annual meeting of the International Monetary Fund at the World Bank in Washington later that same year. As a result, the commission, which was independent, with members serving in a private capacity rather than being under governmental restriction, held its first meeting in Gymnick, Germany, on 9 December 1978. The membership of the twenty-person committee reflected McNamara's intent that it not be dominated by representatives from industrialized countries. After ten meetings, the committee unanimously endorsed a report of their findings entitled *North–South: A Program for Survival*, published in 1980. Among many other issues, the report contained recommendations for changes in the operational procedures and policies of the IMF and the World Bank, indicating a close connection to those institutions. Following the publication, the Commission visited several countries at the invitation of their governments to assess its results. They met in The Hague, Berlin, Kuwait City, Brussels and Ottawa between the spring of 1980 and December 1982. This, in turn, led to an addendum published in 1983.

The Brandt Commission Proposals

The Commission's proposals came at a time when the global economic pendulum had swung in favour of the industrialized countries (following the attempt at autonomy by OPEC a decade earlier), and revolved primarily around the issues of trade and self-sufficiency. The proposals related to the negotiation process between a more affluent, industrial northern hemisphere and a generally less developed southern hemisphere, and although the report inadequately defined the tragic situation of dependency in the developing world, it did succeed in drawing attention to the debilitating spiral of exports produced to offset debt. For the developing countries, the connections between trade and finance make economic management peculiarly difficult. Without adequate finance, imports cannot be paid for; without essential imports, production and exports decline; and without adequate exports, countries are not sufficiently creditworthy to borrow to service their debts. The combined grip of inadequate trade and finance on developing economies has become devastating.

The 'decline' the report recorded became even more manifest shortly after the Commission ended the global assessment of its findings in 1982. Mexico signalled that it could no longer maintain payments, followed by Brazil, Argentina, and other leveraged borrowers in the developing world. This sent shockwaves through the banking community, with economic repercussions that made tangible the inequities between the north and the south discussed in the report. Further collapse of commodity prices soon afterward showed the extent to which the report was prophetic.

Some have felt that the links between the Brandt Commission and the high-level financial institutions, regardless of the independent nature of its composition, made it appear to have been little more than a vehicle to encourage developing borrowers to seek more loans, continuing the destructive spiral of dependence. The Brandt Commission's focus on the oil-producing countries and somewhat abstract attitude toward the extremity of the adverse aspects of trade inequities – the poverty, famine, and death so graphically described at the same time by writers like Susan George – make it difficult to view the contributions of the Commission objectively. Yet it did initiate awareness of the need for global consensus and coordination on environmental policy, through tactics such as 'global negotiations,' to be carried out at the United Nations. Through emphasis on trade, finance, and the essentials of development in the developing world, the Commission began the process of reconciling economics with ecology.

The Brundtland Report

The gap between isolated internal conservationist debate and a higher international possibility of sustainable development was finally bridged by the World Commission on Environment and Development, which was established by the United Nations as a strategic means of compromise between the 'growth' and 'no-growth' factions. The proceedings of the Commission, entitled *Our Common Future* (also known as the 'Brundtland Report', after the president of the panel) were published in 1987. Central to the Commission's findings was the concept of sustainability, which was defined as the principle that economic growth can and should be managed so that natural resources be used in such a way that the 'quality of life' of future generations is ensured. Sustainable development involves 'those paths of social economic and political progress that meet the needs of the present without compromising the ability of future generations to meet their own needs.'

The use of such qualitative, subjective phrases as 'quality of life' left the concept of sustainability open to critical interpretation and speculation as to whether it related to manufactured or natural assets. This means, as some have suggested, that either per capita utility or wellbeing increases over time with free exchange or substitution between natural and human-made capital, or that per capita utility or wellbeing increases over time subject to non-declining wealth. In spite of vagueness on this central issue, the report, by holding out the prospect of the perpetual satisfaction of human needs within a satisfactory natural framework, provided a compelling vision of an attainable middle ground.

A Compromise Between Growth and No-Growth

Our Common Future offered a potential area of rapprochement between agencies, raising official awareness that a realistic compromise might be feasible. By holding out the promise that environmental protection and economic development are compatible or complementary objectives, sustainable development offered a welcome relief from the paradigm of conflict that had characterized the debate on limits of growth during the 1970s. Having been placed at the forefront of the political debate about the feasibility of development, the concept of sustainability offered decision-makers a means with which to reconcile what had previously proved to be an intractable division.

Sustainability, then, has been inextricably linked to development and by extension to economics. From the outset, the focus of the Commission was to determine the general perception of the impact of development, by holding community hearings in key industrialized countries to gauge public opinion. Rather than being made up of environmentalists, the UN Commission members were primarily political figures, with a different agenda: to combine rather than separate environmental and development issues, to attempt to formulate a worldwide view of how this might be achieved, and to bring environmental policy into the political arena. Also adopted as articles of faith were the efficacy of extending production with more efficient technology and conservation, the need to reduce the growth of worldwide population, and, perhaps most important, the definition of a mechanism to allow the distribution of resources from profligate countries predominantly in the northern hemisphere to the poorer nations, predominantly in the south.

The search for such a mechanism was based on a recognition that, since the beginning of the 20th century, the industrially rich countries had thrived at the expense of the poorer ones and had been responsible for a great deal of the environmental damage now evident. It was also recognized that it would be hypocritical to expect the poor, who are now industrializing, to suspend development as a result of this damage. Bringing attention to the dichotomy of both standards of living and values is one of the Brundtland Report's greatest contributions to the current ecological debate. Since the report, important distinctions have been made between development and sustainability. One of these has been the observation that: 'Sustainable development requires a broader view of both economics and ecology than most practitioners in either discipline are prepared to admit, together with a political commitment to ensure that development is "sustainable"… Is it possible to undertake environmental planning and management in a way that does minimum damage to ecological processes without putting a brake on human aspirations for economic and social improvement?'[1] The qualifier in this crucial question is obviously the aspirations of those people at the bottom of the economic ladder in the developed countries involved, as well as those which have been rapidly ascribed the acronyms of RDC (rapidly developing country), LDC (less developed country), and NIC (newly industrialized country).

The Earth Summit: *Agenda 21*

The more recent impetus for the concept of sustainability has been the Earth Summit held at Serrado Mar, near Rio de Janeiro, Brazil, in the late spring of 1992. As an extension of the work of the Brundtland Report, this conference, also sponsored by the UN Commission on Environment and Development, was organized by Maurice Strong, who unequivocally stated, when he was appointed head of the Earth Summit in 1989, that his intention was to use it as a vehicle to further explore the idea of sustainable development and 'to move the environment into the centre of the economic policy.'

Strong's background as a self-made businessman is relevant to the shaping of the outcome of the Rio Summit. Starting as an executive with the Western Canadian Oil Company, Dome Exploration (where he became vice-president at the age of twenty-five), he became vice-president of Power Corporation of Canada in 1962, head of Canada's foreign aid programme under Prime Minister Lester Pearson in 1966, which he reformed into the Canadian

Museum of Fantasy, Bernried, Behnisch, Behnisch &
Partner, 2000
Built to house an important collection of Expressionist
paintings and graphics, among other things, the most
important consideration was how to connect the
building to the park landscape, and give the owner low-
tech flexibility.

Development Agency (CIDA), and head of Petro Canada. Petro Canada had been formed by
Prime Minister Pierre Trudeau in 1976, on Strong's advice, to negotiate directly with the
OPEC cartel following the price rises of that decade. Strong's experience in helping to
organize the UN World Conference on the Human Environment, held in Stockholm in 1972,
which resulted in a consensus by 112 nations on a global environmental plan, and his
background as head of the UN famine relief effort in 1985 made him the proper choice to
tackle the daunting task of organizing the heads of state from 175 member countries to forge
what Strong described as 'an environmental bill of rights.' As a first step in achieving a fusion
between economics and the environment, Strong expressed his belief in typically businesslike
terms that it is necessary to 'put a price tag on the elements of nature' and that 'depreciation of
natural resources has to be taken into account, literally, by nations all over the world. The loss
of a country's natural resources must be subtracted from the GNP. When businesses have to
pay for the loss of things, they have a powerful incentive not to pollute or over-consume.'

The 1992 Rio Earth Summit, in which more than one hundred world leaders participated
– with the notable exception of the President of the United States, who claimed that research
into environmental damage was inconclusive and untrustworthy – did not produce Strong's
much desired 'Earth Charter.' However, the publication of its proceedings, *Agenda 21* (named
after the century in which it would be implemented), has provided a much more
comprehensive outline of the possible scope of sustainable development, as conceptualized by
its most powerful proponents. Based on the fundamental premise that the developed world
must subsidize the development of poorer nations in order to redress past inequities and
reverse the destructive cycle of resource depletion, *Agenda 21* is a complex document with
forty separate sections addressing different areas of concern. It also has 120 programme
outlines, and one thousand proposals, grouped under a directive best expressed in the first
paragraph of introduction to the document:

> Humanity stands at a defining moment in history. We are confronted with a perpetuation
> of disparities between and within nations, a worsening of poverty, hunger, ill health, and

illiteracy and the continuing deterioration of the ecosystems on which we depend for our well-being. However, integration of environment and development concerns and greater attention to them will lead to the fulfilment of basic needs, improve living standards for all, better protected and managed ecosystems and a safer, more prosperous future. No nation can achieve this on its own, but together we can in global partnership for sustainable development.[2]

The daunting complexity of the multivolume document can best be summarized by conceptualizing it in six subject areas, corresponding to the terminology used by the report. These areas are: the quality of life on earth; efficient use of the earth's materials; the protection of our global commons; the management of human settlements; chemicals and the management of waste; and sustainable economic growth.

Quality of Life

Quality of life on earth, which is conceptually as indebted to the Brundtland Report as the idea of sustainable development itself, relates primarily to the disparity between the rich nations of the world, now characterized by conspicuous, wasteful consumption, and poor nations, characterized by poverty, starvation, preventable disease and nonexistent or inadequate health care and education. This part of *Agenda 21* focuses on strategies to alleviate poverty, changing patterns of consumption, and improving standards of health, all within the framework of reducing population growth. The document advocates programmes which will assist the 'most vulnerable' social groups: 'women, children, indigenous people, minority communities, landless households, refugees, and migrants.' The report proposes to achieve this by changes in systems of landownership in poor counties to allow more equitable access to resources and the free exchange of 'environmentally sound technologies' from the developed to the developing world, provided that these are adaptable to particular circumstances. *Agenda 21*, elaborating on the dilemma of population growth, examines the difficulties involved in social change, especially given the pervasive influence of mobility (which makes a lifestyle revolving around high levels of consumption seem so appealing to those in the developing world), and the intrinsic connection in the industrialized world between economic growth and resource depletion.

Using Earth's Resources

Agenda 21 divides the second main theme, the efficient use of the earth's natural resources, into renewable and non-renewable resources, such as land, water, energy, biological, and genetic resources, and here it becomes clear that a single philosophical framework guided recommendations for programmes and activities in each of the six subject areas. This section consists of largely decentralized policies and advocates putting control into the hands of local rather than national authorities, encouraging public participation in decision making, identifying ecosystems as unit to be managed uniformly, developing new technologies to halt and combat degradation and depletion and increase productivity and efficiency, and implementing extensive research in each area of development.

Translated into policy recommendations, these principles, when applied to land and water resources, result in a plea for an awareness of the finite capacity of each and the systematic characteristics that produce complex interaction. This complexity, the report reiterates, argues for an integral approach to land management. This integration has two components: the need for a comprehensive assessment of the negative impact of any proposed human intervention into the environment or use of natural resources, and the careful balance that must be maintained when economic and environmental factors are weighted against each other, with social welfare as a primary criterion. Specific recommendations relating to land are surprisingly inspired for a document of this scope.

Traditional Approaches to Land Use Encouraged
One proposal calls for a study of traditional approaches to land use – as exemplified in terraced agriculture practice in Yemen and Indonesia, the *Hema* reserves used in Islamic societies, and 'pastoralism' (seasonal patterns of pasture use practised by nomadic societies) – as possible solutions for appropriately scaled areas. Another series of proposals, which restate the emphasis on analysis, recommend establishment of detailed land inventories to determine local capacities and ecosystems, to be collected by individual communities and pilot projects for curricular changes at the vocational, technical and university level to expand education about land use and other avenues of public participation. The subject of water, which is given extensive coverage in *Agenda 21*, includes emphasis on its importance for the environment, its manifestations within the ecological network, and its geopolitical implications.

The Global Commons
The third main thrust of *Agenda 21*, related to what has been referred to as a 'global commons,' views the atmosphere and the oceans as belonging to everyone, whereas it characterizes resources as falling into geopolitical jurisdictions. The proceedings refer to industrial development and transportation, as well as the energy used in each and land use, in terms of their negative impact on air and water and looks at 'marine living resources' in a view toward encouraging increased international cooperation in their use.

Managing Human Settlements
Of all sections of the report, the fourth area of concern – management of human settlements – is of most interest to architects and urban planners, since it refers in detail to the need for adequate environmental infrastructure and changes in the construction industry. This section advocates international environmental conferences to address directly issues of the built environment, examines the present structure of the construction industry, and notes its destructive capacity, which it identifies as 'a major source of environmental damage through the degradation of fragile ecological zones, damage to natural resources, chemical pollution, and the use of building materials which are harmful to human health.' A corrective, the report recommends:

1. The use of local materials and indigenous building sources.
2. Incentives to promote the continuation of traditional techniques, with regional resources and self-help strategies.
3. Recognition of the toll that natural disasters take on developing countries, due to unregulated construction and use of inadequate materials and the need for improvements both in use and manufacture of materials and in construction techniques, as well as training programmes.

4   Regulation of energy-efficient design principles.

5   Standards that would discourage construction in moronically inappropriate areas.

6   The use of labour-intensive rather than energy-intensive construction techniques.

7   The restructuring of credit institutions to allow the poor to buy building materials and services, or the proliferation of micro-credit.

8   International information exchange on all aspects of construction related to the environment, among architects and contractors, particularly about non-renewable resources.

9   Exploration of methods to encourage and facilitate the recycling and reuse of building materials, especially those requiring intensive energy consumption in their manufacture.

10 Financial penalties to discourage the use of materials that damage the environment.

11 Decentralization of the construction industry, through the establishment of smaller firms.

12 The use of 'clean technologies'.

A Flurry of Conferences after Rio

Since the watershed Earth Summit in Rio, there have been numerous conferences that have focused on specific issues identified as key components of sustainability. A year after Rio, the World Conference on Human Rights, held in Vienna, addressed the need to promote and protect human rights, and to integrate policies related to this basic need into economic and social development worldwide. The resulting document of the conference, *The Vienna Declaration and Programme of Action*, outlines a comprehensive plan for strengthening the protection of human rights, and defines the connections between development, government and citizens. The declaration addresses the legitimacy of development, the need to protect vulnerable groups such as women, children, indigenous people and refugees, and defines poverty and social exclusion as violations of basic human dignity. As a result of the declaration, the United Nations General Assembly proclaimed 1995 to 2004 the UN Decade of Human Rights. The International Conference on Population and Development held in Cairo in 1994 resulted in a programme of action that establishes what it terms 'reproductive rights', while establishing the goal of making family-planning universally available by 2015. It integrates population concerns into sustainable development, focusing on lowering infant and maternity rates. The World Summit for Social Development held in Copenhagen in 1995 further addressed the eradication of world poverty and social integration and economic imbalance.

The *Beijing Declaration*, adopted in 1995 following the World Conference on Women, recognizes the need to advance the empowerment of women's human rights equality, preventing violence against women and increasing their participation in promoting peace, economic growth and political stability. The Conference recognized that cultural traditions, attitudes and practices all over the world promote inequality and discrimination against women, and called for changes in values and attitudes to correct this. The importance of this conference to sustainability is also in recognizing that truly sustainable development cannot occur until these issues are addressed and corrected.

Habitat II, held in Istanbul in 1996 focused on the issue of rapid urbanization and the need for adequate shelter for all, with recognition that unsustainable patterns of consumption

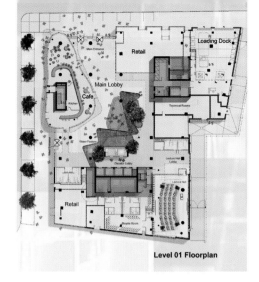

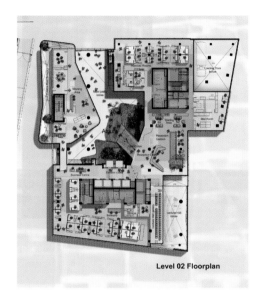

Floor plans and elevation of the Genzyme Center, Cambridge (Mass.), Behnisch, Behnisch & Partner, 2003 Like the Norddeutsche Landesbank Headquarters, the Genzyme Center uses a double façade to stabilize internal temperatures. However, the main focus is on daylighting, through a central atrium and extensive use of light shelves. Around 30 per cent of the materials used in the building are recycled.

production and population growth cause homelessness, unemployment, violence and increased vulnerability to disaster. The *Habitat Agenda*, adopted there, shaped the United Nations' approach toward global sustainable development as related to urbanization for many years afterward. The World Food Summit, held in Rome in 1996, concentrated on ways to eradicate hunger and the general conditions necessary to establish the economic and social frameworks required to insure worldwide 'food security'. And finally, two 'Earth Summits', in New York in 1997 and Johannesburg in 2002, reviewed the provisions adopted in Rio in 1992, and identified the areas that still required further implementation.

A Renewed Focus on Tradition

The breadth of the scope of this ongoing sequence of United Nations initiatives indicates the extent to which the responsibility of design professionals has changed, making it necessary for architects and planners to become more cognizant of and involved in socioeconomic and geopolitical issues. It also explains why sustainability can be characterized as a conference-driven phenomenon.

The Earth Summit in Rio in 1992 as well as the *Beijing Declaration* of 1995 and Habitat II in Istanbul in 1996 also brought home to all of those involved in the design professions, in both practice and academia, that traditional cultures and indigenous architecture were being reprioritized to be considered as important repositories of knowledge about the environment. This has transformed attitudes to vernacular architecture, in ways that are discussed in more detail throughout this book.

left **New Nigerian Capital Project, Abouja,** completed 1974

above **Optimum land use diagram for Plan for the Valleys,** *c.* 1962

This diagram carefully breaks down the area into: valley floors; unforested valley walls; forested valley walls, forested plateau; unforested plateau; hamlets; village centres; country town centres; existing institutional use, currently zoned industrial; lakes; and promontory high-rise location. Such detailed analysis was a new departure, and was to have great influence on later approaches.

18

Ian McHarg: Passionate Steward of the Environment

McHarg decided to work with nature, rather than trying to conquer it, in the process setting the blueprint for ecologically sensitive planning in the West

Biography

Born in Glasgow in 1920, Ian McHarg is one of the most influential figures in ecological architecture. Described as a 'ferocious champion' of ecology and a 'classic old Scottish Bible-thumper [whose] religion was the environment', he was one of the most dedicated and passionate advocates of sensitivity to place.

His philosophy was defined in his first key project, the Plan for the Valleys (1962), which promoted planned growth and offered an alternative to suburban sprawl. It was also characteristically realistic, understanding the market forces that can cause environmental damage. He pioneered the technique of computer modelling, gathering large amounts of data to back up his arguments, and understood the importance of history of place.

A natural leader and proselytizer, his passionate beliefs led to two television series and a successful teaching career, which included establishing the Department of Landscape Architecture at the University of Pennsylvania. He died in 2001.

Ian McHarg redirected the social shift from modernist universality toward the more qualified, populist concerns of the highly radicalized 1960s, as related to landscape architecture. By giving voice to the theoretical issues then emerging in other disciplines in the built environment, he transformed his profession, making it more responsive to the particularity of nature. McHarg was especially effective because he understood the potential power of a newly emerging media as a means of spreading his ideas. His idealism resonated with a post-war generation rapidly becoming disillusioned with the notion of unbounded progress. His basic message was sensitivity to place – that no human intervention into nature should be considered without a thorough analysis of the compatibility between a building and the ecosystem in question, including the specific topographical and microclimatic conditions of the site. These concerns were mirrored in the change in architecture at that time, in a growing interest in regional, vernacular forms, local history, or the 'memory' of a place.[1]

Uniform Development not a Given

McHarg's approach to site selection, at any scale, was revolutionary because he shifted the emphasis away from certitude and the belief that engineering prowess could overcome all natural obstacles, toward a more reflective, selective search that stressed process rather than product. In this process, his most important message was that, unlike the certainty projected

Key Projects

The Plan for the Valleys, 1962

Washington Metropolitan Region Plan, 1967

Plan for Abouja, Nigeria, completed 1974

Signposts

Garden cities Part II: 2, 3, 22

Town planning Part II: 2, 3, 4, 8, 9, 11, 12; Part III: 3

Conservation Part II: 20, 21, 23; Part III: 3

Use of computers Part II: 19; Part III: 1

by modernism, the outcome was not a foregone conclusion. He did not automatically assume that development should occur everywhere. Citing such recurring and devastating natural disasters as the periodic flooding of the Mississippi River Valley and the tragic loss of life and property that it causes, McHarg took the audacious stance that natural forces should be recognized as dominant in such instances, and that these areas should not be inhabited. Instead, he approached each site as a unique physical condition, first determining what physiological features gave it its special identity, and then applying what has become known as the 'McHarg Method' to each of them. After identifying a score of criteria that he considered relevant for any given site, such as water table, topography, woodland, vegetation and wildlife habitat, he would map each of them on a transparent medium and then overlay this set to reveal critical points of coincidence and sensitivity to human intervention. Although it has now been shown to be too simplistic, because it overlooks more complex ecological relationships, his method did make designers aware of the need to consider them. This overlay method also anticipated the computer-based Geographic Information System (GIS) so vital to geographers and those involved in planning the built environment today.

An Unconventional Path

Like fellow Glaswegian Charles Rennie Mackintosh before him, McHarg's early experience of the contrast between that heavily industrialized city and the Highlands nearby was a strong impetus for a life dedicated to protecting nature. Both men took long walks outside the grimy centre into the unspoilt, surrounding hills, drawing the conclusion that pristine nature was preferable to the urban depredation they lived in. McHarg interrupted his studies, first by leaving high school to apprentice with Donald A. Wintersgill, a landscape architect with Austin and McAslan Ltd in Glasgow, at age sixteen. He then enlisted in the British Army two years later, in 1938, just prior to the Second World War. He sailed to Saint-Malo, France, with the Second British Expeditionary Force in 1940, and after being promoted to corporal was sent to Officer Training School, where he received a commission as second lieutenant. After being posted to the Second Parachute Squadron, he fought in the North African Campaign in 1942, the invasion of Italy in 1943 and the south of France in 1944. He was promoted to Captain soon afterward, leading the invasion of Megara, Greece, in September 1944. Just before the end of the war he was promoted to the rank of Major and after being demobilized in September 1946, he entered the landscape architecture programme at the Harvard Graduate School of Design.

It is ironic that he contracted tuberculosis in Boston, while at Harvard, rather than in the industrialized centre of Glasgow or as a result of the hardships of war. After being in the Centre for Consumptives in Edinburgh, he returned to Harvard for a Masters Degree in City Planning in 1951. Having received two degrees, he began offering a lecture course in landscape architecture at the Edinburgh College of Art, while also serving as a planning officer at the Department of Health for Scotland, moving to Glasgow to teach at the College of Art in 1952.

The Perfect Pulpit for an Environmental Fundamentalist

G. Holmes Perkins, who became Dean of the University of Pennsylvania School of Architecture in Philadelphia at the same time McHarg was moving to Glasgow, was determined to transform the School from a Beaux-Arts bastion to the premier modernist

Bird's eye perspective, Plan for the Valleys, 1962

institution in America. His approach was broad based: he believed that the best preparation for an increasingly complex world was an integrated curriculum that would expose all students to each of the three disciplines of architecture, landscape architecture and urban planning. He argued that only such an integrated approach would allow future professionals to deal effectively with a rapidly changing social ethos. This included urban flight and 'renewal,' suburban sprawl, unbridled corporate growth and heightened environmental awareness in the face of mounting evidence of widespread ecological degradation.

Perkins also had a keen eye for emerging talent and a knack for choosing teachers who were just on the brink of greatness. Soon after his appointment, he lured Louis Kahn away from Yale to lead the change of direction he had in mind for the Department of Architecture. He also brought Edmund Bacon into the Department of Urban Planning just as Bacon was implementing his unabashedly modernist plan for Philadelphia. In 1954 he appointed McHarg assistant professor of landscape architecture and city planning, and then worked with him to create a Department of Landscape Architecture at the University of Pennsylvania in 1955.

Kindred Spirits

In retrospect, these three key appointments, more than the many others that Perkins made in the first years of his tenure, were especially serendipitous, since the sensibilities of each were perfectly in tune and were soon to be translated into groundbreaking new ideas for their respective specialties. Louis Kahn, discussed in depth on pp. 115–21, was unquestionably a modernist. He clearly demonstrated his commitment to the ideals of the movement in several low-cost housing projects completed in Philadelphia in the early 1950s, and in his minimalist formal language, initially rendered in steel, glass and concrete. But, beginning with his proposals for improving Philadelphia in 1956, and the Richards Medical Towers in that city in the same year, Kahn made a dramatic shift toward massiveness, or what he called 'monumentality,' as well as an unmistakable reliance on historical sources, both in response to a growing disdain for the formal sterility of high modernism. Kahn was careful to keep his historical sources of inspiration just abstract enough to avoid the damning modernist charge of being derivative, but was undoubtedly encouraged by a similar apostasy by Le Corbusier at Ronchamp in 1956 in his move from Purism to sculptural expression.

In spite of a marked preference for axiality, Edmund Bacon also championed specificity, and the creation of a 'sense of place' in his own field of urban planning. In his influential book *Design of Cities*, Bacon pays homage to such diverse civic achievements as Beijing, Delft, Horyu-ji and Hadrian's Villa, the residence as city in microcosm that also fascinated so many others of his generation. Like Kahn, Bacon also extrapolated the subtle lessons offered by this wide range of cultural expression into his own personal spatial construct. His aesthetic, however, remained more formal since he, of necessity, had to work with many other developers and architects to realize his city-wide plan.

Ian McHarg, then, with his strong opinions about which natural environments were suitable for development and which were not, fitted well with Kahn and Bacon: he shared their respect for history and desire for rebellion against forced uniformity. McHarg lost no time in using his new academic post to best advantage as a platform from which to preach his gospel of how to save the earth. He launched his now legendary 'Man and Environment' course in 1959, inviting geologists, hydrologists, botanists, climatologists, physiologists, anthropologists, theologians, historians and artists as foils for his zealous investigations of planetary problems.[2] The following year, his course was adapted as a television series called 'The House We Live In,' produced by CBS. It ran for two twelve-episode seasons and was then syndicated through PBS. Consistent with his curricular format, the show included guests like biologist Sir Julian Huxley, astronomer Harlow Sharply, psychologist Erich Fromm and anthropologist Margaret Mead, with segment titles such as 'The No Growth Society,' 'The Urban Condition' and 'The Classical Gardens of Suzhou.'

The Plan for the Valleys

In 1962, McHarg co-founded the architecture, urban planning and landscape firm of Wallace–McHarg Associates, reorganized as Wallace, McHarg, Roberts and Todd (WMRT) in 1965. McHarg continued to teach at the University of Pennsylvania after being promoted to professor in 1961. The first commission the firm received, in 1962, was the mandate to plan for the development of the Green Spring and Worthington Valleys near Baltimore, subsequently referred to by the firm as the 'Plan for the Valleys'. In retrospect, this plan can be recognized as a visionary precursor of the sustainable ethic that received official United Nations sanction twenty years later in the Brundtland Report entitled *Our Common Future* (see p. 167), the historic resolution of the bitterly contested growth/no-growth debate of the 1960s and 70s. Like the definition of sustainability put forward in the Brundtland Report – that a point of balance in the environment can be reached by supporting development 'that meets the needs of the present without compromising the ability of future generations to meet their own needs' – the Plan for the Valleys represents a concerted effort to offset idealism against solid business sense. It conveys an understanding that the only way forward in the battle to preserve the environment is to accommodate rather than deny economic realities.

In hindsight, the Plan for the Valleys seems somewhat naive, but it was the first attempt by an architect to confront the reality of uncontrolled suburban growth, which was then in the midst of a boom that began right after the end of the Second World War. Until the plan appeared, architects and urban planners had relinquished a leadership role in guiding this growth, unable to deal with messy market forces and the compromises required by popular taste.[3] Isolated campaigns by architects to come to terms with sprawl, such as the 'Case Study' house programme in California launched by John Entenza in the late 1940s, failed to recognize market forces and popular taste. In its final phase, the programme put forward minimalist Miesian pavilions intended to be produced on assembly lines like automobiles, believing that the public could be educated to prefer transparent steel and glass boxes to the collective, faux-Cape Cod reverie then being built in suburban communities across America.

A Revolutionary Proposition

The Plan for the Valleys is far less idealistic and more realistic than the 'Case Study' house programme because it is tempered with extensively researched alternatives for private landowners to consider when faced with the temptation to sell to developers for quick profit. Since it is so revolutionary, it deserves a detailed overview here. The plan, which McHarg refers to as a 'proposition,' is an iterative, ideological manifesto interspersed with economic proposals intended to ensure serious consideration by farmers being pressured to sell land for development. It has seven main messages, repeated in increasing detail, before it closes with 'recommended controls and devices,' a detailed compensation plan for landowners who do not sell, and 'Action Steps' to ensure controlled growth in the future. In a stirring preamble,

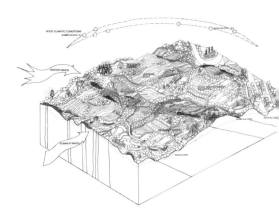

Plan for the Valleys, Spring City, 1960s
'Natural Features and Settlement Patterns': low ground water yields, hydric soils and slopes over 25 per cent are shown, while the arrows show the directions of the summer and winter winds.

McHarg sets the stage for the proposals that follow by saying that: 'the American dream has been substantially achieved: banishment of hunger, control of disease, increased freedom, widened opportunities, accumulation and distribution of wealth are all testimonies to the American way and its success. Yet the dream of life, liberty and the pursuit of happiness do not yet have a physical expression. Today, careless building in city and suburbs destroys natural beauty. Too often, tawdriness, discontinuity, disorder and even anarchy are the result. Nature is destroyed. The image of happiness eludes.'[4]

After warning that 'the urban expansion which menaces the Green Spring and Worthington Valleys today is typical of a national problem,' McHarg introduces the first of the eight messages intended to solve the dilemma. 'The Area is Beautiful and Vulnerable' seems to state the obvious, but the landscape in question is not as overtly imaginable as the Grand Canyon or Florida Everglades. It is significant that McHarg does not automatically assume that local residents appreciate the intrinsic worth of the Valleys, but rather that they take it for granted and must be convinced. He does this with stirringly lyrical prose, underlining his alignment with the emerging post-modern affinity toward history and context in the process. After defining the genius loci (the spirit of the place) of the Valleys as residing in their 'extensive forests, the patterns of the farmlands, the fences and buildings, the heterogeneous free standing trees and copses, the scale of roads, indeed all of the components of the pastoral valley scene', McHarg places the Valleys within the historic context of the Colonial agricultural revolution, and its important historical inheritance. He concludes this message with the caveat that the Valleys are especially vulnerable because they are easy to develop, that there is no possibility of a partial incursion, since even a minor intrusion will destroy their majestic visual sweep. For this reason he proposes that development be confined to the wooded ridges surrounding the valleys since they can absorb it.

In his second message – 'Development is Inevitable and Must be Accommodated' – McHarg paints a grim picture of between 350 to 450 new houses in the Valleys over the next sixteen years, supporting a population of nearly 23,000 and an increase to 150,000 by the year 2000. The third is that 'uncontrolled growth is inevitably destructive', and that it will 'slowly but surely obliterate the Valleys, and exorably cover the landscape with its smear, irrevocably destroying all that is beautiful and memorable.'

The 'Uncontrolled Growth' Model

To graphically covey the consequences of sprawl, an 'uncontrolled growth' model, which is as much an antecedent of current computer modelling as McHarg's overlay method is to the GIS system, is introduced at this point. McHarg justifies the results of the model by citing the availability of vast amounts of accurate information about the Valleys. This contributes substantially to the 'know thy enemy' tone of the report, the willingness of these planners to operate on real-world terms rather than being dismissive of such common, corruptive influences as most architects at the time were. The most essential function of the uncontrolled growth model was to determine aggregate developed land value as a benchmark against which economic gains from future development could be measured, so that a strategy could be formulated to offset the temptation of property owners to take a quick profit. Results from this model confirmed that the Valleys had somehow avoided the growth taking place elsewhere in the region, but predicted that if something was not done immediately, they would soon be filled with homes, destroying their value as 'prestige areas.' This third section of the report ends with McHarg's impassioned exhortation against uncontrolled growth, once again contrasting rational science with emotional, subjective observation in a way that characterizes the entire report.

Sounding distinctly Dickensian, McHarg conjures up the 'Spectre of the Future', the plight of the Valleys if landowner greed prompts them to sell to developers. If this happens, he warns, 'Winding roads, now pastoral, tree lined and fence bordered, will be replaced by bland, straight strips of asphalt or concrete. Trees, hedges, fences will go as will the familiar rural scene. Homes will dot the wooded slopes, little broken teeth. More will appear on the slopes and the serenity of the scene will diminish. A stream will be culvert, as gas stations appear, more houses and suddenly the instinct to protect will be supplanted by the instinct to sell, profit and flee. Deterioration will accelerate, Valleys change to seas of houses, broad faceless highways, commercial development and the Valleys will have gone, submerged in subtopia.'[5]

The McHarg Method Introduced
Realizing that the Valleys cannot remain a natural preserve in the midst of suburban growth forever, McHarg uses part four of the plan to describe how 'Development must Conform to Regional Goals' by clearly striving to bring these goals into line with a model of concentrated growth called 'Metrotown' then being proposed as an alternative to suburban sprawl in many planning journals.

In part five – 'Observance of Conservation Principles can Avert Destruction and Ensure Enhancement' – the daunting McHarg method is introduced to full effect, with underground water supply, areas of surface water, flood plains, steep slopes and forest cover chosen as the critical elements for analysis in this context. Consistent with the tone of realistic idealism woven throughout the plan, the conclusions drawn from this analysis presented in part six, 'the Area can Absorb all Prospective Growth without Despoliation,' are that development should be forbidden over porous marble deposits, aquifers, fifty-year flood plains, soils unsuitable for septic systems and natural surface water courses, all located in the Valleys. But, it also concludes with future population growth estimated to result in 27,000 new dwellings by 2000, saying that expansion can be accommodated on forested slopes using higher densities, saving 7,000 acres in the Valleys for open space. If building must occur there, it must be restricted to agricultural or institutional use, large estates, or parks for recreation.

The Main Recommendation
These sections of the plan incrementally build up to its crescendo, thinly veiled behind yet another ungainly title: 'Planned Growth is more Desirable and Just as Profitable as Uncontrolled Growth.' In addition to reiterating the recommendation that 7,000 acres be permanently withdrawn from development, and that all forested areas should be used to absorb the majority of new growth, at a cost to residents of about fourteen million US dollars, this final section calls for a new 'County Town' with fourteen smaller villages clustered around it to accommodate population growth. While this may seem to some simply to be a bid for an expanded brief, this unexpected recommendation may also be viewed as a final attempt to ensure that all previous recommendations be carried out, and a defence against any possible charge that the plan is too vague on the issue of how to physically deal with future growth.

Not content with introducing this surprise, however, McHarg concludes with two additional strategies that further reinforce his proposals. These are an exhaustive description

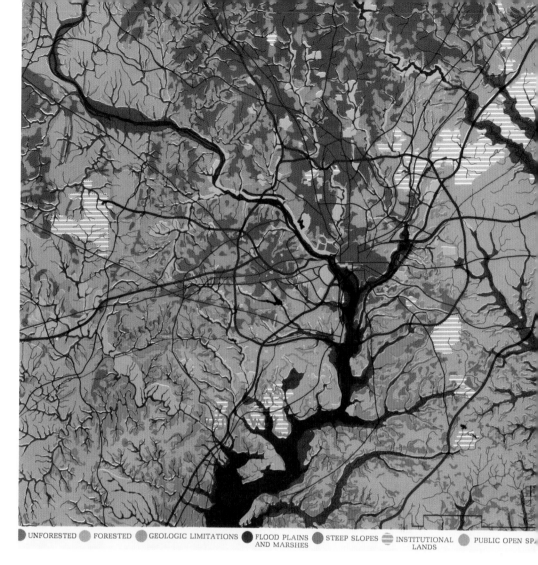

UNFORESTED   FORESTED   GEOLOGIC LIMITATIONS   FLOOD PLAINS AND MARSHES   STEEP SLOPES   INSTITUTIONAL LANDS   PUBLIC OPEN SP.

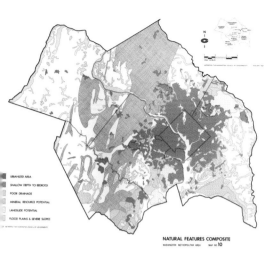

top **Natural features composite diagram, Washington Metropolitan Region Plan, begun 1967**
The various shadings show: urbanized areas, shallow depth to bedrock; poor drainage; mineral resource potential; landslide potential; and flood plains and severe slopes.

above **Diagram showing woodlands, Washington Metropolitan Area**

right **Relative suitability of lands for urbanization, Washington Metropolitan Area**
Features shown are: unforested areas; forested areas; areas with geological limitations; flood plains and marshes; steep slopes; institutional lands; and public open spaces.

of existing and new state laws that both do and could compensate the public for the sale of land, and the proposal for a 'Real Estate Syndicate' that would oversee the orderly development of the wooded slopes, use the profit to purchase land in the Valleys to save it from development and ensure the equitable distribution of finances.

The Historical Significance of the Plan for the Valleys

With its novel mixture of revivalist semantics, idealistic vision and corporate pragmatism, the Plan for the Valleys establishes a more realistic benchmark for regional studies to follow. While it can be faulted for being contradictory in places, and for not being value-free in its selection and use of an 'ecological inventory' (which is skewed to support its conclusions), it is a landmark because of the breadth of issues that it addresses. It builds toward an imposing multifaceted finale, its conclusion that a network of 'physiographic' principles for conservation and development should guide development: a County Town centre with constellation villages to counter sprawl; that the community should utilize legislative as well as zoning strategies as controls; and that the device of a Real Estate Syndicate be established among members of the local community to oversee implementation. Its attitude of educated compromise – the need to establish the costs of environmental protection and amelioration, to meet developers on their own terms with an economic rationale in addition to aesthetic principles, and the critical realization that their plan must contain a financial incentive powerful enough to divert the compelling commercial forces then at work in the region – all predict the sustainable ethos that emerged two decades later. Its emphasis on a populist, rather than elitist, stance – a public–private partnership expressed in community rather than individual action – also predicts New Urbanist tactics, echoed in the calls for changes in zoning controls and state legislation to achieve more humane urban and suburban habitats rather than concentrating on formal configuration alone.

The Washington Metropolitan Region Study

In 1967, five years after the Plan for the Valleys was completed, the newly expanded firm of Wallace, McHarg, Roberts and Todd was commissioned to undertake a study of the entire 1,550 square kilometre (600 square mile) metropolitan region surrounding Washington, D.C., with Ian McHarg designated as partner in charge. The prestige involved in planning the region around the United States capital, and the dramatically large scale of the enterprise, indicate the growing reputation of the firm as well as the success of their technique of physiographic analysis.

As one of the first of the large-scale regional studies carried out after the Plan for the Valleys, the Washington Metropolitan survey sets a pattern of expanding on the approach introduced at Green Spring, becoming a replicable formula that builds on this first early success. The basic elements of that formula were: an eloquent introduction that sets the scene or 'sense of place' within the global context; the use of a mathematical model to then compare controlled and uncontrolled growth in that area; the identification of the specific 'physiographic' features unique to the site through mapping to establish the criteria for urban growth; meticulous delineation of this 'ecological inventory'; and overlays to determine zones of 'prohibition and permissiveness,' and their effect on densities.

Once these zones are determined, the principles that should determine urban form are defined, followed by a concluding 'work programme' or 'action plan' to implement the concepts involved. In the Washington Metropolitan Plan, as in the Plan for the Valleys before it and the scores of plans that follow, McHarg begins with a stirring exhortation that involves active historical processes, the meaning of ecology and the importance of respecting local identity. His definition of ecology here as: 'that branch of science which investigates the relation of organism, environment and peace', indicates his complete belief in his doctrine of environmental particularity. The firm would complete more than 150 landscape projects before McHarg finally resigned in 1979, ranging in scale from a prototypical environmental analysis and management plan for the Woodlands (a community for 50,000 people outside Houston, Texas), to a new capital for Nigeria, both completed in 1974.

Design with Nature

Design with Nature, published in 1969, introduced McHarg as well as his doctrines and method to an international, non-professional audience. It has been consistently reprinted since, becoming a classic, a potent reminder of the passions that drove the ecological sensibilities of the late 1960s and early 70s. His peroration at the beginning of the Washington Metropolitan Region Plan, in favour of 'a search for identity' in the landscape around the national capital predicts the magisterial sweep of his prose in *Design with Nature*, which was soon to follow, and also captures the spirit of his unforgettable lectures at the University of Pennsylvania.

'Processes alone,' he maintains in the Washington Metropolitan Region Plan, 'explain physical and biological evolution, mountains and oceans, plains and plateaus, uplifting and sinking, erosion and sedimentation. When these are understood, then form and differentiation become comprehensible. Ocean and land, arctic and equator, mountains and marshes, volcano and iceberg. These are dynamic. Coastlines, deserts, ice sheets advance and recede, lakes fill while others form, mountains succumb to erosion and others rise. The lake becomes a marsh, the estuary a delta, the prairie a desert, scrub a forest, a volcano creates an island and continents sink. Plants and animals respond to environmental variety, climate, water, soils and occupy various habitats, revealing by their presence, their morphology, and their associations with the character and diversity of environments. The arctic differs from the tropical rain forest, tundra from the ocean, temperate forest from dessert, plateau from delta. Thus Rio differs from Kansas, New York from Amsterdam, and Washington from them all.'[6]

Relevance for Today

Because many of his ideas have been absorbed into the mainstream of the theory of landscape architecture, architecture and urban planning, Ian McHarg is now either taken for granted, dismissed as a part of the activism of the late 1960s, or else forgotten. But as this overview indicates, he was an important catalyst in the constitution of a new approach to the environment in each of these professional disciplines.

In terms of his relationship to each of the topics being used as a framework here, he made a sustained and eloquent plea for a return to a pre-industrial sensitivity to nature and its nearly infinite variations, including the respect, verging on awe, which traditional societies had for its extremes. He offered a counterpoint to the arrogance of modernists who disregarded regional differences and unpredictable natural events, such as floods, landslides and fires, predicting the growing awareness of diversity that was soon to follow.

His 'method' of separating out certain ecological aspects of sites that he considered appropriate to build on was decidedly low-tech, as well as being oversimplified, but has also been the basis for far more technological approaches to categorizing ecosystems and the appropriate level of architectural intervention into them, such as the Geographic Information System and Ken Yeang's updated version of McHarg's method, described on pp. 194–5.

McHarg's classic Plan for the Valleys clearly places him on Ebenezer Howard's anti-density side of the urbanistic debate, yet many of the provisions of the plan prefigure those later adopted by the New Urbanists, who are also discussed here. All of this suggests that he certainly is relevant and that it is necessary to understand his role in changing the direction of all the design disciplines in order to fully appreciate attitudes that are prevalent today.

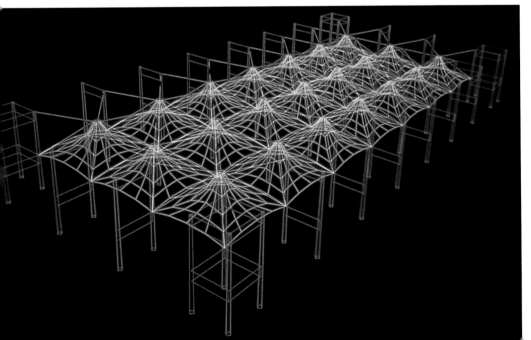

above and left **Hajj Terminal, Jeddah Airport**,
Skidmore, Owings and Merrill, 1975–82
Built to deal with the annual influx of millions of
Makkah pilgrims, the new terminal revolutionized fabric
construction. A new tensile fabric, Teflon-coated
fibreglass, was designed to cope with the extreme
climate.

19

A Revolution in Tent Technology

Tensile membrane structures offer one of the most efficient forms of covering, and are particularly suited to hot climates

Background

Tensile membrane design is an area in which the line of demarcation between high and appropriate technology is difficult to draw. The manufacturing, construction techniques and processes used in fabric structures are becoming increasingly sophisticated, but the results are a model of maximum environmental effect using minimal means.

Early on the technique was used almost exclusively in the Middle East, beginning with the Hajj Terminal at Riyadh Airport (for which Frei Otto acted as a consultant), where it suits the climate perfectly, and fits in with a tent tradition. The High-Tech element came in the creation of an appropriate covering material. However, the tensile membrane technique was also used at Denver International Airport, with great success: there the white peaks of the structure echo the forms of the nearby mountains, showing sensitivity to context as well as efficient use of materials.

The advantages of this technique, then, lie in improved air circulation and low solar gain, but also in creating large, unbroken spaces that can be lit from above – and, as seen in Denver Airport, can be used anywhere.

Key Projects

Hajj Terminal, Jeddah Airport, 1975–82

King Fahd International Stadium, Riyadh, completed 1986

Prophet's Mosque courtyard project, 1992

Denver Municipal Airport, 1989–95

Signposts

Energy efficiency Part II: 1, 11, 13, 16

Local traditions Part II: 20, 21, 23, 24; Part III: 2

Climate control Part II: 7, 8, 9, 10, 12, 15

'Eco-Tech' Part II: 11, 17

Use of computers Part II: 18; Part III: 1

Any discussion of tensile membrane design inevitably must begin with the engineer Frei Otto. Born in Saxony in 1925, he served as a pilot in the German Air Force in the Second World War and was captured near the end of the conflict. He experimented with tensile canopies as coverings for buildings destroyed in the prison camp in Chartres, France, where he was held, and had very little material to work with. After his release he studied architecture at the Technical University of Berlin in 1947 and soon after graduation he founded the Development Centre for Lightweight Construction there, which had a large developmental laboratory and workshop where he could experiment with lightweight structures.

Biological Forms

Otto was fascinated by the fact that while tensile structures are near weightless, they are also structurally strong and stable, especially when combined with high-strength steel cables. Determined to use fabric structure to create environmentally responsive shelter, he pioneered computer-based procedures for determining the optimum shapes and reactions to material forces, studying biological forms such as bubbles and shells for inspiration. His experiments with pneumatic membranes stabilized by air and gas pressure were a breakthrough in greenhouse, grain-silo and storage-tank structures. He conceptualized an entirely different kind of architecture that would rely on tension, rather than compression (which has been the historical norm), focusing instead on stress placed on a material to cause extension, or a force or combination of forces exerting a pull against the resistance of a material. Tensile structures can be subdivided into freely suspended and pre-stressed systems, each with a different shape. The unstressed tent has evenly distributed forces, while those on a pre-stressed form are not. Both can cover large spans economically and require fewer materials than conventional buildings.

A Breakthrough

The pavilion Otto designed for the Federal Republic of Germany at Expo '67 in Montreal was an important step forward in tensile construction, as was his open-air theatre at Bad Hersfeld, Germany, in the same year, in which he introduced a convertible roof that mechanically extended and retracted. These projects and others were the training ground for the next generation of tensile engineers, including Bodo Rasch, David Geiger and Horst Berger, some of whom started to work with him at the Institute of Lightweight Structures in Stuttgart.

The Hajj Terminal

Rasch, Geiger and Berger were involved with Otto as consultants on the Hajj Terminal at the Jeddah International Airport in Saudi Arabia, commissioned by project architects Skidmore, Owings and Merrill to help find a solution to the staggeringly difficult problem of providing a comfortable, welcoming facility to efficiently process and provide shelter for the human ocean of pilgrims that arrive in their country for the Hajj each year. At the time a shelter was being contemplated in late 1975, 530,000 Pilgrims were arriving at Jeddah Airport, and the authorities there found that this number was swelling at an annual rate of 50,000 people during the peak eighteen-hour arrival period. The existing airport was barely able to cope with its normal passenger load, let alone the clearance formalities and detailed requirements of the growing numbers of pilgrims that had to remain at the airport while waiting for their government-appointed Saudi guides to process their visas and arrange transportation to their final destination of Makkah, which is about 65 kilometres (40 miles) from Jeddah.

Skidmore, Owings and Merrill were commissioned by the Saudis in 1975 to alleviate this problem with a new terminal to be located on the western corner of the airport and to be used solely by the pilgrims. The architects made an initial decision that would most affect the form of the new Terminal by determining that the processing and waiting functions were significantly exclusive to be divided from each other. While the processing portion of the Terminal seemed to require an enclosed, air-conditioned space, there was no reason for such control in the waiting portion, which could be flexible and totally open.

Early concepts from Skidmore, Owings and Merrill show rather straightforward design approaches to the processing element, but the morphology of the cover over the waiting area ran the gamut in evaluation from steel vaults to giant, open, ribbed concrete mushrooms. All early directions in this portion, while yielding some interesting ideas, proved to be unsatisfactory environmentally because of the heat transfer through each material into the space below. The concrete mushrooms, for example, while very promising formally, tended to absorb heat during the day and then pump it into the interior at night due to the time delay through their thermal mass.

Rediscovering a Local Traditional Form

With all standard approaches eliminated, the way was left open for the designers to venture into what was then the rather murky domain of fabric covering. In late 1975 the state of the art in membrane structures consisted mainly of polyester coated with polyvinyl chloride, a symbiotic combination in which the polyester fibres contributed to the strength of the material and the vinyl coating over it provided the wearability. The fabric that resulted was thin and flexible, with a stretch factor of up to 12 per cent. This great suppleness gave it a distinct advantage in a situation where disassembly and storage of the shelter were required, but was not desirable for a permanent structure.

Serious Disadvantages

Vinyl-coated polyester has other serious disadvantages. The composition of the vinyl begins to change over time, stretching in hot climates and cracking in cold. In protracted warmth, the surface becomes sticky, attracting wind-blown debris like flypaper, causing either high maintenance costs or the expensive option of replacement of the fabric after five years or so. Vinyl-coated polyester is also highly flammable, producing a thick, black noxious smoke when it burns. The material is also not very insulative, with low reflectivity making heat gain high, so that it is necessary to use another fabric as a liner, which increases construction cost.

A New Material

The engineering consultant on the Hajj Terminal project, working with the architects and the Dupont Chemical Company in the United States, helped to develop a new tensile fabric called Teflon-coated fibreglass. In this fabric, Dupont's Teflon is used as a covering for Beta glass fibre by Owens Corning. The Beta filament differs from polyester in that it has an elongation or stretch capacity of only about one per cent. By twisting two or three of the filaments together, what had been a straight line is reshaped like a spring and stretches about twice as much as the straight filament. The weaving generally adds about two and a half percent to the elongation of the yarns. The space between the warp and fill yarns represents a tiny rectangular window. The diagonal of that window is the weakest direction. The first task of the Teflon coating is to fill that window and control the stretch on the bias. Tension is applied to the fabric as the wide belt of material passes through a vat of milky Teflon. Increasing the tension will elongate the window and decrease its width. Opacifiers can be added to the Teflon, which will make it more opaque and more reflective. The final layer of coating chemically permits fabric widths to be joined by heat sealing.

An average coated fibreglass fabric reflects 70–75 per cent of the solar energy that strikes it; about 6 per cent passes through, and 20 per cent is absorbed by the fabric. Half of the absorbed heat is re-radiated outward and half is re-radiated inward. The fabric that is created in this process is remarkably tough, with a tensile strength of 800 pounds per linear inch. In addition it can withstand temperatures of up to 700°C (1,500°F) without undergoing any compositional change and has a lifespan of about thirty years.

The engineering procedure consisted of computer analysis, which was still in its infancy at that time, as well as wind-tunnel testing and the full-scale construction of two sample units of the structure which were tested to failure. This procedure was the first time that empirical data from wind-tunnel testing and a full-size mock up could be compared with computer analysis, with funds allocated by the Saudi government making this breakthrough possible.

The King Fahd International Stadium in Riyadh

The Hajj Terminal and the new technology used to build it generated a great deal of excitement among architects and engineers everywhere, especially in Saudi Arabia, where the Teflon-coated fibreglass tensile structure seemed to be the ideal, environmentally responsive building system for its extreme climatic conditions. Soon after the completion of the Hajj Terminal, Ian Fraser, John Roberts and Partners were commissioned to design a new international sports stadium in Riyadh, using the same system. The fabric tension roof they designed is a ring with an outer diameter of 288 metres (945 feet) and a centre opening of 134 metres (440 feet), with twenty-four tents formed by a 60-metre (200-foot) high vertical mesh. The interior edge of the membrane is formed by a huge circular ring cable, while the outside edges are pulled back by a series of catenary cables supported by sloping edge mesh, anchored to a berm.

As at the Hajj Terminal, the fabric cover of the International Stadium performs extremely well in the extreme, hot arid climate of Saudi Arabia, keeping football fans relatively cool by reflecting near two-thirds of the sun's radiation, and absorbing most of the rest, so that both the Jeddah Terminal and this stadium stand as good as examples of high technology serving an appropriate environmental purpose and performing brilliantly.

Kinetic Umbrellas

After he finished his work on the Hajj Terminal, Bodo Rasch, as part of S and L Engineers (Sander Konstruktionen und Leichtbau GmbH) designed a shading system for the King Fahd Bin Abdul Aziz extension to the Prophet's Holy Mosque, using 17 by 18 metre (56 by 59 foot) convertible umbrellas. These are covered by the same Teflon-coated fibreglass fabric as was used in the Hajj Terminal and International Sports Stadium. They close at night to allow cold

above, left **Roofs, Hajj Terminal, Jeddah Airport**, Skidmore, Owings and Merrill, 1975–82

above, right **Prophet's Holy Mosque**, Madinah, 1992
These 'kinetic umbrellas', which cover a historically sensitive courtyard, are opened during the day to provide shade for pilgrims, but then close at night to allow cool air to circulate. The convertible shade structures are by Bodo Rasch, of S and L Engineers, while the architectural design is by Dr Kamal Ismail.

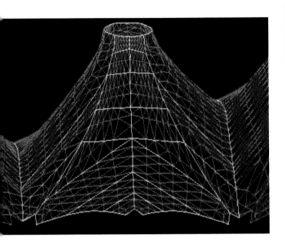

above and right **Denver International Airport**,
Fentress Bradburn Architects, 1989–95
Computer analysis has played an important role in the
development of fabric structures, being able to model
stresses and heating effects, and predict stable or
efficient forms.

evening air to fill the courts, and then open at dawn to trap it and shade the court during the
day. These kinetic structures are a fitting legacy of the convertible roof that Frei Otto
introduced at Bad Hersfeld in the late 1960s and bring this tradition full circle as the end of
the first phase of the tensile revolution.

A Second Phase
Between the late 1970s, when the research and development of the Teflon fibreglass fabric for
the Hajj Terminal roof was begun, and the Prophet's Holy Mosque extension in the early
1990s, this new membrane and the technology necessary to support it was primarily confined
to Saudi Arabia, and to several smaller projects outside the Kingdom. Its profile literally
increased dramatically in the early 1990s, however, when Fentress Bradburn Architects in

Denver International Airport, Fentress Bradburn Architects, 1989–95
The peaks of the structure mimic the Rocky Mountains, just behind, an acknowledgment of the setting. The fabric structure was chosen for its efficiency in spanning large areas, but it also proved to have great daylighting benefits.

Denver, Colorado, selected it as the primary structural system for the Denver International Airport, its largest public application outside of Jeddah.

The process involved in selecting the material for the Denver Airport reveals much about the coming of age of this membrane and its supportive technology. The Rocky Mountains blocked air traffic to Denver in the early days of aviation in the United States, until Mayor Benjamin Stapleton ordered construction of the City of Denver Municipal Airport which opened in October, 1929. By 1934, it was an important national hub and was renamed after the mayor that had foreseen the change in aircraft technology that would make it so. A series of public hearings, beginning in 1972, was initiated to determine how Stapleton Airport could be expanded to handle a large increase in traffic and by the time these ended, in 1987, the decision had been made to build a new airport to the northeast of Denver. Federico Peña, who was elected Mayor in 1983, dedicated himself to implementing this plan.

In 1989, the City and County of Denver selected and commissioned Fentress Bradburn Architects to design the Passenger Terminal Complex at Denver International Airport, and they led a team consisting of Lam Associates, Severud Associates, with Horst Berger, Rowan, Williams, Davis and Irwin, Shen Milson Wilke, Black and Ventch and the Architectural Energy Corporation.

Responding to Mayor Peña's mandate to build an airport with six airways and 110 gates to accommodate 72 million people a year (which would make it America's second busiest airport), and to open by 1992, Curtis Fentress arrived at a concept idea of a peaked profile that would mirror the ridges of the Rocky Mountains in the background. Early model studies of possible roof structures that could be used to achieve this profile indicate a design evolution that is surprisingly similar to that followed by Skidmore, Owings and Merrill twenty years earlier, in which concrete folded plates or steel was tried first, before Jim Bradburn suggested that a fabric structure would be more efficient.[1] He contacted Horst Berger, who had recently joined Severud Engineers, to consult, and Berger, who had also been instrumental in the development of the Teflon-coated fibreglass fabric for the Hajj Terminal project, brought all of his experience and expertise to bear on this new challenge. Computer modelling had improved a great deal in the two-decade interval between the two groundbreaking projects, allowing even more stringent parameters to be established, so that the configuration of the peaks is far from arbitrary, but take into account structural considerations.

The architects and their team arrived at a straightforward solution of two rows of seventeen masts flanking a central space called the Great Hall, supported by two sets of primary cables which allowed the 300-metre (1,000-foot) long roof to be subdivided into three sections, allowing the raising of the central section to accommodate bridges running underneath the roof. The Great Hall is a reference to the large-span railroad stations made possible by the new materials introduced to engineers during the Industrial Revolution and the airport terminals of the 1930s, but the use of translucent fabric in this instance introduces the clear light of this region, reinforcing the sense of place. Skylights were placed on the tops of the masts to increase this sense of lightness and to allow vegetation in the interior, underscoring another characteristic of the region. This also reduced the amount of artificial light needed in the ticketing and check-in areas in the Great Hall during the day, substantially reducing energy costs.

Advantages Confirmed

All of the environmental advantages of Teflon-coated fibreglass first realized in Jeddah were confirmed in Denver, with some notable variations and additions. Its high reflectivity prevented heat gain, as before, but this is not desirable for much of the year in a region that gets cold, and experiences heavy snow storms. Insulation was considered but was rejected because quality control could not be guaranteed and the translucent quality of the membrane, which is such a desirable feature in this region, would have been lost, along with energy and cost savings realized by reducing artificial lighting during the day. During the summer, however, increased research capacity has allowed confirmation of the effect of heat stratification in the tent-like forms, in which hot air rises and cool air falls, allowing air conditioning to be directed to where it is needed. In addition, according to the engineers the fabric roof has so little mass it acts exothermically, allowing the dissipation of heat.[2]

Construction techniques instituted in Jeddah, where the fabric was attached to collars around the base of each mast which were then lifted simultaneously to maintain the required tension in an entire twenty-one tent ensemble were also followed and improved upon in Denver. Roof construction there was completed in less than ten months between February and October 1992. The masts were erected in pairs, moving from north to south on either side of the Great Hall. The mast tops were stabilized by steel trusses as the sequence progressed. The fabric was then laid out on the floor and the outer panels were raised first, followed by the inner panels to retain stability. The fast construction time also saved energy, adding to the environmental advantages of using fabric membrane structures. The architects and engineers have estimated that it also avoided using 300 tons of steel and 61,000 linear metres (200,000 linear feet) of concrete shear wall that their earlier non-fabric concepts would have required.[3]

The Largest Fabric Structure

When completed in February 1995, the Denver Airport was 'the largest structurally integrated Teflon-coated fibreglass tensile membrane roof in the world'.[4] The Passenger Terminal Complex, at 185,000 square metres (two million square feet) in area, could accommodate up to 55 million passengers a year, its thirty-four distinctive peaks held up by more than 16 kilometres (ten miles) of steel cable and 30,000 clamps. It is another important milestone in the ongoing development of a promising technological system replete with environmental advantages and traditional precedents.

left and above **Menara Mesiniaga**, Kuala Lumpur, 1989–92

One of Yeang's best-known projects is this fourteen-storey tower just outside Kuala Lumpur. A series of 'sky courts' are cut deep into the tower, while wide aluminium bands are used to prevent glare. The swimming pool on the roof (above) is used by local families at the weekend.

20

Kenneth Yeang: The Bioclimatic Skyscraper

The 'green' skyscrapers of Yeang reinvent a modern form to create a future typology that blends economy of space with improved standards of living

Biography

Kenneth Yeang is one of the best-known architects working with an environmental sensitivity today. Born in Malaysia, he studied with Ian McHarg, who encouraged him to design according to regional microclimate.

Central to his practice is the skyscraper, an unusual choice for an architect concerned with ecological issues. However, Yeang believes that due to pressures of space the skyscraper is inevitable, in which case it might as well be improved. He has made some decisive changes to the standard design, introducing greenery through 'sky courts', encouraging patterns of behaviour similar to those seen in the street (though vertically), using the height of his buildings to harness solar energy more efficiently and to use wind for effective natural ventilation, and moving the core to the outside of the structure.

Yeang's use of 'sky courts' in particular has been highly influential on a new generation of environmentally responsive tall buildings, including Foster's Swiss Re tower. He continues to practice in Malaysia as the design partner of T. R. Hamzah and Yeang, and is the recipient of an Aga Khan Award.

Key Projects

Menara Mesiniaga, Kuala Lumpur, 1989–92
Menara UMNO, Penang, 1995–8
BATC Masterplan, Kuala Lumpur, 1998
EDITT Tower, Singapore, begun 1998

Signposts

Local traditions Part II: 19, 21, 23, 24; Part III: 2
Natural ventilation Part II: 6, 7, 11, 16, 23, 24
Sustainability Part II: 11, 15, 17, 21, 23
Conservation Part II: 18, 21, 23; Part III: 3
Ecological skyscrapers Part II: 11, 23

The skyscraper has become more lovable since it was carnally personified by Rem Koolhaas in *Delirious New York*. But it still seems an unlikely object of ecological desire after having been reviled by environmentalists as an energy glutton for so long. Kenneth Yeang, however, is determined to make it so. The pragmatism of his position is revelatory: since this typology, like the automobile, seems to be a fact of life of our rapidly urbanizing future, why not try to improve it and make it environmentally sound?

Yeang is fond of using the metaphor of a young tennis player discovered by a coach to justify his specialization. Seeing great promise in the strength of the young man's backhand, the coach made the player a star by perfecting that stroke, while making the rest of his game average. The skyscraper is Yeang's backhand: he has perfected it through writing as well as building, refining the descriptive and theoretical sides of his approach in *The Skyscraper Bioclimatically Considered* (1996) and *The Green Skyscraper* (1999). In the first, he describes 'bioclimatic' architecture as the use of passive, low-energy techniques such as building configuration, shading, component placement, material selection, solar- and wind-related orientation, natural ventilation, 'sky courts' and vertical landscaping. He argues that using the climatic and meteorological data of a specific site, one can create an environmentally interactive building that provides greater physiological comfort for its occupants.[1]

Yeang is an equal mixture of visionary altruist and pragmatic rationalist. A bioclimatic approach is important, in his view, not just because it benefits the environment generally, but because 'designing with climate results in the reduction of the overall energy consumption of the building through the use of passive devices… This results in operational cost savings.'[2] This, in turn, cuts electrical energy which reduces the use of non-renewable fossil fuels, carbon dioxide emissions, air pollution and temperature inversions: a scenario that no client or ecologist can fault.

This measured balance between broader environmental goals and the special interests of clients and developers characterizes Yeang's rationale, while making him a perfect example of the sustainable ethic described in detail on pp. 165–73. Defined by its detractors as capitalism with a green face, sustainability has, at its best, provided a middle ground, or compromise position, that allows development to continue within a framework of environmental sensibility. Yeang's second justification for a 'bioclimatic' architecture is that it results in a more humane, healthy environment, accompanied by client-consoling assurances that natural ventilation also increases business productivity.

A Debt to McHarg

Yeang's theoretical debt to his teacher and mentor Ian McHarg is most evident in his third and final rationale for using bioclimatic design: that it allows for greater variation in built form because of the possibility of responding to regional microclimates. The enormous contribution of Ian McHarg, discussed in detail on pp. 175–83, did much to demolish the International Style fiction that a uniform response to global climatic extremes was not only made possible by new technologies, but was also an essential, politically symbolic statement. The regionally adaptive response that McHarg advocated has only recently been adopted at the governmental level, most visibly in the United States.[3]

Yeang expands his three-part definition of bioclimatic architecture – of passive techniques, environmental amelioration and regional expression – into specific strategies he identifies as: vertical circulation; 'Life in the Sky'; vertical landscape; ventilation; cladding; sub- and superstructure; and geography and services. By design or not, each of his most recent major skyscrapers seems to emphasize a different one of the sub-sets of tactics, almost as if each is being offered as an instalment or pedagogical example of the broad agenda he has in mind. Four clear examples are the EDITT Tower (for the core), Menara Mesiniaga (for sky courts), the Nara Tower (for vertical greenery) and UMNO (for natural ventilation).

The EDITT Tower Illustrates the New Use of a Core

The strategy of vertical circulation predominates in the EDITT (Ecological Design In The Tropics) Tower, where an external core is placed on the perimeter to free up the inside as an atria and also to act as a shield against heat gain during the hottest part of the day. Typically placed in the centre of either a rectangular or square shaft in the past, the core was considered an immutable given in skyscraper design until recently. Its new role in Yeang's syntax will be described here. In the EDITT Tower, as in many of Yeang's other skyscrapers, while the core is located on the perimeter, it is not entirely freestanding due to structural and code requirements. This allows the centre to be opened up as an expanding and contracting vertical courtyard, fringed with lush vegetation, which entices natural ventilation up through the middle of the tower, promoting transpiration.

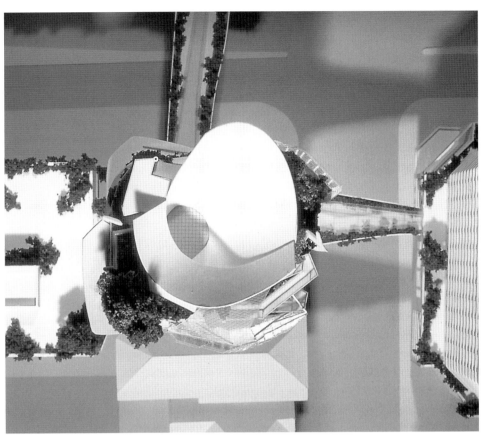

above, left and right **Model of the EDITT Tower**, Singapore, begun 1998

Yeang begins with a site analysis, identifying local flora and fauna that might be incorporated into the building. In this case the dense urban context meant that it was classified as 'zero culture'. The aim, then, was to create biodiversity where there was none. A ramp ensures continuous space between the street and the floors of the skyscraper. The façades are heavily planted, as can be seen in the bird's-eye view of the model, right.

'Life in the Sky' in the Menara Mesiniaga

The 'Life in the Sky' consideration is a more qualitative strategy, shifting the focus from the technological advances that have made it possible to build taller buildings to the physiological well-being of the users. Yeang argues that 'conventional urban design carried out at the ground plane is concerned with such aspects as place-making, vistas, creating public realms, civic zones, linkages, figure-ground and the massing of built form. This type of thinking must now be extended upwards.'[4] To humanize floor slabs disconnected from the ground, Yeang's sense of sustainable compromise again comes into play, prompting him to recommend plan layouts that address 'human habits' and 'logical cultural patterns' as well as meeting commercial requirement. He feels that these patterns, which in Kuala Lumpur include easy access to prayer rooms (*surau*) and hawkers' stalls , are best accommodated in 'sky courts', open, transitional spaces between the inside and outside of the skyscraper.

The Menara Mesiniaga (1989–92), which is arguably the architect's best-known project since it won an Aga Khan Award in 1999, displays the most overt use of the 'sky court' concept of any of Yeang's completed buildings. This headquarters for the IBM representative in Malaysia, which is now a highly visible landmark on the highway connecting Kuala Lumpur with its international airport, attracts attention because it is so obviously different in appearance from other high-rise towers in the city. The 'sky courts,' which are three-storey-high recessed terraces cut deep into the façade, begin at the top of a high, heavily planted earth-bermed base, and spiral around the face of the circular tower. These were originally intended to be planted, to carry the vegetation on the base in a verdant coil up through the middle of the metal capsule. This has not yet happened, due to cost, but in any case these atriums are successful in directing the convective currents of cool air rising from the planted mound up, around and into the building.

Conventional curtain-wall glazing is used only on the cooler north and south façades of the Menara; all east- and west-facing windows are shaded by wide aluminium bands projected out from the building above them, positioned by solar angles. This animates the tower, making it a three-dimensional description of diurnal patterns, a High-Tech sundial that shows how mute skyscraper façades have been in the past. There is a substantial amount of landscaping involved in a tower this size, magnifying questions about maintenance. Yeang has anticipated the support necessary to keep plants growing by providing specially designed robot arms mounted on tracks that follow the spiral and also double as window and cladding washers. He has also used the spiral form to best advantage by having higher floors shade those below, facilitating the growth of shade-giving planting.

A Hanging Gardens for the 21st Century

These High-Tech Hanging Gardens of Babylon, relocated to South-East Asia and upgraded for the 21st century, have a hierarchy of green spaces in the air, including large interior atria, terraces, interior courtyards and private gardens. Each of these is intended to be surrounded by plants and flowers that change with the seasons. These regularly spaced and carefully integrated 'sky-court oases', which Yeang calls 'the lungs' of the tower, are also expected to act as sound breaks between floors, ensuring privacy for those using this hierarchy of outdoor gardens in the sky. The atria, which are the largest spaces in this ranked order, are envisioned as a vertical, interlocking network of spaces, criss-crossed with bridges that connect the elevator and service cores at the periphery, which have also been reconfigured to be less confining. These lift cores are strategically aligned along the east–west axis to block the most extreme solar gain and to allow the north and south façades to receive the best light from these directions. The east–west façades are shielded with both cast concrete and perforated metal cladding, while the east and west sides have clear glazing, and open louvers on tiered sun shades.

The Plan Voisin in a Vertical Tube

The Nara Tower in Japan is the most overt and startling statement to date of Yeang's third strategy of using planting on his skyscrapers to counteract the biological imbalance caused by urban conurbation. It is a startling expansion on Le Corbusier's principle of roof gardens, one of his 'Five Points' for a new architecture. These five points were predicated upon the transfer from the predominance of the bearing wall prior to the Industrial Revolution, to the gridded frame system made possible by the introduction of reinforced concrete. But even Le Corbusier, in his revolutionary use of this principle in his Plan Voisin for Paris (1925), in which he proposed replacing all of the medieval quarter with towers hovering over a park, fell short of the vertical scale envisioned by Yeang in the Nara Tower.

Natural Ventilation for UMNO

Natural ventilation is the fourth of Yeang's bioclimatic strategies, important for improved health, enhanced physiological perception and better energy conservation. The UMNO Tower in Penang, Malaysia, the headquarters of the United Malaysian National Organization, is the most graphic, tangible, expression of Yeang's commitment to this strategy and currently

above and right **Menara UMNO**, Penang, 1995–8
This tower is all about natural ventilation. Wind catches direct fresh air deep into the structure, turning wind-load – normally seen as a hindrance to high-rise building – into an asset.

the tallest skyscraper in the city. Described by the architect as a 'vertical cantilever beam', the UMNO Tower is positioned to take advantage of the wind generated by far-away natural features and terrain such as the South China Sea surrounding Penang Island and the mountains in the interior. Yeang calls this the 'wing profile', which results from the shape and gradient of the wind, including turbulence and eddies in the boundary layer high above the ground. The boundary layer is the point of demarcation between variations in air flow caused by differences in the condition of the terrain, and the uniform air flow above it.

Yeang's vision is to turn wind load, which has always been viewed as a problem by skyscraper designers, into an advantage. This has required much closer attention to wind-tunnel testing and data collection, including wind-rose studies. Such studies have also encouraged the use of different cladding on the leeward and windward sides of towers, to offset the different weathering conditions on each, rather than attempting to derive a uniform skin of the John Hancock Tower variety. In that case uniformity led to disastrous results, when negative pressure pulled glass panels from the slick surface of the building. Yeang also takes full aesthetic advantage of this differentiation, exaggerating the use of different materials rather than suppressing them in the modernist manner, to make each tower a three-dimensional translation of climate. Yeang believes that the skin of a tower should not be a barrier, hermetically sealed against the elements, but a permeable 'sieve' which has adjustable openings to control cross ventilation, provide solar protection, regulate natural ventilation and direct wind-swept rain to the proper channels.

The 'vertical cantilever beam' at the UMNO is a large fin, or 'wind wing wall' angled to create an artificial pressure zone and pull wind in through and out of each office floor, providing an estimated thirty air changes per hour. This ventilation is not meant to replace air conditioning, but to augment about thirty per cent of it, depending upon the prevailing temperature distribution and air-pressure differential between the inside and outside of the tower at any given time.

Appearances aren't Always Deceptive

There are any number of candidates among Yeang's latest projects that could be used to illustrate Yeang's fifth bioclimatic strategy – cladding – as well as, or even better than, UMNO. But his selection of grey aluminium for the majority of that tower, ostensibly because it balances temperature distribution and air-pressure differential better than any other colour, is easily the most serendipitous. When combined with the vertical, wing-like fin that directs wind to its interior, the decidedly aeronautical cladding creates a memorable, soaring image that dominates the rest of the city, spread out at unassuming scale beneath it.

Geography is a Critical Factor

Of Yeang's remaining strategies, which he identifies as 'sub and superstructure', 'services' and 'geography', the last seems to be the most forceful prediction of form, especially in the way that it affects the environment in the city.

Defined by him as the relationship of a building with pedestrians, street, city block and city, this factor relates to the greater environmental impact of the high-rise tower in the city, its contextual implications and its physical presence. This wider awareness is evident in the BATC (Business Advancement and Technology Centre) project completed in 2000, since the entire ground plane around the tower has been treated as its horizontal counterpart. Accelerating computer capability has guided exploration of contextual potential and further possibilities for the integration between horizontal and vertical environments. At BATC, the transition appears to be seamless, largely due to the designer's willingness and ability to let the computer lead. The physical realization of this apparent integration will be the true test of such determinism.

A Theoretical Foundation for Bioclimatic Strategies

Yeang is extremely cognizant of the current causal relationship between theory and practice, which has increased dramatically since the formative period of the influence of theory on architecture in the 1950s. *The Green Skyscraper: the Basis for Designing Sustainable Intensive Buildings*, is Yeang's topologically specific riposte to Ian McHarg's *Design with Nature*, with more science. It reiterates his justification for the focus on the skyscraper, which he rationalizes to be an efficient means of ecological amelioration given the predominance of such towers in rapidly growing cities throughout the world, and the exponential potential of urban growth to affect ecological systems. 'My contention', he maintains, 'is simply that the

Model of the BATC Signature Tower, 1998
This sixty-five storey tower is actually a high-rise park, with a hierarchy of landscaped 'places in the sky'. Yeang's 'sky courts' have been widely imitated as a way of humanizing these giant structures.

Model of the BATC Masterplan, seen from above, 1998
A nine-hectare campus of mixed development, an example of Yeang's 'bioclimatic city', his explorations into urban fabric. His approach owes much to Ian McHarg's 'ecological land-use analysis', discussed on pp. 175–83.

issue of the ecological design of large buildings (whether we like these buildings or not) is just as vital as the ecological design of the small building types – in fact more crucial, because of their scale and volume and consumption of energy and materials.'[5] His rationale, beyond this initial contention, is based on the assumption that the skyscraper is the most ubiquitous building type in all major cities today and demands more attention because of its capacity to consume resources and pollute the environment. Rather than writing the skyscraper off as a detriment to the environment, Yeang sees the building type as having great potential for resource recycling, as well as being a possible catalyst for a reduction of automobile use and pollution, because of the higher densities and mixed-use occupancy that it can accommodate.

The Green Skyscraper, in addition to being a personal, theory-based manifesto, also reads like a primer of ecological design, in parts, especially in a section in which Yeang puts forward the main points that, in his view, comprise green design. In abbreviated form, these are: a recognition of the interdependency between architecture and ecology; a realization of the resilience and the limits of the natural environment; acknowledgment of the importance of biodiversity; awareness of the connectivity of ecological systems; the understanding that synthetic ecological systems can never replicate the complexity of natural systems; a determination to use architecture as a means of repairing and restoring ecosystems; the search for symbiosis between constructed and natural systems, accounting for entropy; acknowledgment that the environment is the final context for all design; conceding that the built environment is dependent upon the energy and resources that the earth supplies, using renewable resources more efficiently; acknowledging the global impact resulting from ecosystem connectivity; controlling the recycling of the built environment back into the ecosystem; using the principles of life-cycle design; sensitivity to ecosystem displacement that construction causes; having a holistic view and being willing to work with other disciplines.[6]

The Environmental Impact of Urban Growth

Yeang's theory of ecological design, which derives from all of these points, is based on the implementation of a set of 'interdependent interactions' that are as complex as the environment itself. To do this, he proposes 'a general framework that structures the entire set of ecological interactions between a designed system and the earth's ecosystems and resources.'[7] This necessitates tracking the flow of natural resources – from extraction, through the building process and then back to the environment – as a lifecycle mechanism. The framework for the tracking model must include a complete description of the built system, the ecosystem and natural resource used, and a mapping of the interactions between the two systems. Yeang believes that systems theory, specifically a partitioned matrix, is the only method of achieving such mapping: he calls this matrix the 'Law of Ecological Design'. The correctness of his assumptions is important because each of them have enormous implications for the way that urban areas will grow in the future and subsequently for the environment, which they share.

left and above **Ministry of Foreign Affairs, Riyadh**,
Henning Larsen, 1989
The Aga Khan Award recognizes work either by Muslim
architects or in a Muslim context. In this case the
architect was from Europe, but made many studies of
local Islamic and vernacular architecture to arrive at a
synthetic approach.

21

The Aga Khan Award for Architecture: A Paradigm Shift

The Aga Khan Award has played a crucial role in encouraging, recognizing and promoting environmentally and culturally sympathetic architecture in the Muslim world

Background

His Highness the Aga Khan, the hereditary Imam of the Shia Ismaili Muslims, established an award for architecture in 1976. It was intended to increase public awareness of Islamic culture and create a forum for debating the appropriateness of contemporary architecture in an increasingly diverse worldwide Muslim community.

Since 1980, this award has been given every three years and in selecting winners, which have varied in number in each cycle, the jury has typically considered project context, social and economic factors and environmental responsiveness as being of primary importance. In retrospect, there has been a consistent pattern of recognizing the balanced and innovative utilization of available resources in meeting cultural needs, as well as choosing projects that set a high standard of excellence for the future.

Past winners include Kenneth Yeang and Abdel Wahed El Wakil, but also some non-Muslims who have made a contribution to architecture in Muslim countries, such as Henning Larsen, for his Ministry of Foreign Affairs in Riyadh.

Key Projects

Citra Niaga Urban Development, 1986
Grameen Bank Housing Programme, 1984–
Ministry of Foreign Affairs, Riyadh,
Henning Larsen, 1989

Signposts

Local traditions Part II: 19, 20, 23, 24; Part III: 2

Community building Part II: 2, 4, 12, 22

Self-build Part II: 6, 7, 9, 12

Sustainability Part II: 11, 15, 17, 20, 23

Conservation Part II: 18, 20, 23; Part III: 3

Few competitions have had as much influence on the development of an ecologically sound architecture, nor are quite as rigorous, as the Aga Khan Award. Just the scale of the Award is staggering. A Steering Committee, chaired by the Aga Khan himself, governs the Award and oversees the distribution of prizes totalling nearly five hundred thousand dollars as designated by the independent Master Jury, the largest architectural prize in the world. The awards include architects, construction professionals, crafts experts and clients considered most responsible for the final realization of each project. At the completion of its eighth cycle the Award had documented over 6,000 projects which had been nominated from all over the world. No other award archive is as wealthy in data and as well cared for. The jury meets twice. At its first meeting it reviews approximately five hundred submissions enrolled through the Awards Nomination Programme. The jurors examine the documentation on each project and typically retain about thirty, which are then analysed on site by technical review teams selected by the Award.

The technical review teams are made up of architectural professionals from various disciplines, including housing, urban planning, landscape design and restoration. In examining each shortlisted project, they verify an original date, add new information corresponding to a detailed set of criteria, and solicit user reactions. The reviewers also respond to specific concerns and questions posed by the Master Jury. To ensure maximum objectivity, reviewers are assigned to projects located outside their native countries. The comprehensive documentation generated by this process is itself a singular achievement, incrementally representing not only a substantial history of Muslim architecture, but also a profile of an emerging environmental sensibility and social consciousness that other, non-Muslim architects can follow.

The Aga Khan Trust for Culture

In addition to designating prizes, the Award also organizes international and regional seminars during each cycle that address issues relevant to the Muslim built environment. The Aga Khan's concern with the cultural dimension of development and the experience gained through the Award and all of its activities, led to the establishment of the Aga Khan Trust for Culture in 1988. The Trust now incorporates the Award as well as an Education and Culture Programme and a Historic Cities Support Programme. The Education and Cultural Programme focuses on improving the training of architectural professionals working in the Islamic world, increasing cross-cultural understanding of the close connection between architecture and culture in Islamic civilizations and raising awareness of Muslim cultural plurality. The Historic Cities Support Programme, established in 1992, concentrates on the revitalization of historic urban settlements in the Islamic world. Physical rehabilitation is achieved by organizing community participation, training, and local institution building, as well as the construction of landmarks, and strategic planning assistance to local authorities. The medieval core of Cairo, as well as Zanzibar, Samarkand and Granada are only a few of the historical Muslim enclaves that have benefited from the Historic Cities Support Programme.

Recording and Inspiring Change

Since the Award was first established, the quality of architecture in the developing regions of the world in which Muslims predominate has increased substantially, in tandem with progressive growth. The physical, social and economic complications of community building have also increased, as has public awareness of the expanding interaction between Muslim and non-Muslim cultures, which has substantially raised the profile and scope of influence of the Award.

Four General Categories

Lines of distinction are not always clear, but the awards presented since 1980 fall into four general categories, although those have never been officially mandated by the Steering Committee. In addition to what the Aga Khan has referred to as an 'architecture of quality,' these are: community improvement; conservation, restoration and preservation; and the reversal of environmental degradation – all of which are germane to the three themes that guide this book.

An Architecture of Quality

Promoting quality seems an obvious aim of any award, but takes an added significance in relationship to contemporary Muslim architecture. Because these projects are predominantly located in the developing world, Muslim architecture was once perceived as being of a lower standard – reversing this perception has been a key strategy for the Award. A selective list of past winners, arguably considered to be in this category, include such translations of tradition as Fathy's disciple Abdel Wahed El Wakil's Halawa House in Agamy, Egypt (1980 award) and the Corniche Mosque in Jeddah (1989), Jean Nouvel's Institute du Monde Arabe in Paris (1989), the Ministry of Foreign Affairs in Riyadh by Henning Larsen (1989), and the reinvention of the Malaysian vernacular in the Salinger House by Jimmy Lim (1998). 'Quality' is also represented by technological breakthroughs such as Skidmore, Owings and Merrill's Hajj Terminal in Jeddah (1983), discussed on pp. 186–7 as a catalyst in the revolution in membrane structures, and by the Tuwaiq Palace (1998), in which this technology is wedded to a curvilinear rendition of traditional Najdi forms. There are many other instances, such as the National Assembly Building (1989) in Dhaka, Bangladesh, by Louis Kahn, and the Menara Mesiniaga by Kenneth Yeang in Kuala Lumpur, Malaysia (1995), in which form was primarily generated by environmental considerations, but in which the excellence of the execution of these forms is an overwhelming consideration.

Inclusiveness

The Aga Khan Award has recognized non-Muslim architects as long as the project concerned meets their general criteria and is in an appropriate context. One unspoken dichotomy involved in 'an architecture of quality' is that Muslim architects are better able to interpret their own cultural tradition, but often lack the technical support and resources to do so, due to the limitations of working in the developing world. The Ministry of Foreign Affairs in Riyadh, by Larsen, for example, is a building of exceptional quality, but is also illustrative of the lack of sensitivity with which architects from outside the Islamic tradition often approach the task of designing within it, and so is a valuable case study of this paradox.

In 1979, the Project Ministry of Foreign Affairs sponsored a limited competition, inviting twelve well-known architectural firms to participate. The programme issued to the competitors stressed the desire for an exemplary building that would be a model for other ministries in the future. The programme also made clear the desire to depart as much as possible from the Westernized export architecture that had tended to prevail in Saudi Arabia before the competition was organized. After Larsen was commissioned, the Project Ministry suggested that he visit as many historical Islamic sites, inside and outside the Kingdom, as possible, and although he is a Corbusian modernist, he obviously made a sincere effort to incorporate many of the lessons learned from that trip, as well as to reflect a traditionally Najdi language in the design.

This has resulted in a closed-down, massive exterior, reminiscent of historical monuments in the region around Riyadh, which also provides the thermal mass necessary to protect against extremely high summer temperatures. Anticipating a time in the future when the oil that once led to a profligate attitude toward energy use in the Kingdom is depleted, the Project Ministry encouraged Larsen to create an advertisement of a new attitude toward conservation. The massiveness is due to a thick cavity wall that absorbs most of the heat gain, with only a few small windows punched through it to reduce glare and allow diffuse golden light to penetrate into the interior. The Ministry was officially dedicated by King Fahad Ibu Abdul Aziz on 25 November, 1984.

The Ministry rises only four storeys above its raised plinth base, but the massiveness of its walls, combined with the small, repetitive, punched-out windows, conveys the impression of a Najdi fortress. Its external severity contrasts dramatically with the episodic spatial sequencing of the interior syncopated by the mysterious half light, filtered by locally carved tamarisk *mushrabbiya* screens covering the punched windows on the interior. A misting fountain in the centre of a triangular *majlis*, in which visitors gather before they are screened and selectively directed to the specific department or official they seek, reinforces the traditional contrast between hard exterior and soft interior typical of Islamic architecture in the past. Long, wide banquettes, built into the side of a raised arcaded walkway that follows the perimeter of the central court, symbolize the offer of rest that by Bedouin tradition a host must offer a guest. Small open-air courtyards also penetrate each of the office sectors strung out along the building perimeter separated from the triangular *majlis* court by an internal 'street.' These small courts keep the offices from being cut off from natural light and are colour coded for ease of orientation and to promote identification with each sector. The intense colours, balanced against tamarisk pergolas and *mushrabbiyas*, palm trees and small fountains contribute to a sense of peace and privacy, quietly closing the cycle of public and semi-public space leading to them.

Avoiding Didactic Reinterpretation

Henning Larsen has used what he has referred to as an 'international formal language meant to reflect the Islamic culture within global forces', and has managed to straddle the fine line between the respectful reinterpretation and historicist didacticism. In spite of his efforts, however, Iraqi artist Waddah Faris was subsequently commissioned to cover what the client perceived to be large expanses of white wall with three-dimensional designs in plaster, and to provide more ornate grillwork and entrance doors that those Larsen had designed. Larsen had stressed 'global cultural forces' and Corbusian modernism too much, in the client's view. This subsequent change demonstrates that, in spite of the architect's best intentions, and of his real contribution in providing an environmentally responsive building based on traditional prototypes, he misread his client's wishes, because he was not a part of that culture.

Community Improvement

A substantial number of projects selected by the Aga Khan Award since its inception fall into the second category of 'community improvement', a prosaic title that does not begin to convey the nearly miraculous, life-changing achievement that they collectively represent. The numerous Kampong improvement schemes, neighbourhood-rebuilding housing projects and institutional restructuring programmes that have been recognized are all indicators of what has been euphemistically called 'empowerment' but translates as people giving up on government and public institutions and working together to improve their lives.

A cluster of Awards which arguably fall into this category were given in 1989, and are indicative of the level of initiative involved, which is of a very different degree to that usually encountered in the developed world. Three in particular – the upgrading of the village of Asilah in Morocco, the Grameen Bank Housing Programme in Bangladesh, and Citra Niaga Urban Development in Samarinda, Indonesia – are instructive both of the intention of the Award, and of its subsequent pervasive influence.

Bracketing Parameters

The municipality of Asilah in Morocco was recognized for community efforts involving the rehabilitation of a small town on the Atlantic coast. Two local men, Mohammed Benaissa and

top **Salinger House**, Jimmy Lim, 1992
above **National Assembly, Capital Complex, Dhaka**, Louis Kahn, 1962–83

The geographical area covered by the Aga Khan Award is vast, stretching from the Near East to South-East Asia. The Award also recognizes non-Muslim architects working in Muslim countries, such as Louis Kahn.

Mohammed Melehi, came back to Asilah after graduate studies abroad, determined to improve their town. The highly personalized way in which they did so began with the question of how the innate creativity of a community can be marshalled for positive change. The first steps that they took in attempting to answer that question are an object lesson in the effectiveness of straightforward tactics, and have served as an inspiration for other such communities throughout the world. They began by organizing a small cultural festival in the town in the summer of 1978, which attracted nearly one thousand visitors from the local area. This modest event gave the townspeople a renewed sense of civic pride and self-worth that has continued to grow as rapidly as the festival itself, which now attracts nearly 125,000 people, and is one of the biggest cultural events in the Middle East. The overall rehabilitation of the town has also encouraged many private individuals to build new houses in the traditional manner throughout the fabric of the *medina*, and to replace others which had deteriorated beyond the point of possible restoration.

The Grameen Bank

Another inspiring example of community building, the Grameen Bank Housing Programme, challenges past theories of how to assist in providing self-help housing for the poor throughout the developing world. The project was initiated in Bangladesh (one of the poorest and most populous countries in the world, where nearly fifty per cent of the rural population is both landless and homeless) by Muhamed Yunus, the managing director of the Bank. He began to offer small loans to the rural poor without requiring any collateral, in direct contradiction of the customary reluctance of the financial community to do so in the past. In his view, every human being, regardless of social position, deserves a life of dignity and should be given the opportunity to care for themselves if they have the commitment to do so. Personal commitment, not financial resources, then, becomes the main criterion in determining creditworthiness, and this initial programme has served as a model for the micro-credit organizations which have now revolutionized the way that shelter is provided in indigenous communities throughout the developing world.

With this small housing loan, each borrower is provided with a prefabricated concrete slab, four concrete columns, and twenty-six corrugated metal sheets for a roof. The pre-cast building materials are mass-produced and made available to the borrowers at very low prices. The residents build their houses themselves, typically enlisting the help of all of the members of the family to do so, in order to keep costs low. The end result is a unit that usually consists of a rectangular, 20 square metre (215 square foot) area that is dry and sanitary. Whatever else those inhabitants want to include is usually added on an incremental basis. Since the programme has been in effect, hundreds of thousands of Bangladeshis have benefited from it and nearly 45,000 such homes have been built. With a payback rate of nearly ninety-eight per cent during this time, the Grameen, or 'rural peoples' project has also demonstrated that institutional changes must precede any significant progress in housing for the poor.

Citra Niaga

In comparison to the wide-ranging institutional implications of the Grameen Bank initiative, the major achievement of Citra Niaga is the lesson it offers in the effectiveness of a self-controlling system of cross-subsidies. A democratic management board represents the interests of the local government, as well as the shopkeepers and street pedlars, and both

Grameen Bank Housing Project, 1984–
Owners build the exterior panels of their basic units according to the available resources, using small loans from the Grameen Bank.

equity and benefits have been shared by all three. This project has totally transformed a former slum area – previously occupied by low-income, migratory settlers – into a well-planned urban and commercial complex. The programme has been implemented in three stages, concentrating primarily on a commercial development, which was sold to finance the second stage related to the informal sector. Smaller shops, to be offered for sale, were built in the third phase. As built, the centre is now made up of 224 stalls that have been provided without cost to the street pedlars, as well as 220 shops of various sizes that are incorporated within a series of arcades that cater to medium and high-income shoppers.

Restoration, Conservation and Rehabilitation

Conserving cities and monuments from a culturally rich and stylistically diverse Islamic past is also an obvious priority for an Award that seeks to preserve and promote this heritage. The projects permeated in this broad category, which also overlay community improvements, range from the preservation of entire districts, such as in Istanbul, Turkey (1986), Kairouan, Tunisia (1992), the restoration of Bukhara Old City, Uzbekistan, and the conservation of Old Sana'a (1995), to the concentration of special skills in saving the Ali Qapu, Chehel Sutun and Hasht Behest in Isfahan, Iran (1980). What all the projects share, regardless of scope and scale, is realization through a concentration of communal care and sparse resources, rather than a single, wealthy institution.

The Environment

Each of the categories just described imply sustainable responsiveness to some degree even in 'an architecture of quality.' But increasingly, the Aga Khan Award has encouraged the nomination of projects which employ large-scale landscaping strategies and foster environmental awareness. The Hayy Assafarat Landscaping Programme, awarded in combination with Al-Kindi Plaza, in Riyadh, Saudi Arabia (1989) marked the start of the expansion of this category. The Reforestation Programme of the Middle East Technical University (1995) is perhaps its most remarkable realization since it involves the replanting of thousands of acres of deforested slopes around the Ankara campus of that university. It was courageous for the Award to accept – and the Master Jury to select – such a landscaping project, especially of such magnitude, and its selection confirms that the Aga Khan Award is

above, left **Detail of restored tilework of the Nadir Divan Begi Madrasa, Bukhara**
above, right **Typical Sana'a multistorey dwellings, Old Sana'a, Yemen**

The Aga Khan Trust has long supported conservation projects involving historic Islamic sites. This seems farsighted, since such buildings offer valuable lessons to modern-day architects on low-tech solutions to recurrent problems of heat, humidity and ventilation.

Reforestation Programme of the Middle East Technical University, Ankara, 1995
The Award has also recognized projects that go beyond straightforward architecture to other interventions or environmental improvements.

not just backing new trends, but is also formulating and confirming global awareness of environmental issues. It is significant that such awareness should be generated from an initial motivation to promote a specific socio-cultural position: further verification of the increasing interrelationship between global diversity and ecological stewardship as an alternative to ineffective or non-existent national initiatives.

The Aga Khan alluded to this shift when he said, in his opening address at the Award Presentation Ceremony at the Alhambra in Granada, Spain in October, 1998, that he:

would offer several propositions based on lessons drawn from the twenty-year experience of the Aga Khan Award for Architecture. They are relevant to its future work, and perhaps, more globally, to the process of cultural development and change. The loss of our inheritance of cultural pluralism – the identity it conveys to members of diverse societies, and the originality it represents and stimulates in all of them – will impoverish our societies now and into the future. Sustaining this inheritance will require conscious and concerted efforts involving the best minds and most creative institutions around the world, efforts that must be grounded in an informed understanding of history and cultural context, and yet be forward looking and imaginative as they address the needs of contemporary societies. This work will require an enabling environment, characterized by open and unfettered debate of ideas, a trust in cultural diversity, the celebration and reward of innovation, and a commitment to civil society and pluralistic government.

Permeating Tradition, Technology and Cities

As the Award moves into the 21st century, these ideals continue to guide it. It is at the forefront of the new environmentally sensitive and historically respectful sensibility that it encourages, in direct contrast to the eradication of collective memory that seems to be defining feature of the electronic revolution. In the projects it has permeated, as well as through an ongoing series of conferences and symposia, the Award has shed new light on the same basic issues which are the main focus of this book: the false dichotomy between tradition and technology, the rising importance of urbanism, and the ways in which each of these currently impact the environment. Its contribution has been significant, widespread and sustained, especially in making the public aware of the value of heritage, the need for conservation and the seemingly obvious (but often overlooked) fact that people and the social networks that support them matter far more than egotistical architectural statements.

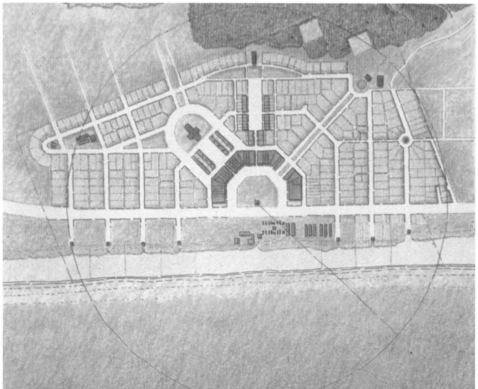

left and above **Seaside development**, Florida, planned by A. Duany and E. Plater-Zyberk, 1984–91
For the New Urbanists, one of the paths to return to traditional community values was to return to traditional vernacular architecture – though not necessarily the vernacular of the region. Many have accused them of indulging in rather sugary nostalgia, and it is difficult to brand Seaside an overwhelmingly successful development.

22

The New Urbanists: Building the Model Community

Dismayed by the rise of anonymous and antisocial suburban sprawl, the New Urbanists developed a set of formal principles to reintroduce a sense of community and place

Background

By the late 1960s urban flight by those in search of a home of their own in something resembling the countryside had become formalized into suburbia. Row upon row of hybridized houses built quickly and cheaply along winding asphalt streets sprang up on the periphery of rapidly industrializing cities, the Garden Cities of tomorrow envisioned by Ebenezer Howard gone horrifically awry. In the United States, where the trend first caught on like wildfire, these suburbs invariably boasted carefully manicured lawns, large two-car garages and a regional mall within convenient driving distance. The result was sprawl, an area neither urban nor suburban.

The New Urbanism emerged in the 1980s as a result of this sprawl, a coherent movement with a Manifesto. Seeking order over placelessness and identity over anonymity, it advocated mixed-use development to create a new sense of community, and a more efficient use of land to take pressure off the further development of land outside the city. Specific strategies include avoiding wide streets, building in vernacular styles, local production and sustainability.

By the end of the 20th century suburbia had reached saturation point: something had to change. The Brookings Institution in Washington, D.C., which has officially declared suburbia as outdated, explains this critical period as occurring in the 1990s, when 'the first ring of suburbs densified. The central cities started to become stronger. And much of the suburban growth leapfrogged into the far fringes, spreading out over a much larger land mass.'[1] Sometime during this 'leapfrogging' phenomenon, suburbia died and sprawl began: the distinct place that the suburbs had occupied, between the city and the country, became difficult, if not impossible, to distinguish. In each of the 65,443 tracts covered in the 2000 United States census, for example, configurations once identified as suburban were found far from urban centres – the essence of sprawl.[2]

Sprawl Reaches Limits

Just as it finally registered in the international consciousness as an issue of grave environmental concern, sprawl ran out of further space to grow. In Los Angeles, usually a barometer of American trends, 'the epicentre of sprawl' has run out of room.[3] The urban core, fattened by immigration, now overlaps legal distinctions between city and country and it is here that planners say 'the significant changes in the economy and demography of Southern

Key Project

Seaside (Florida), planned by A. Duany and
E. Plater-Zyberk, various architects, 1984–91

Signposts

Garden cities Part II: 2, 3, 18

Community building Part II: 2, 4, 12, 21

Urban renewal Part II: 25; Part III: 3

California are seen most strikingly…This is where most of the region's growing working poor population live. Immigration and first generation births have increased the number of low skilled workers in the wage jobs. As a result, having a job does not guarantee rising to the middle class, but more likely staying in the ranks of the working poor'.[4]

Environmental Distress

The inevitable result of this densification and the gobbling up of open space that has resulted from it has been increased conflict between natural and human-made environments. Brush fires, which once occurred on an extended natural cycle as a cleansing and fertilizing mechanism, have become much more frequent and devastating, as people push into environmentally fragile zones without adequate controls. Soil erosion, triggered by development, has accelerated flooding during the torrential rainstorms that are typical of the region and catastrophic landslides are now common. Wildlife and their habitats have been seriously disrupted – cougar and coyote sightings, for example, are increasing in urban areas in and around Los Angeles, a sign of an ecological network under stress.

New Urbanism to the Rescue

Los Angeles, like many other metropolitan regions across America is running out of room to grow, while older housing stock deteriorates and little new low- or middle-income housing is being built. Increasingly restrictive governmental policies and ownership constraints, as well as heightened environmental activism, stronger conservation movements and severe shortages of the resources that are needed for growth, such as water, are all contributing to a crisis condition as population increases.

The New Urbanism was put forward in the early 1980s as an antidote to the relentless spread of sprawl and the rootlessness of a condition identified by Joel Garreau in 1991 in *Edge City: Life on the New Frontier*. In this Garreau examined the conurbations that typically appear when land around a newly completed highway is designated a commercial zone, where strips of services, office and industrial parks then grow to define a new type of soulless city. Garreau defines an 'Edge City' as a worker centre rather than a suburb, with a critical mass of at least five million square feet of leasable office space and over 600,000 square feet of 'destination' retail space, located in an area that used to be either rural or residential. When his book was published, Garreau estimated that by these criteria there were 123 such Edge Cities in North America, with another 78 roadside strips about to achieve this dubious distinction.[5]

To combat such uncontrolled growth driven exclusively by market forces, the founders of the New Urbanism – Andrés Duany, Elizabeth Plater-Zyberk, Peter Calthorpe, Daniel Solomon, Stefanos Polyzoides and Elizabeth Moule, as well as Buzz Yudell and John Ruble – proposed communities planned according to a strict set of guidelines or rules, under the general heading of 'Traditional Neighborhood Developments' (TND).[6] As the name implies, these principles were intended to promote a return to less fragmented, pre-suburban community patterns, ways of making settlements that pre-date the post-war spread of peripheral suburbs. In spite of its traditionalist leaning, the movement tellingly modelled itself on the International Congress of Modern Architecture (CIAM), formulating a manifesto (the first since the end of the Modern Movement) and holding regular congresses. Chronicler Peter Katz has summarized the beliefs of the New Urbanists as a conviction that 'the best way to change suburban patterns is to change the rules of the game. They have concentrated on crafting subdivision regulations, zoning codes and regional plans and on building the consensus necessary to win grass roots and political approval for their proposals.'[7]

Fundamental Organizing Elements

The New Urbanists stress the importance of neighbourhoods, districts and corridors as the basics for any new community. Echoing previous investigations carried out by well-known urbanologists Kevin Lynch and Jane Jacobs, they define neighbourhoods as 'urbanized areas with a balanced mix of human activity', districts as 'areas dominated by a single activity', and corridors as 'connectors and separators of neighbourhoods and districts'. By beginning with the structure of the neighbourhood, the New Urbanists hope to grow communities with self-generating limits and a built-in framework in which population may vary but the relative percentages of living, working, shopping, recreational and civic uses remain the same. Citing a 'natural logic' behind healthy (as opposed to purely economic) growth, they identify the critical parts of an ideal neighbourhood as a recognizable centre and edge, with no more than a 400-metre (quarter mile) distance between the two, as well as a balanced mix of uses, a hierarchical network of streets and appropriate priority given to civic institutions and parks.[8]

Mixed Use

To ensure a balanced mix of uses and to reduce land coverage and sprawl, to save the environment, another of the most important principles of New Urbanism is re-zoning land to allow for mixed-use so that residential, office or commercial uses can be located next to, or stacked above, one another. Integration of people of different economic levels is also part of this mixed-use principle because, like proximity of use, it promotes interaction and breaks down the branding device of exclusivity used by suburban developers in the past to set mass-produced housing apart as a desirable product.

Streets and Street grounds

Streets also rank high among New Urbanist priorities. They identify the four- to six-lane arterial roads serving older suburban developments as the prime reason for isolation, traffic congestion and air pollution. The vast parking lots that such feeder streets require also push buildings far away from property lines, creating large expanses of paved space that discourage walking. In contrast to what they characterize as a 'socially disruptive' pattern of traffic flow, the New Urbanists advocate a hierarchical network of gridded streets, drawing attention to the increased connectivity and ease of orientation that such geometric discipline imposes.[9]

Citing the key place of the grid in formulating the American urban experience, New Urbanism Manifesto signatories Elizabeth Moule and Stefanos Polyzoides recall that 'the cutting of a grid is the first presence of urban structure in the landscape. In this act of making a place, space is allocated for both public and private use – for buildings and open spaces. Shaping this void in the city is an act of democratic responsibility.'[10] The New Urbanists favour reducing setbacks to eliminate the empty expanses of asphalt typical of suburban developments, and placing buildings closer to narrower streets with garages and parking lots moved behind them to give each street a vertical enclosure that makes it feel more like an outdoor room or place. They cite the ideal ratio between the height of this enclosure on either side of a street and the distance between them, including street and sidewalk, as one to three. Moving buildings closer to the street also encourages walking since it increases visual interest.

Streetwalls

Architecture, in this catechism, becomes 'built fabric', an envelope that provides visual character with elevations, mandated setbacks and building projections all helping to define the enclosure of the street. The architectural parts that make up this enclosure, such as porches, stairs, doors and windows are all 'interface' that contribute to the 'life of the street'.[11] Seen in this way, architecture is the final piece of the New Urbanist hierarchy, conceived as a kit of parts to be combined with other strategies to determine urban character.

This favouring of type over function is defended as also allowing changes in use over time, facilitating a mix-and-match approach to planning that makes a richer visual scenography possible. The types New Urbanists now typically cite are homes, cottages, sideyard houses, courtyard apartments and live-work units with shops or offices below and housing above, with control achieved by the building type allocated for each lot and the setback requirements that are stipulated for it. In discussing this basic difference between a New Urbanist scheme and its suburban predecessor, Andrés Duany and Elizabeth Plater-Zyberk explain that 'inside, the plans are almost exactly the same. What makes them different is that they are much closer to the street. The porch is just a few feet from the sidewalk and as you walk along the street you can see how pleasant it is because you constantly see houses.'[12]

A Complex Pedigree

This emphasis on types and façades underscores the complicated theoretical pedigree of a movement that ostensibly rejects modernist functionalism and universal flexibility of space in order to make urbanism more humane, and yet has resuscitated its polemical devices of affordable housing, manifestos and congresses and uses the typological methods of its most extreme, rationalist strain as a basis for planning. This apparent paradox is further confused by a reliance on tactics reminiscent of the 'decorated shed' as well as references to historicism, contexturalism and sustainability, all of which are products of the same global sensibilities that initiated post-modernism. This contradiction can only be explained by Fredric Jameson's thesis that, rather than being disjunctive, the transition from the early phase of heroic modernism, through late modernism, to post-modernism and deconstruction is really a continuum, with increasingly expansive commodification as its basic denominator. Seen in this way, the New Urbanism is simply symptomatic of the conspicuous consumption that began to increase in the late 1980s. Its typologies are far removed from the rigour of Purist discipline, or the regimentation of Giorgio Grassi or Aldo Rossi, in spite of overlapping with the notion of perpetuating permanence, or survival through generality, that Rossi puts forward in *The Architecture of the City*. It is ironic that, while claiming to remove community planning from crass market forces in their search for more humane and liveable places, the New Urbanists have simply replaced the developers' sales pitch with a subliminal appeal to the hearts, minds and wallets of more sophisticated, upwardly mobile, upper-middle-class consumers. Suburban developers sought to hide boring, but lucrative, uniformity behind a seductive mask of exclusivity through skilful marketing. The New Urbanist 'typologies' don't stand up to Quatremère de Quincy's key distinction between a type and a model.

Seaside

Completed in 1981 on the shore of the Florida 'panhandle', the eighty-acre community of Seaside is one of the most enduring representations of New Urbanist ethics. Designed by a

top, left **Diagram setting the maximum distance from core amenities**

top, right **Typical houses at Seaside**

above **The sea front at Seaside**

New Urbanist theory is based on creating pedestrian-friendly sustainable communities. Houses at Seaside have porches that face directly onto the street, in an attempt to create a sense of community, while planning takes into account the need for easy pedestrian access to the town centre. However, while the setting may be perfect, Seaside lacks soul, and year-round occupancy is too low to sustain any sort of community life.

team of New Urbanists, and featuring buildings by Steven Holl and Leon Krier, it established a pattern of rigorous rules, or overall code framework, to which other architects could later contribute. Local sources, such as the clapboard houses of the nearby town of Grayton Beach provide a strong influence, but other picturesque historical strains are welcomed, such as Charleston, Key West and the New Orleans French Quarter. In true post-modern tradition, these last have little to do with the immediate context (other than being vaguely Southern), but were probably chosen because they would sell well, especially when rendered in the pastel, cotton-candy colours that visitors to Disneyland are most familiar with. It is no coincidence that Seaside was chosen as the set for the film *The Truman Show*, in which the unwitting star Truman has his every move from birth broadcast live twenty-four hours a day. Seaside provides the perfect backdrop for what Truman believes to be an ideal existence until boredom sets in and he decides to escape.

But rather than evolving into a viable community as it was intended to, Seaside has now become a resort: its 350 detached houses and 300 additional dwelling units house only about thirty year-round residents, while thousands rent them during high season. The town hall, market, school and club remain symbols of the planner's intention, as much visual landmarks for tourists to photograph as they are functioning institutions.

Criticism

New Urbanism has been criticized on several levels, most severely for drawing attention away from the housing crisis that continues to grow in both the industrialized and the developing world. Instead of focusing on renovating and expanding the deteriorating housing stock in existing neighbourhoods in the inner cities, or providing new, low-cost housing there for the burgeoning members of working poor, it concentrates on recasting suburbia. Although statements of intent typically include the provision of a mixture of housing types for different economic levels, this mix is rarely implemented, because market forces prevail, making New Urbanist communities enclaves for the middle classes. The historical styles favoured by the New Urbanists reinforce this self-perpetuating, inbred exclusivity, since they refer back to a time of social segregation, rather than attempting to represent the racial diversity evident in urban centres today. Instead of being the palliative to the growing list of civic problems that it claims to be, New Urbanism is a slickly marketed diversion that threatens to exacerbate them, and deflect official attention away from their serious environmental consequences.

CROSS SECTION

PROPOSED
BUNGALO...
Bukit Mas, Ku...
for WALIAN ...
CSL Associate...

above **Walian House**, Kuala Lumpur, 1978–80
far left **Pacific Bank Tower**, Kuala Lumpur,
completed 2000
left **Jimmy Lim's residence**, Kuala Lumpur, ongoing

Climate has been the single most important factor in the
development of Lim's architecture, informing all his
experiments from the early wooden-frame projects to
his recent 'e-towers'.

23

Jimmy Lim: The Tropical House

Lim has produced an architecture that responds to place in both cultural and climatic terms, but which also seeks to reconcile the traditional with the modern

Biography

Born in Penang, Malaysia, in 1945, Jimmy Lim was educated in Australia, where he travelled extensively. After practising in that country for five years, he returned to Kuala Lumpur, where in 1978 he established CSL Associates, and concentrated mainly on residential design, formulating such subtle interweavings of modern and traditional architecture as the well-known Salinger House, which was built using traditional methods with local materials and a minimum of technology. His work is characterized by a response to climate and environment, and a continuing attempt to define the national character of Malaysian architecture. He has been involved in the Malaysian Institute of Architects as its president, and his interest in conservation issues extend to his being a founding member of the Friends of Heritage of Malaysia and the Director of the Heritage Trust of Malaysia. Lim has received several awards including one for the use of timber in building from the Malaysian Timber Industry Board in 1988, and the Aga Khan Award in 1998. He has also been responsible for conserving and restoring some important heritage buildings. More recently he has turned his attention to tall buildings, taking the fusion of East and West a step further.

Key Projects

Walian House, Kuala Lumpur, 1978–80
Salinger House, Kuala Lumpur, 1992
Jimmy Lim Residence, Kuala Lumpur, ongoing
100 Cintra Street development, Penang, 1999–2001

Signposts

Local traditions Part II: 19, 20, 21, 24; Part III: 2
Natural ventilation Part II: 6, 7, 11, 16, 20, 24
Sustainability Part II: 11, 15, 17, 20, 21
Material recycling Part II: 14
Conservation Part II: 18, 20, 21; Part III: 3
Ecological skyscrapers Part II: 11, 20

Taking a page from *Tropical Architecture* by Jane Drew and Maxwell Fry, Jimmy Lim Cheok Siang has been virtually alone in designing according to what he calls the 'rites of the tropics' in South-East Asia. On his travels he was particularly affected by the Balinese view of the environment as something sacred, not to be squandered wantonly. He noticed that water among all natural elements is treated with special respect there as a form of sustenance. He also visited New Zealand often, and was impressed by stories of the sustainable way in which New Zealanders logged the giant Kauri trees from the forests of the North Island at the end of the 19th century, using very primitive tools. He compares this to the destruction of the rainforest in his own region, with chainsaws that can fell a centuries-old tree in a matter of minutes and bulldozers that can pull it away in the same amount of time. He has written articles comparing these saws and bulldozers to lethal weapons in the hands of untrained people, who should not be permitted to use them unless they are licensed to do so.

The Rites of the Tropics
Turning his critical eye toward the prevailing architectural responses to the extreme climatic conditions in his region he wrote: 'tropical architecture is at a crossroads because the

NORTH ELEVATION

above, left and right **Jimmy Lim's Residence**, Kuala Lumpur, ongoing

Lim's own residence, which has enveloped an existing residence he bought in the hills around Kuala Lumpur, has been an ongoing labour of love used to test ideas (such as the extending wooden baffles seen above) that he has gone on to use in other projects.

environment is now being threatened as never before. The traditional quarters of cities are being destroyed and replaced with inappropriate architecture. It is like influenza, an epidemic that has swept across Asia, and every urban area now suffers from it. The wholesale importation of Western ideas and icons should be questioned instead of being simplistically accepted'. He sought to derive a more appropriate response to the hot, humid environment that he had to deal with, and went back to basics, bucking the trend toward modernist, sealed, air-conditioned buildings in Malaysia. He saw that the first requirements of tropical architecture have always been 'a roof to keep the sun and the rain out', and then to introduce as few walls as possible to allow cross ventilation: the 'primitive hut' for a hot-humid climate.

He imagined what he calls 'the rites of the tropics', a lyrical checklist that he uses to create a more responsive, open architecture. 'The "tropics"' he says, 'is a celebration of colours in nature, of differing intensity and variation, shape and size and the play of light against darkness. It is also a celebration of sounds: of water, rainfall, rivers and flowing streams; of smells; of nature, of the ground, as the heat surrenders itself to the rain; of decay and death as the sun and the heat sap the life out of the forest. Tropical heat and humidity accentuate sensuality, and add a sense of mysticism to the unseen and unanticipated'.[1] For Lim, tropical architecture is as cerebral as it is physical, an intertwining of nature and human-made structures that celebrates this symbiotic relationship. It should allow for the replication of natural structures, in roof forms and building elements. Light, shade and shadow should be accentuated by the layering of forms and surfaces, blurring the conventional distinctions between spaces. Lim sees history as an important part of this process since by juxtaposing memory over these qualitative elements, they can be put into proper perspective. And Malaysia is full of examples of effective traditional responses to its extreme climate.

The Malay House

A good example of this juxtaposition of memory and function is Lim's interpretation of the traditional Malay house in a contemporary residence in Selangor, completed in 1992, for

above, left and right **100 Cintra Street Development**, Penang, 1999–2001

This late 19th-century mansion was gutted by fire, but rebuilt by Lim and now functions as a small museum, antiques market and café. The walls are original, though reinforced with concrete, while all other materials used in the project are recycled.

which he won an Aga Khan Award in 1998. The traditional Malay house is a lightweight wood construction with a palm-leaf or attap roof that acts as an excellent thermal insulator. The wooden structure is prefabricated, using modular dimensions, based on a centre-post or *triang*, using wood joints only, and wooden window screens instead of glass windows. It is raised on columns and has freely distributed living mass or zones, with as few interior walls as possible. These zones are the *Rumah Ibu* for meeting, praying and sleeping, the *Seramai Gantung* for entertaining guests, the *Rumah Tengah* for dining, and the *Dapar* for cooking. Large roof eaves protect against the heavy rains that are typical in this region and allow for planting around the house, which also contributes to cooling.

The Salinger House

In the Salinger House, built in 1992 for Rudin and Monica Salinger, Lim used the ideas from 'the rites of the tropics' and the principles from the traditional Malay house to arrive at a contemporary expression of tropical architecture. Working with a local master carpenter, Abraham Bin Adam, Lim selected three large Chengal trees, that were approved for cutting, from the national forest, which the carpenter then cut into all of the components needed, and assembled, using no nails, clamps or screws. This process took over six years, due to the size of the trees and the determination of both architect and carpenter not to waste any of the wood and to harvest these trees with minimum environmental impact. Following Malay custom, the house was raised on columns to allow as much natural ventilation as possible, and oriented on its hillside site to catch prevailing breezes. Unlike traditional Malay houses, the house was organized as two interlocking triangles in plan, with a stone hexagonal circulation core. In spite of this organizational difference, however, the Salinger House is an innovative translation of the Malay vernacular form, showing that it not only has validity for the present, but also can withstand alteration. Looking at Lim's extensive body of work, prior to this project, it is obvious that the Salinger House is the culmination of Lim's ideas, though with much less of a Malay orientation, which requires a bit of explanation.

Malayan Architecture and its Politics

Modern-day Malaysia is a racially mixed country: at the beginning of this century, the proportions were more or less sixty per cent Malay, thirty per cent Chinese and ten per cent Indian. This mix, which was augmented by colonial immigration policies prior to independence in 1957, was arguably benign until a race riot erupted in 1969, following a general election. This riot, which has retrospectively taken on the dimension of a collective national trauma (since it offers an example of what could happen if the fragile ties of racial harmony were to break down again), prompted the New Economic Policy (NEP) in the following year. This affirmative action programme (favouring Malays) has arguably increased marginalization among the other two minority groups. Putrajaya, the new capital, has augmented this, because it is a move away from a historically multi-racial capital at Kuala Lumpur. The Petronas Towers, Kuala Lumpur's major symbol that can be viewed as either a stupa, pagoda or minaret, depending on the religious orientation of the viewer, has been replaced, in the predominantly Muslim capital of Putrajaya, with a huge mosque in the centre that leaves no room for other interpretations.

This shift prompted an epiphany in Lim, which coincided with an important breakthrough in residential design, and his response was to call for a Malayan (rather than a Malaysian) architecture that looked back to a time prior to 1969 when all of the races of the nation coexisted peacefully. At the same time many of the other architects in the region in the early 1990s began to look to Bali – which, of course, had been so influential on Lim early on – as an important stylistic resource. This contemporary interest in Bali came about, in large part, due to publications on resorts on that island by Singaporean architect and writer Tay Keng Soon. A decade later, a new generation of architects in Singapore, such as Kerry Hill, began independently to formulate a new kind of tropical architecture which differs markedly from Lim's more rustic approach.

The Singapore School

So similar that they may be referred to as a 'school' of the kind seen in Chicago in the 1940s or Philadelphia in the late 1950s, this group in Singapore adapted the Balinese elements that were becoming increasingly common, and layered a strain of new modernism over them. In ways that are very reminiscent of the Case Study houses that appeared in Los Angeles in the post-war period, houses of the 'Singapore School' share steel frames supporting large expanses of glass, few integral walls and soaring vertical spaces. Some Balinese vestiges still remain, such as the requisite open bathrooms and showers, strategically placed pools and rock gardens, but the emphasis has switched from wood to glass.

The Datai Resort by Kerry Hill, on Langkawi Island in Malaysia (1991–3), marks a mid-point in this transition, when the models chosen by the more prominent members of the school were still traditional rather than technological. The resort, which is built of local stone and wood, is so well integrated into its steep hillside site that is seems to have grown there and presents a convincing case for translating historical forms in an abstract way. In best Balinese tradition, the lobby is completely open, an elemental shelter covered by a long eaved roof that allows long views to the mountains on each side and the Andaman Sea stretching out in the distance. The rooms do have air conditioning, but also have wide verandas that invite guests to spend an equal amount of time outside, when not involved in one of the many sybaritic attractions that the resort provides.

The Datai is so skilfully designed that it seems to have single-handedly reversed a national denial of a brilliant vernacular heritage. However, the nostalgia for *kampungs* (informal, low-income housing throughout South-East Asia) life does not extend to an admiration for the ingenuity of traditional Malaysian houses. By extrapolating many of the key pieces of the Malay house and reconfiguring them at a much larger scale with refined materials and details, Kerry Hill has demonstrated to those local residents rich enough to afford to stay there that there is intrinsic beauty in vernacular tradition. For many Malaysians, resort architecture such as the Datai is the only experience of their own vernacular, since the *kampungs* that generated this once agrarian society are fast disappearing, and so what Kerry Hill has achieved is nothing less than a revival of a vernacular tradition in a very upmarket retreat, frequented mostly by foreigners.

The Tai Chi of Architecture

In the midst of this transition, from the rage for all things Balinese in the early 1990s to the cool steel and glass minimalism of the 'Singapore School' that followed, Jimmy Lim continues to practice what he refers to as the *Tai Chi* of architecture, deriving inspiration from natural elements and forces and transforming them into diaphanous spaces and forms that fit in comfortably in their individual ecosystems. But there is a fine line between *Tai Chi* and *Kung Fu* in a region in which architectural style has been aligned with racial, religious or political affiliation, and Lim has had to walk it very carefully. In such a highly charged atmosphere, it is not enough to have good intentions toward the environment: those intentions must also be described with all of the appropriate metaphors, too.

Ecological Towers

As if such factional considerations were not difficult enough to negotiate, there is intense competition within them as well, especially for recognition as the region's greenest architect. Jimmy Lim has had to vie with Ken Yeang for this and their rivalry has become a local legend. Yeang, who also has an entire section allocated to him in this book, has strategically adopted an effective marketing approach in his effort to capture the title, using branding as his tactic by concentrating on the design of what he has called the 'bioclimatic skyscraper'. However, in the late 1990s, Jimmy Lim also began to receive several commissions for high-rise towers, allowing him to explore a new medium. He has called these 'ecological', or 'e-towers', his own attempt at a tropical skyscraper. It will be fascinating to see where this constructive rivalry takes Malaysian architecture in the future.

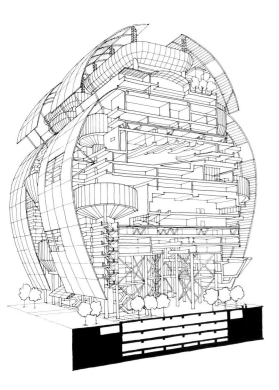

'Ecological Tower' project, late 1990s
This section shows how Lim is now adopting a more High-Tech approach, without losing the formal language or functionality of his more traditional projects.

above and far left **Justice Palace and Great Mosque, Riyadh**, Rasem Badran, to 1992

left **Ruwais Mosque**, Abdel Wahed El Wakil, 1989

Both Rasem Badran and Abdel Wahed El Wakil have been seen as the natural heirs of Hassan Fathy – indeed, El Wakil worked in his studio. However, each has forged a different method of deriving a specifically Middle Eastern architecture, and each is careful to incorporate the lessons of tradition.

24

Rasem Badran and Abdel Wahed El Wakil: The New Traditionalists

For practical as well as religious and social reasons, the Islamic world has been particularly quick to re-establish connections with its vernacular, while successfully adapting traditional forms

Biographies

Abdel Wahed El Wakil   Rasem Badran

Key Projects

Rasem Badran

Sana'a Housing Development, Yemen, 1983

Justice Palace and Great Mosque, Riyadh, to 1992

Abdel Wahed El Wakil

Halawa House, Agamy, Egypt, 1975

Island Mosque, Jeddah, 1986

Ruwais Mosque, Jeddah, 1989

Corniche Mosque, Jeddah, 1990

Signposts

Local materials and techniques Part II: 1, 3, 4, 7, 9, 12

Local traditions Part II: 19, 20, 21, 23; Part III: 2

Natural ventilation Part II: 6, 7, 11, 16, 20, 23

Rasem Badran

Born in Jerusalem in 1945, Rasem Badran studied architecture in Germany, graduating in 1970. After working in that country for three years, and winning a competition to design low-income housing, he returned to Jordan in 1973 where he has remained in practice since 1979 through the firm Dar Al Omran. His work bridges the gap between East and West, to create a highly popular synthesis that has resulted in many important commissions, particularly in the area of religious architecture. His personal philosophy sees architecture as a 'continuous dialogue between contemporary needs and historical inherited values'.

Abdel Wahed El Wakil

Coming originally from Egypt, El Wakil graduated from Aim-Shams University in Cairo, where, from 1965 to 1970, he lectured in the Department of Architecture. He has always acknowledged the influence of Hassan Fathy on his design development, and along with Fathy El Wakil is arguably the most important proponent of Islamic architecture in the modern-day Middle East. Importantly, he has also adopted many of Fathy's working practices, such as using local craftsmen or techniques. Since 1971 he has worked on housing projects, mosques, and civic centres. In 1980 he won the Aga Khan Award, and he is a respected scholar of Islamic architecture.

Since the death of Hassan Fathy in 1988, there has been wide speculation about the survival of his principles and the possibility of a viable successor to perpetuate them. One likely candidate is Rasem Badran, even though he did not work directly with Fathy and even though he approaches the question of the appropriation of tradition in a completely different way. Because of his architectural education in Germany, he is more systematic than others in his study of the appropriateness of precedents, approximating a rational typological method tempered by a heuristic empirical sensibility that gives it broader appeal. His assimilation of regional patterns in each of the areas in which he has worked gives his architecture great authority and a sense of inevitability that is missing from the attempts of those that simply copy forms without exploring the hierarchy of function and meaning that lies behind them.

Graphic Exploration

Badran carries out this exploration graphically through an exhaustive observation of the existing historical fabric to better explain it to himself and others. His graphic skills allow him both to record and to compare across national boundaries, exposing similarities and implying continuities. In this way, he closely approximates the spirit of Fathy's definition of tradition as 'the social analogy of personal habit' which is extinct once it ceases to be vital and useful. Describing this as a 'dialectic methodology' of investigation, Badran sees it as being bound up in a set of interconnected factors, which include social, cultural, and environmental issues.

Sana'a

A recent project for housing in Sana'a, Yemen, demonstrates his approach. His studies there began with an analysis of the process of urbanization relative to defensive requirements and tribal divisions. Badran compared urban growth in Sana'a with that in other cities, such as Cairo and Baghdad, to find points of similarity and difference. He found that a recognizable centre along with a large mosque and related commercial functions are constant, but that housing in Yemeni cities is different. Rather than spreading out horizontally, with individual courtyards, residential groups in Yemen are stacked vertically and clustered around a common garden, or *Bustan*. Badran and others have traced this vertical residential cell to earlier houses created by a nomadic agricultural society to adapt to a hilly topography where terracing is used and tower houses help to save land, as well as serving a defensive function.

As they evolved, tower houses increasingly related to sun and natural ventilation, with the highest room, the *Mafraj*, articulated with openings to create a direct visual relationship with the outside. The ornamentation used on these openings, in addition to being a means of controlling glare, also became an indication of socio-economic status, much as the richness of decor in the internal courtyards of houses throughout other cities in the Middle East have been used to indicate familial wealth, while the outside remains plain. Badran's sketches, typically moving from macro to micro scale, reflect this evaluation. The rooms in the tower house below the *Mafraj* are less ceremonial, with family quarters and bedrooms located in the middle, and the ground floor used for reception, cooking and storage. Because of the importance accorded to view and orientation, Badran found that south-facing elevations are more highly prized than others and that houses with this aspect are called 'complete.'

Tracing the house to the urban setting, Badran identified other topological elements historically associated with it. In addition to the *Bustan* and mosque already mentioned, he found these additional elements to be: a commercial district or *Souk*; a specialized commercial centre, or *Samsara*; a water well, *Abjyar*; and defensive walls and gates. In this system he discovered that residential units usually occupy about thirty to forty per cent of the land available, in linear organization, and he attempted a similar proportion and configuration in the 100,000 square metres (1,080,000 square feet) of housing he was asked to provide. Using the same linear, vertically stacked organization he had seen elsewhere, grouped around common gardens, he located housing away from public streets for privacy, using shops, offices, and hotel accommodations as a buffer. The mosque was used as an intermediate element, linking public and private areas.

As a result, his design for housing in Sana'a is contemporary in appearance, yet historically and culturally responsive and specific, as well as environmentally sensitive, and thus serves as a vital example for those faced with the task of adapting to a specialized social and topological context. While he has changed the materials and methods of construction, reflecting a change in local practice and his realistic assessment of the difficulties involved in perpetuating moribund trades, he has retained the essential attributes that are viable.

Old Sana'a, Yemen
When devising his own scheme for housing in Sana'a (see opposite), Badran first analysed the traditional houses there, and identified certain key characteristics relating to urban setting, siting and vertical stacking and repetitive typologies.

Ideas for housing, Sana'a

Having studied the old fabric, Badran then gave ancient principles a facelift, to create an environmentally responsive and socially responsible scheme.

The Justice Palace in Riyadh

This approach is even more apparent in his re-design of the Great Mosque and Justice Palace complex in Riyadh, Saudi Arabia, in which Badran has established significant design parameters revolving around key questions of the position of the mosque in the fabric of the contemporary city in general, and the specific relationship that the mosque should have with the Justice Palace in this instance.

This was accompanied by the architect's wish also to clarify persistent questions about the appropriateness of natural environmental systems in this region and the interpretation of a distinctive historical style. By researching old photographs of the five-block site, laden with symbolic associations because of the proximity of the historic Musmak fort, Badran was able to begin to confirm topological proportions. Not wanting mindlessly to copy Najdi forms of the past, he approached the problem as a planning issue, testing for meaningful spatial interrelationships. In the course of his studies, Badran found scale to be a key criterion of the earlier architecture of the district, combined with environmental considerations related to the extremely hot, arid climate. In direct contrast to a current trend toward lightweight detached structures, he identified a consistent pattern of massiveness and clustering to reduce heat gain. Badran was determined to recreate this aspect of density in his new complex, believing it also to be a far more effective way of increasing comprehensibility by establishing physical and symbolic connections between the disparate parts of this enormous project.

Going beyond replication, Badran has employed symbolism in more general ways, such as using a bridge between the mosque and the Palace of Justice (the two major elements of the project), to represent the degree of accessibility that has traditionally existed between the government and the people in the Kingdom. This is carried over into the design of the Justice Palace, which is integrated with the rest of the complex, with clusters of administrative buildings attached to a new wall that the architect created, in several places, but pulls away from it in others, to reinforce the analogy.

Returning the Mosque to its Urban Role

The mosque, however, is the primary focus of his design. As the architect's copious preparatory sketches show, many alternatives were considered before a final configuration was chosen. Drawing on his own thorough surveys of relevant monuments throughout the Islamic world, Badran was able to arrive at a solution which returns this building type to its primary location in the city form, without isolating it. Looking back to the hypostyle structure of the first mosque, generated from the trunks of palm trees which were used as columns, Badran has developed a system that guides attention toward the *qibla*, rather than obstructing it, and that naturally accommodates prayer rows, instead of working against them, in addition to incorporating supplementary mechanical air delivery ducts. Rows of towers on the roof, which correspond to the column spacing below, provide natural lighting and ventilation as a primary source, indicating the architect's emphasis on natural environmental systems. A visual bonus in the interior is that cumbersome horizontal ductwork has been eliminated. No detail has been left to chance here, with each design decision subjected to a high degree of thorough, rational analysis. The minarets, for example, rather than following the trend toward public address systems, are treated with the symbolic power embodied in the traditional tower. The architect determined that using two of them, in this instance, would emphasize the stature of the building based on local precedents. The result of his thorough attention to contemporary needs is a building that fits perfectly with its context and is dignified and yet approachable, as it must be.

A similar strategy was adopted in the Justice Palace, which used building elements, materials and details that respond positively to precedent and climatic conditions. Ventilation towers were used in the main halls and offices, increasing air movement. These also provide indirect lighting, which eliminates the need for windows on exterior walls and increases thermal mass, as well as security and privacy. Taken as a whole, the complex in Riyadh provides a compelling example of effective large-scale intervention into a sensitive urban context, and has valuable lessons to teach those faced with similar problems worldwide.

Abdel Wahed El Wakil

Another disciple of Hassan Fathy, who has done much to perpetuate his ideals and principles as an alternative architectural language, is Abdel Wahed El Wakil. When he received an Aga Khan Award in 1980 for the Halawa House in Agamy, Egypt, he insisted that the Nubian mason Aladdin Moustafa, who had also assisted Fathy on many of his projects, share it with him. He did this in recognition of the fact that traditional architecture is frequently designed and built by anonymous contributors whose indigenous constructional wisdom must be acknowledged, as well as the fact that such builders have been responsible for transferring knowledge in the past through an apprentice system, by example.

A Trickle-down Theory

Soon after he finished the Halawa House, El Wakil moved to Jeddah, Saudi Arabia, in the late 1970s. He decided to work at the top of the economic ladder (rather than at the bottom, as his mentor did) so that his ideas would have greater currency. He began working with the enlightened mayor of Jeddah at that time, Said Farsi. Farsi had decided to build a series of three small mosques along the Corniche, running beside the Red Sea, as part of a beautification plan that transformed this gateway city from a medieval enclave surrounded by a defensive wall into an urban model for all of Saudi Arabia. The Island Mosque, which is the first of these, is described by El Wakil as 'religious sculpture' intended to visually evoke an emotional reaction as well as serving in a religious capacity. A severely restricted budget meant that El Wakil had to devise effective means of natural ventilation that would utilize sea breezes to provide the same level of comfort as mechanical cooling. For this reason, each of these mosques is a case study in ways in which design strategies can be effectively developed to combine thermal mass, orientation and form so that natural convective cooling can be achieved. In the Island Mosque, that involved placing the prayer area behind an arcade and an open courtyard to capture the cool sea breeze and filter it before it is directed into the interior. Once inside the prayer area, which is built of thick clay bricks with a tile floor to retain coolness, it rises as it is gradually heated by the people using the space, slowly going up and out of the opening provided for it in the dome above, so that the dome has an environmental as well as a symbolic purpose.

The Ruwais Mosque Improves on Fathy's New Baris

The Ruwais Mosque is very different. It occupies a high knoll and is a dominant landmark when seen from the north in spite of its small scale. The necessity for natural ventilation here results in an eloquent formal response, a rhythmical double rank of catenary vaults which are

top **Halawa House**, Abdel Wahed El Wakil, 1975
above **Island Mosque**, Abdel Wahed El Wakil, 1986
The series of mosques by El Wakil by the Red Sea are striking reinventions of an old form.

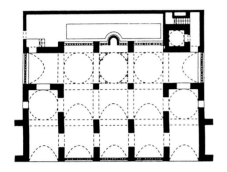

The Ruwais Mosque, Abdel Wahed El Wakil, 1989
Large catenary vaults facing in three different directions
ensure a constant breeze in the mosque, as well as
creating a striking visual language. The most obvious
precedent for the wind catches are the those at New Baris
Market, by Hassan Fathy.

stacked to capture the maximum amount of sea breeze coming in their direction. Behind
them, the main dome above the *mihrab* has been joined with other domes on each side of it
to create an extremely effective system of air circulation as well as a memorable massing of
forms. At over 240 square metres (2,700 square feet) in size, the Ruwais Mosque is larger than
either the Island or Corniche mosques and is also less obviously reliant on specific historical
prototypes in its forms, which are functionally derived rather than iconographic. One
obvious precedent, however, is the New Baris market, built by Hassan Fathy a few years earlier
in the central Egyptian desert, near Kharga, in which a similar stacking of air vents is used to
cool the perishables. Both New Baris and its diminutive heir demonstrate the effectiveness of
traditional cooling strategies in extreme environmental conditions.

Perpetuating Appropriate Technology in Urban and Non-Urban Settings
Badran and El Wakil are the most prominent of the first generation of Fathy followers, but
there are several more in the generation after them. All are dedicated to his ideas of a socially
and environmentally responsive architecture based on traditional principles and appropriate
technologies. Badran, through choice as well as by chance, has primarily explored the urban
typologies of traditional societies throughout the Middle East, reassuringly arriving at many
of the same conclusions that have been codified in the New Urbanist Manifesto: mixing rather
than segregating uses to increase activity and environmental efficiency; reinterpreting
historical languages and materials to re-establish social connectivity; and re-examining the
place that the automobile should occupy in the city.

El Wakil, on the other hand, has primarily built outside the urban fabric, to the extent that
he has been accused of being anti-urban. He responds to this criticism by pointing out several
projects such as a mosque in Manama, Badrain, which have been closely integrated into their
urban surroundings. In any event, there is no disputing his skill at implementing the
environmental techniques and wisdom that he received from Hassan Fathy. Both he and
Badran have been faithful to Fathy's principles, if not all of his methods, and have perpetuated
his search for appropriate technologies that preserve meaningful traditions.

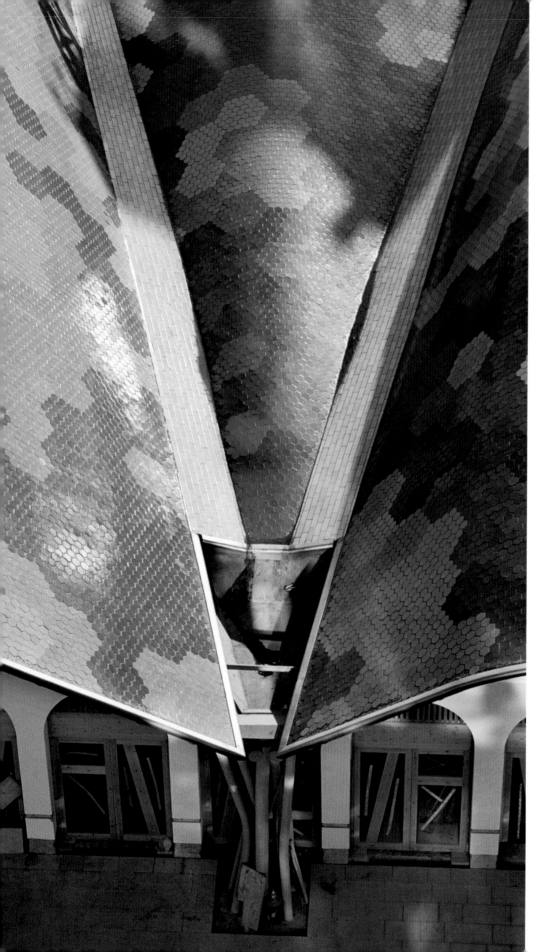

left and above **Santa Caterina Market**, Barcelona, EMBT, 1997–2004

A classic case of renewing or recycling an old structure to preserve the physical and cultural fabric of the city. Structural pyrotechnics in Miralles's work often obscure his great respect for the integrity of a site.

25

Enric Miralles: A Critical Response to Place

Miralles fused landscape with architecture, showing a respect for location and tradition

Biography

The meteoric career of Enric Miralles was tragically cut short when he died of a brain tumour in Barcelona in July, 2000 at the age of forty-five. He had given up the possibility of becoming a professional basketball player to study architecture in Barcelona, graduating in 1978, followed by postgraduate work at Columbia University, where he later taught as well as at Harvard and the Architectural Association in London. As an architect he worked for Helio Piñon and Albert Viaplana before opening his own office with Carme Piños and, later, Benedetta Tagliabue. Miralles's architectural interests included both the international and the local, encompassing Le Corbusier and the Catalan advocate Gaudí.

His work shows an unfailing interest in place, in reusing buildings, or developing land that other architects would avoid, to create a fusion of landscape and architecture: see, for example, the archery pavilion for the Barcelona Olympics, the sports hall in Huesca, and what is perhaps his most significant and memorable work: the Cemetery in Igualada. More recently he renovated the Santa Caterina market and created the Diagonal seaside park, both in Barcelona, as well as designing the Scottish National Parliment buildings.

The work of Enric Miralles is arguably among the most discursive in modern times, in the sense of incorporating a wide range of themes and influences and proceeding through them argumentatively, rather than being digressive. The themes themselves, however, all progress from a deep sensitivity to context and environment: the tendency to embrace far-from-ideal sites, either in urban areas, or on what others might consider unbuildable topography on the periphery; the recycling or reuse of existing buildings; the integration of landscape with architecture (which is typically avoided by most architects); the attempt to perpetuate natural cycles in built form expressing the passage of time in materials; the use of a 'route', or a procession as a way of explication. Peter Buchanan has succinctly described this last, patently modernist, tendency as being attractive to Miralles because 'the route not only shows off the building, as well as the contents, but also exposes the place itself, making unlikely new connections to the surroundings and reestablishing a reverence for nature'.[1]

Igualada Cemetery, Barcelona

Miralles's ability to evoke the quality of a place is clearly evident in one of his earliest projects, won in a national competition in 1985: the design of the Igualada Cemetery, located in a

Key Projects

Igualada Cemetery, Barcelona, 1985
Sports Hall, Huesca, 1989–90
Archery Pavilion, Barcelona, 1989–90
Santa Caterina Market, Barcelona, 1997–2004
Diagonal Mar Park, Barcelona, 1997–2004

Signposts

Sensitivity to site Part II: 6, 10; Part III: 2

Urban renewal Part II: 22; III: 3

Underground construction Part II: 14; Part III: 1

heavily industrialized neighbourhood of Barcelona. The cemetery, which traverses down its sloping site in an elongated Z-shaped gash, cut into the hillside, defines Miralles's commitment to beginning with what he referred to as 'the journey'. 'My working strategy', he explained 'has been to look for relationships between different constructions which accept the specific characteristics called for by each program and every concrete place, and to look for lines of trajectories, to repeat some movements and above all…in establishing a dialogue with the body of work that slowly builds up over time.'[2]

The line of trajectory in this case both defines the hillside into which it is cut, and is defined by it, with the angled ossuaries facing the route on one side, and acting as retaining walls on the other. The route, which follows the path of least resistance down the hill, is paved with concrete with wooden planks randomly embedded in it, appearing to be the flotsam and jetsam carried in a floor, prompting one of Miralles's friends to liken this internal street to a 'river of souls'.[3] Cutting the ossuaries and the pathway into the hill not only creates a powerful metaphor of pain, death and permanence, but also effectively negates the gritty industrial presence around the site allowing visitors and mourners to focus on the natural landscape and on either remembrance, or on forgetting, as Miralles himself hoped they would.

The termination of the 'river of souls' in a cross-shaped axis of two intersecting walls at the bottom of the slope recalls Gunnar Asplund's equally moving Woodland Cemetery Crematorium in Stockholm of 1939, which also relies upon a linear datum of sequential crematoria which each have their own chapel, placed behind a continuous low wall that joins them all and similarly ends at a cross, for its profound symbolic effect.

Huesca Sports Hall

Excavation, the use of mounds, and a retaining wall are design strategies also used in the Sports Hall in Huesca (1989–90). The excavation allows people to access the seating for the sunken sports hall at grade and move down into the stands, or up exposed stairways to seating above, which makes orientation and circulation very clear. The entire hall is covered by a gently curved tubular steel truss system from which a flat steel deck roof is suspended, with a minimal number of compression members exposed below it. The roof as built is much more conventional than the undulating shells (with steel grilles inserted at the base of each vault), shown in the preliminary sections, but the concept of a large, covered, protected space of assembly nestled securely into the earth has remained intact, as has the gradual revelation of the sheer scale of the Hall caused by the mildly circuitous road leading up to it. The exposed roof trusses, which fan out slightly from the entrance as they cross the lowered floor, and a canted second roof that is suspended from a row of concrete masts to cover the mezzanine seating, contribute to the 'machine in the garden' appearance that is a Miralles trademark, even when that garden, as we shall soon see, is a concrete jungle.

A similar approach, of nestling a large-scale building into the earth, is evident at the National Centre for Rhythmic Gymnastics, Alicante, fast tracked for completion prior to the opening of the World Gymnastics Championships in 1993. However, the centre, which is also spanned by large steel trusses that fan out across the main floor, was built on a steep slope, curving in a long arc along its north-eastern edge. Miralles and Piños used this curve to best advantage to both juxtapose the various components of the programme in a tenuous state of equilibrium that mimics the rhythmic exercises performed inside, and to direct the public up onto an elevated entry ramp. This ramp becomes a balcony running along the entire exposed

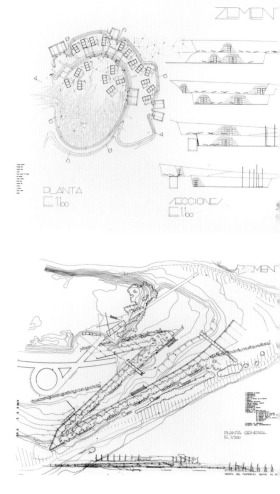

Plan and view of Igualada Cemetery, Barcelona, 1985
Here Miralles plays with levels to create an oasis, a place of peace and reflection, in a highly industrialized part of the city.

long elevation of the main stadium, a counterpoint to its opposite edge, facing the slope, where the dressing rooms, bathrooms and showers are located.

The Alicante building is arguably the most obvious example of the mechanistic contrast with natural forms and forces that Miralles liked to establish, and which is present, to some degree, in each of his projects. And yet, it also highlights his unwillingness to completely embrace the full potential of technology, since the tight timeframe for construction suggested a complete acceptance of prefabrication that was not entirely possible because of atypical design conditions.

The Archery Pavilion, Barcelona

Response to the site and natural forces was also a primary generator of the forms of the Olympic Archery Pavilion (1989–90) in the old urban neighbourhood of Vall d'Hebron in Barcelona. The Pavilion includes two complexes, for training and competition, which each have an outdoor archery range and indoor locker room facilities. Once again there was a steep slope to deal with, as well as the irregular street pattern of the pre-existing neighbourhood. Using the service buildings as retaining walls as in the projects just described, the architects created the level surface needed for the ranges themselves, which are oriented toward the east so that the sun would not be in the athletes' eyes during the afternoon practice sessions and competitions. These flat areas flip on the site plan, like the turning of the page of a book, in a way that once again reflects the special conditions of the site. The architects refer to the flat portion of the Olympic 'park' as being 'primitive', which raises the question of what the term means to them and speculation about possibilities which can no longer be conformed. The flatness of the African veld is the first thing that comes to mind and the stereotypical image of seemingly by endless savannah with snow-capped mountains in the distance.

The bow-shaped configuration of the gang shower enclosures in the competition building (as well as of the precast roofs that cover them) provides another clue that a metaphorical sensibility was at work here, related to archery as one of the most ancient hunting techniques. The elliptical sectional profile of the enclosed portion of the competition portion of the archery complex, which also serves as an arcade in certain parts of its length, is most reminiscent of the retaining walls above the Greek Theatre in the Park Güell by Antoni Gaudí, built between 1900 and 1914, as noted by Juan José Lahuerta. Lahuerta has also commented that the thought of Gaudí 'marked' in 'Miralles double triple memory, because his is a memory of earth removed…'.[4]

Santa Caterina Market, Barcelona

The tendency to embrace far-from-ideal sites and to recycle or reuse existing buildings mentioned earlier here, as well as in relation to the work Eric Moss is doing in Culver City near Los Angeles, is best exemplified in Miralles's career by his restoration of the Santa Caterina Market (1997–2004), in the old quarter of Barcelona, while he was in partnership with Benedetta Tagliabue. As in Moss's case, this aspect of his work also has direct relevance to ecological issues because recycling is one of the most basic principles of sustainability. Interpreting an existing building with a new design is not an attractive option for many architects, because they see this as a compromise and a threat to their creativity.

The EMBT approach to the complex problem of the restoration of the Santa Caterina Market was the opposite of what one might expect from a firm with such a design-oriented reputation; they insisted on keeping the entire perimeter wall of the historical landmark, located near Barcelona Cathedral, and working within it to establish an image of continuity. Their competition-winning scheme offers a sensitive alternative to the all too frequently seen development model of 'urban renewal': demolishing parts of a city that have contributed to the collective memory for centuries and replacing them with soulless, anonymous boxes, which in this case might have meant a mall. EMBT instead chose to weave the old and the new together, reorganizing the interior of the market to make sales and service more efficient, and introducing more public space to support the market's traditional role as a neighbourhood meeting place. They also expanded services below grade making accessibility easier, without increasing the scale or drastically changing the appearance of this much-loved Barcelona icon. A new clear-span truss roof, covering most of the interior space enclosed by the existing perimeter walls, protects vendors and shoppers alike from the sun and rain, and two new residential blocks project like fingers into the remainder, left uncovered, to inject even more life and intimate scale into this revived environment.

Santa Caterina Market, Barcelona, 1997–2004

Seaside Park

Miralles's penchant for gritty, passed-over urban sites is abundantly evident in two park projects he did in collaboration with Benedetta Tagliabue in Barcelona and Mollet del Vallès. Diagonal Mar Park was the grittier of the two, identified by the Barcelona City Council as a potential asset to the Forum of Cultures held in that city in 2004. The site is comprised of a string of partially abandoned industrial plots near the Mediterranean coastline. EMBT took design cues from the aptly named Avinguda Diagonal which dominates the neighbourhood and cuts across the rectilinear grid of streets that identifies it, and leads to the sea, via a pedestrian bridge over the Ronda Litoral road that circles Barcelona. The intersections created by the dendritic street pattern became the inspiration for a contrapuntal series of lines and planes that echo the surrounding streets in reverse order, turning the lines of force from the north to the coastline, on the south. This is no mean feat, given the entrenched movement patterns that the streets have established in the collective civic memory, representing nothing less than an equal and opposite alternative model to a contemporary automobile-dominated society, which permeates people instead of cars.

opposite, above and below **Diagonal Mar Park**, Barcelona, 1997–2004
Landscape projects such as the Diagonal Mar park demonstrate an ability to unify many diverse elements within a binding lexicon that points the way for others confronted with ameliorating the urban wasteland.

In this new pedestrian utopia, procession, as always, is Miralles's main concern, away from the busiest of all the external intersections at the Carrer Josep Pla–Avinguda Diagonal roundabout, in a tangential, serpentine path toward the sea. Along the way, in this metaphorical, as well as literal, transition from the human-made industrial debris of the past back to nature, there is a wonderland of landscape elements used in a very unconventional way. Instead of providing a lush, paradisical garden as an obvious method of contrast, Miralles intentionally mixes materials that remind us of the industrial wasteland left behind, with the waterbodies of various sizes and trees and plants of different types that we have come to expect in a typical park. Steel pipes snake overhead in biomorphic curves that at first appear to be random but are in fact subtly directional, helping to establish an alternative, diagonal path. Steel reinforcing bars, which are left exposed and allowed to rust, are laid along the edge of a pond to discourage people from coming too close and possibly falling in, but also as a reminder that the effects of industry are always with us and cannot be left behind.

As a microcosm of Miralles's view of nature, Diagonal Mar Park confirms his desire for coexistence rather than domination: most of the land remains hardscape, with a sparse

number of trees, planted in wells, all looking rather sad and lonely. Like the Parc de la Vilette by Bernard Tschumi, this is a public landscape for the 21st century, tough and technical, rather than an idyllic Eden meant to serve as a respite from urban woes. Like Tschumi, Miralles chooses to replicate nature in metal, but backs away from its complete exclusion.

The Parc dels Colors, in Mollet del Vallès, north of Barcelona, also joins unlikely urban elements together, in this case linking three existing neighbourhoods that were previously separated. The design cue was a single Romanesque building of exceptional character which prompted a series of proto-medieval, suitably labyrinthine passageways. These lead to various gardens and playgrounds for children, as well as a skating rink and a pitch for bowls. The gardens have various pools and ponds, just as Diagonal Mar does, but here they are a bit more orchestrated, in keeping with the Roberto Burle Marx approach to the site plan. In the best tradition of the Brazilian master landscaper, EMBT first did an abstract painting using the site plan as the canvas, also thinking of Chagall's graphic substitutions of people and nature. As they describe their intention, 'maybe the people living here, the emigrants, the old people, will substitute with their own bodies, the land and topography, sustaining the building on top of themselves, as we can learn through Chagall's paintings.' The colours of the materials transferred from the painting, which give the park its name, are then intended to give the souls of those using it flight, permitting them to soar above the industrial slums just as Chagall's characters do, yet another form of escape from urban reality.

The difficulty with the technique of painting as landscape plan is the legibility of intention on the ground, where the point of perspective is different. EMBT have obviously kept that difficulty in mind, using vertical brick and concrete planes raised up on skewed tripods and other types of piloti to define areas, act as barriers, or guide the eye to a specific feature. Water replaces amorphous blue blobs on the painting, and leaves are rendered in grass. The colours are intended to extend to walls intentionally left blank so that they can be filled by graffiti artists in the future, bringing the urban park idea full circle.

Similar Approaches outside Spain

In their addition to the Town Hall of Utrecht, in the Netherlands, Miralles and Tagliabue demonstrated their concern for existing urban context and their willingness, even eagerness, to work within it and transform it. The Town Hall is essentially one medieval enclosure that has been added to over the centuries and EMBT wanted to accentuate the cumulative character of the structure, rather than suppressing it. To do so, they used a variety of materials, and exposed others in the older parts of the building as well, creating a mixture of old and new, recycled and replaced, to emphasize the eclectic character of the building as well as the culture from which it has derived.

Eclecticism was also the intention behind the design of a Music School in Hamburg, Germany, with the additional agenda of integrating the new building carefully into the surrounding woodland: the 'machine in the garden' aesthetic once again. The building is organized along an internal 'street' that negotiates its way around and through several large trees on the site, with the various offices and classrooms strung out along this vertiginous spine. These relatively small projects among many others outside Spain show that Miralles's ecological sensibilities travel well, and are applicable to a wide range of conditions, but that the constants – of establishing a dialogue with nature in the form of a discourse about contemporary necessities, and to explain intentions – remain the same throughout.

Conclusion: Different Approaches to the Same Problem

Each of the attempts to find commonality between architecture and the environment that have been discussed in Part II presents a different response to the growing sense of loss of a connection to nature caused by the growth of industrialization. Each may also be argued to be based in a nationalistic, ideological, religious or economic agenda, and not on purely altruistic motives. Has this now changed? Are there now those who put the environment first, regardless of other motives? Who are the role models for new generations of design professionals to follow?

The Rural Studio

The obvious candidate among several that can be identified worldwide is Samuel Mockbee (1944–2001) who has achieved near canonical status among students and professionals alike in America for his dedication to the ideal of returning a sense of social commitment to architecture. In 1993 he co-founded, with Dennis K. Ruth, the Rural Studio at the Auburn University College of Architecture. The home base for the Studio, however, is 260 kilometres (160 miles) from the campus, in the small town of Newbern, in Hale County, Alabama. It is one of the poorest regions in the United States, with more than 1,400 substandard dwellings at the time that Mockbee and Ruth became involved there.

Hale County gained national recognition in 1941, when writer James Agee and photographer Walker Evans collaborated on *Let Us Now Praise Famous Men*, which graphically publicized the squalor there. The Rural Studio, which was half-jokingly referred to as Taliesin South by people at Auburn, does share Wright's belief in experimental pedagogy, including hands-on involvement in the building process and working within a restricted budget. Mockbee wanted to return architecture to its original community roots, believing that when people were made the top priority, costs could be taken care of, somehow. He used whatever materials were at hand, such as salvaged wood and metal and similar bits and pieces that other architects would not normally consider suitable for construction, to help the poor families in this region.

Above all, however, he saw his role as that of a teacher, and wanted to convey the importance of people and place to his students, believing that each of these have been forgotten in contemporary architecture and the schools that prepare young people to practise it. While he encouraged the use of unconventional materials and methods to keep costs low, since the clients that the Rural Studio selected were very poor, he did not believe that this justified a lowering of aesthetic standards, but rather that it demanded a higher level of inventiveness, to meet new criteria.

Mason's Bend Community Center

Within seven years of its founding, the participants of the Rural Studio had built five houses, two community centres, a chapel and a playground in and around Newbern, using whatever materials they could afford. One of the community centres, at Mason's Bend, is a good example of Mockbee's approach. The small village, in the middle of what used to be the cotton belt of western Alabama, is populated mostly by four extended African-American families, and the triangular site for the centre is formed by the intersecting property lines of three of them. Mockbee raised $20,000 from the Potrero Nuevo Fund in San Francisco for the centre, which was designed and built as a thesis project by fifth-year students at Auburn University. It is located on the main road through the village and houses a main meeting and worship space and social area inside its small 4.5 x 9 metre (15 x 30 foot) perimeter. A wall extending outside marks a transit stop for a bookmobile, healthcare bus, mobile computer lab and a delivery point for meals for the elderly and disabled. When not being used for gatherings, the central hall also serves as an indoor play space for children, fulfilling the entire wish list that the residents gave the student designer-builders before the project began.

Their wish, to make a lasting contribution to the community, directed their material choices, which varied from the usual neo-vernacular rusted-tin language that Mockbee was known for. The walls were made from earth from the site, mixed with cement and a polymer preservative and compressed in plywood forms. The site also provided the timber for the roof: the students cut down cypress trees on the property, milled them into planks and then glue-laminated these into beams that provide the main structural supports. Columns and secondary structural members were made from scrap metal donated by a local company, which the students had to hand-sand to remove rust and then also paint themselves. A large glass wall, which has became the symbol of the Studio's intentions and inventiveness, is made from the side windows of 1989 General Motors automobiles, retrieved from a salvage yard in Chicago.

Ideological Baggage

It would seem that Sam Mockbee fulfils the criteria for a role model for environmentally conscious architects of the future, due to his deep commitment to social priorities. And yet even he was not free of the additional, overriding motives of the kind also seen to be directing the decisions of the architects, landscape architects, urban planners and institutions that have just been discussed in Part II. He shared not only Frank Lloyd Wright's pedagogical methods, but also his desire to derive a national architecture based on founding principles. As he said in an interview just before he died, 'I don't want to be pigeonholed as a regionalist, yet I am. I pay attention to my region; I keep my eyes open. Then I see how I can take that and, using modern technology, reinterpret certain principles that are going to be true 200 years from now. I want the work to be looked at as contemporary American architecture, and in that sense, it has to have a certain honesty to it. That's what is wonderful about really great American architecture, its honesty'.[1]

Moral Architecture

Mockbee went on, in that interview, to equate architecture with morality, claiming that the 'gluttonous affluence' now evident in America has seduced the profession, tempting it away from its moral mandate toward 'stage-set design' that no longer takes people or place into

consideration. He also alluded to one of his main motives in establishing the Rural Studio, which was to 'reinstitute Reconstruction': rehabilitation of the South enacted as political policy after the Civil War.[2]

These are noble sentiments which nevertheless place Mockbee squarely within the mental framework of each of the individuals and/or institutions discussed in Part II. Like them, he was also primarily driven by sectarian nationalistic motives and within these he sought to redress social debts that he believed to still be outstanding. His work also clearly falls into the sustainable category: local, often recycled, materials assembled with the most appropriate technology possible to meet social needs. Environmental architecture seems to still await its truly altruistic advocate – or perhaps one of the most important lessons that Mockbee has left behind is that pure altruism is impossible in our increasingly complicated world.

Mason's Bend Community Center, Samuel Mockbee and students of Auburn University, 1999–2000
A model of community self-build, the Mason's Bend development makes much use of recycled and reclaimed materials to create something with great social value.

Part III: Shifting Attitudes toward Tradition, Technology and Urbanism

Introduction: The Changing Landscape of a Natural Future

Awaji Island project, Tadao Ando
The ground being prepared for Ando's Yumebutai
Conference Centre and complex. The island, though the
home to an important Shinto shrine, was mined heavily
for sand, leaving an escarpment. Typically, Ando saw the
sympathetic development of the site as a way of
preventing further erosion, and so worked very closely
with the topography.

As the studies in Part II indicate, the outcome of the battle for the environment by architects and planners with a green sensibility is still far from clear. Each new advance must be weighed against equal and opposite setbacks that seem to occur with increasing frequency. However, there has been heartening progress in the areas of tradition, technology and urbanism, the three general themes of this book, and the changes occurring in each of these point to promising trends in the future.

Reinterpreting Tradition
Japan is one of the most tradition-bound countries in the world, with an especially strong connection to nature, so that any discernable change in attitude toward the interface between architecture and the environment there has heightened significance for the future of this relationship in the rest of the world.

Tadao Ando is widely considered to be one of the most sensitive interpreters of the prevailing mood of his nation, able to weave the past and the present together in an austere way that also recognizes collective debt to foreign influence, which Japan has always been able to assimilate and personify in an identifiable way. Ando has made no secret of his debt to Le Corbusier and Louis Kahn, both of whom, as this book has hopefully shown, had a greater awareness of natural forces than they are usually given credit for, but his borrowing has usually been at the level of their formal language: massive concrete walls and minimal interior space. Ando's Rokko Housing Project goes beyond this mere reliance on language to an approach to the environment, since it has distinct similarities to Le Corbusier's Roq and Rob development intended for Cap Martin (but never built). The Rokko Housing Project, like Le Corbusier's project, turns necessity into a virtue by not merely coping with a difficult, extremely precipitous, site but by having the housing units syncopate with it, in terraces that seem to become a part of the steep slope. Unlike Le Corbusier, however, Ando has deliberately attempted to set up a dialectic with his architecture, to recognize and accentuate the natural world by placing his project in sharp visual contrast to it. This is the unlikely but ultimately effective paradox of showing respect yet underlining the inevitable difference between the human-made and the natural worlds.

While the comparison may not initially seem obvious, Ando's approach in his Rokko Housing project is very similar to that taken by arch-modernist Richard Meier at the Getty Museum in Los Angeles, completed in the late 1990s. Like Ando, Meier also had to deal with a extremely difficult, steep slope. Each architect seems to want to perpetuate the 'machine in the garden' metaphor perfected by their common idol, Le Corbusier, at the Villa Savoye, without

Ciudad de la Cultura de Galicia, near Santiago,
Peter Eisenman, 1999–
The application of computers to architecture has led to
new forms that can respond ever more closely to – or
even imitiate – nature.

recognizing that he moved on from that mechanistic position over the course of his long
career, until he eventually reached a softer, more humane, accommodation with what many
modernists saw as an ancient enemy: nature.

In his reconstruction of a large part of Awaji Island, near Kobe, however, Ando has
reversed the position he took on the Rokko Housing Project. At Rokko, he removed the side of
a mountain and replaced it with a concrete replica, in much the same way that Richard Meier
did in his Getty Museum in Los Angeles, to call attention to the irreconcilable differences
between architecture and nature no matter how well-intentioned the intervention. At
Awajima, Ando uses architecture to repair destruction caused by earlier disuse, so that rather
than designing a commentary about difference, he has contributed a memorial to nature
instead. That memorial is highly controlled in a way that is reminiscent of French 18th-
century landscaping by André Le Nôtre and others, revealing an altered attitude toward the
role that human intervention in nature should play and providing a clear warning for us all.

Digital Recreation
A second identifiable trend, related to the technological question so often raised in this book,
is one of hubris, of believing that our electronic capability now allows us to create architecture
that replicates natural systems, to the point of also being able to select for dominant traits, as
humans, animals and plants do in the evolutionary process. Rather than simply designing
buildings that respond to natural forces to conserve energy, architects and engineers are now
investigating ways to replicate those forces through computer programming. John Frazer
pioneered this idea in a studio at the Architectural Association in London, teaching students
how to write their own programmes rather than relying on the limited amount of software
available in the market place. This exercise included the preferencing of selected criteria
related to the design, as will be described in detail in the first study of Part III, 'Digitizing the

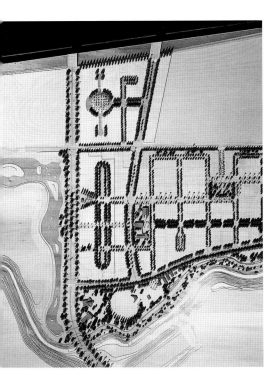

Playa Vista development, Los Angeles
The careful, ecologically sensitive development of Playa Vista, in Los Angeles, was initially intended to bring an important stretch of coast back to life. Parks – and the provision of attractive public spaces – are now seen as key to inner-city areas.

Environment', so that the computer, rather than the student, ended up determining what the final form of the building would be. Climatic, topographical and even stylistic data were translated into each programme and were then allowed to run, to create the architecture.

This process has been adopted, in modified form, by several high-profile architects such as Greg Lynn and Peter Eisenman, whose Santiago de Compostela project, which was designed by using it, is also described in 'Digitizing the Environment'. They differ from Frazer's approach in that they do not go to the extreme of building their own computers, as he and his students did, or creating their own programmes, instead preferring to modify existing software. But the goal is the same: to replicate natural processes in their architecture rather than just responding to them formally.

The implications of this trend are revolutionary, especially when layered over the equally exciting idea of having architecture move to respond to its surroundings through digitally engineered natural selection. Kinetic parts will alter formal configurations beyond our imagining.

Re-Greening the City

A third discernable trend in urbanism is the re-greening of city, with a difference. As cities grew in the industrial age, parks were seen as a necessary respite from the factory floor, but only for those in the managerial class. Hyde Park in London, Central Park in New York City and other such urban enclaves were not located in the blue-collar, poorest areas of the city and while they were not gated, the social proscriptions for their use were clear. Recreational areas for the working class, like Coney Island, New York, were located far from the city limits as a means of economic segregation.

As mentioned elsewhere here, the world is now re-urbanizing after the flight to the suburbs during the post-Second World War period in the developed world, for a multitude of reasons. By 2000, nearly half of the world's population lived in cities and that percentage is rising daily. Much of that proportion, especially in the post-industrial countries, is middle class or below and this constituency is now demanding recreational parkland nearby. Due to demographics and numbers this segment of the new city has a great deal of political clout, even though it is often economically disadvantaged, and politicians are now racing to jump on this bandwagon to provide parks for inner-city residents.

Los Angeles has such an exemplary demographic profile that it is an ideal case study of this phenomenon, and accordingly is discussed here in detail, along with the efforts by various quangos throughout the city to restore damaged natural resources, such as the Los Angeles River, so that its returning residents can have respite from the harsh realities of higher densities, heavy traffic, crime, gangs, pollution, fires, earthquakes, floods and increasing isolation.

Ciudad de la Cultura de Galicia, Peter Eisenman, 1999–
With computers able to mimic natural forms, architects
are able to think in terms of smooth unbroken surfaces.
In this project Eisenman has converted the existing
topography into binary form, then integrated the
structure virtually. The result is an architecture fully
integrated with its surroundings.

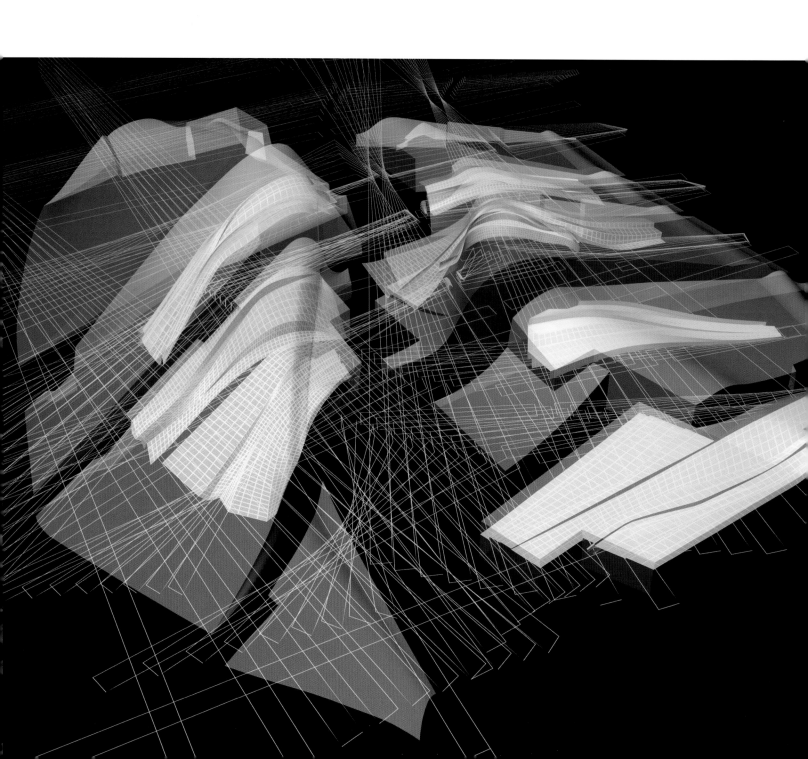

Digitizing the Environment

The advent of the computer has heralded a new age in ecological architecture, allowing architects to develop forms that are closer to nature

Background

Since Charles Babbage invented the 'Analytical Engine' in 1819, computers have been invaluable for processing large amounts of data. By the late 20th century they had begun to dominate architecture, ushering in a new, ahistorical style that could mimic natural processes, and replace biological evolution with technical systems.

Led by pioneers such as John Frazer, the computer allows architects to compare different models, to test for efficiency and performance. An applied example of this approach is the Ciudad de la Cultura, in Galicia, Spain, by Peter Eisenman, an underground cultural centre. Computers were used to factor in environment and topography, to allow the final result to be part of something approaching a natural process.

The use of the computer in architecture is still in its infancy, but it is clear that there is great potential for imitating the complexity and rhythms of nature, to create a marriage between the built environment and the natural one.

Just over a century after its invention, Babbage's modest counting machine had been transformed into ENIAC, the Electronic Numeric Integrator and Computer that by the end of the Second World War had become a key component of the United States Air Defense Command, controlling the trajectories of nuclear weapons that might be used during the Cold War. Fifty years after that, the computer was the catalyst in what is generally referred to as the electronic revolution and entered the realm of what behavioural scientists call a 'social structure': that is, it is part of a technological process that has become the equivalent of a 'form of law; an authoritative or binding expression of social norms and values from which the individual or group may have no immediate recourse'.[1] It qualifies as such, scientists argue, because its use has caused unintended social consequences, has affected politics and culture, has shaped social behaviour through 'coercive mandates', has reconfigured prior social patterns (as well as technologies peripheral to it) and has influenced individual psychological development, prompting subconscious compliance with its systems.[2]

Little Debate this Time Around

Despite these profound social consequences, there has been little reaction to this technological revolution, unlike the epic philosophical battles that were waged in the wake of the Industrial Revolution of the 19th century. The reasons for this are complex, but the

Key Project

Ciudad de la Cultura de Galicia, Peter Eisenman, 1999–

Signposts

Underground construction Part II: 14, 25

Use of computers Part II: 18, 19

upshot for the design professions is significant, nothing less than a complete transformation of the way the built environment is conceived, designed, documented and constructed.

Whatever criticism has been formulated against the unthinking acceptance of electronic technology has primarily been focused on the further detachment from reality and context that it encourages. Virtual reality is an abstract universe, created by a programmer, in which the basic law is simplification, the editing of empirical data which does not comply with the originator's conceptual guidelines. As such, virtual reality has been characterized as the direct descendant of objective experimentation, or the rejection of direct experience, which was one of the principal tenets of modern science until critics such as Karl Popper cast doubt on the possibility of any empirical process being completely value free.[3]

In the early 1990s, when the recurring human fantasy of being able to replace biological evolution with technical systems, or of replacing people with cyborgs, finally seemed capable of being fulfilled, an architect who was then teaching at the Architectural Association in London put forward an inventive alternative to the increasing detachment from the environment that many sceptics believe cybernetics will cause.

The Universal Constructor

Rather than accepting the limitation of allowing the design process to be restricted by available programmes, John H. Frazer questioned current practice itself and the human factor in design. In 1995, he wrote *An Evolutionary Architecture*, which documented a module he had taught at the Architectural Association of London, based on the premise that existing CAD programmes were useful for repetitive transformation, but inadequate for producing new forms.[4] In AA Diploma Unit 11, in 1990, he worked with students to derive what he called a 'Universal Constructor', in which computer modelling was used to develop prototypical forms, which were then tested under various simulated environments and evaluated. The problem he set for his students was to work out a way to code structural form, to find a computer language to describe conflicting criteria, rather than using one predetermined framework, to let these criteria then operate for selection, mimicking natural, morphological and metabolic processes, using the computer as a generating force that would differ in each context.

An Evolutionary Model

This developed into a technique in which the key parameters of a design concept, including topography and environmental factors, were translated into a code script comparable to that of life, encoded in DNA, and the parameters were allowed to evolve naturally. This code script was then subjected to crossover and mutation and the forms that emerged were further exposed to selection, during which significant differences began to occur. In a method that is analogous to natural selection, genetic codes were chosen to simulate evolution, in which functional efficiency is the predominant criteria. Where selection criteria were more qualitative, intuitive criteria were used, a technique Frazer compares to artificial selection, in which experience and personal judgment come into play. In design, this is done by examining a population of genetic variants which are delineated, with selection made after visual inspection, supported by statistical data, so that conflicting criteria can be weighted.

The evolutionary model that Frazer has developed requires that a design concept be described in a genetic code, which is then mutated and developed in a computer programme into a series of models, in response to a simulated environment, with the successful model being the one that performs best. By using a method similar that of life itself, architecture not only responds to its environment, it becomes one with it, the final marriage of nature and the machine.

A New Allegiance

Frazer's theory has yet to be tested in quite the way he has proposed, but there are signs that his ideas are beginning to take hold. The increased connection between architecture and theory has helped in this, since Gilles Deleuze's *The Fold* has heightened interest in the possibility of the extrapolation of form from a digital source among these who have become bored with deconstruction and are looking for the next new thing. It is appropriate that the most promising applications of Deleuze's vision, which is a far less specific version of Frazer's hypothesis, should be attempted by Peter Eisenman, who introduced Jacques Derrida to a trend-hungry public at the end of the 1980s. There is considerable irony in Eisenman's change of allegiance, since Deconstructivism is inherently nihilistic, being predicated on the end of social institutions by undermining the authority of the texts that support them, as well as being predictive of the complete replacement of all human endeavour by technology, so that people are marginalized, if not eliminated, in the architectural equation. As such, Deconstructivism in architecture is space negative, giving preference to structure rather than the people who use a building, rather than being space positive as modernism was. Folding, on the other hand, implies integration rather than eradication, the synthesis of biology and technology that Frazer has been experimenting with.

Ciudad de la Cultura de Galicia as Built Theory

Eisenman's Wexner Center built on the campus of Oberlin College in Ohio in the early 1990s was his attempt to explain Deconstructivism to a confused public in built form, and it did so very effectively by occupying the space between two existing institutions, primarily with an open-gridded structure, or non-space. A gallery beneath this frame, which represents the increasing domination of technology, contains exhibition areas which are marginal, the eradication of the institution of the museum.

Eisenman has attempted a similar explanation of the theory of Folding in his Ciudad de la Cultura de Galicia (City of Culture of Galicia), 15 kilometres (9 miles) south of Santiago de Compostela, Spain, on the top of Monte Gaias. The project, which Eisenman won in competition with such illustrious firms as Manuel Gallego, César Portela, Ricardo Bofill, Juan Navarro Baldeweg, Gigon Guyer, Steven Holl, Rem Koolhaas, Daniel Libeskind, Dominique Perrault and Jean Nouvel, includes a library, archive, media centre, museum and theatre, which this time have not negated, but have been united with, the mountain.

Landform Architecture

More than just an underground museum, the Ciudad de la Cultura is a reinterpretation of the site, a translation of the mountaintop into a binary code in an attempt to finally marry the human-made artefact with its natural context. The site parameters were not translated into digital code to the same extent as they have been by John Frazer, in his attempt to create a 'Universal Constructor', and then allowed to operate according to natural selection, but topography and environment were factored into the computer programme, in a hybrid fashion, to allow the result to be part of a natural process rather than a product. Eisenman

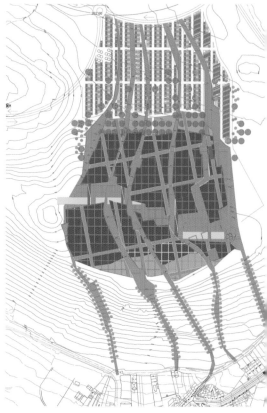

Ciudad de la Cultura de Galicia

The undulating forms of the 'City of Culture' imitate the existing forms of the mountain, and also the undulations of the scallop shell traditionally worn by pilgrims to Santiago. The paths through the development are based on those in the centre of the city, meaning that the building is entirely related to its surroundings. Left: the complex in relation to the city; above: a diagram showing the paths through the complex.

has described his intention on Monte Gaias as the 'production of architecture from the dominating space reference. A temporal change factor was introduced through the construction principles of the fold, which manifests itself as a continuous variation of the forms, and avoiding an object event'.[5]

No Stone Left Unturned

As part of this process, Eisenman intended to use part of the one million cubic metres (35 million cubic feet) of material that had to be removed from the mountain as aggregate for the concrete structure, but was dissuaded by the cost of cutting the rock and its physical

Ciudad de la Cultura de Galicia

The complex is made up an a series of 'ribbons', which house six different buildings for different museums and administration. Above: a model showing the volume of the project; right: the entrance to one of the museums.

characteristics. The stone, a green-veneered anfibolite, is very hard and can only be cut with diamond-covered saws and drills. It also weathers badly, its surface oxidizing very quickly and its physical properties changing as chemical reactions caused by exposure to air continue, causing it to become softer and change colour. Because of the chemical reactions and loss of load-bearing capacity and stability, the rock cannot be used as aggregate for concrete to be used in buildings. Oxidation also makes it difficult to use it as cladding or paving since it would have to be treated to prevent this, which on top of the cost for extraction, would have been prohibitively expensive.[6]

The rock that was dynamited from the mountain was broken into pieces no larger than one metre (three foot) square, mixed with soil and compacted as a sub-base for roads, parking areas and walkways, as well as being stockpiled for future use. Consequently materials used for construction on the site, as well as for the concrete, were brought in from outside.[7]

Awaiting the Verdict of History

Whether the Ciudad de la Cultura de Galicia represents a real breakthrough in the protracted human attempt to replicate nature (or to at least integrate seamlessly with it), or whether it is yet another pedagogical model of the latest theory that is soon to become extinct, remains to be seen. Peter Eisenman has tried to avoid the production of an 'object event', but by tying the Ciudad de la Cultura to the ephemeral rules of commodification, he has insured its eventual eclipse.

Awaji Yumebutai Park, Hyogo, 1993–9
The strong links and symbiotic relationship between Ando's work and the landscape in which it is set is self-evident in this project. The complex includes a conference centre, hotel, series of parks and plazas, and an open-air theatre (left).

Tadao Ando: Perfecting Nature

The work of Tadao Ando builds on the traditional Japanese sensitivity towards the relationship between architecture and nature, even if his materials are often far from natural

Biography

Tadao Ando was born in Osaka, Japan, in 1941. Unusually for an architect of his generation, he did not receive any formal architectural training, instead teaching himself by reading and travelling extensively through Africa, Europe, and the United States. In 1970, after a series of short apprenticeships with planners, architects and designers, he set up Tadao Ando Architect & Associates. His early work shows a radical approach, relying on unfinished reinforced concrete – he cites Le Corbusier and Mies van der Rohe as particular heroes. His work is most notable, however, for retaining a strong connection to the landscape – in Ando's own words : 'My effort is to preserve Japanese residential architecture's intimate connection with nature and the openness to the natural world that I call enclosed Modern Architecture, a restoration of the unity between house and nature'. Over the years he has completed several housing projects, a church, the Japanese pavilion for Expo '92 (where the Grimshaw pavilion was also displayed), and many planning projects. He has been awarded numerous prizes, including the Pritzker Prize, a RIBA Gold Medal and the AIA Prize.

The architecture of Tadao Ando is often described as being quintessentially Japanese. If so, what do his landscape-conscious works that began in the late 1980s tell us about changing attitudes toward nature in a country that is recognized as having a finely tuned appreciation of and response to each of the four seasons? Ando's Rokko Housing Project (1983) and its subsequent addition, followed by his Raika Group Headquarters Building (1989), Garden of Fine Arts (1990), Kumamoto Prefectural Forest of Tombs Museum (1994), all in Osaka, as well as his Naoshima Contemporary Art Museum (1992–95) and the Awaji Yumebutai Park in Hyogo (1993–99) all predict a sea change in a national (and subsequently international) attitude toward the interaction between nature and the public realm.

Controlled, Respectful Restraint

Ando's approach to placing architecture in nature, which perhaps is the characteristic he shares most with Japanese tradition, is not only to show respect for the environment in which he is building, but to amplify its essential quality by showing restraint in what he does, a classically minimalist strategy. As Kenneth Frampton has described it, 'Ando's perception of landscape is two-faceted. He is aware of the incongruity of building in a landscape, but also realizes that by limiting the building as something to be "seen", architecture may function as an apparatus from

Key Projects

Rokko Housing Project, completed 1983
Rokko II, mid-1990s
Yumebutai Conference Centre, Awaji Island, 1993–9

Signposts

Local traditions Part II: 19, 20, 21, 23, 24
Japanese influence Part II: 1, 5, 6, 12
Sensitivity to site Part II: 6, 10, 25

which to "see" the landscape. Landscape is thus accorded higher value than architecture, which
becomes part of the landscape – embraced within it'.[1] This strikes at the heart of the ancient
dilemma of architecture, since it has always basically been both a replication of, and an
intrusion into, the natural world – and in the 21st century frequently an insult to it.

By showing respect and restraint, Ando makes this intrusion a compliment to nature,
a gesture similar to the Shinto recognition that there is an anima to be placated before
construction can begin. Ando's belief, like that of a physician's, is to do no harm. Even where
the need for intervention is inescapable, as it was in the Rokko Housing Project in which high
densities were required and the site was a fragile, steeply sloping hillside plot, he was able to
successfully integrate the natural profile and the built form in such a way that the result looks
more inevitable than intrusive. And Rokko, like all of the other 'landscape conscious' projects
that come after it, also concentrates on the important issue of view that Frampton raises, the
difference being that Ando does not focus on view for its own sake but as a means of evoking
responses and emotions about nature in relationship to his architecture.

Rokko I and II and Yumebutai Offer Insights

The Rokko Housing Project, which has unexpectedly unfolded in three successive phases for
the architect, provides an incisive view, along with the much larger Yumebutai Conference
Centre on Awaji Island, of Ando's attitude toward nature and so it is useful to compare these
two projects in some detail.

Rokko I, completed in 1983, is located in the foothills of the Rokko Mountains, in the
suburb of Osaka. Working within the confines of a very small site, drastically sloped at a 60-
degree angle, Ando organized the units along a circulation spine that in a way is reminiscent
of Le Corbusier's Roq and Rob housing project, designed for an equally steep slope along the
Cote d'Azure but never realized.[2] Rokko I is clustered into two segments of terraced flats
respectively, as it moves up the cliff-like slope, with its service stair flanking the first set on the
far western side and then moving into the middle of the second cluster at the top of the cliff.
Each of the apartments has a different floor plan, consistent with Ando's concept of
irregularity within a strict order, which he sees as the basis of natural form. A third cluster,
Rokko II, was added in the mid-1990s, to the west of the first two. Unlike them, it follows the

grid plan of the streets beneath it, due to a fortuitous shift in the contours of the cliff on this side of the site, and more generous property lines also allowed Ando greater freedom in organizing the units on the lot. This freedom made it even more possible for Ando to express clearly his overall intention for this project, which was 'to create a new relationship between nature and architecture by taking into account the special condition of the site, namely the 60 degrees gradient'.[3] The entire project is based on a 5.2 by 5.2 metre (17 by 17 foot) grid, and each unit has a square enclosure. Moving up the central stairway, which is used as an axis, each of the three blocks is viewed in sequence. With this progression in mind, Ando has deliberately made the elevations of each of the units solid in the lower floors and more open on the upper levels, to underscore the symbolic position of architecture, between earth and sky.

Awaji Yumebutai

The Yumebutai Conference Centre, built on Awaji Island in 1999, may be said to complete a cycle of projects by Ando that amplify nature in this way, serving as a predictor of an attitude about the environment in the 21st century. Pulling back from the stark abyss conjured up in the 1980s by Arata Isozaki, by the paved elliptical void in the middle of his Tsukuba Civic Centre, intended to symbolize the poverty of the public realm in contemporary cities, Ando seeks to use the interrelationship between architecture and nature as a way of restoring public confidence in institutions and built form. By happy coincidence, Awaji Island is closely associated with the myth about the birth of Japan from the sea, and also is home to the Izanagi Shrine, which is the oldest Shinto shrine in the nation.

Located at the far eastern end of the Inland Sea, Awaji Island is legendary for its scenic beauty and temperate climatic, an ideal location in which to reinitiate an institutional, public relationship with nature, and to revive an area destroyed by human intrusion. During the high-growth post-war period, the area was used as a sand pit to provide land fill for the reclamation of Osaka Bay, with about 106 million cubic metres (3.7 billion cubic feet) removed from a 140-hectare area over a fifty-year period. An entire mountain was taken away, leaving a sheer, exposed bedrock cliff in its place. In 1994, the islanders started to try to reclaim the sand mine, planting 250,000 seedlings on the scarred cliff. The large mixed-use facility that Tadao Ando provided takes advantage of the topography, in his invincible way, making a virtue of the remaining escarpment and replacing it with an international conference centre, a hotel, a number of parks and plazas, a conservatory and an open-air theatre. The complex angles used in the project, which covers a vast area, were dictated by an overlay of considerations, to provide the kinds of essential views just discussed as well as to follow previous lines of cut and fill. The names of the various open-air gardens and plazas tell the story: the Chapel of the Sea, the Water Plaza of the Shells, the Circular Forum, the Oval Forum, the Seaside Gallery, the Hillside Gallery, the Sky Garden, the Water Garden. Perhaps the most revealing of all of them, as a window into the architect's mind and intent, is the Hyakuden-En, or Hundred Level Garden, an Escher-like series of planted terraces that are so closely manicured that they seem to be more of an exercise in keeping nature under control than in harmony with people.

Rokko and Awaji as Predictions of Change

The first phase of the Rokko Housing Project was completed during a period of high optimism in Japan. The economy was strong and the bubble had not yet burst. While Ando is not part of the older generation of architects who have ridden the tidal wave of growth that Japan has experienced since the disaster of the Second World War, he has benefited from the same latitude of design freedom that they have enjoyed, until the 'Asian flu' broke out in 1996–7. That downturn caused a drastic lowering of expectations for most Japanese architects, with the exception of those tied into an escalating cycle of urban construction in and around Tokyo that will be discussed later.

The Yumebutai Conference Centre on Awaji Island was begun several years after the economic bubble burst and in spite of the fact that it is much larger than the Rokko Housing Project, it is a fitting mirror of the structural social changes that have taken place in Japan in the decade or so since the first phase of Rokko was completed. Rokko conveys confidence in technology, the ability to take on the most difficult problem that can be encountered in nature and to solve it. This site, previously considered unbuildable, has been tamed in ways that Ando believes can reconcile architecture and the earth it is built on. These ways, as enumerated by him, are: (1) to 'express in sharper form the relationship between the structure and nature [since] this site lies in a valley and the building will sit more deeply in nature';[4] (2) to shift the siting of the blocks to allow them to be seen in rotating perspective when seen from the bottom of the axis stair. This shift also intended to allow natural light into all of them, from the east; (3) the units are each cut 'into east and west sections by spans running north to south, resolving problems of ventilation and lighting';[5] and (4) by gradually opening up the elevations of the units, as previously mentioned, from solid wall to trabeation that frames the sky, the repetitive volumes not only join earth and air, but 'the masses of concrete rising on the hillside, in being thoroughly man-made in form, have the power to confront nature and create their own distinctive world'.[6]

Awaji, on the other hand, was fitted into groups cut out of a mountain, not so much intended to complement nature as to replace it with an architectural prosthesis. Given the history of the site, this garden is a powerful symbol of regeneration and renewal and a people's awareness of the need to correct the mistakes of the past. And yet, it is just as confrontational and controlling, in an expanded way, as the Rokko complex is on its tightly circumscribed lot.

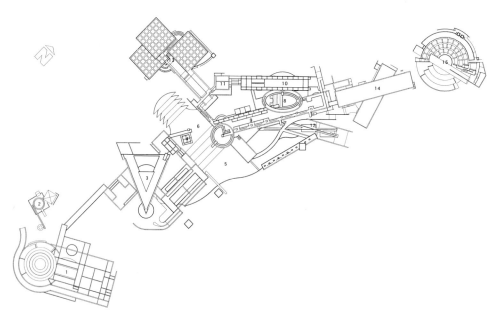

A plan of the Awaji Yumebutai Complex

1   International Conference Centre
2   Tea-Ceremony Room
3   Hotel
4   Chapel of the Sea
5   Water Plaza of the Shells
6   Circular Forum
7   Garden of 1,000 Fountains
8   Oval Forum
9   Seaside Gallery
10 Hillside Gallery
11 Sky Garden
12 Water Garden
13 Hundred Level Garden
14 Greenhouse
15 Open-air Theatre

'Hundred Level Garden', Awaji Yumebutai Park
The spectacular garden created by Ando at Awaji Island integrates itself with its surroundings, yet clearly tries to improve on nature, or to reach a compromise with its surroundings.

Unbridled optimism and unlimited faith in the ability of engineering technology to alter nature may have been mitigated by fundamental changes brought about by economic shifts, causing more sensitivity to social needs and a concern for correcting the human destruction of nature, but the underlying urge to control the environment remains the same, and that is the lesson for the rest of us.

The Japanese, who have historically demonstrated a heightened sensitivity to nature in their architecture, seem to have become caught up in an equally strong relationship with commodity bringing about the progressive destruction of the natural world they profess to love. By the early 1990s, when Yumebutai was begun, nearly fifty per cent of the Gross National Product of Japan was spent on construction in Tokyo alone, evidence of a desire for growth gone out of control.[7] Mega-projects such as the Tokyo Forum by Rafael Viñoly and the Tokyo City Hall by Kenzo Tange hint at this excess, which still awaits a definitive explanation.

The range of responses to the siren call of progress, from Ando's admittedly skilful 'confrontations' to Tange's concrete-and-steel Metropolitan behemoth do not bode well for the future, since this radical shift has taken place in a nation which once had such a spiritual connection to nature and should have been able to provide an example to others.

Playa Vista development
The Playa Vista development is bringing new life to a
neglected part of Los Angeles, providing high-density
usage while increasing the space available for marshland
wildlife.

3

The Greening of Los Angeles

More than any other city in the West, Los Angeles is perceived as a direct affront on nature. Its particular sprawl has acted as a magnet to urban planners, each with their own solution

Background

Along with Las Vegas, Los Angeles has been a perennial source of interest for architects and planners around the world. The settlement of Los Angeles began in the 19th century, with the destruction of indigenous Indian populations. Initially the area was used for pasture, but with the influx of European settlers was increasingly cultivated and used for wheat and orchards. Between 1910 and 1950 the area was the greatest food producer in the United States. However, being situated in the middle of a desert meant that many things had to be imported – even water had to be brought in from elsewhere. By the mid-20th century, agriculture was disappearing to other areas with cheaper labour, while by the end of the century heavy industry had all but vanished. Over the same period poverty increased dramatically.

Today the population of Los Angeles is growing at an astonishing rate, and this in turn has led to pollution reaching catastrophic levels. Furthermore, with the increased deregulation of labour markets, now for the first time since colonization over half the population is of Hispanic origin, leading to a further cultural shift. Today the city and its surrounding area have over sixteen million inhabitants, making it the sixth largest conurbation in the world.

Key Projects

Playa Vista development, initially Maguire Thomas Partners (developers), 1980s–
Pershing Square renewal, Maguire Thomas Partners, with Ricardo Legorreta, 1980s–1990s
Los Angeles River Greenway Programme, 1996–
Baldwin Hills Park, Mia Lehrer + Associates, Hood Design, 2001–

Signposts

Town planning Part II: 2, 3, 4, 8, 9, 11, 12, 18
Conservation Part II: 18, 20, 21, 23
Urban renewal Part II: 22, 25

Now that the industrial cycle in the developed world has almost been completed, the 'brownfields' left in the wake of the urban manufacturing boom that lasted for most of the 20th century offer the promise of a new wave of park-building in inner cities all over the world. Brownfields, defined by the United States Environmental Protection Agency (EPA) as 'abandoned, idled or under-used industrial and commercial facilities where expansion or redevelopment is complicated by real or perceived environmental contamination', hold the promise of generating an environmental revolution in America since the Small Business Liability Relief and Brownfields Revitalization Act was signed into law on 11 January 2002. The law systematizes the approach being taken by the EPA toward urban sites polluted by industry at all levels and doubles government funds available for clean-up from $98 million in 2002 to $200 million a year, beginning in 2003.[1] Guidelines for using this money have also been expanded to include site assessment, clean-up, and removal of underground storage tanks. The new law mitigates the more draconian provisions of the so-called 'Superfund' law, the Comprehensive Environmental Response, Compensation and Liability Act (CERCLA) passed in 1980.

The Polluter No Longer Pays

The Superfund law imposed a tax on oil and chemical industries that was used to finance a trust fund to be used for clean-up, in return for exemption from liability for petroleum contamination.[2] The Superfund law specifies three ways that toxic sites could be cleaned up: by those responsible, by the EPA using the Superfund and recouping costs from those responsible, or by the EPA only, using the Superfund when those responsible could not be held accountable. One way or another, the law operated on the principle that 'the polluter pays'. Proponents argue that it has been an effective tool for financing clean-ups, with more than six hundred completed during the eight years of the Clinton administration. However, the end of the law does not end the shield against liability that the oil and chemical companies enjoy under it, though critics also point out that stopping the Superfund tax also amounts to a huge financial gain for these industries.

The Superfund law also made little distinction between lightly polluted small businesses and highly toxic heavy industries. It held new owners liable for clean-up even if they unwittingly bought properties they did not know were polluted as well as contiguous owners, and this over-regulation caused lenders, developers and insurers to steer clear of any sites that may have been industrialized in the past, mostly in or near the inner city. The EPA estimates that there are now about 450,000 such sites across America, ranging from abandoned rural landfills, gas stations and dry cleaners to rail yards on the urban periphery, factories, chemical plants and refineries.

The Promise of New Parks

With indemnity from liability and the doubling of federal funding, which will come primarily through higher state taxes, there is now more of an incentive for developers in the United States to reconsider brownfield sites they would have avoided in the past, especially since state and city governments, anxious to return these properties to the tax rolls, are offering additional incentives. Since such sites must be developed according to stringent environmental standards also imposed by the EPA, more open space and park land are an inevitable result. The Northeast-Midwest Institute estimates that each brownfield reclaimed generates about four times as much green space to support it.[3]

Engineering firms have been instrumental in bridging the gap between the new technical requirements of clean-up and heightened intent, finding innovative ways to adhere to the letter of the law while still meeting developer's budgets. Local communities, however, are often even more demanding in their expectations than the EPA, making each remediation a political and legal battlefield.

Los Angeles as a Test Case of Urban Greening

Los Angeles seems an unlikely representative of other post-industrial American cities because of the prevalence of agriculture, oil and real estate speculation there in the past, and the concentration of high-technology companies, financial institutions and entertainment industries there today. But, as social geographer Edward Soja argues: 'Seemingly paradoxical and functionally interdependent juxtaposition' epitomizes this city, since 'Frostbelt and Sunbelt dynamics come together in Los Angeles, interweaving to produce a complex mix of selective industrial decline and industrial expansion'.[4] While it has never had the same kind of centralized, concentrated factory production as cities in the northeastern part of the United

Development by the Los Angeles River,
Moore, Ruble, Yudell
The New Urbanists have been instrumental in focusing public attention on revitalizing green spaces in existing cities, such as Los Angeles.

States, Soja asserts that this also made Los Angeles a prime candidate for the 'Fordist urban industrialization of the interwar years' when four major automobile manufacturers opened assembly plants there in the 1920s, drawing all of the support industries that these factories require.[5] These, in turn, drew aircraft industries, which fed on automobile production, and rapidly evolved into an aerospace specialty, relying on defence contracts. This rare mixture of Frostbelt–Sunbelt and industrial–post-industrial characteristics, then, makes Los Angeles a compelling model for city growth elsewhere today.

The visible aftermath in the centre of Los Angeles is certainly familiar: high-density low or lower middle income, demographically diverse residential areas that lack parks and recreational areas. For this reason, what is happening there is indicative of similar initiatives in other post-industrial cities throughout the world. As Kenneth Frampton has said: 'The American megalopolis has already been built and there is little chance of recasting it. The alienating non-place urban realm is already a ubiquitous condition covering vast areas of the continent and clearly there is little that can be done to humanize this ruinous situation except possibly the gradual application of fragmentary landscape interventions. This may be the most fundamental reason why landscape design is of greater cultural consequence today than the other traditional environmental disciplines'.[6]

The Crisis that Confronts the People

The idea of a green Los Angeles seems incongruous, since the city is best known for freeways, acres of asphalt, smog, suburban sprawl and an entire river encased in concrete. But incredibly, almost imperceptibly, Los Angeles is moving toward the verdant vision outlined by the Olmsted Brothers in a little known report submitted to the Citizens Committee on Parks, Playgrounds and Beaches in 1930. In their report, the Olmsteds characterized the lack of parks in the region as 'The crisis that confronts the people', and bluntly identified the economic priority of providing infrastructure as the major obstacle to nurturing open space. Los Angeles is now one of the fastest growing and most racially diverse cities in the United States. Its phenomenal growth, change in population mix and the lack of green space to serve it seems to have been prophesied by the Olmsteds' observation that: 'The rapid growth of population, which makes the rapid expansion of park facilities so urgent, also makes its financing particularly difficult. The rapid influx creates an exceptionally insistent need for capital to invest in those private and public improvements which are always the first requirements of a new population.'[7]

Twenty years after their report was submitted, the economic forces that the Olmsteds described had spawned a region consisting almost entirely of speculative development, linked by freeways. Originally one of the first cities in America to install a public transportation system, Los Angeles drastically changed direction soon after the Second World War. A shift in public policy in favour of freeways over public transport intensified urban flight and communities established near the original Pueblo core were abandoned for the suburbs.

Plan for Los Angeles, 1930

The Olmsted brothers, who are perhaps best known for their design of Central Park in NYC, also prepared this recently discovered ecological battleplan for Los Angeles in 1930.

Reassessment

After five decades of almost unlimited growth, the slow realization of what rampant speculation has wrought has brought public attention back to the green space issue. The increasing diversity of the region has made the older communities, which had been abandoned during the rush to Orange County and the San Fernando Valley in the 1950s and

1960s, popular once more, and the residents of these communities, demanding amenities, are forming committees. Politicians, sensing a critical shift in popular will, are now making alliances with these community groups, leading to the passage of several Environmental Improvement Bonds in 2000 and 2001.

Open Space Angels

These initiatives have resulted in what landscape architect Mia Lehrer has called a 'concentrated series of strategic interventions' led by 'open space angels' who have consequently become identified with causes that are beginning to have a startling cumulative effect. The significant thing about this effect is that it will not only make a substantial difference to the environmental quality and urban character of Los Angeles, but also means that this pattern is likely to occur in other American cities as well, just as suburban sprawl did fifty years ago. The angels that Lehrer refers to run the gamut from enlightened developers, administrators of the California Resources Agency and the Santa Monica Conservancy, and activists who are fighting to clean up Santa Monica Bay, to the Friends of the Los Angeles River (FoLAR).

Resurrecting the River

The Los Angeles River Greenway campaign, which is working with private landowners, local communities and public agencies to acquire land along the entire 80-kilometre (50-mile) length of a river that was largely diverted into a concrete culvert in the 1930s and 40s, has been using strategies that are typical of all the activists trying to provide badly needed recreational facilities in the most densely populated part of Los Angeles. The Los Angeles River begins in the San Fernando foothills, and once supported wide ribbons of lush vegetation as it meandered across the coastal plain on its way to the Pacific Ocean. Because it was a dependable water source, it was responsible for the founding of the Pueblo that eventually grew into the city of Los Angeles. After a disastrous flood in 1930, the United States Army Corps of Engineers lined the entire river basin with concrete to control overflow, and as separate communities began to grow around it, the river became invisible.

Ironically, if the riverside system of small parks recommended by the Olmsted Brothers in their 1930 plan had been implemented, the flooding would have been mitigated, making a concrete channel unnecessary. As the city grows and open spaces become even more limited, the wisdom of the Olmsted proposal – of providing greenways that would connect neighbourhoods to larger parks – is becoming obvious. The pressing need for more open space led Mayor Thomas Bradley to form the Los Angeles River Task Force in 1990, made up of Council District representatives, City Commissioners, Environmentalists, members of County, State and Federal agencies and concerned citizens. The Los Angeles River Master Plan, completed in 1996, outlines a network of parks, community spaces and trails along the entire length of the river, to be implemented by non-profit community action groups and public agencies that have identified sites for parks and have also designed and paid for them.

The Los Angeles and San Gabriel Watershed and Open Space Plan developed by the California Resources Agency and the Santa Monica Mountains Conservancy is based on the recognition that, in order to address the problems of the river in the inner city, the upper part had to be studied as well, and it takes a holistic approach toward the coordination of the treatment of both, to be dovetailed with planning efforts in the region tied to parks and open

space being considered in individual cities. The intention of the plan is to extend the focus from the river to the entire watershed and to involve each community within it (affecting more than seven million people). The problems that the joint commission initially encountered were typical of the symptoms of an ecosystem put under strain by human activity: restricted movement of wildlife, scarce habitat for it, and pollution of groundwater. However, they were faced with the additional challenges of improving these conditions while providing people with more park space and the chance to experience nature at first hand.

The Los Angeles and San Gabriel Watershed and Open Space plan attempts to establish a balance between natural systems and human activity throughout the watershed, and to establish a set of principles to guide space planning inside it that apply to both land and water. Land planning creates, expands and improves open space throughout the region, and improves community access to it through a network of pedestrian pathways in ways that preserve the quality of natural habitat and improve connectivity. Since concern about flood control has been the cause of the current condition of the Los Angeles River, planners have returned to the original Olmsted notion of creating riverfront 'greenways' as natural filters to hold floodwaters, extend open space and to clean and improve the quality of ground and surface water. Planning has been predicated upon integrating these strategies for both land and water through coordination across jurisdictional boundaries and ongoing management that ensures effective implementation and public involvement.[8]

Pershing Square

In the 1980s and 1990s Robert Maguire, then partner in Maguire Thomas Partners, helped establish a precedent for the kind of community involvement that is now transforming Los Angeles, by organizing local residents to support the restoration of Pershing Square in the downtown area. Once a lush, elegant park full of King palms and criss-crossed with fine gravel paths, Pershing Square had deteriorated into a crime-ridden no-go zone by the late 1960s, isolated from its neighbourhood by an inaccessible concrete perimeter and wide entrances to a parking garage that had been built beneath it.

Maguire coordinated a community regeneration effort, raising enough capital to commission landscape architect Laurie Olin and architect Ricardo Legorreta to transform it into an urban asset once again. Laurie Olin tracked down the King palms which had been removed from the park, miraculously finding them still alive in a conservatory forty years after transplanting, and returned them to their original positions. Curb heights were reduced and subterranean parking entrances relocated to allow easier access into the city-block sized green space. Ricardo Legorreta provided large-scaled geometric landmarks in vibrant hues, reminiscent of those used by his mentor, Luis Barragán as gateways to El Pedregal in Mexico City, to clearly declare that Pershing Square had been returned to public use, by a far more pluralistic populace.

Playa Vista

Once owned by Howard Hughes, and used as a landing strip and aircraft assembly plant for his experimental projects, the 1,087-acre Playa Vista property near the Pacific Ocean is another complex case study in urban greening. Determined to break the string of mismanagement and misfortune that had prevented previous developers from completing their plans for the site, upon acquiring the site Maguire Thomas Partners characteristically

PLAYA VIS

adopted a more reflexive approach to the problem of addressing the myriad objectives of public agencies and local special interest groups in designing this project. The key objections they addressed were the preservation of a wetland and freshwater marsh on a large portion of the site, and the issue of more than 180 acres of severely degraded fresh- and saltwater wetlands, which were bulldozed and compacted by Howard Hughes during the construction of the runaway for Hughes Aircraft.

This restoration programme would have allowed the wetland to increase to about 260 acres, a forty per cent increase over existing acreage, and nearly half of the total site to be dedicated in common as open space, neighbourhood parks, waterways and habitat reserve. Maguire Thomas Partners had also committed to restoring the 260-acre Ballona Wetlands, one of the region's few remaining wildlife sanctuaries, connecting it to a freshwater marsh that includes a riparian corridor extending over two kilometres along the base of the Westchester bluffs, to the south. The programme of wetland restoration and the provision for its implementation are embodied in a settlement agreement of a lawsuit which led to the establishment of the Ballona Wetlands Committee, charged with formulating detailed plans for wetlands expansion and restoration. In addition to Maguire Thomas Partners, the committee consisted of representatives of the Comptroller of California, the Sixth District Council Office, and the Friends of the Ballona Wetlands. But Maguire Thomas exceeded the intent of the agreement, and planned, through the density of distribution of the building footprint on the entire site, to keep a great deal of the site as open space.

Runoff

Increase in rainwater runoff is a frequently heard criticism of the Playa Vista proposal, but the development will actually greatly improve the situation that existed prior to development. Polluted urban runoff from over 265,000 acres surrounding the site now makes its way through coastal wetlands habitats into Santa Monica Bay through concrete viaducts. Lax land-use regulations have previously allowed runoff from residential neighbourhoods, commercial and industrial areas and surface streets and freeways to drain directly into habitats on its way

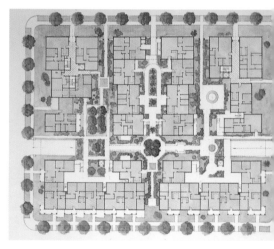

Playa Vista residential development
Under the eye of real estate developer Maguire Thomas and architects Moore Ruble Yudell, Playa Vista promised to be a model of sustainable community in the New Urbanism mould. These drawings show an overview of the residential development and a typical residential block.

to the bay, without filtration. The attention that has been focused on Playa Vista has been partially responsible for a change in federal, state, county and municipal laws related to runoff. Still, polluted runoff from the areas above Playa Vista, comprising more than 1000 acres, flow directly down on the site, which has low permeability because it is silt and clay that has been tightly compacted by past activity. Because it cannot absorb surface water, this unheated runoff remains on the surface and then drains into the Ballona flood control channel and Marina del Rey before discharge into the Santa Monica Bay. This runoff is now being dealt with by control at the source, filter treatment and temporary flow interruption to encourage settling the pollutants out as sediments which can degrade organically.

To maximize green space in the new community, the Maguire Thomas masterplan for Playa Vista was based on a New Urbanist model of mixed-use, and a hierarchical street system as a network for a series of district neighbourhoods, joined by a low-emission internal transit system intended to encourage walking and reduce dependency on the automobile. A wide variety of housing types within each neighbourhood were intended to encourage a mix of income levels.

From Egalitarian Experiment to Campus Plan

After the Playa Vista development changed hands in the late 1990s, there was a substantial re-evaluation of the goals of the project. As a result, some essential elements stayed the same, while others were radically changed. The contract that had been forged with the local community and with environmental activists dictated that the visionary position taken by Maguire Thomas on the restoration and maintenance of the wetland remain unchanged. The riparian corridor, which feeds the newly restored marsh, has remained the focus of the developer's consideration of natural systems. The changes, instituted by landscape architect Mia Lehrer + Associates have hinged on the switch to a 'campus' plan, as a device for allowing office and residential uses to coexist on the large site. The lynch pin for this new 'campus' plan is to be nearly one million square feet of office space for the film industry and other related high-tech support services. In sharp contrast to the previous Maguire Thomas wish to create a more economically diverse, mixed-income community, this more socially specific office campus is expected to draw professional residents who want to live near their workplace.

Plan showing maximum walking distances

The Playa Vista plans, now changed, were originally predicated upon walking distances from residences to local services, to avoid car use.

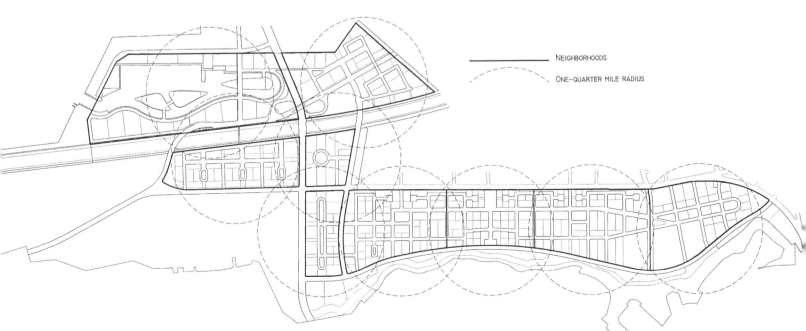

NEIGHBORHOODS

ONE–QUARTER MILE RADIUS

While the New Urbanists' emphasis on working and living in the same community, to eliminate commuting, and the provision of schools, parks and commercial centres nearby remains the same, resistance to individual architectural expression seen in other communities, such as Seaside Florida, was discouraged in the new Playa Vista plan. There is also a more clearly defined approach to green areas inside the development, based on Sustainable Performance Guidelines prepared by Mia Lehrer + Associates. In the new scheme, no lawn is allowed except in a park in its centre, which Lehrer describes as 'the glue of the campus,' with green fingers that extend into housing areas. Decomposed granite paving is used to offset albedo and drainage problems, and many strategically located fountains help to clean and disperse standing water.

The Ballona Creek

The Maguire Thomas idea to extend Playa Vista across the Ballona Creek, which runs along the northern edge of where the community stops today, became a contentious issue, due to increased pressure from environmentalists and local residents. Encased in concrete like most of the Los Angeles River that feeds it, the Ballona Creek is now little more than a glorified open sewer. But Mia Lehrer was also determined to change that. The Ballona Creek has become a test case of what the Los Angeles River itself can become: community workshops, mostly made up of full-time participants, are working on cleaning up the Creek, breaking up its concrete container, and making it a tree-lined waterway that can support recreation, wildlife and fish. Lehrer is using the community process that these workshops represent as a way of funnelling information and educating people about the potential of landscape architecture to dramatically change the environment they live in. The new axis that has been established here, between the communities that adjoin the Creek and the newly responsive city agencies that represent them, has been highly effective in generating the money needed to make this idyllic vision reality, giving everyone involved a feeling of empowerment. What began as a simple bikeway study has now been transformed into a major urban planning strategy, a test case for more extensive action along the river.

Baldwin Hills as the Urban Park of the 21st Century

Contrary to the common belief that all the great city parks have been designed and that opportunities to implement ideas on the grand scale of Central or Hyde Park cannot come again because of code changes and urban growth, Mia Lehrer, in conjunction with Community Conservancy International and Hood Design also designed a masterplan for a two square mile urban park in Baldwin Hills, the last undeveloped open space in Los Angeles. Because it is contiguous to the Playa Vista development to the west, as well as to the Los Angeles River and Ballona Creek, Baldwin Hills is generating a great deal of excitement as a model for the urban park of the 21st century, as well as being a large, significant piece of the open-space puzzle of the greening of Los Angeles. Much of this interest has to do with the circumstances of its location, as well as shifting demographics and social change.

As cities grew during the Industrial Revolution and overcrowding and unhealthy housing conditions increased, parks were viewed as picturesque releases from urban ills, as well as a way for speculators to generate high property values along their periphery. When industrialization slowed in the developed world, the need to provide open spaces in built-up areas became glaringly obvious, and brownfields such as Baldwin Hills, the residual of past industrial activity defined earlier, were seen as ideal opportunities to do so. New questions of equitable distribution now also come into play, as does the refined expectation of empowerment: neighbourhoods creating community associations to raise funds and to resist development in favour of green space that they finance themselves. Tracking these raised expectations, politicians are now positioning themselves as the advocates of inner-city residents, seeking to rectify what has historically been an unbalanced distribution of park land in and around inner-city neighbourhoods.

The Baldwin Hills were originally part of the Rancho La Ballona, Rancho Rincón de los Bueyes and Rancho Cienega Paso de la Tijera, when Mexico stilled occupied this part of California. These ranchos were acquired by the City of Los Angeles and subsequently put into production when oil was discovered there in 1924. In 1975 Kenneth Hahn (who went on to become mayor of Los Angeles in 2001) approved the concept of a regional park within Baldwin Hills, on behalf of the Los Angeles County Board of Supervisors, and 500 acres of parkland were purchased from the property in 1982, designated the Kenneth Hahn Recreation Area by State legislation in 1989. By 1990, one million people lived within an 8-kilometre (5-mile) radius of Baldwin Hills, divided into nearly equal sections of the community, and the pressure for access to Baldwin Hills began to grow, indirectly in conflict with the increased oil production in the 900-acre portion of the property still privately held.

After Stocker Resources, Inc. took over oil production in 1990, activity increased so that by 2000 there were 420 wells producing 6,900 barrels of oil and 3.2 million cubic feet of natural gas daily. The increased pressure for more recreational facilities in the area prompted Community Conservancy International to push for a park in the Baldwin Hills. After State Senator Kevin Murray secured $4 million in state funds for Baldwin Hills' planning and acquisition in 1999, he and Assemblyman Herbert Wesson sponsored state legislation for expansion of the Kenneth Hahn Recreation Area, leading to the allocation of $32.5 million for park acquisition in the Baldwin Hills, approved by Governor Grey Davis in 2000. This significantly increased the existing equation of less than one acre of parkland per thousand residents, creating a new precedent for urban parks nationwide.

The Plan for Baldwin Hills, as a New Model for Urban Parks
The plan by Community Conservancy International, Mia Lehrer + Associates and Hood Design preserves, conserves and restores sensitive native habitats concentrated on hill canyons and slopes. It balances recreation, community, education and cultural facilities as well as features that will improve the economy of the surrounding area. Preserving and protecting ecology while providing the kinds of recreational facilities needed by all segments of the surrounding community was an essential part of the design challenge. The planners recognized that the new park is a key component of the 329 square kilometre (127 square mile) Ballona Creek watershed, since it is bounded on the west by Ballona Creek and the Ballona Creek Trail. In addition to connecting with the Ballona Creek, restoring natural landscapes and promoting 'recreation-based economic development', they wanted to establish a comprehensive trail system and protect scenic vistas. These include stunning views of the entire Los Angeles Basin, from the 10,000-foot Mount Baldy in the San Gabriel Mountains to all of the Santa Monica Bay, and provide community gathering areas. They made this a natural amenity for all of the ethnic groups represented in the area, not just one, and in doing so, have changed the entire concept of an urban park.

Conclusion: Architecture in the Global Commons

Social scientist Garrett Hardin has provided one of the most memorable and enduring analogies for the unrelenting pressure now being put on global resources in his classic article 'The Tragedy of the Commons'. In it, he equates these resources to the common in an English village, a park-like green space to which everyone in the village has access and on which they may all graze their livestock. The continuing viability of the common depends upon the discipline and restraint of each resident – overgrazing by one jeopardizes the use of this shared resource for all.

The concept of sustainability which has been described in detail here and has informed the attitudes of many of the individuals and movements that have been presented, is the institutionalized version of responsible action by all of those using the 'common'. It is the antidote to the tragedy that Hardin describes, which is no less then the total destruction of the natural environment and the exhaustion of precious resources which are open to everyone, but controlled by no-one.

Sustainability requires that people sacrifice short-term interests for long-term gain, but there are many instances of human greed lurking behind the tragedy of the commons, still running rampant at a global scale. Exploitation of the rainforest is one of the most obvious of these – the destruction of the key resource that helps to stabilize and cleanse the earth's climate and combat global warming. Slash-and-burn techniques used to clear forests for farm land are responsible for much of the destruction, in spite of past proof that in the rainforest, the nutrients are in the trees, not in the soil, and that farming on this land is never profitable past the first few growing seasons.

Often destruction such as this is also driven by structural debt throughout the developing world, which is disproportionate there.[1] Caught in a vicious cycle, less-developed countries incur debt to large financial institutions in the West based on export revenues to produce goods and services for survival at home and for export abroad and to repay bank debt. Scarce resources, such as rainforest timber are seen as expendable by countries caught in this cycle and are often priced far below their inestimable value as an irreplaceable commodity out of sheer expediency. Less-developed countries export such raw materials in order to import high value-added products that they desperately need, like farm equipment and machinery, but the demand for the products they export is elastic. During an economic recession in the developed world demand for such exports falls dramatically and so more must be sold at a lower cost to maintain economic equilibrium. This condition, called declining terms of trade, results in the accelerated depletion of such precious non-renewable resources, exacerbating an already alarming situation.

A Post-Everything Era Begins

Although Charles Jencks was not the first to use the term 'post-modern', he did initiate a wider understanding of the connection between the sociological phenomenon that this term attempts to capture and its architectural manifestations. Widespread disillusionment with the notions of progress and technology (as well as the institutions that embody it in the developed world) that has been brought on by increasing evidence of environmental problems and the democracy scenario during the Cold War, caused cynicism to replace sincerity as the social norm. This cynicism and lack of trust in institutions has deepened as revelations about new scandals in government, business and religion increase.

It is important to realize, however, that the post-modern condition that has been brought on by this progressive failure of social institutions, as well as the tightening grip of commodification and the media, has not been uniformly experienced. The constant refrain in this book has been that nation-building still has meaning throughout the developing world, and this includes trust in the institutions that make this construction possible.

A Post-Global World?

This sale of precious, non-renewable resources, along with growing proof of accelerating economic inequality between the rich and poor in both the developing and the developed worlds, has led some to question the 'rising tide raises all boats' theory of globalization. While the measure of increasing income disparity varies depending on which statistical method is used, World Bank data of changes in household income of its member nations, which amounts to about 85 per cent of the world's population, shows that 'the share of world income going to the poorest 10% of this group has fallen by over 25% while the share of the richest 10% has risen by 8%. This represents a startling move away from the median in both the positive and negative direction. The reasons for this change in global inequality are: (1) developed countries have grown faster than developing countries; (2) faster population growth in developing countries that anticipated; (3) slow economic growth in rural China, rural India, and Africa; and (4) a widening income disparity between rural areas in both China and India.'[2]

The frustration caused by this disparity, as well as the increasing polemical polarization that began to accelerate after 11 September 2001, have eroded the multicultural, utopian image of a global village put forward in the 1990s, and a hegemonic war of ideological attrition has taken its place. A cultural Balkanization, which was admittedly discernable before this hardening began to grow, has now gone into high gear, as a way of protecting beliefs and values from threat. Beneath these new circumstances, the future of traditionally based initiatives and the environmental strategies that are inextricably tied to them is increasingly unclear.

A Post-Traditional World Too?

This murkiness is compounded by the increased pace of change brought on by the electronic revolution. While the economic benefits of this revelation are now in question, the impact it has had on our perception of space and time is not. It has radically changed the pace of our lives as well as our expectations, to the extent that younger generations, who have experienced nothing else, seem to abhor reflection and the complete silence that it requires and always need electronic distraction instead. Cell phones, the internet, DVD players and similar paraphernalia help fend off introspection, as well as an awareness of the outside world. Some argue that this increasing reliance on simulacra has had an even more fundamental effect, going beyond our new perception of time, and its electronic compression, to our connection to space and place. The accelerating pace of change has erased the moment, destroying previous distinctions between now and then, past and present, and essentially weakening our relationship to history and context. In this reordering of space and time, as one observer has described it, 'the present is assumed to be the past, and the past is forgotten, referents (in architecture) now have no relationship to a fixed moment in history, no relationship to place, nation or ethnicity; all connections to history and geography have been severed'.[3]

Due to this rupture, the role of tradition itself must now be redefined, since the entire process of the cultural transmission of social and physical rituals and habits has been compromised. Individual aspirations are becoming increasingly disassociated from both nation and place. Identity as a connection to place is no longer determined by tradition, and is increasingly related to imagability, the life-changing legacy of the electronic age, so that the final distancing from nature is now underway.

Notes

PART I

Introduction
pp. 10–14
1   United Nations Human Settlement Programme, *The State of World Cities: Globalization and Urban Culture*, New York, 2004, p. 168

2   The Technological Imperative
pp. 19–22
1   D. Bell, *The Future of Technology*, Kuala Lumpur, 2001, p. 25
2   Ibid., p. 27

3   Facing up to an Urban Future
pp. 23–29
1   D. Sudjic, *100 Mile City*, New York, 1999, p. 15
2   Z. Quinan, 'Professionalism in the Conflict Between Globalization and Rooted Cultures', *Architectural Society of China*, 1996. Draft, p. 3
3   Ibid., p. 6
4   K. Ohmae, *The End of the Nation State: The Rise of Regional Economics*, New York, 1995, p. 16
5   S. Sassen, *Global City*, New York, 1991, p. 3
6   Ibid., p. 6
7   Ibid., p. 8
8   E. O. Moss, 'Conjunctive Points', office publication, 1999, p. 26
9   K. Yeang, *The Bioclimatic Skyscraper*, London, 2000, p. 18
10 Ibid., p. 36

PART II

Introduction
pp. 32–37
1   F. MacCarthy, *William Morris*, London, 1994, p. 63
2   Ibid., p. 65
3   Ibid., p. 66
4   S. Suleri, *The Rhetoric of English India*, Chicago, 1972, p. 47
5   F. Fanon, *The Wretched of the Earth*, New York, 1996, p. 150
6   Ibid., p. 137
7   Ibid., p. 56

1   Charles Rennie Mackintosh
pp. 39–47
1   John Ruskin in G. Naylor, *The Arts and Crafts Movement*, London, 1980, p. 26
2   J. Harris, 'The Primacy of Hardware', in *William Morris Revisited: Questioning the Legacy*, exh. cat. of 'Paradise Postponed, William Morris in the Twentieth Century', Birmingham Art Museum. 1997, p. 36
3   J. Harris, 'Rural Romanticism', in ibid., p. 63

2   Ebenezer Howard
pp. 49–55
1   *The Building News*, Dec. 29, 1875 quoted in M. J. Bolsterli, *The Early Community of Bedford Park*, Ohio University Press, 1983, p. 46
2   Ibid., p. 55
3   Ibid., p. 17
4   D. Macfayden, *Sir Ebenezer Howard and the Town Planning Movement*, Cambridge (Mass.), 1970, p. 32
5   C. B. Purdam, *The Garden City*, London, 1913, p. 56
6   'Letchworth: The World's First Garden City', North Hertfordshire District Council and Letchworth Garden City Corporation, undated brochure, p. 2
7   Ibid., p. 4

3   Finland
pp. 57–61
1   J. Pallasmas: *Hvittrask: The Home as a Work of Art*, Museum of Finnish Architecture, Helsinki, 1987, p. 16
2   L. Rossi (ed.), *Kunnantalo Saynatsalo*, Alvar Aalto Museum, Jyvaskyla, 1997
3   P. Korvenmaa, 'Destruction, Scarcity and a New Rise', *20th Century Architecture: Finland*, Museum of Finnish Architecture, 2000, p. 79
4   S. Jetsonen, 'Humane Rationalism', in *20th Century Architecture: Finland*, op. cit., p. 85
5   See T. Tuomi, *Tapiola: A History an Architectural Guide*, Espoo, 1992

4   The Amsterdam School
pp. 63–69
1   J. Buch, *A Century of Architecture in the Netherlands 1890–1990*, Netherlands Architecture Institute, Rotterdam, 1990, p. 279
2   Ibid., p. 57
3   R. Banham, *The Age of the Masters*, London, 1975, p. 66
4   J. G. Wattjes and F. A. Warners, *Amsterdamse Bouwkunst en Stadsschoon 1306–1947*, Amsterdam, 1949
5   Buch, op. cit., p. 169: 'De Stije was not forsaking nature, but they saw that it was necessary to take their inspiration from the nature described by Einstein, Kamerlingh, Onnes and Bohr'.
6   Ibid., p. 142

5   Frank Lloyd Wright
pp. 71–75
1   N. Levine, *Frank Lloyd Wright's Taliesin West*, New York, 1999, p. 10
2   Ibid., p. 11
3   H. Hugh, *Wright for Wright*, New York, 2001, p. 119
4   Levine, op. cit., p. 2

6   Rudolf Schindler
pp. 77–83
1   K. Smith, *R. M. Schindler House: 1921–22*, Los Angeles, 1987, p. 8
2   Ibid., p. 18
3   A. Vidler, *Warped Space*, Cambridge (Mass.), 2000, p. 53

7   Hassan Fathy
pp. 85–93
1   H. Fathy, 'An Ekistic Approach to Roofing', *Ekistics*, 1954, p. 3
2   The University of Chicago Press, Correspondence with the author, July 1993. Unpaginated
3   Ibid.
4   Constantinos Doxiadis, internal memo to Hassan Fathy while he served on the 'City of the Future' project in Athens, June, 1960

8   Le Corbusier
pp. 95–105
1   Y. Tominaga, 'The Houses of Le Corbusier and the Images of Movement' *GA Houses*, 39, November 1993, p. 20
2   P. Sereny, 'Timeless but of its time: Le Corbusier's Architecture in India', *Architectural Design*, 55, 1985, p. 60
3   W. Rubin (ed.), *Primitivism in 20th Century Art*, vol. I, Museum of Modern Art, New York, 1984. See 'Modernist Primitivism', p. 3
4   Ibid., K. Varnedoe, 'Gauguin', p. 180
5   Ibid., p. 183; see also E. Lipton, *Picasso 1901–1939*, London, 1976, and A. Gleizes and J. Metzinger, *Cubism*, London, 1913
6   Sereny, op. cit., p. 55
7   Ibid., p. 56

8 W. Curtis, *Le Corbusier: Ideas and Forms*, London, 1986, p. 212
9 Sereny, op. cit., p. 55
10 A. Prakash, *Chandigarh, The City Beautiful*, New Delhi, 1973, p. 18
11 N. Evanson, *Chandigarh*, Berkeley, 1966, p. 43
12 Ibid., p. 44
13 S. Hurtt, 'Le Corbusier: Type, Architecture and Iconography', in G. Rockcastle (ed.), *Type and the (Im)Possibilities of Convention*, New York, 1991, p. 306
14 Ibid. p. 307

9 Balkrishna Doshi
pp. 107–113
1 B. Doshi, 'Urbanization and Cultural Continuity' (keynote address), Proceedings, Indian Institute of Architects Convention, Mumbai, 1984, p. 17

11 Rogers, Foster, Hopkins, Grimshaw
pp. 123–133
1 'Inland Revenue', *Arups Journal*, Fall 1995, p. 22
2 R. Haryott and N. Grimshaw, 'Solar Powered Pavilion', *RIBA Journal*, October 1992, p. 37

12 Paolo Soleri
pp. 135–141
1 P. Bonvicini, 'Soleri Dialogues', interview with Paolo Soleri in *L'Architettura*, no. 422, 1990, p. 871–4
2 E. Callenbach, *Ecotopia*, Berkeley (Calif.), 1975, p. 22
3 S. M. Davis, *The Integrated Urban Complex*, unpublished Masters Thesis, College of Architecture and Environmental Design, Tempe, Arizona, 1986, p. 117
4 J. Alper, 'Biosphere II: Out of Oxygen', *American Chemical Society Journal*, 1999, pp. 1–5. This chapter was also assisted by advice from Rafael Pizzaro and his unpublished manuscript 'Arcosanti', which he produced while a Doctoral Candidate at USC in 1999. I am grateful for his help.

13 Buckminster Fuller
pp. 143–147
1 All quotations in this chapter taken from R. W. Marks: *The Dymaxion World of Buckminster Fuller* New York, 1960, and J. Baldwin, *BuckyWorks: Buckminster Fuller's Ideas for Today*, New York, 1996

15 Edward Mazria
pp. 155–159
1 J. Sullivan, *The American Environment*, New York, 1984, p. 54
2 Ibid., p. 75
3 Ibid., p. 32
4 Ibid., p. 37

5 Ibid., p. 37
6 E. Mazria and M. Riskin, 'Architectural Design Nature's Way', *Public Garden*, vol. 14, no. 1, January 1999, p. 26

17 The Source of Sustainability
pp. 165–173
1 J. Steele, *Sustainable Architecture*, New York, 1998, p. 15
2 Ibid., p. 23

18 Ian McHarg
pp. 175–183
1 A. C. Revkin, 'Ian McHarg, 80, Architect Who Valued a Site's National Features', obituary, *New York Times*, March 9, 2001, p. 9
2 Ibid., p. 9
3 D. Scott Brown, 'On Houses and Housing', in *Venturi, Scott Brown*, London, 1990, p. 96
4 'Plan for the Valleys', Towson Maryland, Green Spring and Worthington Valley Planning Council, 1964. David A. Wallace, Ian L. McHarg, Thomas A. Todd, William H. Roberts, Ann Louise Strong, William G. Grigsby, Nohad Toulan, Anthony Tomazinas, 1964, p. 11
5 Ibid., p. 12
6 'Toward a Comprehensive Landscape Plan for Washington, D.C.', National Planning Commission, US Government Printing Office, 1967. Ian McHarg Partner in Charge, p. 15

19 A Revolution in Tent Technology
pp. 185–191
1 J. Sommers, *Fentress Bradburn Architects: Gateway to the West, Designing the Passenger Complex at Denver International Airport*, Images, Australia, 2000, p. 38
2 Ibid., p. 18
3 Ibid., p. 47
4 Ibid., p. 18

20 Kenneth Yeang
pp. 193–199
1 K. Yeang, *The Skyscraper Bioclimatically considered*, London, 1996, p. 15
2 K. Yeang, *T. R. Hamzah and Yeang: Bioclimatic Skyscrapers*, London, 1994, p. 120
3 See Part II:18 of this book
4 K. Yeang, *The Green Skyscraper*, London and New York, 1999, p. 73
5 Ibid., p. 92
6 Ibid., p. 93
7 Ibid., p. 101

22 The New Urbanists
pp. 209–213
1 D. Firestone, 'The New Look Suburbs: Denser or More Far Flung?', *New York Times*, April 17, 2001, p. 2

2 Ibid., p. 14
3 D. J. Waldie, 'Do the Voters Really Hate Sprawl?' *New York Times*, March 3, 2000, p. 25
4 'Sprawl Hits the Wall: Confronting the Realities of Metropolitan Los Angeles.' Southern California Studies Center, Los Angeles. 2001, p. 3
5 J. Garreau, *Edge City*, New York, 1991, p. 103
6 Excerpts from the 'Traditional Neighborhood Development Checklist' in *Suburban Nation: The Rise of Sprawl and the Decline of the American Dream*, New York, 2000. pp. 246–55
7 P. Katz, *The New Urbanism; Toward an Architecture of Communities*, New York, 1994, p. xxxvi
8 A. Duany and E. Plater-Zyberk in *Suburban Nation*. op. cit., p. 48
9 Ibid., p. 43
10 E. Moule and S. Polyzoides, 'The Street, the Block and the Building', in *The New Urbanism*, op. cit., p. xxii
11 Ibid., p. 32
12 Newshour interview: http://www.pbs.org

23 Jimmy Lim
pp. 215–219
1 The ideas in this chapter are based largely on discussions with Jimmy Lim over the last five years.

25 Enric Miralles
pp. 227–231
1 P. Buchanan, *The Architecture of Enric Miralles and Carme Piños*, New York, 1990, p. 3
2 E. Miralles, *Works and Projects, 1975–1995*, (ed. B. Tagliabue Miralles), New York, 1996, p. 7
3 'Cemetery, Igualada, Spain, 1985–96', *AV Monographs*, 95, 5–6, 2002, p. 39
4 Juan José Lahuerta, 'For Now', in *Enric Miralles, Works and Projects*, op. cit., p. 22

Conclusion
pp. 232–234
1 A. O. Dean, 'Sam Mockbee', *Architectural Record*, 2–01, p. 82
2 Ibid., p. 80

PART III

1 Digitizing the Environment
pp. 239–243
1 J. Carroll, 'Participatory Technology,' in *Technology and Man's Future* (ed. A. H. Teich), New York, 1977, p. 36. See also J. Weizenbaum, *Computer Power and Human Reason, From Judgment to Calculation*, San Francisco, 1976
2 J. H. Frazer, *An Evolutionary Architecture*, London, 1995, p. 123

3 Ibid., p. 54
4 Ibid., p. 55
5 K. Englert, 'Ciudad de la Cultura de Galicia', in *Zurich Post*, 2 February, 2001
6 Internal email from Antonio Marono to Cynthia Davidson, forwarded to the author on April 3, 2003
7 Ibid.

2 Tado Ando
pp. 245–249
1 K. Frampton, *Tadao Ando: Buildings, Projects, Writings*, New York, 1984
2 T. Ando, 'Rokko Housing II', *The Japan Architect*, 8707, p. 18
3 Ibid., p. 19
4 Ibid., p. 19
5 Ibid., p. 20

6 Ibid., p. 21
7 Ibid., p. 21

3 The Greening of Los Angeles
pp. 251–259
1 J. Halusha, 'For Developers, Brownfields Look less Risky', *New York Times*, 21 April, 2002, p. 2
2 T. Lawrence Jones, 'Superfund-Superbust', *New York Times*, May 24, 1985, p. 25
3 The Northeast Midwest Institute, www.nemw.org
4 A. J. Scott and E. W. Soja Edo, *The City: Los Angeles and Urban Theory at the End of the Twentieth Century*, University of California Press, 1998, p. 55
5 Ibid., p. 56
6 K. Frampton, 'Technoscience and Environmental Culture: A Provisional Critique', *JAE*, 2001, pp. 123–5
7 G. Hise, *Magnetic Los Angeles: Planning the 20th Century Metropolis*, Baltimore, 1997, p. 67
8 B. Gumprecht, *The Los Angeles River: Its Life, Death and Possible Rebirth*, Baltimore, 2001, p. 44

Conclusion
pp. 260–262
1 T. F. Young and V. Golich, 'Power, Debt and the Environment', Pew Initiative, University of Pittsburgh, 1993, pp. 61–3
2 R. Wade, 'Global Inequality', *The Economist*, April 28, 2001, pp. 72–4
3 IASTE Conference Announcement, 3 Sept., 2003, unpaginated

Selected Bibliography

Aleksander, I., and H. Morton, *An Introduction to Neural Computing*, Reading (Mass.), 1990

Alper, J., 'Biopshere II: Out of Oxygen', *American Chemical Society Journal*, 1999, pp. 1–5

Ando, T. (and Associates), 'Awaji Yumebutai, Hyogo, 1993–99', *GA Japan: Environmental Design*, no. 45, July–Aug., 2000

Baker, G. H., *Le Corbusier: An Analysis of Form*, 2nd edn, New York, 1989

Banham, R., 'Rudolph Schindler – A Pioneer Without Tears', *Architectural Design*, vol. 37, Dec. 1967. pp. 578–9

Baxandall, R., and E. Elizabeth, *Picture Windows: How the Suburb Happened*, New York, 2000

Beavers, R., *The Garden City Utopia, A Critical Biography of Ebenezer Howard*, London, 1988

Bonvicini, P., 'Soleri Dialogues: Interview by Pierluigi Bonvincini', *L'Architettura*, no. 422, 1990, pp. 871–874

Bosterli, M. J., *The Early Community at Bedford Park*, Akron, Ohio, 1967

Buchanan, P., 'Reinventing the Skyscraper', *Architecture and Urbanism*, no. 329, Feb. 1998, pp. 28–67

Callenbach, E., *Ecotopia*, Berkeley (Calif.), 1975

Calthorpe, P., *The Next American Metropolis: Ecology, Community, and the American Dream*, New York, 1993

Calthorpe, P., and W. Fulton, *The Regional City: New Urbanism and the End of Sprawl*, Washington, D.C., 2000

Crates, E., 'The Genesis of the New Eden', *Construction News*, no. 6685, Sept. 28, 2000, pp. 20–1

Creese, W., *The Search for Environment*, New Haven, 1966

——, *The Legacy of Sir Raymond Unwin*, Cambridge (Mass.), 1967

Curtis, W., *Modern Architecture Since 1900*, London, 1982

——, *Le Corbusier Ideas and Forms*, London, 1986

——, *Balkrishna Doshi, An Architecture for India*, New York, 1988

Davey, P., 'Natural Selection', *Architectural Review*, no. 1242, Aug. 2000, pp. 32–3

Davis, S. M., *The Integrated Urban Complex*, Master's Thesis, College of Architecture and Environmental Design, Tempe, Arizona, 1986

Dawkins, R., *The Blind Watchmaker*, London and New York, 1986

Doremus, T., *Frank Lloyd Wright and Le Corbusier the Great Dialogue*, New York, 1985

Duany, A., and E. Plater-Zyberk, *The Rise of Sprawl and the Decline of the American Dream*, New York, 2000

Dutton, J. A., *New American Urbanism: Re–Forming the Suburban Metropolis*, New York, 2000

Easterling, K., and D. Mahoney (eds), *Seaside: Making a town in America*, New York, 1991

Evenson, N., *Chandigargh*, Berkeley and Los Angeles, 1966

Ferguson, F., *Architecture, Cities and the System Approach*, New York, 1975

Fishman, R., *Bourgeois Utopias: The Rise and Fall of Suburbia*, New York, 1987

——, *Urban Utopias in the Twentieth Century*, Cambridge (Mass.), 1982

Forsyth, R. (ed.), *Machine Learning*, Reading (Mass.), 1989

Frampton, K., *Modern Architecture: A Critical History*, London, 1973

——, *Tadao Ando: Buildings, Projects, Writings*, New York, 1984

Frazer, J. H., *An Evolutionary Architecture*, London, 1995

——, *Datastructures for Rule Based and Genetic Design*, Tokyo, 1992

Fulton, W., *The Reluctant Metropolis, The Politics of Urban growth in Los Angeles*, Point Arena (Calif.), 1997, pp. 139–41

Futagawa, Y. (ed.), *Tadao Ando. Vol. 3: 1994–2000*, Tokyo, 2000

Gebhard, D., and R. Winter, *A Guide to Architecture in Los Angeles and Southern California*, Salt Lake City, 1977

Girsberger Boesigner, W., *Le Corbusier 1910–1965*, Zurich, 1967

Glaeser, L., *The Work of Frei Otto*, The Museum of Modern Art, New York, 1972

Goldberg, D. E., *Genetic Algorithms in Search Optimization and Machine Learning*, Reading (Mass.), 1989

Grimshaw, N., and R. Haryott, 'Solar-powered pavilion', *RIBA Journal*, 99 (10), Oct 1992, pp. 32–8

Holland, J., *Adaptation in Natural and Artificial Systems*, University of Michigan, 1975

Jencks, C., *Le Corbusier and the Continual Revolution in Architecture*, New York, 2000

Johnson, K., *The Book of Letchworth*, London, 1975

Jordan, R. F., *Le Corbusier*, London and New York, 1972

Katz, P., *The New Urbanism: Toward an Architecture of Community*, New York, 1994

Krieger, A. (ed.), *Andres Duany and Elizabeth Plater–Zyberk: Towns and Town Making Principles*, New York, 1991

McCoy, E., 'Four Schindler Houses of the 1920s', *California Arts and Architecture*, San Francisco, vol. 70, Sept. 30, 1953, pp. 12–14

McFayden, D., *Sir Ebenezer Howard and the Town Planning Movement*, Cambridge (Mass.), 1970

Miller, M., *Letchworth, The First Garden City*, London, 1989

Mitchell, W. J., *The Logic of Architecture, Design, Computation and Cognition*, Cambridge (Mass.), 1990

Negroponte, N., *The Architecture Machine*, Cambridge (Mass.), 1970

Nicholas, G., and I. Prigogine, *Exploring Complexity*, London, 1993

Nikula, R., 'Erik Bryggman and His Architecture', in *Erik Bryggman, 1891–1955* (ed. R. Nikula), Museum of Finnish Architecture, 1991

Norri, M.-R., et al. (eds), *20th Century Architecture: Finland*, Museum of Finnish Architecture, The German Architecture Museum, Frankfurt, 2000

Osborn, F. J. (ed.), *Ebenezer Howard, Garden Cities of Tomorrow*, New York, 1946

Paavilainen, S., *Nordic Classicism*, Museum of Finnish Architecture, 1982

Palazzolo, C., and R. Vio, *In the Footsteps of Le Corbusier*, New York, 1991

Pallasmaa, J., *Alvar Aalto: Villa Mairea*, Helsinki, 1998

Polyzoides, S., 'Schindler, Lovell, and the Newport Beach House, Los Angeles, 1921–1926', *Oppositions*, no. 18, Fall 1979, pp. 60–73

——, and P. Koulermos, 'R. M. Schindler – Notes on His Work: Five Houses by R. M. Schindler', *Architecture and Urbanism*, Tokyo, Nov. 1975, pp. 61–126

Powell, R., *Rethinking The Skyscraper: The Complete Architecture of Ken Yeang*, London and New York, 1999

Purdam, C. B., *The Building of Satellite Towns*, London, 1949

——, *The Letchworth Achievement*, London, 1963

——, *The Garden City*, London, 1913

Rhodes, C., *Primitivism and Modern Art*, London, 1994

Risselada, M. (ed.), *Raumplan versus Plan Libre: Adolf Loos and Le Corbusier 1919–1930*, New York, 1987

Roland, C., *Frei Otto: Tension Structures*, New York, 1970

Rubin, W. (ed.), *Primitivism in Twentieth Century Art*, vol. 1, Museum of Modern Art, New York, 1984

Ryan, R., 'Justice being seen', *Architectural Review*, no. 1229, July 1999, pp. 48–54

Sarnitz, A., 'Rudolph Michael Schindler – Theory and Design', Thesis, MIT, Cambridge (Mass.), 1982

Schildt, G., 'Alvar Aalto and the Classical Tradition', *Classical Tradition and the Modern Movement*, the Second International Alvar Aalto Symposium, 1982 Asko Salokomi, Helsinki, 1985

——, *Alvar Aalto: The Early Years*, New York, 1984

Segal, W., 'The Least Appreciated: Rudolph Schindler, 1887–1953', *The Architect's Journal*, London, vol. 149, Feb. 196, pp. 476–79

Skowlimoski, H., 'Arcology', *AA Quarterly* 4, 1:30, 1971, pp. 36–43

Smith, K. *The R. M. Schindler House, 1921–22*, Los Angeles, 1987

Taideteoksena, K., *Hvitträsk: The Home as a Work of Art*, Helsinki, 2000

Thornton, J. A., 'The New Parliamentary building – Portcullis House', *Structural Engineer*, 78 (18), Sept. 19, 2000, pp. 17–23

Todd, S., and W. Latham, *Evolutionary Art and Computers*, London, 1992

Tuomi, T., *Tapiola: a History and Architectural Guide*, Espoo, 1992

Unwin, R., *Town Planning in Practice*, London, 1909

Wäre, R., 'How Nationalism was Expressed in Finnish Architecture at the Turn of the Century', in N. Gordon Bowe (ed.), *Art and the National Dream*, Dublin, 1993

Yeang, K., *The Tropical Verandah City*, Kuala Lumpur, 1987

——, *The Skyscraper Bioclimatically Considered*, London, 1996

——, *The Green Skyscraper*, Munich, 1999

Acknowledgments for Illustrations

pp. 2-3: Moore Ruble Yudell Collection. **Part I, Introduction:** 11(t): James Steele; 11(m): Tom Bonner; 11(b): Tom Bonner; 12(t): The Architectural Archives, University of Pennsylvania; 12(b): James Steele; 13: T.R. Hamzah and Yeang. **Part I, 1:** 15, 17(t), 17(bl), 17(br): James Steele. **Part I, 2:** 19: Tom Bonner; 21(l), 21(r): Tom Bonner; 22: Behnisch, Behnisch and Partner. **Part I, 3:** 23: © FLC/ADAGP, Paris and DACS, London, 2005 [FLC L2(14)46]; 25: Tom Bonner; 28(t): Eric Owen Moss; 28(b): Eric Owen Moss. **Part II, Introduction:** 32: ; 33: ; 34(t): James Steele; 34(br): T.R. Hamzah and Yeang; 35: AKAA; 36: Malcolm Wells. **Part II, 1:** 38(t): Alan Crawford; 38(b): James Steele; 39: T.R. Annan & Sons Ltd, Glasgow; 43(tl), 43(ml), 43(tr), 43(br): T.R. Annan & Sons Ltd, Glasgow; 44: James Steele; 46(t), 46(b): Alan Crawford; 47: T.R. Annan & Sons Ltd, Glasgow. **Part II, 2:** 48(t): Photo: Clutterbuck photographers; 48(b): Photo: E.A. Fleming Hewitt; 49: © First Garden City Heritage Museum, image supplied courtesy of Letchworth Garden City Heritage Foundation; 50: © First Garden City Heritage Museum, image supplied courtesy of Letchworth Garden City Heritage Foundation; 51: Photo: Quentin Hughes; 52: from Ebenezer Howard's *Garden Cities of Tomorrow*, 1902; © First Garden City Heritage Museum, image supplied courtesy of Letchworth Garden City Heritage Foundation 53: © First Garden City Heritage Museum, image supplied courtesy of Letchworth Garden City Heritage Foundation; 54: © First Garden City Heritage Museum, image supplied courtesy of Letchworth Garden City Heritage Foundation; 55(t), 55(b): From C. S. Stein, *Towards New Towns for America*. **Part II, 3:** 56(l), 56(r): James Steele; 58(t), 58(b), 59, 60(b), 60(t): Museum of Finnish Architecture; 61: James Steele. **Part II, 4:** 62(t), 62(b), 65, 66: Netherlands Architecture Institute; 67(t), 67(b): James Steele; 68: Netherlands Architecture Institute. **Part II, 5:** 70(t), 73(tl), 73(tr), 73(b):

Frank Lloyd Wright Foundation, Taliesin West/DACS, London, 2005; 74(t), 74(b): James Steele, 75(t), 75(b): Frank Lloyd Wright Foundation, Taliesin West/DACS, London, 2005. **Part II, 6:** 76: Grant Mudford; 77: University of California Archives; 78: Grant Mudford; 79(t): University of California Archives; 79(b): Grant Mudford; 81, 82(t), 82(b): Grant Mudford. **Part II, 7:** 84: AKAA (Photo: Chant Avedissian); 85: AKAA; 86: James Steele; 87, 88: AKAA; 90(l): AKAA (Photo: Chant Avedissian); 90(r), 91: AKAA (Photo: Chant Avedissian); 92(l): James Steele; 92(r): James Steele; 93: AKAA (Photo: Chant Avedissian). **Part II, 8:** 94: James Steele; 95, 96: © FLC/ADAGP, Paris and DACS, London, 2005; 97(l), 97(r), 99, 100(t), 100(b): © FLC/ADAGP, Paris and DACS, London, 2005; 102, 103: James Steele; 104(t), 104(b): © FLC/ADAGP, Paris and DACS, London. **Part II, 9:** 106(tl): Yatin Pandya; 106(b): James Steele; 107: Ram Kumar; 108: James Steele; 109(t): Anne Hong; 109(b): Ram Kumar; 111(t): Jo Newson; 111(bl): Anne Hong; 111(br): Joseph St Anne (courtesy AKAA); 112: Yatin Pandya; 113: Yatin Pandya. **Part II, 10:** 114(t): Courrtesy The Salk Institute, San Diego, California; 114(b): Kahn Collection, Architectural Archives, University of Pennsylvania; 117: Kahn Collection, Architectural Archives, University of Pennsylvania; 118: John Ebstel Collection, Courtesy of the Keith de Lillis Gallery, New York; 119(l), 119(r): James Steele; 120: George Pohl Collection, Architectural Archives, University of Pennsylvania.
Part II, 11: 122: Jo Reid and John Peck; 123(tl): Foster and Partners; 123(tr): Nicholas Grimshaw & Partners; 123(bl): Hopkins Architects Limited; 123(br); 126(t), 126(br), 127: Richard Rogers Partnership; 128: Foster and Partners; 131(t), 131(bl), 131(br): Hopkins Architects Limited; 133: Photo: Andrew Sanigar. **Part II, 12:** 134, 135, 136, 137, 138, 139(tl), 139(tr), 139(b), 140: Cosanti Foundation. **Part II, 13:** 142:

145(t), 145(b), 147: Stanford University Libraries, Department of Special Collections and Archives. **Part II, 14:** 148(t), 148(b): Timothy Hursley; 150, 151(t), 151(b), 152: Malcolm Wells; 153: Timothy Hursley. **Part II, 15:** 154, 156(t), 156(b), 157(l), 157(r): Edward Mazria. **Part II, 16:** 160(l), 160(r): Peter Cook/VIEW; 162(t), 162(b), 163: Short & Associates. **Part II, 17:** 164(t), 164(b), 169(t), 169(b), 173(tl), 173(bl), 173(r): Behnisch, Behnisch & Partner. **Part II, 18:** 174(l), 174(r), 175, 177, 178, 181(tl), 181(bl), 181(r): Architectural Archives, University of Pennsylvania. **Part II, 19:** 184(t), 184(b), 188(l): Skidmore, Owings and Merrill, 188(r): SL GMBH; 189(l), 189(r), 190: Fentress Bradburn Architects, Denver. **Part II, 20:** 192(l), 192(r), 195(l), 195(r), 197(l), 197(r), 198, 199: T.R Hamzah and Yeang. **Part II, 21:** 200(l), 200(r), 204(t), 204(b), 205, 206(l), 206(r), 207: AKAA. **Part II, 22:** 208(t), 208(b), 213(tl), 213(tr), 213(bl): Duany Plater-Zyberk & Company. **Part II, 23:** 214(t), 214(bl), 214(br), 216(l), 216, 217(l), 217(r), 219: CSL Associates. **Part II, 24:** 220(t), 220(bl): Dar-al-Omran Architects, Amman, Jordan; 220(br): Abdel Wahed El Wakil; 221(l): James Steele; 221(r), 222, 223: Dar-al-Omran Architects, Amman, Jordan; 224(t), 224(b), 225(l), 225(r): Abdel Wahed El Wakil. **Part II, 25:** 226(l): Alex Gaultier; 226(r): Alex Gaultier; 227: Eric Morin; 228(t), 228(b), 230: EMBT Architects; 231(t): Duccio Malagamba; 231(b): EMBT Architects. **Part II, Conclusion:** 234: Timothy Hursley. **Part III, Introduction:** 235: Shigeo Ogawa; 236: Eisenman Architects; 237: Tom Bonner. **Part III, 1:** 238, 242(l), 242(r), 243(l), 243(r): Peter Eisenman. **Part III, 2:** 244(t), 244(b): Mitsuo Matsuoka; 245: Kinji Kanno; 246(l), 246(r), 248: Tadao Ando Architects and Associates; 249: Mitsuo Matsuoka. **Part III, 3:** 250: Moore Ruble Yudell; 252(t), 252(b), 254(t), 254(b): Mia Lehrer; 256(t): Moore Ruble Yudell; 256(b): Moore Ruble Yudell; 257: Moore Ruble Yudell

Index

Illustrations are indexed by page number and are indicated by *italics*.

Aalto, Aino 59
Aalto, Alvar 56, 58–60, 61; Paimio Sanatorium 58–9; Saynatsalo Town Hall 56, 59–60, 61; Sunila housing development 60–1; Villa Mairea 59, 60
Aesthetic Movement 50
Aga Khan Trust for Culture 202; Aga Khan Award 11, 18, 37, 201–7; Historic Cities Support Programme 202
Agenda 21 see Earth Summit
agriculture 13, 23
Ahmedabad 100–102, 107, 108, 119; Institute of Indology *12*, 108, *108*; School of Architecture 107, 108; Sarabhai house 97, 100–2, 110
al Fayez, Zuhair 29
Alberts, A. 69; NMB Bank, Amsterdam 69
Amsterdam 62–9; Stock Exchange (Beurs) 64, *65*; NMB Bank, Amsterdam 69; Shipping House 66, *66*; Spaarndammer development 66, *67*; De Dageraad *62*, 66
Ando, Tadao 235–6, 245–9; Yumebutai Park, Awaji Island *244*, 245, 247–8, *249*; Japanese pavilion, Expo '92 245; Garden of Fine Arts 245; 'Hundred Level Garden' 247, *249*; Kumamoto Prefectural Forest of Tombs Museum 245; Rokko Housing 235, 236, 245, 246–7, *246*, 247–8
Aranya Low-Cost Housing *106*, 110, 112–13, *112*, *113*; *see also* Doshi, Balkrishna
Arcologies *see* Soleri, Paolo
Arts and Architecture (magazine) 80
Arts and Crafts movement 10–11, 33, 39, 40–7; Austria and Germany 45, 47; Netherlands 64, 68; see also Morris, William
Ashbee, C. R. 42, 46
Asplund, Gunnar: Woodland Cemetery Crematorium 228
Awaji Island *235*, 236; *see also* Ando, Tadao

Bacon, Edmund: *Design of Cities* 177
Badran, Rasem 11, 220, 221–4; Old Sana'a, Yemen 206, *206*, 222, 223, *222*, *223*; Justice Palace and Great Mosque, Riyadh *220*, 223
Bakema, Jacob Berend 68, 69
Banham, Reyner 55, 66, 145
Barcelona: Archery Pavilion 229; Diagonal Mar Park 230–1, 231, *231*; Mies van der Rohe Pavilion 32, 161; Santa Caterina Market *226*, 227, 229–30
Barkow Leibinger: Biosphere and Flower

Pavilion, Potsdam 141
Bartram, John 155
Bass, Edward P. 140, 147; *see also* biospheres
Bauhaus: Dessau 10, 85; Weimer 10, 34
Bazel, K. P. de 64
Behnisch, Behnisch and Partner 22, 169; Genzyme Center *173*; Museum of Fantasy *169*; Norddeutsche Landesbank Headquarters, Hanover 22, *164*
Beijing Declaration 172, 173
Bell, Daniel: *The Coming of the Post-Industrial Society* 19–20, 30
Bellamy, Edward: *Looking Backward* 51
Benaissa, Mohammed 204
Berger, Horst 186, 190
Berlage, Hendrik 64, 65, 66, 67, 68; Holland House, London 66
Bharat, Diamond Bourse *see* Doshi, Balkrishna
Bijvoet, Bernard 67, 68; Open Air School for the Healthy Child 67, *68*, 69
bioclimatic skyscrapers 193–9, 219
biospheres 140–41, 147; Biosphere II 147
Birkert, Gunnar: University of Michigan Library 153
Blomstedt, Aulis 60
Bordeaux, Law Courts *see* Rogers, Richard
Bournville 49
Bradburn, Jim *see* Fentress Bradburn Architects
Brandt Commission 165, 166–7
Broadacre City 55, 116
Brookings Institution, Washington, D.C. 209
brownfield sites 251, 252, 258
Brundtland Report 6, 9, 165, 167–8, 178
Building News 49
Bukhara, Nadir Divan Begi Madrasa 206, *206*

Cadbury, Edward 49, 52; *see also* Bournville
Cairo 24, 85, 86–7, 91
Calthorpe, Peter 210; *see also* New Urbanism
Carlyle, Thomas 40
Carr, Jonathan 49, 50, 51, 55
'Case Study' architects 81, 82–3, 145, 178
Chace, Clyde 78
Chagall, Marc 231
Chandigarh 12, *94*, 100, 102–5, *103*, *104*, 107, 108; *see also* Le Corbusier
Cheap Cottage Exhibition 52–3
Chimanbhai, Chinubhai 101
CIAM (Congrès Internationaux d'Architecture Moderne) 68, 210
cities 23–31; and agriculture 23; and 'arcology' 137; 'City as a House' 105; and climate 103–5; and globalization 24–7; greening 237; growth

199; and industry 23, 24, 30; modern views of 23–4; and nature 178–83; as organisms 137; planning 88–9, 92, 102–5, 110, 112–13, 125–6, 178; and population 14, 39; post-colonial 30–31; and 'producer' services 26–7; renewal of 110, 112; urban sprawl 138, 179, 209–10, 254; and work patterns 27; *see also* forest cities; garden cities
Citra Niaga Urban Development 204, 205–6
Ciudad de la Cultura de Galicia *see* Eisenman, Peter
Clean Air and Federal Water Pollution Act (USA) *see* legislation
climate 74, 75, 86; bioclimatic skyscrapers 193–9, 219; desert 137; of Egypt 11, 86; of India 101–2, 103–5, 108; Mediterranean 124; Midwest 73, 74, 75; tropical 215–16
Club of Rome: *Limits to Growth* 165
colonialism 18, 24–5, 34–5
Commoner, Barry 8, 156
Comprehensive Environmental Response, Compensation and Liability Act (CERCLA) *see* legislation
computers, use of in architectural practice 20–1, 187, 236–7, 239–43
Congrès Internationaux d'Architecture Moderne *see* CIAM
Conservation Movement (USA) 155
conservatories 36, 132–3, *154*
Correa, Charles 16
Cosanti *see* Soleri, Paolo
Culver City *see* Moss, Eric Owen; Los Angeles
Cuypers, E. (nephew of P. J. H. Cuypers) 66
Cuypers, P. J. H. 64

Dar Al Islam 92, *92*; *see also* Fathy, Hassan
Datai Resort *see* Hill, Kerry
De Dageraad (The Dawn) *see* De Klerk, Michael
De Klerk, Michael 62, 66, 67; De Dageraad *62*, 66; Shipping House, Amsterdam 66, *66*; Spaarndammer development 66, *67*
De Montfort University, School of Engineering *see* Short, Alan
De Stijl group 67, 68
deconstructivism 19, 241
Deleuze, Gilles: *The Fold* 241
Denver International Airport *see* Fentress Bradburn Architects
Derrida, Jacques 241
desert environments 137, 140–1
developing countries: 31; debt 166–7, 260; and resources 168, 169–70
Development Centre for Lightweight

Construction, University of Berlin 185
Dipoli Student Union, Otaniemi University *see*
    Pietila, Raili and Reima 60, 61
Doesburg, Theo van 67
Doshi, Balkrishna 12, 16, 101, 106–13; Bharat
    Diamond Bourse 109, *109*; Hussein-Doshi
    Gufa *106*, 108–9; Institute of Indology,
    Ahmedabad *12*, 108, *108*; School of
    Architecture, Ahmedabad 107, 108; Sangath
    12, *106*, 109–10, *111*, 113; *see also* Aranya
    Low-Cost Housing
Doxiadis, Constantinos 88–9; 'City of the
    Future' 88–9, 147
Drew, Jane: *Tropical Architecture* 215
Duany, Andrés 11, 208, 210, 212; *see also* New
    Urbanism
Dudok, William Marinus 62, 67; Hilversum City
    Hall *62*, 67
Duiker, Johannes 67, 68, 69; Open Air School
    for the Healthy Child 67, *68*, 69

earth construction 135–6; *see also* underground
    structures
Earth Day 8, 146, 156, 165–6
Earth Summit: *Agenda 21* 6, 9, 165, 168–72, 173
ecology: definition 8; and economics 7, 167;
    integrated construction 87
Ecology Party *see* Green Party
Eden Project, Cornwall *see* Grimshaw, Nicholas
Egypt 11, 16, 33, 36, 85–93
Eigen Haard (A Hearth of One's Own), housing
    foundation 66
Eisenman, Peter 236, 237, *238*, 239, 241, 242–3;
    Ciudad de la Cultura de Galicia *236*, *238*,
    239–43, *242*, *243*; Wexner Center 241
El Wakil, Abdel Wahed 11, 201, 203, 220, 224,
    225; Corniche Mosque 203, 224; Halawa
    House 203, 224, *224*; Island Mosque 224, *224*;
    Ruwais Mosque *220*, 224–5, *225*;
Eldem, Sedad Hakki 16
electronic revolution 18, 19, 20–1, 24, 27, *see*
    also computers, use of in architectural
    practice
embodied energy 7, 71
EMBT Architects 229–30; *see also* Miralles,
    Enric; Tagliabue, Benedetta
Emerson, Ralph Waldo 155
energy efficiency 73, 132, 151, 159, 162–3, 171
Entenza, John 55, 80, 82, 178; *see also* 'Case
    Study' architects
environment, sensitivity to 44, 45, 216–18; in
    Finland 56, 57–8, 60; in Hong Kong 128; in
    USA 72–4; and Kenneth Yeang 199
Environmental Protection Agency (EPA, USA)
    8, 251, 252
Ervi, Aarne 60, 61
European Union 9, 130
Expo '67 (Montreal) *142*, 143, 146, 147, 186
Expo '92 (Seville) *122*, 132, 245,
Eyck, Aldo van 68–9

Fanon, Frantz 30, 35
Fathy, Hassan 16, 23–4, 33, 36, 84–93, 224,
    225; *Architecture for the Poor* 11, 85, 87, 88;
    Dar Al Islam 92, *92*; Fuad Riad house 91;
    New Baris *33*, *84*, 89, *90*, *91*, 92, 224, 225;
    New Gourna Village 88; Sadat Resthouse,
    Gharb Husayn 93
Federal Forest Reserve 155
Fentress Bradburn Architects 189, 190, *189*, *190*;
    Denver International Airport 185, 189–91,
    189, *190*
'Fertile Crescent' 13
Finland 11, 33, 56–61; 'carpenter' style in 61;
    'handicraft' style in 58
Ford, Brian 161, 162, 163
Fordham, Max 161
forest cities 11, 60, 61; *see also* garden cities
Foster, Norman 123, 126–8; Commerzbank
    Tower 128, *128*; Hong Kong Shanghai Bank
    Tower 127, 128; Sainsbury Centre, Norwich
    127; Swiss Re building, London 123, 128, 193;
    Willis Faber Headquarters 127
Frampton, Kenneth 245–6, 253
Fraser, Ian 188; International Stadium,
    Riyadh 188
Frazer, John H. 236, 239, 240–1, 241–2
Fry, Maxwell: *Tropical Architecture* 215
Fuller, Buckminster 89, 140, 141, 142–7, 159;
    Beach Aircraft 145; Dymaxion House 143,
    144–5, *145*; Expo '67 Dome *142*, 143, 146,
    147; Harlem Redevelopment Plan *147*;
    Tetrahedronal City 147; Two-Mile Diameter
    Dome 147

garden cities 11, 14, 23, 48–55, *48*, *51*; *see also*
    forest cities; Hampstead Garden Suburb;
    Letchworth Garden City; Radburn New
    Town; Welwyn Garden City
Garreau, Joel: *Edge City: Life on the New Frontier*
    210
Gaudí, Antoni 227, 229
Geiger, David 186
Geographic Information System (GIS) 176
geothermal power 156
Gesellius, Herman 57; Villa Hvittrask *34*, *56*, 57,
    58, *58*; Villa Karsten 57
Gill, Bredan 74
Gill, Irving 78
'global cities' 26
'global commons' 171
'global community' 7
global warming 141
globalization 24–7, 261
Godwin, E. W. 50
Goldrick, Anne 161; *see also* Short, Alan
Gothic architecture 40, 41, 163
Grameen Bank Housing Programme 7, 204,
    205, *205*
'green' (as a term) 6
'Green National Product' 6

Green Party 8, 9
greenhouse gases 141
greening cities 237; Los Angeles 250–59
Greenpeace 9
Grimshaw, Nicholas 92, 122, 123, 132–3, 141,
    147; Eden Project, Cornwall 123, 132–3, *133*,
    141, 147; UK Pavilion, Expo '92 *122*, 132
Gropius, Walter 10, 34
growth/no-growth debate 6, 124, 156, 165, 166,
    167–8, 178
Grüne Aktion Zukunft 8
Grüne Listen 8

Habitat II, Istanbul 172–3
Hamdi Sief Al-Nasr Villa 87, *87*
Hampstead Garden Suburb 49, 51, *53*; *see also*
    Unwin, Raymond; garden cities
Hamzah, T. R. 28–9; *see also* Yeang, Kenneth
Hardin, Garrett: 'The Tragedy of the Commons'
    260
Haussman, Baron 23
Hayy Assafarat Landscaping Programme 206
Hertzberger, Herman 69; Central Beheer,
    Apeldorn 69
Hertzen, Heikki von: 'A Home or a Barracks for
    Our Children?' 60
Hewlett, James Monroe 143, 144
'High-Tech' architecture 123–33
Hill, Kerry 218–19; Datai Resort 218–19
Historic Cities Support Programme *see* Aga
    Khan Trust
Hoff, Robert van't 67; Villa Nora 67
Hoffmann, Josef 10, 45
Holl, Steven 213, 241
Hollein, Hans 153; Guggenheim Museum,
    Salzburg 153; Museum of Vulcanology,
    Auvergne 153
Hopkins, Michael 123, 128–30, 131; Bracken
    House 128; David Mellor Cutlery Factory
    128, 130; Glyndebourne Opera House 128;
    Inland Revenue Centre, Nottingham 128–30;
    Lord's Cricket Ground 128, 130; Portcullis
    House 123, 130, *131*;
housing *see under individual architects*
Howard, Sir Ebenezer 10–11, 14, 23, 49–55, 183,
    209; 'Three Magnets' diagram 52
human rights 172, 173
human settlements: management of 171–2
humanism 58, 59
Hunt, M. van 69; NMB Bank, Amsterdam 69
Hussein, M. F. 108, 109

India 100–102, 103, 106–13, 119
industrialization 14, 19–20; in London 39–40; of
    the Netherlands 63–4
Institute of Lightweight Structures, Stuttgart
    186
interior-exterior spaces 71, 78, 80–1, 83, 86–7
International Conference on Population and
    Development, Cairo 172

International Congress of Modern Architecture *see* CIAM

'International Style' 11, 16, 19, 31, 33; exhibition at MoMA 77, 82

irrigation 13, 124

Islamic architecture, traditional 223–5

Isozaki, Arata 110, 247

Jacobs, Jane 211

Jameson, Fredric 15, 212

Japan 21–2, 36, 45, 74, 244–9; influence of in architecture 45, 71, 80, 83

Jeddah: Hajj Terminal, Airport *184*, 186–8, *188*, 203

Jencks, Charles 261

Johnson, Philip 77, 82

Kabul, International Trade Fair (1956) 146

Kahn, Louis 11–12, 23, 110, 114–21, 159, 177, 203; Alfred Newton Richard Medical Research Building 117; American Federation of Labor Medical Services Building 117; City Tower Project, Philadelphia 117, *117*; Erdman Hall, Bryn Mawr College 118, 119; housing projects 116; Dominican Mother house of St Catherine de Ricci 120; Fine Arts Center, Fort Wayne 118; First Unitarian Church, Rochester 118, *118*; Hurva Synagogue 120, *120*; Indian Institute of Management 119, *119*; Jewish Community Center, Trenton 117; Kimbell Art Museum 12, 110, 118; Levy Memorial Playground 118; Memorial to the Six Million Jewish Martyrs 120; Mikveh Israel Synagogue 119, 120; National Assembly Building, Dhaka 203, *204*; Richards Medical Towers, Philadelphia 177; Salk Institute *114*, 118; Temple Beth-El 120; Tribune Review Publishing Company Building, Greensburg 117; US Consulate in Luanda, Angola 12, *12*, *114*, 117–18; Yale Center for British Art 121; Yale University Art Gallery 115, 117

Katsura Villa, Japan *11*, 15, *15*, *17*

Katz, Peter 210–11

Koninklijt Istitut van Ingeniers (KIVI) 64–5

Koolhaas, Rem 193, 241

Kramer, Pieter Lodewijk 66; Shipping House, Amsterdam 66, *66*

Krier, Léon 213

Kromhaut, William 64

Kuala Lumpur 218: BATC project 198, *198*, *199* Menara Mesiniaga 29, *192*, 195–6, 203; Petronas Towers 218; Salinger House 203, *204*, 215, 216–17

Kurokawa, Kisho 21

Kyoto declaration 141

Lahuerta, Juan José 229

Land Art movement 151

land use 174, 176, 178–9

landform architecture 241

landscape 60, 176–7, 178–80, 182–3, 206; higher value than architecture 245–6; and planning 174–83

Larsen, Henning 201, 203, 204; Ministry of Foreign Affairs, Riyadh *35*, 203

Lauwerks, J. L. M. 64

Lawson, Thomas 161

Le Corbusier 23, 68, 83, 94–105, 196, 235, 246; Cherchell, North Africa 97; and Doshi 107, 110; and Kahn 11, 12; *Dom-i-no* 95, 96, 97, 98, 110; Fueter House, Constance 97; La Roche/Jeanneret house 96; La Tourade 97; Maison Citrohan 101; Maison de 'weekend', Saint-Cloud 97, *97*; Maisons Jaoul 97, 100, *100*, 101; Millowners' Building 101, 102, *102*; *Monol* 95–6, 97, 98; Plan Voisin 23, *23*, 103, 196; Roq and Rob, Cap Martin 97, 98–100, *99*, 235, 246; Sarabhai house, Ahmedabad 97, 100–2, 110; Unité d'Habitation, Marseilles 100; Villa Savoye, Poissy 95, 96, *96*, 161, 235

Le Nôtre, André 236

legislation 155–6: Clean Air and Federal Water Pollution Act (USA) 8; Comprehensive Environmental Response, Compensation and Liability Act (CERCLA) 251, 252; National Environmental Policy Act (USA) 8; Small Business Liability Relief and Brownfields Revitalization Act 251

Legorreta, Ricardo 255

Lehrer, Mia 258

Letchworth Garden City 11, *48*, 49, 51–3, *51*; Rushby Mead *48*; *see also* Parker, Barry; Unwin, Raymond

Lethaby, W. R. 11, 51

Lever, W. H. 49, 52

Licht en Waarheid 64

Lim, Jimmy 203, 204, 215–19; 100 Cintra Street, Penang *217*; Salinger House, Kuala Lumpur 203, *204*, 215, 216–17; Walian House *214*;

Lindgren, Armas 57; Villa Hvittrask *34*, *56*, 57, 58, *58*; Villa Karsten 57

London 39, 66, 123, 128, 129–30; Bedford Park 49–50; Hampstead Garden Suburb 49, 51, *53*; Shaftesbury Park Estate 49; Turnham Green 49, 50

Loos, Adolf 32, 58, 81, 83; *Raumplan* 81, 82

Los Angeles 27–8, 55, 78, 81, 82, 126, 237, *237*; Baldwin Hills 258–9; Ballona Creek 258; Ballona Wetlands 256, 257 greening of 250–9; Culver City 11, 27–8, *28*, 229 'Conjunctive Points' 28; Pershing Square 255; Playa Vista development *237*, *250*, 255–7, *256*, *257*; urban sprawl in 209–10, 254

Los Angeles and San Gabriel Watershed and Open Space Plan 254–5

Los Angeles River Greenway 254–5

Los Angeles River Master Plan 254

low-cost housing 110, 112–13, 144–5

Lynch, Kevin 211

McHarg, Ian 10, 11, 156, 175–83, 194; *Design with Nature* 182–3; 'Man and Environment' course 177; plan for Abouja *174*; Plan for the Valleys 11, 55, *174*, 175, *177*, 178–82, *178*;

Mackintosh, Charles Rennie 10, 32, 38–47, 81; Glasgow School of Art 42–3, 46, *47*, 64; House for an Art Lover *32*, *43*; Hill House *38*, 44, *44*, 46, 81; Windyhill *43*, 44–5

McNamara, Robert S. 166

Maguire Thomas Partners 255, 257, 258

Malayan architecture 216–18

Malaysia 28–9, 37

malkaf 86, *91*; *see also* windcatches

Mallorca, Development Project *see* Rogers, Richard

Mason's Bend Community Centre *see* Mockbee, Sam

materials: aluminium 144; costs 87; geometric building blocks 146; local 108, 109, 171; in tent technology 184–91; waste reduction 78, 79, 80

Mazria, Edward 154–9; *Passive Solar Energy Book* 155, 157, 158; Mt. Airy Public Library 155, *157*, 158; Rio Grande Botanic Garden Conservatory *154*; Stockebrand Residence *156*, 157, 158

Mead, Margaret 89, 178

Meier, Richard 235; Getty Museum, Los Angeles 235, 236

Meurman, Otto I. 60

Mey, Johan Melchior van der 66, 67; Shipping House, Amsterdam 66, *66*

Middle East 85–93

Mies van der Rohe, Ludwig 83, 115; Barcelona Pavilion 32, 161; Farnsworth House 83

Miralles, Enric 227–31; Archery Pavilion, Barcelona 229; Diagonal Mar Park, Barcelona 230–1, 231, *231*; Hamburg Music School 231; Huesca Sports Hall 227, 228–9; Igualada Cemetery 227–8, *228*; National Centre for Rhythmic Gymnastics 228–9; Parc dels Colors 231; Santa Caterina Market, Barcelona *226*, 227, 229–30; Utrecht Town Hall 231; *see also* EMBT Architects; Tagliabue, Benedetta

Mockbee, Samuel 232; Mason's Bend Community Centre 233, *234*

modernism 11, 36, 37, 64, 65; and the environment 83; and Kahn 115–16; and Le Corbusier 96; and post-modernism 121; and tradition 107–8, 113

Molière, Marinus Jan Granpré 68

Morphosis: Diamond Ranch High School *11*, *19*, *21*

Morris, William 33, 39, 40, 41–2, 98; *News from Nowhere* 34, 41

Moss, Eric Owen: Culver City 11, 27–8, *28*, 229

Moule, Elizabeth 210, 211; *see also* New Urbanism

Muthesius, Hermann 10, 45